The Foundations of Small Business Enterprise

The Foundations of Small Business Enterprise provides an extended, and novel, entrepreneurial analysis of small firm inception and growth. Gavin C. Reid develops a new kind of 'micro–micro' analysis, applying rigorous methods from economics, accounting and finance to gain a deeper understanding of micro-firms, by examining their performance, hierarchy, strategy, capital structure, monitoring and control, flexibility, innovation, and information systems.

Using statistical, econometric and qualitative methods of empirical research, *The Foundations of Small Business Enterprise* tracks and analyses the evolution of firms from their early years through to maturity.

Gavin C. Reid is Professor of Economics, School of Economics & Finance, University of St Andrews, Scotland, UK. He is the Founder/Director of the Centre for Research into Industry, Enterprise, Finance and the Firm (CRIEFF). The author of over 60 papers in the leading economics, accounting and finance journals, he has published eight books, including *Small Business Enterprise, Theories of Industrial Organization, Classical Economic Growth* and *Venture Capital Investment.*

Routledge studies in small business
Edited by David J. Storey
Centre for Small and Medium Sized Enterprises, Warwick Business School, UK.

The Foundations of Small Business Enterprise

An entrepreneurial analysis of small firm inception and growth

Gavin C. Reid

 Routledge
Taylor & Francis Group

LONDON AND NEW YORK

First published 2007 by Routledge
2 Park Square, Milton Park, Abingdon, Oxon OX14 4RN

Simultaneously published in the USA and Canada
by Routledge
270 Madison Ave, New York, NY 10016

Routledge is an imprint of the Taylor & Francis Group

© 2007 Gavin C. Reid

Typeset in Times by Keyword Group Ltd
Printed and bound in Great Britain by TJI Digital, Padstow, Cornwall

British Library Cataloguing in Publication Data
A catalogue record for this book is available from the British Library

Library of Congress Cataloging in Publication Data
A catalog record for this book has been requested

ISBN10: 0-415-33877-8 (hbk)
ISBN10: 0-203-44843-X (ebk)

ISBN13: 978-0-415-33877-6(hbk)
ISBN13: 978-0-203-44843-4(ebk)

Gavin C. Reid. Portrait by John Mackie.

To Annabel Macfarlane Reid

Thrice happy she that is so well assur'd
Unto herself, and settled so to heart,
That neither will for better be allured,
Ne fears to worse with any chance to start,
But like a steady ship doth strongly part
The raging waves, and keeps her course aright.

Edmund Spenser (1553–1599), *The True Woman* *

* In *A Thousand and One Gems of English Poetry*, selected and arranged by Charles Mackay, 1890, Routledge, London, p. 28.

Contents

Figures

Tables

Preface

This is a book about founders of small business enterprise that is, entrepreneurs. In this sense, it is about the foundations of enterprise – like business strategy, financial structure and organisational form. I think it fair to say that I am now a veteran of book writing. Even so, the task of writing this one has become no easier with experience, nor with the passage of time. It is the most ambitious undertaking with which I have been concerned, in an intellectual sense. This is true largely because of the scale and duration of the projects on which this book is based, the long period of scientific analysis of the evidence, and the patient exposure of ideas derived thereof to the community of scientific specialists – in economics (especially industrial organisation and business economics), of course, as I am at root an economist, but also in emerging fields like entrepreneurship and business strategy, in subfields like innovation, R & D, intellectual property and information systems, and finally in large adjacent and cognate fields, like accounting and finance. What has finally emerged is more than a study in economics, hence the use of the phrase 'an entrepreneurial analysis' in the subtitle.

The genesis of this work is coincident with my founding of the Centre for Research into Industry, Enterprise, Finance and the Firm (CRIEFF) in 1991, when I moved from a Readership in Economics at Edinburgh University to the post of Professor of Economics at the University of St Andrews. It is in CRIEFF, of which I have been the Director since its inception, that almost all of this work has been performed, often to the accompaniment of seagulls' cries, from its superb location overlooking the West Sands of St Andrews. I can think of no better location for research than this beautiful physical environment. It has been a continued source of inspiration. The founding of CRIEFF was an 'entrepreneurial event' in itself, and helped me to acquire insights into the trials and tribulations of a new entrepreneurial start-up.

Entrepreneurship as an interdisciplinary field has taken great strides since the work upon which this book is based was started, cf. Brock and Evans (1989). On occasions in the past, I felt quite isolated in my willingness to engage with sister disciplines, especially those of accounting and finance. However, this kind of approach is now much more accepted, and it has been of comfort to feel that, to use a Scottish phrase, one has been drawn further 'into the Kirk', as time has gone by – with this 'broad Kirk' being the study of entrepreneurship itself. In the process of sharing the experience of the expanding field of entrepreneurship, my contact with Babson College, MA, has been particularly inspiring in an academic sense. At the practitioner level, the Scottish Institute for Enterprise (SIE) has been part of a larger, deliberative, dynamic process of cultural transformation in Scotland. This has seen the social standing of entrepreneurs rise in 20 years from being below that of ex-prisoners to having parity with (or even superiority to) establishment figures like lawyers and accountants. We now have many entrepreneur-heroes in Scotland, a number of whom have emerged, to fame and fortune, from the small firms studied in this book.

The underlying scientific work required many years of toil. This started from its early conceptualisation in 1993 (and the quest for funding from the Leverhulme Trust), to its inception in 1994 (once that funding having been acquired), and then to its labour-intensive execution in the early phases, from 1994 through to 1997, by visits to small enterprises throughout Scotland. My research assistants on this work were (briefly) Marianne Nilkes and (for the entire project) Julia Smith. An additional round of funding from the Research Foundation of the Chartered Institute of Management Accountants (CIMA) made another year of fieldwork possible, extending the original framework to information systems, monitoring and control. Falconer Mitchell, of Edinburgh University, joined the team at this stage.

All this fieldwork took the data-gathering process into the major cities of Scotland, and also, to my delight, to its roads and pathways, its hamlets, villages and towns, and past the meadows, woods, hills, glens, river sides and burn banks of this bonnie land. This was followed by the long haul of analysis of evidence in the subsequent years. This veritable saga included the publication of discussion papers, seminar and conference presentations, and early forms of publishing, in many academic journals and book chapters. I was assisted in this endeavour by grants from the Nuffield Foundation, and the British Academy, during which period my research assistant within CRIEFF was Kirsty Hopkins.

Finally, a number of the firms in the original sample were re-visited, using a grant from Enterprise Ireland, in 2002–03. And so the fieldwork began again; and it was a pleasure to re-visit small businesses – now rather changed from my earliest time of contact. My co-worker on this was Bernadette Power, of University College Cork, who has also played a major role in my recent scientific work on this body of evidence.

It would not have been possible to accomplish all of this without the cheerful cooperation of many people in 'the enterprise game' in Scotland, from my earliest contacts with the likes of Peter Carmichael (then SDA) and John Moorhouse (then ScotBIC) and Directors of Enterprise Trusts, to my later contacts with key individuals in the emerging new enterprise based institutions, like Scottish Enterprise, the Enterprise Companies (LECs), and the Scottish Institute for Enterprise (SIE). Above all, the 'stars of the piece' have been the entrepreneurs. It was these entrepreneurs, or as they often preferred to be called, 'owner-managers', of small businesses, who made the whole thing worth while, and fostered a deep concern on my part for their business existence, including their successes and failures.

In undertaking this work, the generous sponsorship of the Leverhulme Trust with a major grant over the period 1993–97 is gratefully acknowledged, as is the further financial support over the period 1997-98 by the Research Foundation of the Chartered Institute of Management Accounts (CIMA). Dr Julia Smith was a steady and positive influence on the project work behind this research, as a research assistant, research associate, and then finally in 1997–98, as research fellow within the Centre for Research into Industry, Enterprise, Finance and the Firm (CRIEFF) of the (then) Department of Economics, University of St Andrews. As the years have gone by, this research assistance has grown and developed into a creative and productive joint scientific and authorship relationship, as Dr Smith has moved from CRIEFF, St Andrews, to the Institute of Economics and Statistics (IES), University of Oxford, to the Cardiff University Business School (CARBS), and finally, to the Strathclyde University Business School. For both this early support, and our continued collaboration, I am most grateful.

Part of what is contained in this book has seen earlier light in a variety of published forms, and has been the basis of extensive discussion and debate in conferences, seminars, round tables and network meetings. Amongst the most important of these have been the Network of Industrial Economists (NIE), the European Association for Research in Industrial Economics (EARIE), the Babson/Kauffman Entrepreneurship Research Conference, the British Accounting Association, the European Accounting Association, the Royal Economic Society, the Scottish Economic Society, EIM (Business and Economics Policy Research) Rotterdam, and the Business and Economics Society International (B&ESI). Many comments and criticisms from individuals at these forums have been helpful and useful, and I have tried to learn from them all, and to adapt my scientific agenda accordingly.

Of all these, and there are, alas, too many to name individually, I should like specifically to mention Robert Cressy and Simon Parker, for an insistence on rigour, Andrew Burke for an unremitting sense of purpose in entrepreneurship research, Alan Hughes and David Storey for a keen strategic sense of what is important, Zoltan Acs and David Audretsch for seeing the 'big picture' in a welter of detail, Bill Bygrave and Paul Reynolds for reminding me that the United Sates is the land of enterprise, and two Dutch colleagues: Ingrid Verhuel, for the most joyful adherence to the research endeavour I have ever witnessed, and Roy Thurik for long, insightful, often lugubrious, but ultimately amusing, conversations on what constitutes leading edge research in entrepreneurship. They, and the many others who have influenced my thought and ultimately my drafting of this book, are absolved from responsibility for any errors of omission or commission I may have committed in the following pages.

I am grateful to the following publishers for permission to draw on previously published material: the Cambridge University Press, Springer and Elsevier. Details of such materials are given in the section on 'Acknowledgments'. My own publishers, Routledge, have been bastions of support for over 15 years, and through three earlier books. Rob Langham commissioned the present volume, and Terry Clague, as Economics Editor, has successfully steered it through to publication, being encouraging and supportive, especially in the final stages.

I should specifically mention again two key co-workers, Julia Smith and Bernadette Power. Where they have played a significant role in the material of particular chapters, an acknowledgement has been made at the chapter head. A list of principal sponsors of the research is as follows: Leverhulme Trust, Carnegie Trust, CIMA Research Foundation, British Academy, Enterprise Ireland. Their funding has been crucial to my sustaining this long-term research, over a period of 13 years, and my debt of gratitude to them is indeed deep.

Finally, now this long haul is over, I should mention my patient daughter, Annabel. Though not the youngest, she has waited with tolerance for some years for this book dedication. I can only say that I wanted it to be as worthy of her name as my humble offering could merit. It is this thought that has helped me to strive towards, and to achieve, the completion of this book.

Gavin C. Reid, CRIEFF
School of Economics & Finance
University of St Andrews

Acknowledgements

In writing this book, the author has been able to draw on his published works with permission of the following publishers.

With kind permission of Springer Science and Business Media:

1. Reid, G.C. (1996) 'Mature micro-firms and their experience of funding shortages', *Small Business Economics* 8(1), 27–37.
2. Reid, G.C. (1996) 'Financial structure and the growing small firm: theoretical underpinning and current evidence', *Small Business Economics* 8(1), 1–7.
3. Reid, G.C. (1999) 'Complex actions and simple outcomes: how new entrepreneurs stay in business', *Small Business Economics* 13(4), 303–315.
4. Reid, G.C. and J.A. Smith (2000) 'What makes a new business start-up successful?', *Small Business Economics* 14(3), 165–82.
5. Reid, G.C. (2003) 'Trajectories of small business financial structure', *Small Business Economics* 20(4), 273–85.
6. Power, B. and G.C. Reid (2005) 'Flexibility, firm-specific turbulence and the performance of the long-lived small firm', *Review of Industrial Organization* 26, 15–43.

And with kind permission of Elsevier Ltd:

7. Reid, G.C. and J.A. Smith (2000) 'The impact of contingencies on management accounting system development', *Management Accounting Research* 11(4), 427–450.

And with kind permission of Cambridge University Press:

8. Reid, G.C. (1999) 'Capital structure at inception and the short-run performance of micro firms', in Z.J. Acs, B. Carlsson and C. Karlsson (eds), *Entrepreneurship, Small and Medium-Sized Enterprises and The Macroeconomy*, pp.186–205.

Abbreviations

ABC	Activity based costing
AGV	Automated guided vehicle
AIS	Accounting information system
AQ	Administered questionnaire – As in AQ1 for Year 1, AQ2 for Year 2, etc.
BS	British standard
CBIS	Computer based information systems
CIMA	Chartered institute of management accountants
CRIEFF	Centre for research into industry, enterprise, finance and the firm
DDBMS	Distributed database management system
ET	Enterprise trust
FIML	Full information maximum likelihood
HIDB	Highlands and islands development board
HIE	Highlands and islands enterprise
IS	Information system
ISO	International organization for standardization
IT	Information technology
JIT	Just-in-time
LISREL	Linear structural relationship
MA	Massachusetts
MAS	Management accounting system
MCR	Money capital requirements
MIS	Management information system
MM	Modigliani-Miller
R & D	Research and development
ROCE	Return on capital employed
SBE	Small business enterprise
SDA	Scottish development agency
SE	Scottish enterprise
SIC	Standard industrial classification
SIE	Scottish institute for enterprise

SME	Small and medium-sized enterprise
SPSS	Statistical package for the social sciences
SWOT	Strengths, weaknesses, opportunities and threats
TQM	Total quality management
UK	United Kingdom of Great Britain and Northern Ireland
VAT	Value added tax

Part 1

Background

1 Small firm inception and growth

1.1 Introduction

The theme of this book is small business inception and growth. The approach adopted is entrepreneurial. Thus the focus is on the entrepreneur, or more prosaically, on the owner-manager (Blanchflower and Oswald, 1990). But more than this, the methodology used is entrepreneurial. Whilst grounded in economics, and specifically in industrial organisation, it extensively utilises research methods from accounting (especially management accounting), finance (especially capital structure) and information systems (especially monitoring and control systems). Also much in evidence are ideas from business strategy (especially competitive advantage) and political economy (especially enterprise policy). Entrepreneurship is itself an inter-disciplinary field, and this book therefore deliberately reflects its sub-title, in being 'an entrepreneurial analysis'.

A final distinctive feature of the book is to be noted. It is that every chapter is based on the same approach to evidence and its analysis; and indeed, the book is exclusively concerned with one body of evidence. Thus the wide variety of issues explored (e.g. financial structure, flexibility, business strategy) from an entrepreneurial perspective, is nevertheless through the use of the same body of evidence. This evidence is fieldwork-based (Woolcott, 2005; Burgess, 1984), and 'the field', in this instance, is the economy of Scotland. One of the privileges of living and working in Scotland is that it is the birthplace of economics (or, as it was first known, political economy). The writings of Smith (1776) and Hume (1752) are surely an inspiration to the analysis of the enterprise economy. As it turns out, Scotland has indeed deep roots as an enterprise economy, and this makes it an ideal 'laboratory' for testing a wide variety of small business hypotheses.

Finally, the compact nature of Scotland makes it well suited to fieldwork. Geographically, it is an almost contiguous reverse L-shaped set of centres of high population density (e.g. Glasgow, Edinburgh, Dundee, Aberdeen). This makes it possible to travel relatively easily to small businesses (as fieldwork 'sites') to conduct detailed interviews with entrepreneurs. Thus the final distinctive feature of this book is that all the analysis is based on primary source data. Data were obtained with a view to testing a variety of hypotheses, some of which were received hypotheses, and some of which were emergent. Most often this evidence was obtained by fieldwork, and occasionally (e.g. because of problems of access) by postal questionnaire or by telephone interview (see Chapter 5, for example). This conviction that primary source data are essential to testing theories of the small business goes some way towards the approach of 'grounded theory' (Glaser and Strauss, 1967), in its advocacy of fieldwork methods, but does not embrace their approach to 'testing' theories by 'filling categories'. Rather, a more positivist approach is adopted to theory construction and testing, and methods of statistical inference and econometrics are used extensively.

To summarise, the approach adopted is well rooted in fieldwork methods. Though unfamiliar to some economists, it was in fact adopted by the greatest of economists, Adam Smith, Alfred Marshall (see Groenewegen, 1995) and Ronald Coase (see Coase, 1988), all of whom were highly creative theorists, but also inveterate fieldworkers. To that perspective is added a commitment to theory formulation and empirical testing. In treating theory in this way, the subject of entrepreneurship has been my guide, because, being inter-disciplinary in approach, it is well suited to being guided by influences from economics, accounting, finance, management and much more besides. Given the richness and complexity of small business activity, this diversity of approach seems essential.

This chapter will cover three things. First, an overview of the fieldwork undertaken is provided, which gives a preliminary account that will be more fully developed in Chapters 2 and 3. Second, an overview is provided of the key features (e.g. markets, finance, costs) of the small businesses analysed, over four successive years. There, reference is made to the preliminary evidence which was returned to entrepreneurs as a *quid pro quo* for their involvement in interviews. Such data were subject to correction, completion and revision, but they provide an interesting view, as shared with the subjects of the research, of small firm dynamics, in the early years after inception. Third, an overview is provided of the book itself, and of its essential structure (namely background, existing evidence, finance, performance, information and contingency, flexibility).

1.2   Sampling

As indicated earlier, the evidence on which the models of this book were estimated was obtained by fieldwork methods (Woolcott, 2005; Werner and Schoepfle, 1987). This fieldwork involved 'face-to-face' interviews (Willis, 2005; Sudman and Bradburn, 1982) with owner-managers of new business start-ups in Scotland. As is usual with fieldwork methods it is necessary to find 'gate keepers' who provide 'ports of entry' to the field (Burgess, 1984; Woolcott, 2005). Here, the gate keepers were directors of enterprise incubators, known as Enterprise Trusts (ETs) in Scotland (Reid and Jacobsen, 1988). They provide a range of business inception facilities including training, advice on sites, access to finance and more generally networking opportunities.[1] Directors of ETs were asked to provide random samples of new business start-ups from their case loads. The only restriction set was that the exact inception date of the enterprise needed to be known, and that not more than 3 years should have elapsed since inception. A random sample of approximately half of the ETs in existence in Scotland in 1993 was taken.

The sampling area extended from the main metropolitan area concentrations on the West Coast of Scotland (including Glasgow) through the Central Belt to the metropolitan areas of the East including Edinburgh and then up North through the main population centres including Stirling, Perth, Dundee, Aberdeen, finally extending as far north as Inverurie. Thus the main population concentrations of Scotland were largely covered by a sampling area which had, roughly speaking, a thick, reverse L-shaped configuration.

The initial sample size was 150 small firms in the base year of 1994. The same (surviving) firms were re-interviewed for three successive years under the same conditions, using three variants of an administered questionnaire (Oppenheim, 1992) (denoted AQ1, AQ2 and AQ3 – see, for example, appendix to this book for the instrumentation of AQ1). Then a further year's data were collected using the modified administered questionnaire (AQ4) which is re-printed in the appendix at the end of this book. Only the final year variant of the questionnaire is reproduced, for reasons of space, but it gives an accurate indication of how data were gathered for all years, including the last. Finally, in a set of long-term re-interviews, in 2002, data were gathered on a sub-set of surviving small firms, examining their flexibility and performance in the face of firm-specific turbulence. Results on the latter are reported upon in the final chapter of this book (Chapter 18).

For the main body of evidence, extensive data were gathered on a wide range of attributes, including markets, finance, costs, business strategy, human capital, internal organisation and technical change (AQ1, appendix to this book). Additional data were gathered on information systems, monitoring and control in a fourth annual round of interviewing in the field (See Section 5, Development of MAS, in AQ4 of appendix to this book). In this chapter a limited view of these data will be presented, in order that a good indication is given of the general characteristics of the small firms which were sampled. Its purpose is not to be comprehensive, but rather to set the scene for the empirical work that ensues. A more detailed analysis of the database, as it relates to the first 4 years of fieldwork, is available in Reid (1999a), and in the following Chapter 2. Furthermore, every chapter of this book will also add to the information about the database, as is necessary to an understanding of its design or content, in any specific context.

1.3   Summary evidence from first year

In the first year, each entrepreneur was kind enough to consent to being interviewed about their new business, and indeed agreed to being approached on a follow-up basis. In those interviews of the first phase, it was also agreed that the field workers would report back to the entrepreneurs on their first year's findings, concerning the state of new small firms in Scotland. This section provides a summary of (provisional) results as they stood after 1 year.[2] Data were obtained from 18 areas in Scotland, providing a comprehensive and balanced coverage of new small firms' activity during the fieldwork period. The following sections will trace the development of the fieldwork year by year, in order to provide a general perspective on the investigative methods, and the general nature of the fieldwork findings. Essentially, they present the emerging picture of the (slightly imperfect) evidence as reported back to those entrepreneurs who had participated in the study. Headings for each sub-section are based on the corresponding sections in the administered questionnaire (AQ) as given in the appendix to this book (where AQ1 and AQ4 are reproduced).

1.3.1   *Market data*

The average or typical firm in the sample had been in existence for 19 months. Thus the evidence provided a picture of the early stage of the small firm's life-cycle. Typically it was run by one entrepreneur, who had three full-time and three part-time workers. Gross sales were an average of £192,000. The number of products sold was about 36, and these could be put into five main product groups. There was a wide variation in what the typical small firm regarded as its main market. More entrepreneurs thought they operated in a local market, rather than in any other market, and the ranking of markets, in order of importance, was from local, to regional, to Scottish, to British and finally to international. Although the typical firm found that most of its sales (about two-thirds) arose from just one leading product group, about one-fifth came from the next most important product group. The market share for the main product group was about one-fifth. Overall, competition in the firm's main market was perceived to be 'strong to fierce'. It was thought that competition was strongest on price, followed by quality, and then salesmanship. Most entrepreneurs expected to 'grow on' their businesses over the next few years.

1.3.2   *Finance*

The average level of gross profit for a small firm in the sample was about £55,000. This was based on estimated average sales of about £184,000. Just over half the firms had debt, but only a small percentage had any outside ownership. About 95 per cent of entrepreneurs had founded their business using their own cash, often in conjunction with other funding. The average size of the entrepreneur's personal financial injection was £13,000. Other sources of finance which had been important in the life of the average firm were mainly grants, subsidies, or bank loans, followed by family or friends.

1.3.3   *Costs*

About two-thirds of entrepreneurs could identify a capacity output. Normal capacity operation was thought to be about two-thirds of peak capacity. Even though the firms were very young, about two-thirds claimed to be enjoying increasing returns to scale (i.e. their costs were rising less rapidly than their outputs, implying falling costs per unit as their scales of operations increased). About one-third of the entrepreneurs thought they had a good idea of what their rivals' costs were, and of these, about two-thirds thought they had lower costs than rivals. In terms of the breakdown of costs into components, the most important was wages (about one-quarter), followed by raw materials and rents (about one-eighth each).

1.3.4 Business strategy

The main aims of entrepreneurs were, first, to achieve long-run profit, and second, to promote the growth of their firm. Few specified that they mainly sought short-run profit, and only a small proportion expressed the view that they merely wanted to survive. The main reason for getting involved in running a business was, first, as an alternative to unemployment, and second, to be one's own boss.

Firms typically (nine out of ten) had a business plan, and this was reviewed every 6 months. Firms looked 18 months ahead, on average, when considering the impact of their decisions. Whilst there was a high awareness of the importance of information technology, this was less so of quality management. Few firms (about one-tenth) had thought about or implemented a total quality management (TQM) system. However, various quality controls were commonly adopted (e.g. product quality standards, operations and personnel standards, quality standards for business as a whole). Entrepreneurs identified their major strengths as being product quality, followed by adaptability; and their major weaknesses as lying in their financial resources and market share. The main threat to the entrepreneur's business was thought to be rivals' plant and resources; and the factor that provided the main opportunity to the business was product quality.

1.3.5 Human resources

Just over half of the entrepreneurs had run a business before, usually someone else's, but, for a significant minority, their own. An impressive three-quarters had attended some sort of college or university course. Just over a half had some kind of diploma or certificate qualification, and whilst none had a doctoral degree, about one-seventh had an honours degree. The typical day was mainly spent producing the product, followed by attending to sales and then to management. Of those firms which had employees, about two-thirds had undergone some sort of formal training. About 5 per cent of an employee's time was spent on formal training. The bulk of employees acquired skills 'on the job' as well, and skill acquisition was perceived by nine out of ten entrepreneurs to be 'very important' for employees' productivity.

1.3.6 Organisation

The typical firm in the sample was a sole trader operating from business premises (about one-third). About one-quarter were private limited companies, a quarter partnerships, and the rest sole traders operating from home. Subordinates were reviewed about every 3 months on average, and the discretion over subordinates' activities was extensive. The typical reason for dismissing a subordinate was because of a disciplinary problem, followed by him or her being no longer a suitable employee. Generally (75 per cent of cases), subordinates understood and acted on instructions, but when they did not, the typical reason was that instructions were unclear (two-thirds of cases), followed by inadequate subordinates' skills.

1.3.7   Technical change

In the short lifetimes of these small firms, process innovation (improving an existing process) was typically thought to have been 'slightly important' by owner-managers. Also, product innovation (doing something entirely new) was ranked as having been 'slightly important' on average since start-up. Most entrepreneurs did not feel under pressure from either the product or process innovations undertaken by rivals. Over two-thirds of entrepreneurs had witnessed a lot of technical change in their industry in recent years, and almost one-half had used new technologies. Of those who had, the implementation of new technology had generally been successful. Information technology was thought to be very important by two-thirds of firms and was widely used, with the phone, fax, answering machine and personal computer being commonplace. Less common, but still in significant use, were mobile phones, and electronic databases. However, in specific sectors (e.g. the hotel trade) it may be that acceptance of IT may have been slower than this positive image suggests (Buick, 2003).

1.4   Summary evidence from second year

After a year had gone by, entrepreneurs who had consented to being interviewed about their new small firms were approached again on a follow-up basis. Most (81 per cent), but not all, had survived, and all had experienced material change in numerous respects. This section summarises the results from the perspective of the second year, and makes a number of brief comparative points. As before, the data given were the provisional results passed back to entrepreneurs. Though based on slightly imperfect data (subject initially to slight errors of omission or commission), they do convey well the way in which the evidence unfolded. It should be noted that, because of the common format, year by year, adopted in reporting back to entrepreneurs, there is some repetition of wording.

1.4.1   Market data

By the end of the second year, the average or typical firm in the sample had been in existence for about 34 months. Thus the evidence continues to create a moving picture of the early stage of the small firm's life-cycle. Typically it was run by one owner-manager, or entrepreneur, who had three full-time and two part-time workers. Gross sales were an average of £233,600, only slightly higher than the previous year. Firms had 're-focussed' their product ranges, and the average number of products sold had fallen from 48 to 32. These could be put into four main product groups, as before. There was a wide variation in what the typical firm regarded as its main market. More firms thought they operated in a local market, than in any other market, and the ranking of markets, in order of importance, was from local, to Scottish, to regional, to British and finally to international, the main change being a shift of emphasis from regional to Scottish markets. Although the typical firm found that most of its sales (about two-thirds) arose from just one leading product group, about one-fifth came from the next most important product group. The market share for the main product group was about one-fifth. Overall, competition in the firm's main market was perceived by entrepreneurs to be 'strong to moderate'. It was thought that competition was strongest on price, followed by advertising, and then salesmanship. Quality has become less important as a competitive issue. The great bulk of owner-managers expected to 'grow on' their businesses over the next few years.

1.4.2   Finance

The average level of gross profit for a firm in the sample had risen sharply from about £50,000 to about £67,000. This was based on a similar level of average sales of about £234,000. Just over half the firms had debt, but only a small percentage had any outside ownership. The average size of the owner-manager's personal financial injection was £13,000. Other sources of finance which had been important in the life of the average firm were mainly grants, subsidies, or bank loans, followed by family or friends.

1.4.3   Costs

About two-thirds of firms could identify a capacity output. Normal capacity operations had risen from about two-thirds to about three-quarters of peak capacity. A decreasing proportion (down from two-thirds to one-half) claimed to experience increasing returns to scale, probably reflecting an approach to decreasing returns at higher levels of capacity utilisation. Fewer owner-managers than in the first year (59 per cent) thought they had a good idea of what their rivals' costs were, and of these, fewer again (69 per cent) thought they had lower costs than rivals. In terms of the breakdown of costs into components, the most important were wages (over one-quarter) and raw materials (over one-quarter), followed by rents (about one-eighth).

1.4.4   Business strategy

The main aims of entrepreneurs were, first, to achieve long-run profit, and second, to promote the growth of their firm. Few specified that they mainly sought short-run profit, and only a small proportion expressed the view that they merely wanted to survive. The main reason for running a business was now predominantly to satisfy the need for achievement (36 per cent). Running a business as an alternative to unemployment was now relatively less important, and had been newly joined by the motive 'to get rich'.

Significantly fewer firms (down from nine out of ten to two-thirds) now had a business plan, and this was only reviewed every 6 months. Firms now looked further ahead (on average 19 months), when considering the impact of their decisions. Whilst there was a high awareness of the importance of information technology, this was less so of quality management. Few firms (about one-eighth) had thought about or implemented a TQM system. However, various quality controls were commonly adopted (e.g. product quality standards, operations and personnel standards, quality standards for business as a whole). Entrepreneurs identified their major strengths as being product quality, followed by adaptability; and their major weaknesses as lying in their market share, financial resources and organisation. The main threat to the owner-manager's business was now thought to be rivals' competition (21 per cent) rather than the market share (17 per cent); and adaptability now joined product quality as a factor that provided the main opportunity to the business.

1.4.5   *Human resources*

Just over half of the entrepreneurs had run a business before, usually someone else's, but, for a significant minority, their own. Three per cent had attended some sort of college or university course since the previous year. Almost two-thirds of these had some kind of diploma or certificate qualification, and whilst none had a doctoral degree, again about one-seventh had an honours degree. The typical day was still mainly spent producing the product, followed by attending to sales and then to management. Of those firms which had employees, under half of them had undergone any sort of formal training. About 11 per cent of an employee's time was spent on formal training. The bulk of employees acquired skills 'on the job' as well, and skill acquisition was perceived by eight out of ten owner-managers to be 'very important' for employees' productivity.

1.4.6   *Organisation*

The typical firm in the sample was no longer a sole trader operating from business premises (down since the first year from one-third to one-quarter). About one-quarter were private limited companies, a quarter partnerships, and the rest sole traders operating from home. Subordinates were reviewed about every three months on average, and the discretion over subordinates' activities was extensive. The typical reason for dismissing a subordinate was either because of a disciplinary problem, or because of him or her having become an unsuitable employee. An increasing proportion (87 per cent of cases) of subordinates understood and acted on instructions. When they did not, the typical reason was that instructions were unclear (two-thirds of cases), followed by inadequate subordinates' skills.

1.4.7   Technical change

In the short lifetimes of these firms, process innovation (improving an existing process) was typically thought to have been 'slightly important' by owner managers. Also, product innovation (doing something entirely new) was ranked as having been 'slightly important' on average since start-up. Most entrepreneurs did not feel under pressure from either the product or process innovations undertaken by rivals. Almost two-thirds of entrepreneurs had witnessed a lot of technical change in their industry in recent years, and almost one-half had used new technologies. Of those who had, the implementation of new technology had generally been successful. Information technology was now thought to be very important by rather fewer firms than before (down from two-thirds to a half), but it remained widely used, with the phone, fax, answering machine and personal computer being commonplace. Less common, but still in significant use, were again mobile phones, and electronic databases.

1.5   Summary evidence from third year

Below, the results as they stood in the third year are presented under the same headings as in the two previous sections (which themselves relate to the subsections of the administered questionnaires of the third year of fieldwork). As the picture becomes more complete, the evidence starts to take on the character of a 'bird's eye view' of the development of new small firms in Scotland. By the end of the third year, of the original 150 firms in the sample, 78 per cent were still in business. This represented an annual failure rate of just over 7 per cent, which was below historical trends.

1.5.1   Market data

Typically, the average firm was run by one owner-manager, and had three full-time and three part-time workers. Gross sales were an average of £370,000, some 64 per cent higher than in the previous year. The average number of products (33) and main product groups (4) were much as before. Although there was wide variation in what the typical firm regarded as its main market, more firms thought they operated in a local market, than in any other sort of market. The ranking of markets, in order of importance, was from local, to Scottish, to regional, to British and finally to international, as for the last year. Although the typical firm found that most of its sales (about two-thirds) arose from just one leading product group, about one-fifth came from the next most important product group. The market share for the main product group was stable at about one-quarter. Overall, competition in the firm's main market was perceived to be 'strong to moderate'. It was thought that competition was strongest on price, followed by quality, and then salesmanship. Entrepreneurs thought that quality had become more important as a competitive issue. The great bulk of entrepreneurs expected growth in their businesses over the next few years.

1.5.2   Finance

The average level of gross profit for a firm in the sample had risen sharply from about £67,000 to about £104,000. This was based on a level of average sales of about £370,000. Just over half the firms had debt, but again only a small percentage had any outside ownership. The other main sources of finance which have been important in the life of the average firm were, first, grants, subsidies, or bank loans, followed by family or friends.

1.5.3   Costs

Over 70 per cent of firms could identify a capacity output. Normal operating levels had risen from about two-thirds to about three-quarters of peak capacity, mostly reflecting improved macroeconomic conditions. A decreasing proportion of firms (50 per cent) experienced increasing returns to scale, probably reflecting the decreasing returns induced at higher levels of capacity utilisation. Fewer entrepreneurs than in the previous year (54 per cent) thought they had a good idea of what their rivals' costs were, and of these, slightly more (72 per cent) thought they had lower costs than rivals. In terms of the breakdown of costs into components, the most important were wages (over one-third) and raw materials (about one-third), followed by rents (about one-eleventh).

1.5.4   Business and pricing strategy

The main avowed aims of entrepreneurs were, first, to achieve long-run profit, and second, to promote the growth of their firm. Few specified that they mainly sought short-run profit, and only a small proportion expressed the view that they merely wanted to survive. The main reason for running a business had now predominantly become to satisfy the need for achievement (29 per cent), followed by a desire to be one's own boss (27 per cent). Running a business as an alternative to unemployment had now become relatively unimportant (just 15 per cent), and indeed had been overtaken by the motive 'to get rich' (21 per cent).

Over two-thirds of businesses now had a business plan, and this was now reviewed slightly less frequently than before, every seven months. Firms now looked further ahead (on an average of 20 months), when considering the impact of their decisions. There was a high awareness of the importance of information technology.

Prices were reviewed roughly quarterly, and slightly less often in boom conditions. In boom conditions, if a rival put up its price, firms would not necessarily raise their prices; but in slump conditions if rivals raised prices, they would definitely not be followed. In slump conditions, if rivals cut prices, firms would typically not follow, but in boom conditions, if rivals cut prices, they would certainly not be followed.

1.5.5 Human resources

Seven per cent of entrepreneurs had attended some sort of college or university course since the previous year. All of these had obtained some kind of certificated qualification. The typical day was still mainly spent producing the product, followed by management, and then attending to sales. Just over half of the employees had undergone some sort of formal training. About 8 per cent of an employee's time was spent on formal training. The bulk of employees acquired skills 'on the job' as well, and skill acquisition was perceived by eight out of ten owner-managers to be 'very important' for employees' productivity. The average wage paid to full-time skilled workers had risen by 5 per cent, to £6.27 an hour, or an annual salary of around £12,000.

When skilled labour was scarce, in boom conditions, firms typically raised the wage rates they offered. In slump conditions, when skilled labour was plentiful, firms tended to raise the quality of workers hired.

1.5.6 Organisation

The commonest firm type was a sole trader operating from home or from business premises (50 per cent), followed by private limited companies (about one-quarter), partnerships (about one-quarter) and public companies (just one). Subordinates were reviewed formally about every 8 months on average, and informally about every 3 months, and the discretion over subordinates' activities was less than before, although still considerable. The typical reason for dismissal was either a disciplinary problem, or because the employee was no longer suitable for the job. Most subordinates (86 per cent) understood and acted on instructions. When they did not, the typical reasons nominated were inadequate subordinates' skills (three-quarters), followed by unclear instructions and subordinate indiscipline.

1.5.7 Technical change

Process innovation (improving an existing process) was typically viewed as 'slightly important' by entrepreneurs. Also, product innovation (doing something entirely new) was ranked as having been 'slightly important' on average since start-up. Most entrepreneurs did not feel under pressure from either the product or process innovations undertaken by rivals. Less than one-third of owner-managers had witnessed a lot of technical change in their industry over the last year, but over one-half had used new technologies. Of those who had, the implementation of new technology had generally been successful. Information technology was now thought to be very important by a half of the firms. The phone, fax, answering machine and personal computer were commonplace cf. (Kinder, 2000). Less common, but still in significant use, were mobile phones, and electronic databases.

1.6 Summary evidence from fourth year

The evidence below arises from the fourth phase of the study. By then, of the original 150 firms in the sample, 57 per cent were still in business. This represented an annual failure rate of 11 per cent, which remained below historical trends. Subheadings follow those of the relevant administered questionnaire (in this case AQ4 of the Appendix to this book). For comparability across the years, the new section on management information systems has been omitted here.

1.6.1 Market data

Typically, the average firm was run by one or two owner-managers, and still had five full-time and four part-time workers. Gross sales were an average of £396,000, only 7 per cent higher than in the previous year. The average number of products (32) and main product groups (4) were much as before. Although there was wide variation in what the typical firm regarded as its main market, more firms (41 per cent) thought they operated in a local market, than in any other market. The ranking of markets, in order of importance, was from local, to regional, to Scottish, to British and finally to international. Although the typical firm found that most of its sales (about two-thirds) arose from just one leading product group, about a fifth came from the next most important product group. The market share for the main product group was again stable at about one quarter. Overall, competition in the firm's main market had increased to 'strong'. It was now thought that competition was strongest on price, followed by volume, and then salesmanship. Volume had become more important as a competitive issue. The great bulk of entrepreneurs expected growth in business over the next few years.

1.6.2 Finance

The average level of gross profit for a firm in the sample had risen slightly from about £104,000 to about £109,000. This was based on a level of average sales of about £396,000. Over half the firms (58 per cent) had debt, but only slightly more than previously (7 per cent) had any outside ownership. The main other source of finance which had been important in the life of the average firm was a bank loan (62 per cent). Grants were now held by just 13 per cent; indicating a steady decline in grant support as the small business matured.

1.6.3   Costs

Now 98 per cent of firms could identify a capacity output. Normal operating levels have risen from about three-quarters to about four-fifths of peak capacity, again reflecting good macroeconomic conditions. A slightly higher proportion of firms (55 per cent) now experienced increasing returns to scale. Far fewer entrepreneurs than in the previous year (42 per cent) thought they had a good idea of what their rivals' costs were, and of these, slightly fewer (69 per cent) thought they had lower costs than rivals. These results suggest learning by the entrepreneur, and a more realistic appraisal of the business as time progresses. In terms of the break-down of costs into components, the most important were wages (40 per cent) and raw materials (about 34 per cent), followed by rents (about 10 per cent).

1.6.4   Business and pricing strategy

The main avowed aims of entrepreneurs were still, first, to achieve long-run profit, and second, to promote the growth of their small firms. Few specified that they mainly sought short-run profit or that they merely wanted to survive.

Only one half of the firms now had a business plan, and this was now reviewed slightly less frequently than before, every 8 months. Firms now looked ahead an average of 18 months when considering the impact of their decisions. There was a moderate awareness of the importance of information technology. Overall, there was a greater focus on commercial success, and a lesser focus on more formal ways of achieving this.

1.6.5   Human resources

Only five per cent of entrepreneurs had attended some sort of college or university course since the previous year. All of these had some kind of certificated quali-fication. The typical day was still mainly spent producing the product, followed by management, and then attending to sales. Over half of the employees (sixty per cent) had now undergone some sort of formal training. About eight per cent of an employee's time was still spent on formal training. The bulk of employees (ninety-five per cent) acquired skills 'on the job' as well, and skill acquisition was perceived by eight out of ten owner managers to be 'very important' for employ-ees' productivity. The average wage paid to full-time skilled workers had risen again, by 12 per cent, to £7 an hour, or an annual salary of around £13,400. Overall, though several aspects of human resources changed little, the benefits of earlier human capital investments were becoming evident.

1.6.6   Organisation

The commonest firm type remained a sole trader operating from home or from busi-ness premises (48 per cent), followed by private limited companies (31 per cent), partnerships (22 per cent) and public companies (just one). Subordinates were still reviewed formally about every eight months on average, and informally about every two months, and the discretion over subordinates' activities was still considerable. The typical reasons for dismissal remained either a disciplinary problem, or because the employee was no longer suitable for the job. Most subordinates still understood and acted on instructions. When they did not, the typical reasons nominated were inadequate subordinates' skills, followed by a new factor, dissatisfaction with pay conditions.

1.6.7   *Technical change*

Process innovation (improving an existing process) had been 'slight'. Also, product innovation (doing something entirely new) was not common. Most entrepreneurs did not feel under pressure from either the product or process innovations undertaken by rivals. About 40 per cent of entrepreneurs had witnessed a lot of technical change in their industry over the last year, and over one-half (51 per cent) had implemented new technology, generally successfully. Spreadsheets or other computer software for handling information within the business were commonly used (69 per cent).

1.7   The structure of this book

It has been made clear previously that this book is concerned with an *entrepreneurial* analysis of small business inception and growth. A necessary feature of such an approach is its willingness to embrace inter-disciplinarity. The structure of the book reflects this. Its contents are divided into six parts: background, existing evidence, finance, performance, information and contingency, and flexibility. These parts, and their component chapters, are considered as follows.

Part 1, the *Background*, has two substantive chapters. Chapter 2 sets out in some detail the fieldwork procedures adopted, the sampling frame, and the relation between the sampling frame and the population of small firms. It concludes with a brief characterisation of the typical small entrepreneurial firm, and with key statistics from the small firms database that was created from the fieldwork evidence. In many ways, Chapter 2 extends and amplifies the content of this, the first chapter. Chapter 3 then looks in more detail at the instrumentation, and the data gathered under its main headings, namely markets, finance, costs, strategy, human capital, organisation and technical change. By the end of Part 1, the reader should be thoroughly grounded in the data acquisition process, and the subsequent mounting of such data on a database suitable for statistical and econometric analysis.

Part 2, *Existing Evidence*, is a 'bridging' part of the book, connecting directly related past research and analysis to the current concerns of this book. Many of the principal themes of the book are anticipated in this linking material of Chapters 4 (growth and survival) and 5 (funding shortages). Chapter 4 anticipates the treatment of survival, performance and growth of Part 4; and Chapter 5 anticipates the treatment of capital and financial structure of Part 3. Furthermore, Chapters 4 and 5 introduce techniques to be used later, like the constrained finance problem, and the phase diagram representation of Gibrat's Law, which are used in Chapters 6 and 16, respectively. The approaches of Chapters 4 and 5 also anticipate the general approach of the book as a whole. That is to say, they use primary-source data, to which tools of statistical inference and econometrics are applied. In many ways, these chapters are prototypes for the rest of the book.

Part 3, *Finance*, moves on to the substantive research content of the book, exploring the statics and dynamics of small business financial structure, and testing hypotheses derived therefrom. An important insight is that capital structure is strongly time-dependent: what may be right for the 1-year-old small firm (e.g. as regards gearing) may be quite wrong for the 3-year-old small firm. A novelty of Chapter 8 is its use of calibration (rather than the econometrics of Chapter 7) to test hypotheses about financial trajectories.

Part 4, *Performance* moves into the territory first broached in Chapter 4. It reports upon a detailed investigation into methods of measuring small business performance using so-called 'objective' (as opposed to 'attitudinal') variables. This lays the basis for the introduction of another technique to be used later in the book (in Chapter 14), namely cluster analysis. Here, it is used to rank small firms on a one-dimensional metric, even though the underlying performance attributes are multi-dimensional. This is then used to develop and test a model of performance and strategy, moving this kind of argument considerably further than in Chapter 4. Finally, Chapter 11 looks at entrepreneurial actions, and performance in the sense of staying in business. Underlying this is a general optimising model of the small firm, which allows for quite a finely nuanced view of entrepreneurial actions. Of especial interest is the focus on the organisational shape of the small firm, as represented by the extent to which hierarchy is used, and the way full-time and part-time workers are controlled to achieve flexibility that will both enhance survival prospects and improve performance. This treatment in Chapter 11 anticipates the approach of Part 5, using contingency theory, and of Part 6, focussing on flexibility. It anticipates an approach which places greater emphasis on the organisational form of the small firm, and its adaptability in the face of changed circumstances.

Part 5, *Information and Contingency*, looks at the small entrepreneurial firm as an adaptive entity, with an internal form, and systems of monitoring and control in place. It starts, in Chapter 12, with a rather theoretical (though grounded) approach to information systems and performance, then proceeds to detailed testing in Chapters 13 and 14. The dynamic approach reasserts itself in the empirical analysis of the timing of contingencies, and subsequent organisational adaptation, in Chapter 13. Chapter 14 concludes Part 5, starting first with the use of cluster analysis again (this time to develop a morphology of small firm types), and then investigating in considerable detail the impact that various contingencies (e.g. technology, strategy, markets) have on organisational form.

All the necessary preliminaries are therefore in place for the final Part 6 of the book, *Flexibility*. Part 6 starts by setting out key features of flexibility in

Chapter 15, and then examines two particular forms of flexibility in Chapter 16 (scale flexibility) and Chapter 17 (market niche flexibility). Both the latter forms of flexibility are concerned with adjustment to equilibrium (e.g. speed, and direction of adjustment) and shifts in equilibrium itself. They provide a link between Chapters 4 and 16, this being Gibrat's Law (or the Law of Proportionate Effect). A different concept of equilibrium may seem to be utilised in Chapter 17 (using Markov chains), but actually the approaches are more similar than may appear to be the case at first sight (e.g. both approaches have at their core a stochastic, first-order, linear difference equation as the 'equation of motion'). Finally, Chapter 18 adopts the most general approach in the book, and in many ways melds the principal themes of the book into a unified approach, involving dynamics, performance, organisational form and adaptation. This last chapter also builds on the database behind all the work in the book, in that a further round of fieldwork was undertaken to make possible a perspective on long-lived small firms – going right to the other end of the small business life-cycle, from that introduced in Chapter 1. A new view of flexibility is also advanced, which is only possible because of the detailed view taken of the organisational form of the small firm. This 'new view' is a real options approach, which examines flexibility in terms of the ability both to move forward in investments, and to move back (at minimum cost) should such an investment not fulfil its promise. Such a view of flexibility is very useful for understanding performance over the full life-cycle of the small firm.

1.8   Conclusion

A fairly comprehensive discussion has been provided earlier of the methodology to be used, the types of firms to be examined, and the hypotheses to be addressed (and with what tools). Attention must now be turned to the solid scientific analysis which is at the core of this book. It should be said that, bearing in mind that many readers may want to dip into this book, looking at specific topics (like financial structure, performance or flexibility) each chapter is reasonably self-contained, especially if read in conjunction with Chapter 1 itself. So, there is some slight repetition of material, especially as it relates to the database, between the various chapters. This slight (and deliberate) over-determinacy, is something I am comforted by (and I hope the reader is too), for it is a characteristic of robust, survivable systems, of which the long-lived small firm is an example.

Endnotes

1 For further details on the Enterprise Trust as a business incubator see Reid and Jacobsen (1988, Ch. 5). For an Australian perspective on advice provided to micro-firms, see Leighton and Schaper (2003).
2 These data in Sections 1.3–1.6 are as represented to owner-managers at the time. Slight revisions did occur year by year as small errors of data entry were spotted and corrected, omitted data were retrieved and inserted in the database, and so on. Though imperfect, these data do give a good feel for the magnitudes involved, and a strong sense of the

evolution of firms. Because feedback was provided each year to entrepreneurs on a common basis there is some repetition of wording across the same sections by years. This has been retained, both because it reflects the actual information provided to entrepreneurs, and because the repetition has been found helpful to readers encountering the material of this book for the first time.

2 Fieldwork and database

2.1 Introduction

The evidence presented in this chapter relates to very small firms, technically micro-firms,[1] which are at the smallest end of the reverse J-shaped size distribution of business enterprises (Daly and McCann, 1992). Relatively little is known about these firms, many of which are sole proprietorships. For such firms, annual sales (turnover) may not even exceed the value added tax (VAT) threshold. The evidence to which this chapter refers aims to dispel our ignorance of this relatively unexplored small business constituency by obtaining primary source data using fieldwork methods (Sekaran, 1992; Burgess, 1984).

Here, the aim is to provide an empirically 'rich' characterisation of new business start-up in Scotland ('the foundations of enterprise'), by reference to its more qualitative features (Glaser and Strauss, 1967), like strength of competition, business experience and business planning. As Alam (2005) has argued in a related fieldwork-based research area (namely customer interaction in new product development), such qualitative work can be both scientifically objective and methodologically robust (cf. Glaser and Strauss, 1967; Miles and Huberman, 1984). After brief consideration of fieldwork activity and the sampling frame, this chapter starts the process (in Section 2.4), which is not finished until the end of Chapter 3, of developing a characterisation of the typical, *average* or *modal* new small firm. In a sense, it aims to provide a 'bird's eye view' of a small firm in Scotland.

2.2 Fieldwork activity

To illustrate, such a 'modal small firm' is found to be very small, and subject to strong competition by prices, advertising and salesmanship. It is motivated by long-term profit, and exploits local niche markets by emphasising the quality of its own goods and services over those of its rivals. This kind of detailed characterisation is not typical of work that uses secondary source data. However, it *is* the sort of detail that is typical of fieldwork evidence (Burgess, 1984; Werner and Schoepfle, 1987; Shaffir and Stebbins, 1991), obtained by going directly into the small business. This methodology permeates all the empirical work of this book.

Thus evidence on which conclusions are based derives from three rounds of face-to-face interviews (cf. Sudman and Bradburn, 1982; Neijens, 1987; Willis, 2005), in this case, with 150 Scottish entrepreneurs. As indicated in Chapter 1, in the 'base year' of 1994–95 a sample of entrepreneurs, stratified by region, was interviewed, using an administered questionnaire (AQ1 as in appendix to this book) (Oppenheim, 1992). This chapter now considers the evidence of follow-up interviews, which were made with the entrepreneurs of firms which had survived in 1995–96 and 1996–97.

This stratified sampling procedure (cf. St John and Richardson, 1989) which was adopted has produced a set of firms which represent well the attributes of the larger population of new firms in Scotland over the period in which fieldwork was conducted. For example, by business type, the proportions in the sample were: sole trader (from home) (26 per cent); sole trader (from business premises) (29 per cent); partnership (19 per cent); and private company (27 per cent). The Scottish new business statistics produced by Scottish Enterprise in 1996 were based on a sample of 21,400 new firms in 1995. For this sample, the proportions of business types were: sole proprietorship (50 per cent); partnership (23 per cent); and limited company (27 per cent). Although there are slight category differences, these two sets of percentages are in close concordance. This provides reassurance on the representative nature of the sample used in this chapter, and indeed elsewhere in this book. More detail on the relation between the sample and the population is given in Section 2.3.

Crucial to access to the field are the 'gatekeepers' who effect introductions and provide 'ports of entry'. In this study they were the Directors of ETs (Moore, 1988) in Scotland,[2] these being small enterprise stimulating units which are jointly funded by the private and public sectors (Reid and Jacobsen, 1988: Ch. 5; Reid, 1996b). The Directors of these units provided random samples of entrepreneurs from their client lists, subject to two restrictions, that they should be able to identify the date of inception of the enterprise, and that this date should be no more than 3 years from inception. The fieldwork areas may be represented as a reverse L-shape across Scotland (Figure 2.1), running from the northeast (e.g. Haugh and Pardy, 1999), as far north as Inverurie, down through the main east coast population centres, including Aberdeen, Dundee and Edinburgh, across the Central Belt, to Glasgow and the west coast. The specific sample areas were: Inverurie, Aberdeen, Dundee, Crossgates, Cupar, Alloa, Grangemouth, Edinburgh, Midlothian, Stirling, Angus, Perth, Hamilton, Clydesdale, Cumnock & Doon, Strathkelvin, Glasgow, Gordon and Paisley. The geographical representation in Figure 2.1 (cf. St John and Richardson, 1989) indicates the main fieldwork areas used within Scotland, with radii of circles being proportional to the sizes of strata for which data were generated by fieldwork activity, within sub-regions of Scotland.

2.3 The sample and population

As suggested earlier, the typical firm (in the sense of average or modal) of the sample is a micro-firm (i.e. having not more than 10 employees). This typical

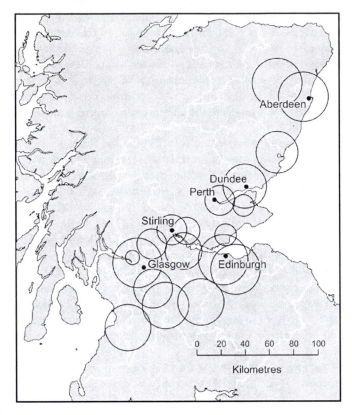

Figure 2.1 Fieldwork areas of Scotland for the study.

firm produced just less than 50 products, which could be classified into four main product groups. Gross sales were around a quarter of a million pounds (for firms which survived), and about half that value for firms which ceased trading. Generally, survival rates were high, with 105 of the original 150 still being in business in the fourth year (1997). The number of firms exiting year by year was low at: 28 in year 2 (1995); another 5 in year 3 (1996); and a further 12 in year 4 (1997)[3] (cf. Smallbone, 1989).

In terms of how well the sample represents the population, Table 2.1 provides a picture which strengthens earlier comment in Section 2.1. Essentially, the representative nature of the sample (as expected from previous discussion) is suggested by its reverse J-shaped firm size distribution, with a high proportion being of the very smallest firm types, as measured by employees. The data presented provide the best comparison that could be made on available statistics. The Scottish data set for 1996 has rather more weight at the bottom end of the size scale (as does the United Kingdom in 1994), compared to the sample as initially selected for the project research in 1994. However, the effect is not marked.

Table 2.1 Size distributions of sample and population

Business size	Sample 1994	UK 1994	Scotland 1996
1–4	61.4	66.5	65.0
5–9	20.5	16.8	17.5
10–19	8.0	9.5	9.9
20–49	8.0	4.5	4.7
50–99	1.1	1.4	1.4
100+	1.1	1.3	1.5

Notes:
(a) Business size is measured by number of employees.
(b) Figures are a percentage of the total number of businesses with 1 or more employees.
(c) 1996 figures for Scotland are the earliest set available with are comparable to the sample.

Based on this, and other evidence, the sample seems to be a reasonable representation of the population of small firms in Scotland, during the period of the fieldwork activity.

2.4 The typical micro-firm

The discussion of this section is largely qualitative, being based on attitudinal variables (often binary in form) in the administered questionnaire (AQ). Table 2.2 provides much of the statistical underpinning for the discussion of this section. The typical small firm[4] in the base year of the study (1994–95) had a headcount of seven (satisfying the micro-firm criterion of ≤ 10 employees), gross sales of £234k at nominal prices, and produced or supplied four ranges of products or services. Its main market was local, and it had about 11 major rivals and 24 minor rivals. Competition was regarded as strong, particularly with respect to price, advertising and salesmanship. The goods or service supplied was differentiated, and the firm competed independently against a dominant rival and a few small firms. Gross profits were about £50k and net profits about £15k, and the entrepreneur had sunk about £13k in the business at inception. Typically, neither a bank loan, nor outside equity was used to help launch the business (cf. Clay and Cowling, 1996).[5]

On an average, the small firm operated at just over two-thirds of capacity and enjoyed falling unit costs. The largest cost component, in percentage terms (25 per cent approx.) was attributed to wages. A formal business plan, prepared using outside help, was reviewed roughly biannually. The time over which the impact of planned decisions was considered was about one and a half years. The two main reasons for running the business were as an alternative to unemployment, and to satisfy the need for achievement; and the main aim of the business was regarded as the pursuit of long-term profit. Both strategic and operational decisions were made, in part, by drawing on the past experience of other similar small businesses, and strategic decisions involved greater consultation within the

Table 2.2 Summary statistics for key variables

Name	n	Mean	SD	Minimum	Maximum
Grprof	124	51,673	82,854	−2500	450×10^3
Grsales	147	227×10^3	0.844×10^6	0	960×10^4
Netprof	131	13,555	28,879	−50,000	151×10^3
Debt	150	0.507	0.501	0	1
Outeq	149	0.054	0.226	0	1
Owncash	143	13,014	2985	0	250×10^3
Bankloan	149	0.322	0.467	0	1
Employ	150	6.400	14.702	1	157
Normcap	104	67.641	27.269	0	140
Impact	148	15.466	18.968	0	120
Involvea	150	0.260	0.440	0	1
Involvee	150	0.187	0.391	0	1
Involvef	150	0.260	0.440	0	1
Mainaima	150	0.167	0.374	0	1
Mainaimc	150	0.320	0.468	0	1
Mainaimd	150	0.213	0.411	0	1
Mainaimf	150	0.127	0.334	0	1
Colluni	149	0.752	0.434	0	1
Techchng	150	0.620	0.487	0	1
Initiata	93	0.430	0.498	0	1
Initiatb	93	0.140	0.349	0	1
Newtecha	150	0.533	0.501	0	1

Note: SD denotes standard deviation

firm than did operational decisions. About two-thirds of decisions were made for purely financial, as opposed to personal, reasons.

For this sample, the typical small firm was not willing to sacrifice a proportion of the stake in the business in order to promote its growth, but it was willing to accept smaller profits for a while to expand the business.[6] Trade intelligence was gathered from rivals, especially about market share and financial performance. This type of information-gathering was done frequently (about every 2 months), largely by word of mouth, but also through newspapers, trade associations and trade journals. Information technology (IT) was important with the phone, fax, personal computer and telephone answering machine being the typical 'cluster' of IT devices (cf. Smith, 1997a: Ch. 5).[7] The main use of IT was for administrative purposes (e.g. keeping track of buyers and suppliers), with producing accounts, networking and producing forecasts and business plans also being important.

TQM systems were not typically adopted, and this was also true for forms of quality assurance which required outside validation (e.g. BS 5750 or ISO 9000). Even so, the typical entrepreneurs regarded their firm's product quality as its strongest attribute, followed by specialist know-how and faith in the business. The principal threats to the business were perceived to be rivals' market shares, competitiveness and rivals' plant or resources. Product quality, adaptability and new ideas were thought to offer the greatest opportunity to the typical entrepreneur.

Experience of running a business before was the norm, though it was typically someone else's business. 'Hands on' experience, and financial and product knowledge were thought to be the most important abilities that the typical entrepreneur 'carried in' to the new business. Developed human capital was in evidence, in the sense that the typical entrepreneur had been to college or even to university and had been awarded a form of accreditation like a certificate or diploma. About 58 h were devoted to the business weekly, of which about 18 h were other than of normal working hours (i.e. other than the time a full-time employee would work).

It was normal to provide formal training for employees, and this accounted for about one-eighth of employees' time. The entrepreneur typically allocated most of his effort (40 per cent) to creating the supply of the main products or services, with sales, management and planning occupying most of his remaining time. Skills were invariably acquired 'on the job' as well as through training, and such experience-based skills were crucial to employees' productivity.

The wage rate for the best skilled full-time worker was about £5.60 per hour, or £900 per month. In the hierarchical organisation which is typical of even the small firm (cf. Reid, 1998), incentives were quite strong across hierarchical levels, with managers being paid about twice the base level, and directors about three times the level. Authority was usually not exercised simply through immediate subordinates, but was typically exercised by selective intervention at the level which was thought to be most appropriate. Superiors reviewed subordinates about every quarter, and they had extensive discretion over their workplace activities. Standard procedures for monitoring subordinates were typically not in place, and monitoring itself was unpredictable rather than regular in its application. Compliance by subordinates was high, and in most circumstances (73 per cent) superiors could get subordinates to understand and act on what was required of them. When this did not happen, typical causes were demarcation disputes and unfair instructions.

Within the small firm, areas of specialisation were typically loosely defined, with different specialists being knowledgeable about each others' skills, and willing to take on each others' tasks in certain circumstances. The entrepreneur typically took the burden of hiring or dismissing personnel upon his own shoulders. The usual reason for dismissal was disciplinary problems.

Innovation was an evident, if not pervasive, feature of these small firms. Typically slight change in process innovation had been undertaken, usually inspired by suggestions made from within the firm itself (e.g. derived by experience or 'learning by doing'), or by customers. Rivals were thought to be undertaking little process innovation, and this was perceived not to create much competitive pressure. Product innovation, however, was the norm, and it was also typically undertaken by rivals, though this too was not thought to create great competitive pressure. Technical change within the industry was normal, with the prime initiator of it being a leader in the industry, which occasionally was the small firm itself. If technical knowledge were sought, which was of relevance to new products or processes, then suppliers and customers played an important role in the provision of it, as did trade journals.

To conclude, this bird's eye view of the new Scottish micro-firm, emphasising typical features, gives insights which may be summarised as follows. These firms are very small, and neither very innovative nor highly profitable, but their owner-managers emphasise their business quality. They are subject to rivalry, especially as manifested by competitive pricing, advertising and salesmanship, and are largely run on a commercial basis. Entrepreneurs are quite skilled and experienced and have well-established organisational structures within the firm which sustain monitoring and provide incentives. Despite the lurid titles of popular books aimed at the would-be entrepreneur, like 'Go for Growth', 'Profit from Your Business' and 'Do the Deal', all of which suggest the fast-track lifestyle of a 'buccaneer capitalist', life in the real world of small business enterprise is more prosaic. The evidence for Scotland is that it involves the quiet application of much time and some skill, under competitive pressure, to deliver a quality product or service in a local market. This sounds platitudinous, but the evidence is that this is how the business world ticks, despite more romantic images of the entrepreneurial economy.

2.5   Key statistics from the database

The account given of small business enterprise in Section 2.4 above was largely qualitative, and aimed to give what was called a bird's eye view of micro-firms in the Scottish economy. In this section, the treatment is more quantitative than qualitative, and aims to look (very briefly) at key statistical features of the evidence, in terms of average outcomes.

In Table 2.2, some of the most important variables of the database are displayed. They are in fact just a small subset of over 600 variables available, but cover key features of size, structure and motives. Definitions of variable names are contained in the appendix to Chapter 3. The table gives sample size n (taking account of missing observations), and the mean ($\bar{x}$), standard deviation (σ) and range (min, max) for each variable. Many of the variables are of binary form, so in this sense the table contains the basis for much of the qualitative analysis of the previous section, and may be useful for buttressing that account with percentages (mean values).

Missing from the table are the variables which give the survival rates. The initial sample size was 150, with 81 per cent of firms still running in the second year, and 78 per cent in the third year. These survival rates are relatively high for new business start-ups [see Reid (1993, pp. 166–167) for various estimates close to the fieldwork period], and this reflects both the screening of the ETs and the generally favourable macroeconomic conditions during the sampling periods. The data in Table 2.2 relate to the base sample period of 1994–95. The way in which key variables change over time for the period 1995–96 and 1996–97 will be considered later, in Chapter 3, under the headings of market, finance, costs, business strategy, human capital, organisation and technical change, where the headings correspond to sections of the administered questionnaire.

As will be clear from Table 2.2, the micro-firm status of these small enterprises is very much in evidence. They generated about a quarter of a million pounds of sales per year, which amounted to £35k (approx.) per person employed, although as sales varied much more widely than employment,[8] this overstates the typical or modal sales generated per employee.

The table provides diverse information on topics like capital structure, internal organisation, costs, motivation, human capital and technical change. General features which are noteworthy include: the marked preference for debt over equity finance (*Debt*, *Outeq*), high capacity utilisation (*Normcap*), the lengthy planning horizon (*Impact*), the ubiquity of obtaining credentials after secondary school (*Colluni*); and the pervasiveness of technological change (*Techchng*).

2.6 Conclusion

This chapter does no more than highlighting the range and form of data that will be discussed subsequently. More detailed analysis follows in Chapter 3. There, the emphasis is on differences between those small firms that continued trading and those small firms that ceased trading, over the 3-year time period of their early life cycles.

Endnotes

1 The upper threshold limit for micro-firms is ten employees – sometimes expressed in full-time equivalent employees (e.g. Part timer = 0.5 full timer).
2 The basis for this policy document is set out in the publication of the Industry Department for Scotland (1989) *Towards Scottish Enterprise*, Edinburgh, HMSO.
3 These relatively high survival rates are partly attributable to the fact that all small firms came through business incubator units (ETs), but no doubt an additional feature was the relatively successful state of the Scottish macroeconomy over this period of time. For more detailed analysis of the positive role played by ETs, in terms of policy regime shift, see Reid (1999).
4 Where this term is used in the following few paragraphs, 'typical' means average or modal firm for the sample. It should be noted that the summary statistics here differ slightly, in some cases, from those presented in Chapter 1 (Sections 1.3–1.6). The latter evidence relates to the feedback given to entrepreneurs immediately after fieldwork had been completed, in an annual phase, and the statistics were preliminary (due to error, incompleteness, etc.) at that point, though useful in an indicative sense. In contrast, the data of this chapter reflect revised figures after the database had been audited, and necessary amendments and corrections made.
5 Though a majority of small firms (51 per cent) had bank loans. Gearing was high at 169 per cent though entrepreneurs expressed the hope that this would be more than halved over a 3 years time horizon.
6 This willingness to sacrifice short-run profit is not inconsistent with long-run profit maximisation: indeed, it may be intrinsic to it.
7 It has been found that whilst no specific IT device, in itself, is crucial to small business performance, certain 'clusters' of IT devices *are* very important. See, for example, the discussion in Chapter 10.
8 The coefficient of variation on sales ($\sigma/\bar{x}$) is 3.72 compared to 2.30 for employment.

3 Main quantitative features of the database

3.1 Introduction

This chapter aims to build upon the empirical evidence for Chapter 2. Making reference to markets, finance, costs, business strategy, human capital, internal organisation and technical change, it uses key components of the database to identify salient differences between surviving and non-surviving small firms over a period of 2–3 years after inception. The empirical evidence, it has been seen, is based upon interview data (Sudman and Bradburn, 1982; Niejens, 1987; Willis, 2005) acquired from 150 entrepreneurs over a 3-year period.

More generally, this chapter aims to address the central concerns of the book, namely, what makes the new small firm tick? Do those that survive have different features from those that close? These are the issues addressed in this chapter. In doing so, it makes reference to the unique body of primary source data on small business inception in Scotland referred to in Chapter 2. This facilitates an examination, to use biological terms, of the morphology and morphogenesis of small firms. This is possible because over 600 quantitative measures are available for each firm, and the data collectively take the form of an unbalanced panel. Many of these key measures are defined in the Appendix to this chapter.

Then the detailed features of the new small firm, as it develops over the next 2 years of its life, are examined by reference to markets, finance, costs, business strategy, human capital, internal organisation and technical change (see Sections 1–7 of the AQ1 in appendix to this book). For each year, firms which survived are compared with firms that closed. Key features are found to have salient differences. The surviving firms are found to be larger, better funded, lower geared and more profit-oriented. They also pay higher wages, and are both more attuned to, and realistic about, new technologies. The conclusion reached is that the small firms which survived generally displayed wider and deeper competencies than firms which closed (cf. Chaston et al., 2001; Huck and McEwan, 1991).[1] This was evident in many ways, including commercial orientation and strategic awareness.

3.2 Markets

The ultimate test of marketplace fitness of a firm is of course whether it survives. Indeed, if π_i is the profit of the i-th firm, the classical criterion for long-run survival is that $\pi_i \geq 0$ in which case survival and profitability are equivalent. Of course, failing to survive does not imply failure in a pejorative sense. For small niche opportunities it is perfectly rational for the entrepreneur to harvest this niche until profit is exhausted and then voluntarily to liquidate the firm. Far from failure in a pejorative sense, this would be efficient exploitation of a limited market opportunity. In the tables of this section (Tables 3.1–3.7) that follow, of which Table 3.1, on market data, is the first example, the distinction is made between firms which 'continued trading' and those which 'ceased trading' to ensure that the above point is carefully accommodated. However, in the narrative that follows, more demotic terms like 'survival' and 'failure' are sometimes used in similar contexts, just because this is common parlance. This is not to suggest that the distinction carefully made between continuing to trade and ceasing to trade is unimportant. In Tables 3.1–3.7, the values reported are mean values, computed for the indicated sample size. Variable names are defined in the Appendix to this chapter.

Table 3.1 indicates that surviving firms were, on average, longer lived than non-survivors (see *Inbus* measure). Though these differences are not marked, they confirm a long-established empirical regularity that fitness to survive depends on having survived (Brock and Evans, 1986). The time over which a firm survives is known to provide the entrepreneur with valuable marketplace experience, which enhances his capabilities, and also permits 'learning by doing' within the firm, which helps to reduce unit costs over time. The figures for gross sales (*Grsales*), gross profit (*Grprof*) and headcount (*Employ*) all indicate that the surviving firms were larger than non-surviving firms. Theories of entrepreneurship due to the likes of Lucas (1978) and Oi (1983) suggest that this implies that the more competent firms survive, as competence is positively related to firm size (Snell and Lau, 1994).

Looking at the sales generated per employee (viz. *Grsales* ÷ *Employ*), one finds that those that remained in business had figures of £36k per year in both years 2 and 3, whilst those going out of business had figures of £29k per year and

Table 3.1 Market data

	Year 2		Year 3	
	Continued trading $n = 122$	*Ceased trading* $n = 28$	*Continued trading* $n = 117$	*Ceased trading* $n = 33$
Inbus	22	18	22	17
Grsales	£252k	£114k	£253k	£133k
Grprof	£56k	£32k	£56k	£37k
Employ	7	4	7	5
Prodgrp	4	4	4	4
Product	47	44	46	47

£27k per year, respectively in each of these years. This difference is not explained by product ranges (*Prodgrp*) or even total number of products (*Product*), which are very similar in magnitude over time, and over survivors and non-survivors. One concludes, therefore, that non-survivors are exploiting niches which are on an average considerably smaller than those for survivors. This too suggests a superior competence of surviving firms (Foss and Mahnke, 2000).

3.3   Finance

Previous detailed work on the financial structure of firms within this database (Reid, 1997a, b) has suggested that 'financial structures were similar whether firms continued trading or not'. A perusal of Table 3.2, which contains more longitudinal data than were available at the time of the earlier study, slightly qualifies this statement. Again, variables are defined in the Appendix to this chapter.

Many financial features *are* similar: net profit (*Netprof*), access to outside equity (*Outeq*), the use of debt (*Debt*), having been awarded a grant at launch (*Grant*) and the debt/equity ratio (i.e. gearing) at start-up (*Gearst*). However, there are also minor and major differences. The first minor one is the greater tendency of non-survivors to use a bank loan to launch the business (*Bankloan*). This suggests a lesser net worth of entrepreneurs of firms which did not survive and/or a lesser willingness to commit financial resources to launch the business. The second minor one is the greater willingness of survivors to sacrifice profit in order to encourage growth of the business (*Smlprof*).

The major differences are as follows. First, the owner-managers of firms which had survived had committed considerably larger sums of money (*Owncash*) to the firm at its launch. Indeed, on an average the cash injection at launch was twice the magnitude of that committed by non-survivors. This also explains the greater need

Table 3.2 Financial data

| | Year 2 | | Year 3 | |
	Continued trading n = 122	Ceased trading n = 28	Continued trading n = 117	Ceased trading n = 33
Netprof	£13,329	£14,514	£13,547	£13,581
Debt	51%	50%	51%	48%
Outeq	6%	4%	5%	6%
Bankloan	31%	36%	30%	39%
Grant	78%	82%	76%	82%
Owncash	£14,331	£7084	£14,687	£6967
Gearst	159%	152%	155%	168%
Gearnow	166%	183%	164%	188%
Sacstak	45%	64%	44%	64%
Smlprof	90%	86%	91%	85%

for non-survivors to have access to bank loans at the stage of launching the business (cf. Fletcher, 1995; Young, 1995). Second, although gearing ratios were somewhat similar at launch (*Gearst*), by the time years 2 and 3 had come around, there was a clear tendency for surviving firms to have lower gearing (*Gearnow*) than non-surviving firms. This meant they were both less risk-exposed, and more shielded from debt servicing crises. Third, non-survivors were much keener than survivors to sacrifice a stake in their business (*Sacstak*). Two-thirds of non-survivors were willing to do this, but less than a half of survivors. The natural interpretation to put on this is that those owner-managers who were relatively confident that the prospective returns to their firms' activities were good would be reluctant to share future benefits with outsiders; whereas those who took a more jaundiced view of future prospects might wish to share the downside risk with outsiders.

3.4   Costs

Previous econometric evidence (Reid, 1992) on the form of cost curves and scale economies in small entrepreneurial firms suggests that short-run scale economies, up to capacity output, are both strong and widespread. However, in the long run, as these firms grow, the tendency to decreasing returns (scale diseconomies) asserts itself. One explanation for this is the fixity of the entrepreneurial input as a specialised factor of production. Table 3.3 cannot address these issues in an econometric fashion, but the data therein do provide useful indicators on the nature of costs and economies within the small firm. Variables are defined in the Appendix to this chapter.

Both survivors and non-survivors recognised a capacity output, it being slightly more common for the latter group. The percentage of this capacity at which firms normally operated was, on an average, just over two-thirds in each case, with a slight tendency for non-survivors to have higher capacity utilisation. Of the five choices for the form of cost curve presented in the questionnaire much the most favoured were: (a) that total cost increased in line with the amount

Table 3.3 Cost data

	Year 2		Year 3	
	Continued trading (%) n = 122	Ceased trading (%) n = 28	Continued trading (%) n = 117	Ceased trading (%) n = 33
Capacity	67	71	67	72
Normcap	67	69	67	70
Coststra	30	36	31	30
Coststrb	59	57	57	64
Rents	11	11	11	11
Wages	24	28	24	30
Rawmat	19	19	19	18

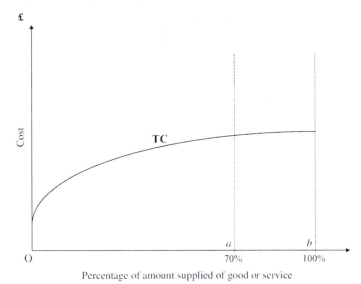

Figure 3.1 Total cost (TC) curve for typical micro-firm.
Note: b = Capacity; a = Normal capacity utilisation.

supplied (*Coststra*); and (b) that total cost did not increase as fast as the amount supplied (*Coststrb*). Roughly, about one-third of all firms nominated the former, and two-thirds the latter. Whilst proportions varied slightly across survivors and non-survivors there is no discernible pattern here. Combining statistics, the most typical form of cost curve was as in Figure 3.1. The concavity from below of this curve implies falling average and marginal costs up to capacity, with the former approaching the latter from above. This form of cost curve appears typical for both survivors and non-survivors.

The break-down of total costs into the percentage of costs allocated to rents (*Rents*), wages (*Wages*) and raw materials (*Rawmat*) is also indicated in Table 3.3. There is a slight tendency for the wage bill to be a higher proportion of costs amongst non-survivors, which suggests, given the tendency noted below for them to pay lower wage rates (Table 3.6), a higher labour intensity of operations in non-surviving firms. To conclude, whilst the cost data are of general interest, and in themselves revealing, they convey little about relative performance, and provide little insight into the question of which new businesses are most likely to survive.

3.5   Strategy

Although the traditional preserve of business strategy is the large corporation, an increasing awareness is emerging that small businesses too confront, and grapple with, serious strategic considerations. In another study of small Scottish firms, this time significantly older than the ones being examined here, Reid *et al.* (1993) identified a number of salient features of small business strategy (see also Reid and Jacobsen, 1988). First, it is generally deployed to achieve competitive advantage in markets which Porter (1980, 1983) would describe as being 'fragmented'. Such markets have low seller concentration, lack dominant or leading firms, and emphasise personal service, trade connections, tightly monitored operations and responsiveness or flexibility in the face of business fluctuations or trends. Second, new small businesses greatly emphasise aggressive, competitive strategies, but take recourse far less to defensive strategies like blocking trade channels. Third, of the various competitive forces which might impinge on the small firm, the rivalry of incumbent firms (i.e. so-called 'intra-industry competition') is most important. Fourth, experience counts. This is often based on a large body of tacit knowledge which is not written down, but rather is based on observation, exchanges of views and a variety of subtle social signals which have to be experienced to be understood, and then turned to strategic advantage.

Table 3.4 takes a rather different look at strategy, by emphasising motivational rather than technical aspects of strategy. If I were an entrepreneur, then instead of asking a technical question like how much rivals would increase advertising if I increased my own advertising, I might ask myself what I expect to get out of running my business.

To explore motivational issues of this sort, each owner-manager was asked what was the main reason for running his business. The answers could be any of the following: an alternative to unemployment (*Involvea*); to 'get rich' (*Involveb*); to take over the family business (*Involvec*); to profit from a hobby (*Involved*); to be one's own boss (*Involvee*); to satisfy the need for achievement (*Involvef*), or to exploit a new market opportunity (*Involveg*). Of these, the responses (c), (d) and (g) were rare and so are not reported in Table 3.4. For the other responses, the different proportions of entrepreneurs nominating them, as between survivors

Table 3.4 Strategy data

	Year 2		Year 3	
	Continued trading (%) n = 122	*Ceased trading (%) n = 28*	*Continued trading (%) n = 117*	*Ceased trading (%) n = 33*
Involvea	24	36	23	36
Involveb	7	4	8	3
Involvee	19	18	18	21
Involvef	25	32	25	30
Mainaima	16	18	16	18
Mainaimb	1	0	1	0
Mainaimc	34	21	35	21
Mainaimd	18	36	18	33
Mainaime	9	7	9	6
Mainaimf	15	4	14	9
Mainaimg	11	0	11	0

and non-survivors, are noteworthy. Non-survivors were more likely to have started a business as an alternative to unemployment (*Involvea*), and less likely to have done so to 'get rich' (*Involveb*). They also placed more emphasis on the way in which running a business satisfied the need for achievement (*Involvef*). Only about one-fifth of both survivors and non-survivors said they ran their businesses to be their own bosses.

Each entrepreneur was also asked what was the main aim of his business. The possible responses were: survival (*Mainaima*); short-term profit (*Mainaimb*); long-term profit (*Mainaimc*); growth (*Mainaimd*); increased sales (*Mainaime*); increased market share (*Mainaimf*); and high rate of return (*Mainaimg*). The most common response was 'long-term profit' (*Mainaimc*), but this was nominated considerably more frequently by the survivors compared to the non-survivors. Whilst there were only slight differences in responses for aims (a), (b) and (e), for other aims the responses differed in ways which were noteworthy. The non-survivors were much more likely to specify growth as an aim (*Mainaimd*), whereas the survivors were much more likely to specify high rate of return (*Mainaimg*). This suggests that survivors had a better awareness of the growth-profitability trade-off (cf. Dobson and Gerrard, 1989) than did non-survivors. A better strategic awareness is also apparent on the part of survivors in that they more frequently nominated the aim of increased market share (*Mainaimf*)which, if achieved, would be likely to increase market power, and thereby profitability.

The differences that emerge between survivors and non-survivors as regards strategy are quite clearly delineated. Non-survivors had tended to be pushed into entrepreneurship, and emphasised the importance of running a business according to their own lights. They tended not to set financial goals, and might have pursued growth to the detriment of profitability. In contrast, survivors were less coy about admitting to wanting to 'get rich', and in setting goals for the business were more likely to invoke strictly economic and financial criteria.

3.6   Human capital

As advanced economies become more service-sector dominated and manufacturing and extractive industries become more innovative in the way they use labour inputs (e.g. quality circles, job rotation), so the relative importance of human capital seems to be emphasised. However, we have yet to discover what the life-cycle consequences there are, within small firms, because of this new emphasis: for example, in terms of enhanced profitability, or even of, more simply, survival, as a consequence of entrepreneurial effort or skill (Hill and McGowan, 1999).

Unfortunately, Table 3.5 does not help us to unravel this mystery. Survivors and non-survivors have rather similar characteristics as regards human capital, and these do not vary much over short time periods. Years of secondary schooling (*Secschl*) are similar, partly because of statutory minimum requirements, but survivors are rather more likely to have gone on to higher education or further education (*Colluni*) than non-survivors. They both worked similar numbers of hours a week (*Hrswk*), though arguably to greater effect for surviving firms, given their higher 'skill intensity'. Habits were also slightly different as regards

Table 3.5 Human capital data

	Year 2		Year 3	
	Continued trading n = 122	Ceased trading n = 28	Continued trading n = 117	Ceased trading n = 33
Secschl	4.8	4.7	4.7	4.8
Colluni	77%	68%	77%	69%
Hrswk	58	57	58	56
Timprod	40%	45%	40%	42%
Timman	16%	14%	16%	13%

time management. Non-survivors allocated relatively more effort to production (*Timprod*), whereas survivors allocated relatively more effort to management (*Timman*). Given that noted longitudinal studies, like Evans and Leighton (1990), have indicated the marked positive consequences for small firm performance of deploying greater human capital, it would be imprudent to diminish or neglect its potential. However, over this short-run time scale, the impact of human capital seems relatively slight, certainly so far as survival is concerned.

3.7 Organisation

Turning to Table 3.6, a number of organisational features are notable. Again, there is considerable similarity between years; but differences between survivors and non-survivors are worthy of comment. The sole proprietorship form of firm (both at home, *Legbusa*, or in business premises, *Legbusb*) has a relatively poor survival record, compared to partnership (*Legbusc*) and company (*Legbuse*) forms. The highest survival rates are for the company form. This reflects several factors, including size, age and evolutionary history.

The use of hierarchy (cf. Williamson, 1975, 1985) is similar between survivors and non-survivors, but it is to be noted that in neither case is hierarchy of the classical pyramid form. Rather, structures tend to be more peaked at the top and less flat at the bottom (cf. numbers at each level, *Nolev*). An obvious difference between those that survived and those that failed is that the former group had more powerful incentives (as measured by salary level, *Salev*, differences) between hierarchical levels. At each salary level (*Salev*), for each year of data, it is to be noted that salary multipliers were higher for surviving firms. For example, at the top level the multiple was 3.6 times the bottom level for survivors, compared to 2.1 for non-survivors in year 2. Further, specialist personnel, in running firms, were more likely to be knowledgeable about each others' skills (*Knowoth*), but less likely to be called upon to perform them (*Takeoth*) in 'special circumstances' (e.g. a negative shock to the business, like plant failure), for survivors, compared to non-survivors.

Table 3.6 Organisational data

	Year 2		Year 3	
	Continued trading $n = 122$	*Ceased trading* $n = 28$	*Continued trading* $n = 117$	*Ceased trading* $n = 33$
Legbusa	25%	32%	24%	33%
Legbusb	27%	36%	28%	30%
Legbusc	20%	14%	20%	15%
Legbuse	29%	18%	28%	21%
Nolev1	1.9	1.5	1.8	1.8
Nolev2	1.8	1.8	1.8	1.9
Nolev3	3.3	3.7	3.4	3.0
Nolev4	2.0	1.4	2.0	1.3
Salev1	3.6	2.1	3.5	3.0
Salev2	2.1	1.6	2.0	1.8
Salev3	1.4	1.0	1.4	1.1
Salev4	1.1	1.0	1.1	1.0
Knowoth	82%	81%	86%	72%
Takeoth	82%	100%	83%	91%
Wagerate	£919	£790	£921	£789

This suggests a higher 'knowledge content' in surviving firms, and a more economic use of the capability best described as flexibility.[2] Non-survivors have personnel who know less about each others' tasks, but nevertheless are more likely to have to take them on (cf. Chaston *et al.*, 2000, 2001). Such personnel are, therefore, less capable in these functions, as well as being more often drawn away from their areas of relatively greater skill (and comparative advantage). To illustrate, if typists and data processors were relatively ignorant of what each did, and how it was done, yet were quite often called upon to switch tasks, the outcome would be likely to be inferior to one in which each was familiar with the other's task and how to do it, but was not so often required to switch tasks. Finally, it is to be noted that the skilled wage rate (typically earned at *Salev3*, the second level up the hierarchy) was higher for survivors compared to non-survivors in each year. As multipliers between hierarchies were also higher for the survivors, the terms of pay were superior across all levels for survivors compared to non-survivors. Whilst there might be an efficiency wage effect at work here, with workers being retained in firms by relatively attractive pay (Yellen, 1984), it is also possible that the best entrepreneurs are being matched with the best workers, as in the analysis of Oi (1985), leading to larger surviving firms whose workers have higher marginal productivities.

3.8   Technical change

Although small firms are thought to be vectors of change and innovation, in terms of the so-called 'new learning' of industrial organisation (Acs and Audretsch, 1993),

Table 3.7 Technical change data

	Year 2		Year 3	
	Continued trading n = 122	Ceased trading n = 28	Continued trading n = 117	Ceased trading n = 33
Procinn	1.4	1.4	1.4	1.4
Prodinn	1.0	1.3	1.0	1.2
Techchng	62%	61%	62%	61%
Initiata	36%	76%	37%	65%
Initiatb	16%	6%	15%	10%
Initiatc	22%	12%	22%	15%
Newtecha	52%	61%	52%	58%
Newtechb	1%	0%	1%	0%
Newtechc	11%	0%	10%	3%
Newtechd	37%	39%	37%	39%

this effect is confined to quite a narrow class of firms (Oakey, 1991). Even venture capital firms, especially in the United Kingdom, are rather reluctant to get involved with high technology companies, which they rather cynically describe as being at the 'bleeding edge' rather than 'leading edge' of technology (cf. Reid, 1996a, b). This, no doubt, has arisen from bad experiences with development companies with highly volatile values that depend on 'long-shot' success with complex, new technologies. In the previous section, cautionary remarks have already been made about the efficacy of innovation and technical change in the new small firm, and Table 3.7 provides further evidence on this issue.

Both product (*Prodinn*) and process (*Procinn*) innovations typically have been introduced by these new small firms, and there is only slight variation in their importance by year or by the survivor/failure divide. For just one-third (approx.) of firms, technical change (*TechChng*) has been important within their industry, and this is fairly constant across years and across success or failure. Firms which did not survive were considerably more likely to trail behind acknowledged leaders in the industry than firms which did survive, as regards initiation of technical change (*Initiata*), presumably because surviving firms were themselves on occasion the initiators of change in their own markets. The significance of newly emerging innovators (*Initiatb*) was better appreciated by surviving firms, as were forces outside the industry (*Initiatc*) (e.g. government incentives). This effect was constant over time. Non-survivors were slightly more likely not to have used new production technologies (*Newtecha*), and survivors were much more likely to admit that they had implemented new production technologies, even if not always successfully (*Newtechc*). There was a similar reported rate of success between survivors and non-survivors in the successful implementation of new technology (*Newtechd*). There is very little evidence in Table 3.7 that the technical change data are particularly sensitive to time period, so over this time scale life-cycle effects appear to be absent as regards new technologies. One can summarise the evidence of Table 3.7 by saying that technical change was generally not a major consideration for all firms over the time scale considered, but that when it was, the surviving firms showed a better awareness of new developments, and of their own limitations in initiating them; and, furthermore, displayed a superior capacity to initiate change (cf. Collinson, 2000).

3.9   Conclusion

This chapter has provided a sharp empirical characterisation of an entity that has been widely discussed, but rarely so precisely measured, the new business start-up. The accuracy of the characterisation, in terms of markets, structure and behaviour, is novel and it provided the starting point for a thorough comparison of surviving and non-surviving firms in the first few years after inception. It was shown that these two classes of firm behaved differently, over several significant dimensions. A parsimonious way of summarising these differences is to say that the competencies of firms (cf. Martin and Staines, 1994; Chaston *et al.*, 2001) which survived were generally superior to those that closed down.

APPENDIX

Definitions of Variables

Variable Name	Definition
Bankloan	=1 firm has used bank loan or overdraft in previous year, =0 otherwise
Capacity	=1 respondent can identify a maximum capacity of output, =0 otherwise
Colluni	=1 respondent went to college or university, =0 otherwise
Coststra	=1 total cost increases at same rate as supply, =0 otherwise
Coststrb	=1 total cost increases at lesser rate than supply, =0 otherwise
Debt	=1 firm has debt, =0 otherwise
Employ	total headcount (directors + managers + full and part-time employees + trainees)
Gearnow	current debt/equity (gearing) ratio of the firm (per cent)
Gearst	debt/equity (gearing) ratio of the firm at inception (per cent)
Grant	=1 firm has received a grant or subsidy, =0 otherwise
Grprof	gross profits (£)
Grsales	gross sales/turnover (£)
Hrswk	no. of hours a week spent by the owner-manager in the business
Impact	planning horizon of the firm (months)

Continued

Definitions of Variables—cont'd

Variable Name	Definition
Inbus	time since business inception at first interview (months)
Initiata	=1 technical change is initiated by an acknowledged leader in the industry, =0 otherwise
Initiatb	=1 technical change is initiated by newly emerging innovators in the industry, =0 otherwise
Initiatc	=1 technical change is initiated by forces outside the industry, =0 otherwise
Involvea	=1 entrepreneur became involved in the business as an alternative to unemployment, =0 otherwise
Involveb	=1 entrepreneur became involved in the business 'to get rich', =0 otherwise
Involvee	=1 entrepreneur became involved in the business to be own boss, =0 otherwise
Involvef	=1 entrepreneur became involved in the business to satisfy the need for achievement, =0 otherwise
Knowoth	=1 employees are knowledgeable about each others' skills, =0 otherwise
Legbusa	=1 firm is sole trader (operating from home), =0 otherwise
Legbusb	=1 firm is sole trader (operating from business premises), =0 otherwise
Legbusc	=1 firm is partnership, =0 otherwise
Legbuse	=1 firm is private limited company, =0 otherwise
Mainaima	=1 main aim of business is survival, =0 otherwise
Mainaimb	=1 main aim of business is short term profit, =0 otherwise
Mainaimc	=1 main aim of business is long term profit, =0 otherwise
Mainaimd	=1 main aim of business is growth, =0 otherwise
Mainaime	=1 main aim of business is increased sales, =0 otherwise
Mainaimf	=1 main aim of business is increased market share, =0 otherwise
Mainaimg	=1 main aim of business is high rate of return, =0 otherwise
Netprof	net profit (£)
Newtecha	=1 firm has not used new production technologies, =0 otherwise
Newtechb	=1 firm has implemented new production technologies, but rarely successfully, =0 otherwise
Newtechc	=1 firm has implemented new production technologies, but not always successfully, =0 otherwise
Newtechd	=1 firm has generally been successful in implementing new production technologies, =0 otherwise
Nolev1	number of staff on level 1 of firm's hierarchy
Nolev2	number of staff on level 2 of firm's hierarchy

Continued

Definitions of Variables—cont'd

Variable name	Definition
Nolev3	number of staff on level 3 of firm's hierarchy
Nolev4	number of staff on level 4 of firm's hierarchy
Normcap	level of capacity at which firm normally operates (per cent of total capacity)
Outeq	=1 firm uses outside equity, =0 otherwise
Owncash	cash injection by owner-manager at business inception (£)
Procinn	level of process innovation undertaken by firm (=0 none, =1 a little, =2 a lot)
Prodgrp	number of product groups or categories firm offers
Prodinn	number of new products introduced by firm (=0 none, =1 '1–5', =2 '6–10', =3 '11–20', =4 'more than twenty')
Product	number of products firm offers
Rawmat	percentage of total costs attributable to raw materials
Rents	percentage of total costs attributable to rents
Sacstak	=1 entrepreneur is willing to give up a share of his stake in the business, =0 otherwise
Salev1	salary multiple over base level 5, at level 1
Salev2	salary multiple over base level 5, at level 2
Salev3	salary multiple over base level 5, at level 3
Salev4	salary multiple over base level 5, at level 4
Secschl	time respondent spent at secondary school (years)
Smlprof	=1 entrepreneur is willing to accept smaller profits for a while to facilitate growth, =0 otherwise
Takeoth	=1 employees take on each others' tasks in certain circumstances, =0 otherwise
Techchng	=1 there has been a lot of technical change in the industry over the previous year, =0 otherwise
Timman	percentage of entrepreneur's time spent on management
Timprod	percentage of entrepreneur's time spent on production
Wagerate	wage paid to highest skilled employees (£ per month)
Wages	percentage of total costs attributable to wages, salaries and directors' remuneration

Endnotes

1 See also the readings edited by Foss and Mahnke (2000) on competence, governance and entrepreneurship.
2 See Lee (1993) for a study of flexibility in small Scottish firms. Flexibility issues are explored in greater depth in Part 6 of this book. Indeed, the findings of this section have partly inspired this later work.

Part 2

Existing evidence

4 Growth and profitability of micro-firms

4.1 Introduction

Essentially, this chapter, and Chapter 5, on funding shortages, are 'scene setting' chapters, which show the ground base of evidence on which all subsequent chapters are predicated. The concerns, techniques and methodology are similar. For example, the evidence used in both chapters is also based on primary-source data collected in Scotland. As another example, the techniques of analysis relating to Gibrat's Law (Almus, 2000; Ganugi *et al.*, 2004, 2005; Hart and Oulton, 1999; Hart, 2000; Weiss, 1998), as expounded and tested fully in Chapter 16, are 'bench tested' first here in Chapter 4.

This chapter reports on extant evidence on young (<3 years old) micro-firms (less than ten employees) in Scotland, early in the life-cycle. In it, two main tests are carried out. The first takes Gibrat's Law (briefly, that growth is independent of size) as the null hypothesis, and a life-cycle effects model as the alternative. The Gibrat's Law model is rejected in favour of the life-cycle model: smaller micro-firms grow faster than larger micro-firms (cf. Liu *et al.*, 1999). Robust non-linear variants of the life-cycle model are discussed, and shown to display stable equilibrium characteristics which are consistent with the sample evidence. The second test takes a Classical simultaneous equations model of growth and profitability as the null hypothesis. For this model, growth and profitability are mutually reinforcing. A Managerial model is set up as the alternative. For this model, growth and profitability are found to be in a trade-off relationship: the Classical model is rejected in favour of the Managerial. In the short-run, it is clear that young micro-firms already experience a trade-off between profitability and growth. This Managerial model is also shown to imply a stable equilibrium, with characteristics consistent with sample evidence.

The purpose of this chapter is to report on an extant body of original research concerned with how young small firms grow shortly after they have started up in business.[1] It aims to provide a link between the new body of evidence analysed in this book and related earlier work on Scottish micro-firms.[2] Thus, as expressed in the opening of this section, this chapter introduces themes (e.g. variants of Gibrat's Law) which will be revisited later.

4.2   The neglect of the micro-firm

In earlier chapters it has been argued that the micro-firm, despite its extreme neglect, even in the small firms literature itself, is of great interest in being (no more or less) the *typical* or *modal* firm (Hughes, 1993). The reason why the micro-firm has been neglected hitherto is quite simple: data are not readily available. The larger the firm, the more likely are its operations to be covered by legislation on public disclosure of its business operations. Furthermore, the more likely are its activities to fall within one or more of various tax regimes. These regimes, as well as playing a fiscal role, also generate data of use to the small firms specialist. However, if an entrepreneur's operations are too small to require public reporting, and for the same reason fall outside of various tax regimes (VAT, corporation tax, etc.), he or she becomes a shadowy figure in national statistics. There are ways of trying to plumb our ignorance in this area. For example, one can use the membership lists of small business associations (e.g. the Federation of Small Businesses, the Forum of Private Business[3]). However, membership lists involve some measure of self-selection. An investigator who wishes to avoid the potential bias that this implies must engage in primary source data collection: such is the focus of this book.

This is the course of action which was taken in acquiring the body of evidence on micro-firms reported upon later. As in the rest of the book, all data were gathered by directly interviewing owner-managers of young (on an average, 3 years old) small entrepreneurial firms in Scotland.[4] This chapter therefore provides benchmark evidence, from which the new analysis, from Chapter 6 onwards, proceeds, using the data described in Chapters 1–3. The average size of these firms was eight employees, and data were gathered over the period 1985–88. During this period, it is known that small firms such as these, lying in the category of 0–19 employees, accounted for 5 per cent of gross output and 7 per cent of total employment in Scotland. A sample of 73 micro-firms was obtained in this early work, from which were acquired very detailed data on each individual firm. This evidence was sufficient indeed to construct 73 case studies, yet the sample was also sufficiently large to permit the legitimate use of large sample techniques of statistical inference and econometrics. In doing so, a middle course was followed between small sample case study methods, in which one learns 'a lot about a little' (cf. Samson, 1990; Pratten, 1991; Lazerson, 1990), and large sample econometric studies, in which one learns 'a little about a lot' (cf. Evans, 1987; Brock and Evans, 1986). Here, the aim was to provide a rich characterisation of each firm, and to do so for a sufficiently large number of firms that mathematical modelling becomes possible. In this way, modelling is 'well grounded' in reality, and sufficient degrees of freedom exist to estimate statistically robust models.

It is this early modelling, and its relative success, that encouraged one to go on to the larger and more detailed work considered in Chapters 6–18 of this book. A representative sample was obtained from the client list of a random sample of Enterprise Trusts, ETs, in the Lothian, Fife and Strathclyde regions (EVENT, GET, LET, ASSET, etc.). The composition by *small business type* was: private companies (50 per cent); partnerships (20 per cent) and sole proprietorships (30 per cent). *Business type* was treated as a categorical variable and this variable played an important role in the modelling reported upon below.

4.3   Variants of Gibrat's Law

This section reports on two aspects of the analysis of this earlier sample. The first explores the relationship between size and growth, taking as the central hypothesis the Law of Proportionate Effect (or Gibrat's Law),[5] according to which growth rates of firms are independent of size. The second explores the simultaneous, mutually causative relationship between growth and profitability. The classical view (Reid, 1989), that growth and profitability go hand-in-hand, is taken as the central hypothesis, with the alternative hypothesis appealing to the growth-profitability trade-off implied by 'managerial theories' of the growth of the firm (of the Penrose–Marris–Richardson–Slater[6]) variety.

Suppose a market is expanding at the rate of 5 per cent per year. Then Gibrat's Law says that all firms in the market will share this expansion rate. Thus a firm with a turnover of £1 million in 1985 would have a turnover of £1.05 million in 1986; and a firm with a turnover of £0.5 million in 1985 would have a turnover of £0.525 million in 1986. This so-called law is weakly confirmed for very large (typically corporate) enterprises (cf. Singh and Whittington, 1968), but in the small firms literature is treated more as a null hypothesis that is formulated with rejection in mind (Liu *et al.*, 1999).[7] It is therefore normally regarded as a special case of a more encompassing hypothesis which adds two elements: first, an endogenous size dependence, with growth dependent partly on base-period size; and second, an exogenous shock component, which says that the basic growth relationship is subject to an independent, multiplicative random shock each time period (cf. Hay and Morris, 1991, Ch. 15).

This leads to an equation suitable for estimating growth effects which expresses size this year as a linear function of size last year, where the size variables are expressed in natural logarithms. Size may be measured by any of the several economic variables such as sales, employment or assets. The coefficient of the lagged natural logarithm of the size variable (call it β) plays a special role. If $\beta = 1$ growth is independent of size; if $\beta > 1$ larger small firms grow faster than smaller small firms; and if $\beta < 1$ smaller small firms grow faster than larger small firms. Of these competing hypotheses, the third is the most plausible ($\beta < 1$) despite the elevation of the status of the first to that of a 'Law'. This is because $\beta < 1$ implies a stability in the growth process, and indeed suggests a type of optimal or equilibrium size for the small firm.

The argument is illustrated by reference to Figure 4.1, which has (log) size in time period t on the horizontal axis and (log) size in time period $t+1$ on the vertical, and a 45° line which can be used to identify a so-called 'fixed point' for the growth process implied by the fitted equation which is superimposed on it. This equation was fitted by least squares using (log) assets in 1988 (i.e. S_{t+1}) as the dependent

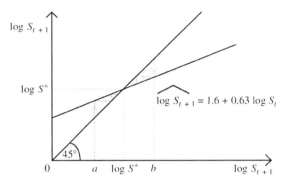

Figure 4.1 Adjustment to equilibrium size.

variable and (log) assets in 1985 (i.e. S_t) as the independent variable.[8] It will be observed that it does indeed imply a stable growth process. In Figure 4.1, $\log S^*$ denotes the equilibrium size of the small firm, in the sense of that (log) size to which small firms will tend. Possible adjustment paths from (log) sizes a and b towards $\log S^*$ are indicated.

When equilibrium is achieved, $\log S^* = 1.6 + 0.63 \log S^*$ which implies $\log S^* = 1.6/0.37 = 4.324$, from which equilibrium size is given by: $S^* = \exp(4.324) = 75.49$. This figure is close to the average nominal asset size within the sample in 1985 of £76.36 thousand. Because β is so unambiguously less than unity, Gibrat's Law ($\beta = 1$) is refuted, and a more general model is accepted with the property that smaller small firms grow faster than larger small firms. This is a model that displays the 'life-cycle' effect noted in the introduction of this chapter: it is thereby established for this sample of young Scottish small firms.

This argument is plausibly neat, but arguably simplistic. The 'mechanism' behind the process (a simple first-order difference equation) is too much in view, and one acquires from it no intuitive sense of why such a life-cycle effect might occur in practice. A convincing story (Jovanovic, 1982; Frank, 1988) makes appeal to an element of 'human capital' theory. Partly the success of a small firm is attributable to the experience of its owner-manager. His experience is accumulated by the practice of running a firm, and even the entrepreneur may initially be ignorant of his ability. Over time, his ability is revealed, at the same time as his skill is being cultivated. This introduces a 'time dependence' into the growth relationship: the age of the small firm is also a determinant of its growth rate, as well as its size.

This dependence of growth on age and size can be assumed to take a quite complex non-linear form, for the purposes of generality. It can again be simplified to facilitate econometric estimation by being re-expressed in a log-linear form, which also incorporates quadratic age and size effects (cf. Evans, 1987; Brock and Evans, 1986; Heshmati, 2001). This flexible functional form can capture, or approximate to, many forms of non-linearity. When estimated on the data, using assets, sales or employment as the size variable, a consistent picture emerges.

It is that growth is negatively related to size *and* to age.[9] Thus younger and smaller small firms grow faster than older and larger small firms. There *is* a life-cycle effect, and the rapidly learning owner-manager running a young small firm which is close to financial inception is able to 'grow on' his firm more successfully than the owner-manager of an older small firm in which the benefits of learning have been exhausted.

Although size and age have been identified as determinants of growth, and their effects have been found to operate in a relatively complex, non-linear fashion, the model specification is still sparse. One could invoke Occam's Razor and say 'do not compound hypotheses unnecessarily', and leave the matter as it stands. However, that would be to ignore a significant body of economic theory which could lay claim to providing a more complex explanation of the growth of the firm.

The initial hypotheses explored above were that growth depended on size, or on size and age. Now these parsimonious hypotheses will be extended to take account of market extent, market share, rivals' pricing policies, capital structure (e.g. gearing) and, above all, profitability. One expects a profitable firm to have a Darwinian advantage over an unprofitable or less profitable firm, and to enjoy superior growth opportunities. But more than this, one might expect growth itself to be a stimulus to profitability, for example, because of learning effects and the consequential dynamic economies of scale. We have developed this argument in some detail elsewhere in an industrial context.[10] It implies a model of 'cumulative causation', with growth fostering profitability, and profitability fostering growth. A necessary condition for this is the existence of increasing returns to scale. When the author first approached hypothesis testing in this area, this was the kind of framework he had in mind, and evidence from fieldwork amongst small firms provided fragments of evidence that seemed to support it. For example, profits were the major source of finance for expansion. Outside equity participation, either formally through venture capital (Reid, 1998), or informally, through 'business angels' (Mason and Harrison, 1994), was non-existent. External finance was invariably debt finance, and was often provided on a matching basis by banks, to a level that corresponded to the owner-manager's personal financial injections. Thus gearing ratios of around unity were common. On the supply side, evidence of scale economies was widespread, across a broad range of industrial activities, up to capacity operations (see also Pratten, 1991). One therefore is led to construct a null hypothesis that says growth and profitability advance hand-in-hand.

4.4   Classical vs. managerial theories

This type of reasoning has its roots in Classical notions of competition, and has been updated by the likes of Kaldor, Currie and Thirlwall (cf. Reid, 1989). However, there is an alternative view. It is based on a theory that is too extensive to bear detailed individual reference in a brief account of this sort. Suffice it to say that it is, generically speaking, of the 'managerial theory of the firm' variety (Hay and Morris, 1991, Chs 9, 10; Reid, 1987, Ch. 9). Here, the key intellectual figures would be Penrose (1959), Marris (1964) and Baumol (1962), with important formalisations being due to Slater (1980) and Richardson (1964). According to this view, there are costs of growth of a managerial sort, which attenuate profitability. The firm must change, in an organisational sense, when it grows; and putting into place new 'organisational technology' involves resource costs. Penrose (1959) argued informally that new managers had to be drawn into the growing firm, and then trained and dovetailed into existing managerial arrangements. Training, and the re-positioning of personnel within the organisational form of the firm are in themselves expensive; and furthermore they are a diversion from direct production, both of which are detrimental to short-run profitability. Slater (1980) has formalised this argument to show that increases in marginal cost will arise from rapidly recruiting managers, when the firm is expanding quickly. Richardson (1964), somewhat less formally, argued that the key constraint to growth was acquiring and assimilating suitable additions of personnel to the managerial team. These arguments are normally directed at the corporate enterprise. The novelty of this chapter is to argue that the logic is no less applicable to the small firm. A firm which starts from home as a sole proprietorship might rapidly become a partnership, and subsequently a private company, all within as little a time as 3 years. This involves major changes in managerial methods, and significant management recruitment as the small firm's form mutates (Reid *et al.*, 1993). For example, it typically involves creating tiers of superior/subordinate relations, organised in a hierarchical fashion [see Reid (1998) for explicit testing of models of hierarchy in small firms]. This usually involves 'control loss' by the founding entrepreneur. As Samson (1990, Ch. 5) points out, it sometimes involves 'organisational crisis'. A '*Business Type*' variable is available for my sample to proxy such effects.

Developing an alternative hypothesis to the 'cumulative causation' (Young, 1928) view of growth and profitability, one comes up with, following 'managerial' lines of reasoning as above, a growth-profitability 'trade-off' view, sometimes known as the 'Penrose Effect'. Summarising, the null hypothesis is that growth and profitability advance hand-in-hand; the alternative hypothesis is that growth and profitability lie in a 'trade-off' relationship to one another.

These alternative hypotheses can be tested using a simultaneous equations model of growth and profitability for the small firm. The estimated equations to be reported upon were:

$$Growth\ Rate = F[Profitability\,(-),\ Main\ Market\,(+),\ Market\ Share\,(+),$$
$$Rivals'\ Pricing\,(-),\ Degree\ of\ Product$$
$$Differentiation\,(-),\ Gearing\ Ratio\,(-)] \tag{4.1}$$

$$Profitability = f[Growth\ Rate\,(-),\ Business\ Type\,(-),\ Rivals'$$
$$Pricing\,(+),\ Gearing\ Ratio\,(-)] \tag{4.2}$$

Under a variety of specifications and methods of estimation,[11] these variables were significant, and generally stable in the signs of their effects on the dependent variables, as indicated by the plus or minus signs in brackets. In Equation (4.1) profitability has a negative effect on the growth rate; and in Equation (4.2) the growth rate has a negative effect on profitability.[12] Thus the evidence refutes the null hypothesis of 'cumulative causation' and accepts the alternative hypothesis of a growth/profitability 'trade-off'. Such conclusions have been reached in other contexts by Cubbin and Leech (1986) and Dobson and Gerrard (1989).

The new evidence reported upon here supports a managerial view of small firm growth. If a concave profitability-growth rate locus exists of the sort indicated in Figure 4.2 by the line GG', and an owner-manager's indifference curve is given by UU', equilibrium (and presumably *observed*) values for growth and profitability will be observed *on the trade-off section*[13] of the locus GG'. Rather than stop short at the growth rate g_1, which maximises profitability (π_{max}), the owner-manager pushes on growth to g_2. This may be quite rational. It could be that whenever the small firm gets a 'toehold' in a new market niche, its primary goal must be to invade that niche, even at the cost of sacrificing short-run profitability, in order that it pre-emptively occupies that niche ahead of rivals. Thus the alternative to rapid niche invasion, with some temporary sacrifice of profit, is no niche occupancy at all, and hence no profit. Once a niche is occupied, the small firm can devise various 'harvest' strategies aimed at maximising long-run profit.[14]

Apart from the 'trade-off' aspect of the model given by Equations (4.1) and (4.2), other features are worth commenting. In the growth rate Equation (4.1), the extent of the main market, and the size of market share correlate positively, as one would expect, with growth. The next two variables have less obvious, perhaps even surprising, effects. Rivals' pricing is based on a dummy variable which is unity when rivals' prices are crucial to the small firm's own pricing (and zero otherwise). Essentially the more elastic is the conjectural cross-price coefficient

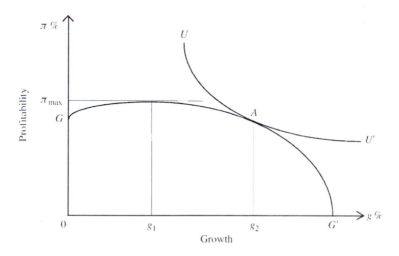

Figure 4.2 Equilibrium of the managerial firm.

$(\Delta P_i/P_i \div \Delta P_j/P_j)$, the lower is the growth rate. This suggests that alert, competitive, and in particular, price-conscious rivals deliberately take pricing actions which impede the growth of other small firms (Cunningham and Hornby, 1993).

The *Degree of Product Differentiation* variable assumes greater values the less homogeneous (i.e. the more differentiated) is the good. Normally, one would think of product differentiation as defining the boundaries of a small firm's niche markets, and to a degree it should act as a barrier to entry. This market protection should foster rather than hinder growth, but apparently that does not occur on an average for these small firms. The reason is likely to be found in the rather extreme form that product differentiation often takes. Small firms frequently supply goods or services on a 'bespoke' basis i.e. custom-designed to a particular buyer's needs (cf. Reid *et al.*, 1993). This removes all substitutability in the marketplace. One buyer's version of the good will not even substitute for another buyer's, let alone meet the needs of a larger potential customer base. This acute, perhaps even excessive, product differentiation has the potential severely to curtail sales growth possibilities. High gearing, especially if it rises above unity, furthermore, will increase the small firm's exposure to risk, and also impose a debt-servicing burden. Not surprisingly, this is to the detriment of growth.

Turning to the profitability Equation (4.2), the gearing ratio is again as expected: high gearing damages profitability. The *Business Type* variable increases as the type goes from sole proprietorship to partnership, to private company, etc. The negative sign on this variable precisely confirms the insights of managerial theorists like Penrose, Slater and Richardson. Increasing the organisational complexity of the small firm creates costs which erode profits. More surprising is the different effect that the *Rivals' Pricing* variable has on profitability, compared to growth. The interpretation to be put on this variable is that rivals act as good monitors of small firms' profitability performance, through their close interdependence in terms of pricing policies. In a sense, they provide a costless monitoring system which keeps the profit orientation lively amongst rivals.

A final interpretation of the model embodied in Equations (4.1) and (4.2) is worth considering. There are two endogenous (or jointly determined) variables in the model: profitability (π) and the growth rate (g). All the other variables are exogenous (or predetermined). The status of these variables has been confirmed by diagnostic testing.[15] To simplify the model, it may be written as just a single-argument profitability equation $\pi = f(g)$ and a single-argument growth rate equation $g = F(\pi)$. Suppose all exogenous variable are assigned to their mean values. Then the linear regressions used to estimate Equations (4.1) and (4.2) enable specific linear functions to be given to $f(.)$ and $F(.)$. Using the estimated coefficients [see Note 9] and mean values for exogenous variables, these functions are found to be (approximately) $\pi = f(g) = 21.9 - 0.04g$ for the profitability equation and $g = F(\pi) = 109.0 - 2.71\pi$ for the growth equation. It is informative to graph these equations, as in Figure 4.3. The equilibrium values for growth (g^*) and profitability (π^*) should mutually satisfy $f(.)$ and $F(.)$, that is: $g^* = F(\pi^*)$ and $\pi^* = f(g^*)$. Solving out using the expressions for these functions, one gets $g^* = 55.7$ per cent which is close to the mean value of the annual

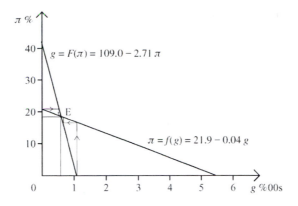

Figure 4.3 Paths to equilibrium profit and growth rates.

real growth rate in the sample of 57.1 per cent, and further $\pi^* = 19.67$ per cent which likewise is close to the mean value of profitability in the sample of 19.43 per cent. It is to be further noted that the equations indicate a stable equilibrium point[16] at (g^*, π^*) which is denoted as E in Figure 4.3. Thus, starting from a growth rate of 109 per cent on the horizontal axis, a convergent path to E can be traced; and likewise starting from a profitability of 21.9 per cent on the vertical axis, one can trace another convergent path to E. These equilibrium values are close to mean values for growth and profitability in the sample, and the growth and profitability values generated in passages to equilibrium are also similar to those observed in the sample.

4.5   Conclusion

To conclude, the earlier Scottish data on young small firms which have been examined in this chapter shows a remarkable coherence, and display clear congruence with several major theories. Two main null hypotheses were set up, with the following consequences after testing.

(a) Gibrat's Law was tested and refuted. The alternative hypothesis, which was accepted, implies a 'life-cycle' effect for the small firm in Scotland. This simple alternative model can be generalised to a more complex non-linear model, which also takes account of entrepreneurial experience. The main conclusion stands under this generalisation: smaller small firms grow faster than larger small firms. Furthermore, this growth process is stable, and tends to an equilibrium value which is close to the mean value of size for small firms in the sample.

(b) A more general simultaneous equations model of growth was formulated. Under the null hypothesis a 'cumulative causation' view was put to the test. It was rejected in favour of an alternative (managerial) hypothesis, which implies a growth/profitability 'trade-off'. This more general model was also shown to be stable, and to generate equilibrium values which were close to the mean values for growth and profitability in the sample.

Endnotes

1 See the preliminary treatment in Reid and Jacobsen (1988), the detailed treatment, appealing to case study, statistical and econometric evidence in Reid (1993), the small business strategy approach in Reid *et al.* (1993), and the market and hierarchies approach of Reid (1998).

2 The focus here is on works which use primary source data, rather than secondary source data: compare the work of Ash *et al.* (1991) on the Scottish economy.

3 See, for example, the work by Binks *et al.* (1988) using data supplied by the Forum of Private Business.

4 The fieldwork design and instrumentation used, are treated in some detail in Reid (1993).

5 The original source is Gibrat (1931) *Les inégalites économiques*. In its simplest form, Gibrat's Law said that if x_t is firm size at time period t, then the growth rate $(x_t - x_{t-1})/x_{t-1} = \varepsilon_t$ is serially uncorrelated random variable. A key paper to develop this model was Kalecki (1945). A good technical treatment is in Aitchison and Brown (1969).

6 Space precludes a detailed individual treatment of authors. For an extensive and thorough survey, see Hay and Morris (1991, Ch. 10).

7 There are some exceptions, however. To illustrate, Audretsch *et al.* (2004) find that the Dutch hospitality industry, which is largely made up of small scale service firms, does follow the Gibrat law. However, this is a rather specialised sub-sector of services.

8 The equation estimated was:

$$\ln(\text{asset}_{t+1}) = 1.6 + \underset{(4.02)}{0.63} \ln(\text{asset}_t); \quad F = 25.87$$

Estimation was by least squares using White's heteroskedastic-consistent covariance matrix, White (1980).

9 An example of the typical model estimated is:

$$g = \underset{(2.02)}{0.37} - \underset{(-1.97)}{0.11S} + \underset{(0.64)}{0.003S^2} - \underset{(-0.78)}{0.06A} - \underset{(-0.14)}{0.001A^2} + \underset{(1.83)}{0.018S.A}$$

with $R^2 = 0.33$, $F = 7.5$, $n = 67$

Here, g is asset growth in real terms, S (for 'size') is the natural logarithm of real assets and A the natural logarithm of age. Estimation was by least squares, using White's heteroskedastic-consistent covariance matrix. Compare Evans (1987), Brock and Evans (1986).

10 See Reid (1989, Ch. 4) where a dynamic model of price leadership is developed, in which the leader sustains an output and profitability advantage over time.

11 Estimation was by ordinary least squares and by iterative three stage least squares.

12 One-iteration three-stage least squares estimators for Equations (4.1) and (4.2), respectively give coefficients and asymptotic t-ratios as follows, where coefficients are in the same order as indicated in the main text, starting with a constant:

$$228, \ -2.7, \ 28.0, \ 18.3, \ -64.8, \ -72.9, \ -0.8 \qquad\qquad (4.1)^*$$
$$(-2.1) \ (1.7) \ (2.2) \ (-1.4) \ (-2.5) \ (-3.0)$$

$$44.7, \ -0.04, \ -9.0, \ 13.0, \ -0.13 \qquad\qquad (4.2)^*$$
$$(-0.8) \ (-1.9) \ (1.3) \ (-2.52)$$

The system $R^2 = 0.52$. When higher iterations are used, the significance on the profitability and growth rate variables in (4.1)* and (4.2)* rises rapidly. For technical details, see Reid (1993, Ch. 11).

13 This would be true, for example, if small firms shared the same profitability-growth locus, but differed by the owner-managers' tastes for growth versus profitability. Various 'identifiability' conditions need to be satisfied if the trade-off case is to be theoretically substantiated along managerial lines. These conditions are analysed in Hay and Morris (1991, Ch. 10).

14 It may be that in the long-run the growth-profitability 'cumulative causation' effect will assert itself, despite any short-run trade-off effects of the sort I have identified.

15 That is by Hausman endogeneity tests (Reid 1987, Ch. 2).

16 This stability condition may be expressed:

$$(d\pi/dg)_f = -0.04 > -0.369 = (d\pi/dg)_F.$$

5 Funding shortages

5.1 Introduction

This chapter provides a further link between established evidence and the developments that flow from it, as developed in Chapters 6–18. This link is achieved in three ways. First, it utilises primary source data on Scottish small firms. Second, its focus is on the long-lived small firm, that is to say the small firm in a mature phase, long-distant from its start-up and early growth phase. This is a theme that will be returned to in Chapter 18. Third, it develops a theory of the financially endowed small firm. Specifically, it models and tests a financially constrained small firm (cf. Jefferson, 1997).

Such funding shortages are analysed in the context of a simple neoclassical model of the very small firm (namely the micro-firm) that uses finance-capital for its operations (cf. Chapter 6). This theory is shown to predict that a response to funding shortages is to substitute part-time workers for full-time workers, under the assumption that the latter are the more finance-capital intensive employees. This finding of what may be described as the 'casualisation of labour' in the small firm will be returned to, and investigated further, in Chapter 11. The experience of funding gaps in the supply of finance-capital to long-lived micro-firms is investigated using data which were obtained by telephone interviews. The micro-firms examined had an average size of six full-time and two part-time workers, and an average age of 15 years. Using probit estimators of the probability of experiencing funding shortages, a strong and significant negative association is shown to exist between the number of part-time workers and the probability of experiencing funding shortages. This refutes a simple neoclassical hypothesis of the free market provision of finance, and suggests an alternative hypothesis, emphasising the flexibility advantages of part-time employees in averting funding shortages. Thus, a 10 per cent increase in part-time employees is shown to reduce the probability of experiencing funding shortages by two and a half per cent. A regional effect is also discovered, and bivariate probits give results which are consistent with univariate probits.

It has been seen in Chapter 2 that the size distribution of firms has a reverse J-shape. This implies not only that the small firm is (of all firms) the modal firm type, but also that the most populous category is itself the very small or micro-firm.

The typical micro-firm examined in the literature (e.g. Mata, 1993; Storey, 1994, Ch. 3) is, in life-cycle terms, very young, being at, or close to, financial inception. It might experience a variety of effects (e.g. very high growth, acute funding shortage) which are a direct consequence of its relative youth (cf. Dunn and Cheatham, 1993). However, youth is only a temporary phase, and one expects a more standard neoclassical view of the micro-firm to be applicable when it becomes mature. Proportionately few micro-firms sustain early high growth rates, and those that survive typically remain small. Thus mature micro-firms are an important object of analysis in their own right. They are the focus of this chapter, and will be returned to again, for even more detailed consideration, in Chapter 18.

A neoclassical view of the mature micro-firm is expounded in Section 5.2, extending the standard analysis to embrace the use of money capital within the enterprise, and to consider the implications of finance-capital scarcity. The acquisition of primary source data to test these implications is discussed in Section 5.3, which shows how telephone interviews generated evidence on experience of funding shortages in long-lived (average age 15 years) very small (average size six employees) enterprises. In Section 5.4, these data are subjected to empirical analysis using probit models to test the core predictions of Section 5.2, as well as a number of auxiliary hypotheses (e.g. on sectoral and regional effects). The main conclusions are summarised in Section 5.5, and emphasise the importance of part-time employees in averting funding shortages in mature micro-firms (cf. Section 11.4 of Chapter 11).

5.2 The funding constraint

The theoretical point of departure in this chapter is a micro-firm which needs financial (i.e. money) capital[1] for its operations (e.g. factor hiring, product sales), but which may not always have enough of it fully to fund its operations (Jefferson, 1997). If it is subject to a finance-capital constraint, the usual neoclassical optimal factor hiring conditions need to be modified. It is shown that the micro-firm will substitute the less finance-capital intensive factor input for the more intensive. Thus if we focus on just two factor inputs, full-time and part-time workers, with the second input being less finance-capital intensive than the first, it is found that the effect of the funding constraint is to encourage the substitution of part-time for full-time workers. Further details on the hypothesis are developed in this section. Then the hypothesis is tested by probit models in Section 5.4, using new primary source data (Section 5.3).

To demonstrate the essential point of the argument, consider a neoclassical micro-firm which sells a single product (Q) at a given price (P) utilising two factor inputs: full-time workers (F) and part-time workers (T). These workers receive competitive wage rates of f and t, respectively. The micro-firm's finance-capital requirements depend positively on the volume of production (Q), and therefore sales (PQ), and on the level of hiring of factors F and T. To simplify, suppose finance-capital requirements are: (a) proportional to factor hiring (with proportions

α and β respectively), these hiring levels being F and T for full-time and part-time workers respectively; and (b) increasing in sales, $G(Q)$, $g' > 0$. Consider $Q = h(F, T)$ as a smooth, concave neoclassical production function, and M, the (given) finance-capital available to the firm. Then (putting aside debt servicing, for simplicity) the quantity sold by the micro-firm, and the level of hiring of factor inputs F and T cannot make a greater call on total finance-capital than the amount available M. Thus the funding constraint is:

$$G[h(F, T)] + \alpha F + \beta T \leq M \tag{5.1}$$

If this constraint is not binding then, following Vickers (1987, Ch. 4), we would describe the micro-firm as being 'saturated' in finance-capital, and the marginal product of finance-capital would be zero. The usual marginal productivity conditions would hold, with the ratio of the marginal product of full-time labour to the marginal product of part-time labour being equal to the ratio of their respective wage rates:

$$(h_F/h_T)_u = f/t \tag{5.2}$$

where the subscript u denotes 'unconstrained'.

However, if the constraint (5.1) *is* binding, then there is an impediment to the fulfilling of the condition (5.2). To simplify further, suppose that only the hired factors make a call on finance-capital. Then the micro-firm's maximand is the constrained profit function:

$$Ph(F, T) - fF - tT + \gamma(M - \alpha F - \beta T)$$

with Lagrange multiplier γ. This is maximised when:

$$(h_F/h_T)_c = (f + \gamma\alpha)/(t + \gamma\beta) \tag{5.3}$$

where the subscript c denotes 'constrained'.

When the funding constrain is binding, finance-capital is a scarce resource to the micro-firm, and its implied marginal product is positive rather than zero. The implication of this for optimal factor hiring is given by comparing conditions (5.2) and (5.3). Clearly we have:

$$(h_F/h_T)_u < (h_F/h_T)_c \tag{5.4}$$

provided $(\alpha/f) > (\beta/t)$. This requires that the finance-capital intensity of full-time workers (measured as the ratio of the full-time worker's finance-capital requirement to its unit hiring cost) exceeds that for part-time workers, which seems an assumption that is likely to be met. If so, this implies, for given Q' and smooth, convex isoquants $Q' = h'(F, T)$, a tendency for part-time workers to be substituted for full-time workers, in the finance-capital constrained case.[2] That is, the micro-firm has a tendency to hire more of the less finance-capital intensive factor input (here, part-time labour T) when it is finance-capital constrained.

The dependent variable of the empirical probit analysis in Section 5.4 is defined by reference to the finance-capital constraint (5.1) above. This dependent variable is unity if the equality holds in (5.1) and zero if the inequality holds. If the strict inequality is satisfied, the micro-firm has *not* experienced a funding shortage. If a funding shortage *is* experienced, then the following argument attaches to the inequality (5.4): for such firms, part-time workers will tend to be substituted for full-time workers. This is the key implication to be tested in Section 5.4. First, the data on which these tests are to be performed are described.

5.3   The data and the questionnaire

The data used for estimation were gathered by telephone interviews using a structured administered questionnaire schedule. The sample was drawn from the membership list of Scottish members of the Federation of Small Business (formerly the National Federation of the Self-employed and Small Businesses).[3]

There were 93 firms in the sample, all of which were chosen from a membership population of 3584 small firms in Scotland. The method of stratified proportional random sampling was used, with the nine regions of Scotland providing the strata.[4] In terms of regional breakdown, the division between the Highlands and islands (Region 1) (25 per cent) and the rest (75 per cent) is the main one of significance.[5] The refusal rate for interviews was approximately 10 per cent. This low figure can be attributed to the use of the Federation of Small Businesses as a 'gatekeeper' to this population of micro-firms. Legitimising access in this way typically enhances response rates, and increases the quality and volume of data.

The sectoral representation within the sample was as follows: agriculture (2 per cent), heavy manufacturing (3 per cent), light manufacturing (20 per cent), construction (12 per cent), wholesale and retail distribution (32 per cent), hotel and catering (9 per cent), repairs, transport and storage (9 per cent) and services (13 per cent). Best represented were distribution and hotel and catering. The full range of sectors by Standard Industrial sector (SIC) codes was represented, with the highest proportion being in SIC category 6, which includes retailing, hotel and catering, repairs and garage services.

Telephone interviews of some 20 min duration were conducted using an administered questionnaire.[6] This investigated, with varying success, the existence (or not) of funding shortages, capital structure (including debt, equity, ownership and risk sharing), awareness and use of venture capital, and the likely benefit of new financial arrangements for small businesses (e.g. easier trade credit).

The key question posed to owner-managers asked whether they had experienced a lack of funding in running their businesses. The evidence from the telephone interview is that a minority of micro-firms (31 per cent ± 10 per cent) had experienced a lack of funding, although it was usually perceived not to be serious. In most cases (66 per cent) this shortfall was met by a bank loan, typically of the order of £12,000. For the 69 per cent of micro-firms which had not experienced lack of funding, the average number of full-time workers was (to the nearest inte-ger) seven ($\sigma = 10.1$) and the average number of part-time workers was three ($\sigma = 5.6$). By contrast, for the 31 per cent of micro-firms which *had* experienced lack of funding, the average number of full-time workers was five ($\sigma = 7.1$) and of part-time workers was one ($\sigma = 1.4$). This suggests that the micro-firms which did not experience funding shortage had a higher ratio of part-time to full-time workers. Putting the latter point more precisely, the average ratio of part-time to full-time workers for micro-firms which had not experienced lack of funding was 0.59566 ($\sigma = 0.80517$) and for those which *had* experienced funding shortage was 0.34124 ($\sigma = 0.61923$). Thus there appears to be almost twice the ratio of part-time to full-time workers for micro-firms which had not experienced lack of funding compared to those which had. A 90 per cent confidence interval for the difference ($\pi_1 - \pi_2$) in this ratio of part-time to full-time workers, between the two types of micro-firms is $\Pr(0.00065 < \pi_1 - \pi_2 < 0.58799) = 0.90$ which does not contain the origin, refuting the hypothesis that the ratios are identical. Taken overall, the clear interpretation of the evidence is therefore that it does not support the neoclassical prediction of Section 5.2. This proposition will be examined in more detail in the next section, using univariate and bivariate probit estimation.

5.4   Probit analysis

The goals of this section are: (a) to test the hypothesis suggested by the model of a finance-capital constrained neoclassical micro-firm developed in Section 5.2; (b) to test auxiliary hypotheses on attitudinal variables and regional/sectoral effects; and (c) to test the robustness of the most satisfactory estimates by embedding them in a bivariate probit model.

The question in the administered questionnaire which generated the dependent variable of the probit analysis was: 'Have you experienced a lack of funding in your business?' A response of 'Yes' was coded as unity ($y = 1$); and a response of 'No' as zero ($y = 0$). The y variable is given as *Fundlack* under variable group I in Table 5.1. The constraint (5.1) above suggests that sales, full-time and part-time workers should provide some explanation of the experience of funding shortage at the firm level. These were therefore prime candidates for inclusion in the x vector of a univariate probit model $y = x'\beta$. The variables used from the questionnaire, *Turnover*, *Fulltime* and *Parttime* respectively, are defined in Table 5.1 under vari-able group II. The *Parttime* variable excluded seasonal and casual workers, thus reducing the measurement error and volatility of this variable, and allowing more systematic effects to show through. To check whether, even for mature micro-firms, life-cycle effects might yet play a prominent role in the experience of funding shortage, *Age* was included as another explanatory variable, being measured in years from financial inception of the micro-firm. The variables under group II in Table 5.1 constitute the core set of explanatory variables, in terms of conventional neoclassical hypotheses about the micro-firm.

Additional variables included in the univariate probit modelling are also listed in Table 5.1, and they can be regarded as further control variables. They are

Table 5.1 Variables used in probit analysis

I	*Fundlack*	Unity for experience of lack of funding, zero otherwise
II	*Age*	Age in years from inception
	Fulltime	Number of full-time employees
	Parttime	Number of part-time employees (excluding seasonal and casual workers)
	Turnover	Annual sales turnover (including VAT) in £million
III	*Famsup*	Unity if benefit from financial support from friends and relatives, zero otherwise
	Laxbank	Unity if benefit from more relaxed attitude to granting loans, zero otherwise
	Tradcred	Unity if benefit from more relaxed attitude to extending trade credit, zero otherwise
	Redbus	Unity if benefit from a reduced level of business rates, zero otherwise
	Hithresh	Unity if benefit from higher threshold for VAT exemption, zero otherwise
	Redtax	Unity if benefit from a reduced level of corporation tax, zero otherwise
	Lowint	Unity if benefit from a reduced level of interest on bank loans, zero otherwise
	Reshed	Unity if benefit from rescheduling of debt, with no change in interest, zero otherwise
	Redint	Unity if benefit from reduction of interest on loan with no rescheduling, zero otherwise
IV	$D1, D2, \ldots, D8$	Sectoral dummies, equal to unity if sector appears, zero otherwise
	D	Sectoral dummy, based on SIC coding equal to unity is SIC $= 0$ to 5, zero otherwise
	Highdum	Sectoral dummy equal to unity for Highlands, zero otherwise
V	*Hearvc*	Unity if heard of venture capital backing of a business
	Knowvc	Unity if understood venture capital

basically of two types: attitudinal and technical. The attitudinal variables fall under the headings of variable groups III and V. Under III are listed a variety of measures which may benefit the micro-firm, and therefore which may play some role in ameliorating experience of funding shortage. For example those micro-firms who believe they might benefit from financial support from friends and relatives are more likely to report experience of funding shortage than those who do not. This attitude is measured by the variable *Famsup*, defined in Table 5.1. Under variable group V are listed two further attitudinal variables, which are concerned with owner-managers' perception and knowledge of venture capital.[7] Finally, under variable group IV of Table 5.1, three types of technical variables are used: first, dummy variables (D_i) for the full range of sectors represented in the sample; second, a service/non-service sector dummy (D); third, a regional dummy (*Highdum*), this being relevant to regime differences between the Highlands and Islands and the rest of Scotland.

The first probit estimates reported upon are given in Table 5.2.[8] The key hypothesis is addressed by the inclusion of the full-time (F) and part-time (T) variables suggested by the constraint (5.1) in the model of Section 5.2 (now appearing in empirical estimates as the variables *Fulltime* and *Parttime*). The money finance constraint is further investigated with the (PQ) variable of Section 5.2 (appearing here as *Turnover*); and possible life-cycle dependency is captured by the *Age* variable. Coefficients, *t*-ratios, and Hencher–Johnson weighted elasticities are given in the table, as are relevant critical values. In this and subsequent tables, C^2 denotes χ^2 divided by degrees of freedom. On a likelihood ratio test the model has a 5 per cent probability level, and the Cragg–Uhler R^2 (0.34) is high for cross-sectional models of this sort. The percentage of correct predictions is also high, at 76 per cent.

Table 5.2 Binary probit for full set of control variables with single sectoral dummy variable

Variable elasticity	Coefficient	t-ratio	Weighted
Age	0.11627×10^{-2}	0.72023×10^{-1}	0.14863×10^{-1}
Fulltime	-0.38573×10^{-1}	-1.3459	-0.17237
Parttime	-0.28245	-2.4998^{***}	-0.25776
Turnover	1.4487	2.1194^{**}	0.38162
Famsup	0.67545	1.6402^{*}	0.10155
Laxbank	0.86761	2.1610^{**}	0.55289
Tradcred	-0.68106	-1.8866^{*}	-0.23444
Redbus	-0.13849	-0.25142	-0.10446
Hithresh	-0.71803×10^{-1}	-0.20310	-0.24472×10^{-1}
Redtax	-0.29928	-0.77198	-0.61974×10^{-1}
Lowint	0.56798	0.71591	0.47288
Reshed	0.36520	0.80431	0.20502
Redint	-0.91286×10^{-1}	-0.18307	-0.59033×10^{-1}
Hearvc	0.20875	0.38780	0.71447×10^{-1}
Knowvc	-0.46672	-0.77877	-0.11338
D	-0.11115	-0.27178	-0.27090×10^{-1}
Constant	-1.2070	-1.1928	-1.0583

Likelihood ratio test: Prob. value $= 0.05 [C^2 = 1.601 = C^2 0.05(16) = 1.64]$
Cragg–Uhler $R^2 = 0.33862$
Log-likelihood $= -44.905$
Binomial estimate $= 0.3118$
Sample size (n) $= 93$
Percentage of correct predictions $= 76\%$
Critical *t*-values: $t_{0.01} = 1.289^{(+)}$, $t_{0.05} = 1.658^{(*)}$, $t_{0.025} = 1.980^{(**)}$, $t_{0.001} = 2.358^{(***)}$

On statistical criteria, therefore, the model is satisfactory. No age-related effect is detected, arguing against a life-cycle dimension to experience of funding shortages by these mature enterprises. *Parttime* as a variable has a highly significant ($\alpha = 0.001$) coefficient with a negative sign, and a relatively high elasticity. This elasticity is unit free and a useful predictive tool. Specifically, a 10 per cent increase in part-time employees within the micro-firm, *ceteris paribus*, is associated with a decrease in the probability of experiencing a funding shortage of 2.5 per cent.

This result rejects the finance-saturated model of Section 5.2, and accepts the alternative, to the effect that the finance-capital constrained micro-firms will have higher levels of part-time employees than will finance-saturated micro-firms.[9] The latter prediction hinges on the presumed lower intensity of the finance-capital requirement for part-time, compared to full-time, employees. An explanation of how such small firm funding shortages arise would emphasise the flexibility which part-time employees offer to the owner-manager. It is easier to adjust part-time employees' hours compared to full-time employees' hours, in response to unexpected shocks. For many micro-firms, the wage bill is a principal cost driver.[10] Fine tuning of this wage bill to lower the probability of experiencing funding shortage can be achieved in a flexible fashion especially by varying that part of it which is attributable to part-time employees. The relative maturity of these microfirms makes such adjustments possible over a considerable period of time. Further evidence on casualisation of the work force to control the wage bill is provided in Chapter 11 (Section 11.4).

Amongst the attitudinal variables three features are noteworthy. (a) The predisposition to want banks to be more liberal in this lending (*Laxbank*) is positively and significantly ($\alpha = 0.025$) associated with the experience of funding shortage. The desire to resolve a funding shortage through greater bank liberality is consistent with the pecking order theory of finance of Myers (1984), according to which firms first look to internal finance, and if a firm requires external finance, it will first start with debt finance, followed by equity finance. The *Laxbank* variable's weighted elasticity is the largest of all in the fourth column of Table 5.2, suggesting the prominence of this form of outside finance in the pecking order. (b) Less obvious in interpretation is the negative association, which is marginally significant ($\alpha = 0.05$), between the desire for a more permissive granting of trade credit (*Tradcred*) and the experience of funding shortage. It suggests marginal costs always exceed marginal benefit for this form of outside finance, with costs arising from loss of good will being particularly serious. (c) The desire for better family support for the business (*Famsup*) is associated positively, and marginally significantly ($\alpha = 0.01$), with experience of funding shortage, but the elasticity is small. In terms of pecking order, one would expect this type of outside equity finance to be less desirable than additional debt finance, and hence to have a lesser quantitative significance for funding shortages. Taken as a group, attitudinal variables like *Laxbank* and *Famsup* suggest that micro-firms find financial slack desirable (e.g. in terms of unused debt capacity) (cf. Fletcher, 1995). All other attitudinal variables are insignificant in this probit model.

The three main results on attitudinal variables imply that an extension of an overdraft facility from a bank, or (less so) an injection of funding by friends and/or family were regarded as sound methods of coping with funding shortages (cf. Michaelas *et al.*, 1999), whereas the extension of trade credit was viewed as unsound. This suggests that owner-managers of micro-firms are relatively happy to negotiate extensions to overdraft facilities, which seems rational given the usual requirement for draft collateral; but that they do not regard trade credit as a substitute for other forms of finance. The problem with trade credit is that its terms are very much in a discretionary or 'grey' area. Failing to honour bills within conventional, but often not legally agreed, limits is very damaging to continued harmonious relations with micro-firms' suppliers. It puts at risk the 'customer goodwill' emphasised in the theory of the firm literature from Marshall (1890) through Andrews (1949) to Loasby (1978) [cf. Reid (1987, Ch. 5)].

It seems that few owner-managers in the sample, when confronted with experience of funding shortage, appeared willing to run the risks, and to bear the costs, associated with prolonging, over time or in magnitude, trade credit. Familiarity with (*Hearvc*) and knowledge of (*Knowvc*) venture capital show no association with experience of funding shortage. Not a single firm in the sample had gained access to venture capital (even of business angel form). This form of equity typically comes bottom of the pecking order of outside finance, Myers (1984), Chittenden *et al.* (1996). The dummy variable (*D*) for the manufactures/services dichotomy performs badly, indicating no significant difference in experience of funding shortages between these broad categories of activities for micro-firms. Of course, this does not rule out the possibility of more disaggregated sectoral effects on funding shortages.

This possibility, amongst others, is investigated in the probit model reported in Table 5.3. None of the dummy variables ($D_1, D_2, \ldots, D_8$), introduced to capture sectoral effects at the single-digit SIC level,[11] had a significant coefficient, and all the corresponding weighted elasticities were small. This amplifies the result of the single sectoral dummy variable in the probit of Table 5.2. Taken together, the evidence does not support any sectoral effects for this sample of Scottish micro-firms. Given this, the view in certain policy quarters that manufacturing might require, or deserve, favoured treatment compared with services, seems unjustified so far as experience of a funding gap is concerned.

Considering the probit of Table 5.3 more generally, the main change in specification is the dropping of a large number of insignificant variables contained in the original specification of Table 5.2. The general diagnostic results in the footnote of Table 5.3, as regards goodness of fit, etc., are again satisfactory. Signs and significance of coefficients, and the relative sizes of weighted elasticities are qualitatively the same as in Table 5.2. There is slightly stronger evidence in Table 5.3 of the general advantage of control of the wage bill in avoiding the strict equality version of (5.1) earlier (i.e. funding shortage). Having resolved the issue of sectoral effects (namely there are none) and shown that major influences on experience of funding shortages are stable in their consequences between alternative specifications, a search for a more parsimonious probit model is indicated.

Table 5.3 Binary probit with subset of control variables and full set of sectoral dummy variables

Variable elasticity	Coefficient	t-ratio	Weighted
Fulltime	-0.44287×10^{-1}	-1.6940	-0.19963
Parttime	-0.25350	-2.2395^{**}	-0.24300
Turnover	1.4833	2.1701^{**}	0.38256
Famsup	0.66952	1.6388^{+}	0.10721
Laxbank	0.95655	2.4547^{***}	0.62203
Tradcred	-0.56021	-1.6301^{*}	-0.19273
D1	0.69793	0.62904	0.18224×10^{-1}
D2	-1.4964	-0.39398×10^{-1}	-0.32299×10^{-5}
D3	0.51872	0.48850	0.13806×10^{-1}
D4	-0.52338×10^{-1}	0.64322×10^{-1}	-0.30206×10^{-2}
D5	0.19096	0.2882	0.24920×10^{-1}
D6	0.92465×10^{-1}	0.16514	0.41182×10^{-1}
D7	0.23177	0.24890	0.68884×10^{-2}
D8	-0.14738	-0.21673	0.14223×10^{-1}
Constant	-1.0366	-1.7131^{*}	-0.92583

Likelihood ratio test: Prob. value $= 0.05 \left[C^2 = 1.68 = C^2 0.05(14) = 1.69 \right]$
Cragg–Uhler $R^2 = 0.31468$
Log-likelihood $= -45.936$
Binomial estimate $= 0.3118$
Sample size $(n) = 93$
Percentage of correct predictions $= 77\%$
Critical t-values: $t_{0.01} = 1.289^{(+)}$, $t_{0.05} = 1.658^{(*)}$, $t_{0.025} = 1.980^{(**)}$, $t_{0.001} = 2.358^{(***)}$

An example of such a 'lean' model is given in Table 5.4, where a probit for just three conventional economic variables and three attitudinal variables is reported. No sectoral effects are incorporated, in view of the results of Tables 5.2 and 5.3. In this 'lean' model, all coefficients are significant, and none at less than the 5 per cent level. On a likelihood ratio test, the model is significant at less than the 0.5 per cent level, the percentage of correct predictions is 74 per cent and the R^2 is high for cross-sectionally estimated models of this sort. No qualitative results are altered by going to this more parsimonious model, and even quantitative results (e.g. the weighted elasticities) are very similar. One can therefore restate the claim with some confidence, using the weighted elasticity for the *Parttime* variable, that a 10 per cent increase in part-time employees is associated, *ceteris paribus*, with a decrease in the probability of experiencing a funding shortage of 2.5 per cent. Comparing the models of Table 5.3 and Table 5.4 using a likelihood ratio test one gets a χ^2 statistic of 0.761, which is very much less than the $\chi^2_{0.01}(8)$ critical value of 20.1 or even its 5 per cent value of 15.5. That is, the data do not accept the extra restrictions imposed in the probit of Table 5.3 compared to Table 5.4. The parsimonious probit of Table 5.4 is therefore preferred.

Table 5.4 Parsimonious binary probit

Variable elasticity	Coefficient	t-ratio	Weighted
Fulltime	−0.04404	−1.7699*	−0.20323
Parttime	−0.25927	−2.4980***	−0.24970
Turnover	1.4489	2.2882**	0.38268
Famsup	0.65217	1.6678*	0.10458
Laxbank	0.93175	2.5826***	0.60705
Tradcred	−0.57061	−1.7572*	−0.19756
Constant	−0.87083	−2.3425**	−0.78508

Likelihood ratio test: Prob. value $= 0.05\left[C^2 = 3.80 = C^2 0.05(6) = 3.09\right]$
Cragg–Uhler $R^2 = 0.30560$
Log-likelihood $= -46.321$
Binomial estimate $= 0.3118$
Sample size (n) $= 93$
Percentage of correct predictions $= 74\%$
Critical t-values: $t_{0.01} = 1.289^{(+)}$, $t_{0.05} = 1.658^{(*)}$, $t_{0.025} = 1.980^{(**)}$, $t_{0.001} = 2.358^{(***)}$

Finally, one is interested in the possibility of regional effects on funding short-ages. Given the small size of some regional strata, it is not always easy to get strong estimates of regional effects, though there is some evidence that they do exist, to varying degrees. Given the institutional arrangements for enterprise stimulation in Scotland, which prevailed during the sampling period, replacing the old planning institutions of the Scottish Development Agency (SDA) and the Highlands and Islands Development Board (HIDB) with the more market-oriented Scottish Enterprise and Highlands and Islands Enterprise, the most important regional distinction is between the Highlands and Islands and the rest of Scotland. To test for a regional effect along these lines, the probit in Table 5.5 has another variable added to it, com-pared to that of Table 5.4, namely a dummy variable (*Highdum*) to represent the effects of the Highlands compared to the rest of Scotland. The Highlands dummy is highly statistically significant, though it does not have as high an elasticity as most other significant control variables. It clearly suggests that micro-firms in the Highlands are significantly less likely to experience funding shortages than their Lowland (i.e. rest of Scotland) counterparts. Exploring this further, one finds that 15 per cent ($=4/26$) (p_1) of the small firms in the Highlands had experienced fund-ing shortages compared to 37 per cent ($=25/67$) (p_2) in the Lowlands. Computing 95 per cent confidence intervals for these proportions one finds they are, respec-tively, $(0.04 < \pi_1 < 0.34)$ and $(0.27 < \pi_2 < 0.50)$, which overlap very little. More precisely, a 95 per cent confidence interval for the difference in proportions between the Highlands and the Lowlands is given by $(-0.40 < \pi_1 - \pi_2 < -0.04)$ which does not contain the origin, implying that this difference is statistically sig-nificant. Explanations of this effect would require a detailed independent study: the main purpose here is to establish that it exists. Whilst the most obvious expla-nation would tend to focus on differences in grant regimes between the regions, differences in entrepreneurial culture may also be important. The farming tradition

Table 5.5 Parsimonious probit with Highlands dummy variable

Variable elasticity	Coefficient	t-ratio	Weighted
Fulltime	−0.03726	−1.5095	−0.16653
Parttime	−0.27479	−2.6792	−0.25697
Turnover	1.2233	1.9397*	0.31619
Famsup	0.58318	1.4363+	0.08381
Laxbank	0.77610	2.1812**	0.46799
Tradcred	−0.70409	−2.0712**	−0.23691
Highdum	−0.92564	−2.3671***	−0.16321
Constant	−0.41193	−1.0969	−0.35481

Likelihood ratio test: Prob. value $= 0.05 \left[C^2 = 3.80 = C^2 0.05(7) = 2.90 \right]$
Cragg–Uhler $R^2 = 0.35016$
Log-likelihood $= -44.400$
Binomial estimate $= 0.3118$
Sample size $(n) = 93$
Percentage of correct predictions $= 74\%$
Critical t-values: $t_{0.01} = 1.289^{(+)}$, $t_{0.05} = 1.658^{(*)}$, $t_{0.025} = 1.980^{(**)}$, $t_{0.001} = 2.358^{(***)}$

is stronger in this area, which tends to foster an entrepreneurial attitude, and part-time working and multiple job holding are more common, emphasising greater labour market flexibility.

A likelihood ratio test for comparing the probits of Tables 5.4 and 5.5 produces a χ^2 statistic of 3.842 which is greater than the $\chi^2_{0.05}(1)$ significance point of 3.840, implying the data accept the additional Highland dummy variable restriction at a probability level of approximately 0.05. Thus the final preferred specification for this chapter is the probit of Table 5.5. Looking at all seven restrictions, this probit stands up well on the likelihood ratio test, having a very small probability of occurring by chance (<0.005). The fading from high significance of the full-time employees' variable is not problematical, for it is consistent with the behaviour of this variable in a variety of alternative specifications. The upshot of this detailed discussion of results is that one ends up with a parsimonious probit model which emphasises the importance of part-time workers and location in explaining the micro-firm's experience of funding shortages.

The probit analysis can be extended in a number of directions, of which the only one reported upon here, for the purpose of robustness testing, is the case of bivariate probits. This method has been previously used in biological and sociological contexts, but is also of interest to economists.[12] The economic focus of interest is still on explaining the lack of funding experienced by micro-firms, and the statistical focus is on the robustness of the probit results reported in Tables 5.2–5.5. It will be noted from Table 5.6 that the between equation error correlation (ρ) is positive and significant, confirming the value of this multivariate extension. In Table 5.6, the first of the pair of probits is based on that of Table 5.4, with even further simplification. Under bivariate estimation, the influence of part-time employees (*Parttime*) is again important, and consistent in its effect, further

Table 5.6 Bivariate probit model: Full information maximum likelihood estimates

Model:
Fundlack $= F_1$ (*Parttime, Turnover, Tradcred*)
Laxbank $= F_2$ (*Lowint, Tradcred*)

Variable	Coefficient	t-ratio
Probit 1		
Parttime	−0.23028	−2.266**
Turnover	0.59373	1.447
Tradcred	−0.32895	−1.059
Constant	−0.23352	0.2432
Probit 2		
Lowint	1.4021	1.951*
Tradcred	0.64898	2.089**
Constant	−1.1256	−1.642+

$\rho = 0.3929(2.225)$**
Critical *t*-values: $t_{0.01} = 1.289^{(+)}$, $t_{0.05} = 1.658^{(*)}$,
$t_{0.025} = 1.980^{(**)}$, $t_{0.001} = 2.358^{(***)}$

emphasising the robustness of this result. The turnover and trade credit variables behave as before in a qualitative sense, but here their coefficients are no longer significant. The second probit is less familiar in conventional economic terms, and is influenced by sociological applications[13] which have used bivariate probits, in that all the variables are attitudinal. The *t*-ratios on the control variables all lie in critical regions. The second probit says that if you have the attitude that lower interest rates or easier trade credit would be good for your kind of micro-firm, you would tend to think that banks should adopt a more lenient attitude towards granting loans to customers who run such businesses. This empirical finding is not trivial, because one knows from earlier probits that the low interest and trade credit variables have opposite effects on the lack of funding. Banks are typically very sensitive to the view that their micro-firm customers take of the conduct of banking business,[14] and the second probit gives some insight into what governs these attitudes.

5.5   Conclusion

The central hypothesis explored in this chapter concerned the response of the neoclassical micro-firm, in terms of its factor hiring (especially of labour), when its supply of finance-capital is constrained. The principal conclusions of the chapter are as follows:

(a)   Variation of part-time employees provided the most powerful leverage on the probability of experiencing a funding shortage. A 10 per cent increase in part-time employees, other things being equal, lowers the probability of experiencing funding shortages by two and a half per cent. This refutes a simple neoclassical hypothesis of the financially saturated micro-firm. It suggests those firms which become financially constrained will favour hiring part-time employees. This suggests a flexibility advantage of part-time employees which is successfully exploited by these mature micro-firms to avert funding shortages. A number of auxiliary hypotheses were also explored, leading to the following further conclusions.

(b)   High-turnover firms are more prone to funding shortages than low-turnover firms, suggesting that a reason for funding shortages could be over-trading.

(c)   Sectoral effects were found to have no bearing on funding shortages, arguing against any sector-specific form of positive discrimination on the policy front (e.g. special help for manufactures).

(d)   Regional differences in experience of funding shortages were detected. Specifically, by reference to regional arrangements at the time of sampling, small firms under Highland and Islands Enterprise experienced funding shortages significantly less often than those under Scottish Enterprise.

(e)   Owner-managers of small firms that had experienced funding shortages tended to think that their plights could be improved by more financial support from friends and family, and by a more permissive bank lending policy, but that they would only be worsened by an extension of trade credit.

Conclusion (b) refutes a neoclassical financial saturated hypothesis and suggests an alternative hypothesis, appealing to the flexibility of part-time employees in averting funding shortages. Conclusions (c) and (d) have significant policy implications for sectoral and regional selectivity, suggesting the relative efficacy of the latter. Conclusion (e) demonstrates the potential usefulness of attitudinal variables. Overall, it is hoped that these conclusions enrich the rather limited evidence available on mature micro-firms.[15]

Endnotes

1   The terms 'money capital', 'finance-capital' and 'financial-capital' will be used interchangeably.

2   Thus flexibility is assumed to be a capability of the micro-firm in the sense of its hiring policy. By exercising a flexible part-time hiring capability, the micro-firm can adapt to a constraint on finance-capital. This notion of flexibility extends that of technological flexibility in the work of authors like Acs *et al.* (1990). More detailed consideration of flexibility will be undertaken in Part 6.

3   A detailed account of the database, covering sample design, instrumentation and summary statistics is available in Reid and Anderson (1992) so here the account will be very much abbreviated. Statistics were obtained from the Federation of Small Businesses' research office in Glasgow.

4   Highlands and Islands (25 per cent), Grampian (13 per cent), Tayside (5 per cent), Central (3 per cent), Fife (2 per cent), Lothian (6 per cent), Strathclyde (43 per cent), Borders (1 per cent), Dumfries and Galloway (3 per cent).

5   The new enterprise arrangements put in place in Scotland after 1989 set up a distinct institutional arrangement for the Highlands and Islands to replace the old HIDB.

Elsewhere in Scotland another new system, Scottish Enterprise, replaced the old Scottish Development Agency (SDA). See *Towards Highlands and Islands Enterprise* (1989) and *Towards Scottish Enterprise* (HMSO, 1989) for further details. They each created a framework for local enterprise companies (LECs) being the focus of delivery for enterprise stimulating policies.

6 A description of the instrument and a reproduction of the full schedule is given in Reid and Anderson (1992).

7 Which, in this case, is almost certainly likely to be of the 'business angel' or informal investor variety, Mason and Harrison (1994).

8 These and other estimates were obtained by the author using the *Shazam 6.2* econometric software package. For the estimates reported, an iterative maximum likelihood procedure, based on the Davidon–Fletcher–Powell algorithm, was used, as implemented by coding due to John Cragg. A tolerance of 0.001 convergence was usually achieved within five or so iterations. The results reported were subjected to independent audit, by Dr Jonathan Seaton, of the University of Loughborough, to whom I am grateful. He used the *LIMDEP 6* econometric package, with coding due to W.H. Greene. There, the algorithm used is Newton–Raphson. Convergence was again rapid, though typically with a somewhat larger number of iterations, and the final estimates obtained agreed with the earlier set to at least four digit accuracy.

9 This hypothesis can also be tested in ratio form. For example, if the parsimonious probit of Table 5.4 is re-estimated using the ratio of part-time to full-time employees (*Pfratio*), rather than the levels of both part-time and full-time employees, variables have similar effects on experience of lack of funding, but *Pfratio* has an asymptotic *t*-ratio of −1.5626 which is just marginally significant. Whilst this indeed suggests that the higher the ratio of part-time to full-time employees, the lower the probability of experiencing a funding shortage, the empirical case is more strongly made by the estimates reported in the main text.

10 There is ample qualitative evidence for this reported in Reid *et al.* (1993, pp. 30, 46, 98, 105). The best quantitative estimate currently available (from the CRIEFF-based Leverhulme project on the life-cycle effects in small firms) on wages as a cost driver for a similar sample of firms (though generally younger), is that wages are the principal cost driver (25 per cent) followed by raw materials (18 per cent), stocks (11 per cent) and rents (11 per cent). See the descriptive evidence in Chapter 3, and the analytical/econometric evidence in Chapter 11.

11 Only eight dummy variables, rather than the usually required nine, were required to represent ten sectors because one sector was unrepresented in this sample (Sector 2: minerals extraction, chemical industry etc.).

12 The method is due to Ashford and Sowden (1970) and a fairly full treatment of theory and extension is available in Amemiya (1985, Ch. 9). In the bivariate probits case, two latent dependent variables which, because of threshold effects, can be mapped into binary variables, are assumed to be distributed as the bivariate normal distribution with zero means, unit variances and correlation coefficient. The parameters of the probits may be jointly estimated by the method of maximum likelihood. The estimates of Table 5.6 were obtained using the software package LIMDEP 6 referred to in Note 7.

13 Ashford and Sowden (1970) applied the model to breathlessness in coal miners, and Muthen (1979) to attitudes of parents towards their children. Greene (1984) gives a mixed sociological/economic example for illustrative purposes, which analyses voting decisions in a school tax referendum.

14 See article (p. 17) in *The Scotsman* newspaper on 15 April 1992.

15 The author is currently conducting work on long-lived micro-firms in Scotland, which aims to remedy this deficiency. This work is being conducted with Bernadette Power of University College, Cork, based on research sponsored by Enterprise Ireland, see Power and Reid (2003). The first fruits of this collaboration are reported in Chapter 18.

Part 3
Finance

6 Modelling financial structure

6.1 Introduction

This chapter introduces the general topic of financial structure in a small firm (Lund and Wright, 1999; Hamilton and Fox, 1998; Tucker and Lean, 2003; Gregory *et al.*, 2005). It starts by considering first the well-known static framework. In this, it recurs to themes of Chapter 5 on funding constraints, and extends that treatment. It then establishes a general underpinning for the analysis of small firm financing over time. This appeals to the control theoretic literature, notably the work of Hilten *et al.* (1993), which permits the specification of 'master trajectories' of key variables over time like output, debt, dividend and capital. Two key trajectories (for cheap debt and cheap equity, respectively) are used to illustrate this type of analysis, showing how financial structure can vary over time, involving phases of growth, consolidation and stationarity. From this perspective, important issues of small firm dynamics and finance are addressed, and then illustrated by reference to selected literature on credit constraints (funding shortages), wealth as collateral, financial structure, target income modelling of start-up, and bank lending during financial liberalisation.

6.2 Analytical underpinning: statics

Vickers (1970) was the first writer to integrate seriously the production aspect of the firm with the financial. An extended and general treatment of this approach, in book form, is contained in Vickers (1987). There, it is argued that the firm needs financial capital to hire inputs and to produce and to sell output. It acquires outside financial capital either in the form of debt (B), for which it pays a rate of interest, or in the form of equity (E), which has a required rate of return, to be interpreted as the cost of equity. The value maximisation problem which the firm solves involves both the production function constraint in a familiar way, but also the financial capital constraint, in a less familiar way. Indeed, the typical exposition of the neoclassical theory of the firm usually ignores the latter constraint. The solution to the more general problem posed here will determine not only what will be sold, and how much will be hired of various factors, but also how much financial capital will be used, and in what ways.

First, following Vickers (1987), consider the following notation: $E =$ equity; $B =$ debt. Furthermore, if X and Y are factors of production, and Q is output, then $Q = f(X, Y)$ is the production function, satisfying the usual neoclassical concavity assumptions. Production and sales cannot occur without money capital, in the form of working capital (W) in the firm. So let $W = g(Q)$ show the dependence of money capital (W) on the firm's output, with g being monotonically increasing in $Q, g' > 0$.

In the same way as one can argue that the net working capital requirements of a firm depend on the level of output (or the level of sales) as mentioned earlier, it is also sensible to hold that every unit of factor employed will need an investment of money capital in fixed assets. In the two-factor case, these may be represented as $\alpha(X)X$ and $\beta(Y)Y$ where α and β are the *money capital requirements coefficients*. Then, what may be called the total money capital requirements (MCR), are:

$$G[f(X, Y)] + \alpha(X)X + \beta(Y)Y \tag{6.1}$$

Furthermore, as in Chapter 5, whatever the level of production, this MCR cannot exceed the money capital to which the firm has access (namely equity plus debt $= E + B$). Thus the financial constraint can be written as:

$$G[f(X, Y)] + \alpha(X)X + \beta(Y)Y \leq E + B \tag{6.2}$$

In general, this will be a binding constraint. To put it in the terminology of Chapter 5, the small firm will typically not be finance capital saturated. A common further simplification is to assume that the functions $\alpha(.)$ and $\beta(.)$ take the simple form of constants α and β.

As a final simplification, consider the case in which no debt capital is used at all, but only equity capital. This is quite a realistic assumption in the present context, see Chapter 1. For example, for the sample of small firms examined in Chapter 8, only about one-third (32 per cent) obtained debt finance at launch. Almost inevitably, firms were launched with equity finance. In the sample of Chapter 8, for example, 95 per cent of firms were launched with inside equity, this being the owner-manager's personal financial injections (averaging about £13,000). To build up the picture from familiar territory, consider first the profit (π) as the maximand for the owner-manager, in the absence of money capital within the firm. It may be written as:

$$\pi = p(Q)f(X, Y) - \gamma_1 X - \gamma_2 Y \tag{6.3}$$

where γ_1 and γ_2 are factor prices, and $p(Q)$ is the monotonically decreasing (inverse) demand function, $p' < 0$. However, it is argued in this chapter that (6.3) is an unrealistic way to proceed. Small firms require finance-capital to function (e.g. to sell good and to hire factors of production). This suggests introducing the finance-capital constraint or MCR constraint. This now has the simplified form $E \geq \alpha X + \beta Y$ where 'fixed proportions' money capital requirements for factor inputs are written in the simplified forms αX, βY. Suppose this constraint to be binding.

To solve this constrained optimization problem,[1] the Lagrangian (Φ), with Lagrange multiplier λ, may be written as:

$$\Phi = p(Q) f(X, Y) - \gamma_1 X - \gamma_2 Y + \lambda(E - \alpha X - \beta Y) \tag{6.4}$$

Taking derivatives, first-order conditions for a maximum are:

$$\partial \Phi / \partial X = (p + Q dp/dQ) f_x - \gamma_1 - \lambda \alpha = 0 \tag{6.5}$$

$$\partial \Phi / \partial Y = (p + Q dp/dQ) f_y - \gamma_2 - \lambda \beta = 0 \tag{6.6}$$

$$E - \alpha X - \beta Y = 0 \tag{6.7}$$

f_x and f_y are the marginal physical products of factors X and Y.

Solving the first-order conditions gives:

$$\frac{f_x}{f_y} = \frac{\gamma_1 + \lambda \alpha}{\gamma_2 + \lambda \beta} \tag{6.8}$$

That is, the ratio of marginal products equals the ratio of their 'effective marginal costs' [cf. equation (5.3) of Chapter 5]. Note that effective marginal costs (when finance-capital is involved) have two components: direct unit costs of γ_1, γ_2 and marginal imputed money capital costs of $\lambda \alpha$, $\lambda \beta$. Note too that this optimality condition differs from the standard neoclassical one of $f_x/f_y = \gamma_1/\gamma_2$ (namely the marginal rate of substitution in production equals the factor price ratio: compare equation (5.2) of Chapter 5). Indeed, the revised formulation suggests that if the money capital constraint is binding, the small firm typically will be taken off its (efficient) expansion path. Its production plan will be (constrained) efficient, but may differ markedly from what it would be in the (assumed) abundant finance-capital environment of neoclassical reasoning. It is easy to show that $\lambda = d\pi/dK$, which is the marginal efficiency, or marginal productivity, of money capital.

6.3 Analytical underpinning: dynamics

Leland (1972) first combined production and finance in a dynamic theory of the firm. In his case, the theory of the firm adopted was based on so-called 'managerial' principles. Therefore, the goal of his firm was to maximise the total discounted value of *sales* (over a finite planning horizon) plus the final value of the equity. However, though this model started an important new line of enquiry, in itself it contained several flaws and inconsistencies.[2]

It remained for writers like Ludwig (1978) and Lesourne and Leban (1982) to provide rigorous and general treatments of the dynamics of a theory of the firm which combined production and financial aspects. A synthesis of these approaches is provided by Hilten *et al.* (1993), to whom reference is made throughout this section. The type of firm being considered is a familiar one to small firms' specialists. It has no access to the stock exchange, has limited access to debt finance and its technology is subject to decreasing returns. It is assumed that production is a proportional function of capital, and sales are a concave function of output. In terms of its balance sheet, the value of capital assets is equal to the sum of debt and equity.[3] Equity can be raised by the retention of earnings, and there is assumed to be a maximum debt to equity ratio (i.e. gearing) determined by the risk class of the enterprise. It is assumed that there is a linear depreciation rate on capital.

It is now possible to set up a dynamic maximisation problem, with the maximand being the shareholders' value of the firm, under the assumption of a finite time horizon on the dividend-stream integral. The constraints of this maximisation problem have been largely covered in the previous paragraph. To them must be added the initialising values of variables, and non-negativity constraints on capital and dividends (i.e. a zero dividend policy is possible). This problem can be solved by the Pontryagin Maximum Principle. The state variables, representing the state of the firm at a point in time, are equity and capital. The control variables are debt, investment and dividend. The derivation of the optimal solution is a distinctively non-trivial matter, as the cases considered by Schütte (1996), discussed later, illustrate.

6.4   The dynamic model

This section presents a dynamic financial model of the small, owner-managed enterprise. The emphasis is upon debt and equity relationships, and their modification, as the small firm goes through various stages of growth. The basis of this modelling is the extant literature on the dynamics of the firm, especially the writings of Feichtinger and Hartl (1986) and Hilten *et al.* (1993). It has previously been utilised in a small firms' context by Reid (1996a, b). It is to be noted that the symbols here differ slightly from the more obvious one adopted in Chapter 5 and in Section 6.3 earlier. This is necessary, because the larger number of symbols used subsequently have to be used without ambiguity (e.g. *D* now refers to dividend; and *B* now refers to debt).

It is assumed that the owner-manager engages in maximising the value of his or her firm according to

$$\max_{D,I,B} \int_0^\tau e^{-it} D \, \mathrm{d}t + e^{-i\tau} E(\tau) \tag{6.9}$$

where $D \geq 0$ is the dividend stream, and i is the owner-manager's rate of time preference. E denotes equity, τ is the planning time horizon, I is gross investment and B is debt. For this model, the state variables are the amount of equity (E) and the capital stock (K); with the control variables being debt (B), investment (I) and dividend (D). It is assumed that the owner-manager pursues the goal of maximisation of value as in (6.1) by its dividend, investment and debt policy, subject to the following constraint upon policy, and therefore upon the state of the firm and its performance:

$$\dot{E} = \pi - rB - D \tag{6.10}$$

$$\dot{K} = I - \delta K \tag{6.11}$$

$$K = E + B \tag{6.12}$$

$$0 \leq B \leq \gamma E \tag{6.13}$$

$$B \geq 0, \ K \geq 0 \tag{6.14}$$

$$E(0) = e_0; \quad K(0) = k_0 \tag{6.15}$$

Equation (6.10) is the state equation for equity, with π being the operating profit, r the interest rate on debt and δ the depreciation rate on capital goods. γ is the maximum gearing ratio permitted for the risk class of debt to which an interest rate r is attached. This approach has become standard since the contribution of Ludwig (1978, p. 51).

Note that what drives this maximum on gearing is a limit on desired risk exposure, *not* a limit on outside finance (which could be expressed as a credit rationing argument). In fact, limits on gearing depend on the debt–equity *ratio* not the *level* to which equity or debt are provided by investors or lenders. It is also notable that small firms often have gearing ratios well in excess of unity, in the early stages of the life-cycle, casting doubt on the credit rationing argument, so far as the provision of debt finance is concerned (the case typically argued).

Like dividends, debt and capital are subject to non-negativity constraints; and the initialising values of equity and capital are e_0 and k_0, respectively. Operating profit (π) is defined as the difference between sales (S) and production costs, given that capital is the only factor input. It is assumed that the output rate of the firm (Q) is proportionately related to the capital input by the capital productivity parameter κ. Thus operating profit may be written as follows:

$$\pi = P \cdot Q - \delta K \tag{6.16}$$

$$= K(\kappa P - \delta)$$

assuming a unit price of capital goods. Finally, the firm's sales are defined by the function $S(Q)$ which is monotonically increasing and concave in Q, with sales being positive for positive outputs. Thus:

$$S(Q) = P(Q) \cdot Q \quad \text{with}$$

$$S' > 0, \ S'' < 0 \quad \text{and} \quad S > 0 \quad \text{for} \quad Q > 0 \tag{6.17}$$

In effect, this small firm is subject to decreasing returns to scale, the source of which may be an imperfect goods market and/or unspecified non-production costs which raise the marginal costs of organising the production plan of the firm as it grows. The evidence for decreasing returns in small firms has been established by Reid (1992, 1993). In some measure, an organisational explanation for it is plausible (cf. Richardson, 1964; Reid, 1995), especially in a growth context. Parameter restrictions for the model are that:

$$i, r \in (0, 1) \quad \text{and} \quad \delta, \gamma, \kappa \geq 0 \tag{6.18}$$

Further restrictions, which make the model more tractable, are that there are constant unit (and hence marginal) costs of finance, which are denoted by c_E, c_D or c_{ED} depending on whether the financial structure of the firm is equity (E) or debt (B) dominated, or a mixture of the two (EB). It is assumed that marginal revenue close to zero output exceeds the greatest of these costs, implying the small firm has a motivation to at least start investing and producing. Finally, it is assumed that operating profit cannot be negative ($\pi \geq 0$) (cf. Reid, 1991), that the prices of debt and equity differ ($r \neq i$) and that equity at time zero is positive ($E(0) > 0$). These last restrictions[4] follow from the assumptions that: (a) making non-negative profit is a survival criterion; (b) debt and equity markets are distinct; (c) holding equity in itself may engender utility (e.g. from owner-management and the control it implies) that makes equity-holders willing to accept less than the return relevant to the investment risk class and (d) the owner-manager has at least a certain amount of equity at inception of the business, $e_0 > 0$. It has been observed that (d) is a reasonable assumption: the vast majority of firms in the sample were launched on equity (average value £13,000).

Using the Pontryagin maximum principle, optimal dividend, investment and debt policies can be derived, and their dependence on the parameter set (6.10) displayed. The complete solution to this dynamic optimisation problem is complex and prolix, without necessarily being economically informative, so here the solution will be outlined, with an emphasis on economic interpretation.

The Hamiltonian for the system is

$$H = D + \lambda_1 \dot{E} + \lambda_2 \dot{K}$$

$$= D + \lambda_1 (\pi - rB - D) + \lambda_2 (I - \delta K) \tag{6.19}$$

and the Lagrangian is

$$L = H + \mu_1 D + \mu_2 (K - E) + \mu_3 \{(1 + \gamma)E - K\} + \mu_4 K \tag{6.20}$$

For optimality the maximum principle requires

$$\frac{\partial L}{\partial I} = \frac{\partial L}{\partial D} = 0 \qquad \text{for all } t \tag{6.21}$$

$$\mu_1 D = 0, \quad \mu_1 \geq 0 \tag{6.22}$$

and

$$\dot{\lambda}_1 = i\lambda_1 - \frac{\partial L}{\partial K} \qquad\qquad \text{for all } t \qquad\qquad (6.23)$$

$$\dot{\lambda}_2 = i\lambda_2 - \frac{\partial L}{\partial E} \qquad\qquad \text{for all } t \qquad\qquad (6.24)$$

$$\mu_2(K - E) = 0, \quad \mu_3\{(1 + \gamma)E - K\} = 0, \quad \mu_4 K = 0 \qquad (6.25)$$

and $\qquad\qquad\qquad\qquad \mu_2, \ \mu_3, \ \mu_4 \geq 0 \qquad\qquad\qquad (6.26)$

where λ_1 is the shadow price of equity and λ_2 the shadow price of capital. For example, λ_1 is the rate of change of the maximand's optimum for a marginal change in equity, and similarly for λ_2 with regard to capital.

The detailed derivation of feasible paths for the above model is omitted (Hilten *et al.*, 1993, Part B), but the implications can be summarised as follows (cf. Reid, 1996a, b). If debt is cheap ($i > r$) maximum debt finance is used, and no dividend is paid until a stationary state is reached (Figure 6.1). Then there is no further growth in output, debt or capital stock, and a positive dividend is paid. Whilst growth occurs, marginal revenue from sales exceeds the marginal cost of debt, that is $S' > c_B$. This implies that the marginal return to equity exceeds the owner-manager's time preference, so all earnings will be re-invested. When this inequality ceases, because of decreasing returns, the optimal output (Q_B^*) has been reached.

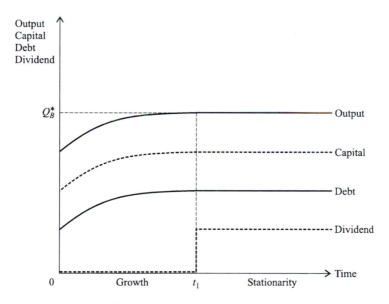

Figure 6.1 Trajectories if debt is cheap.

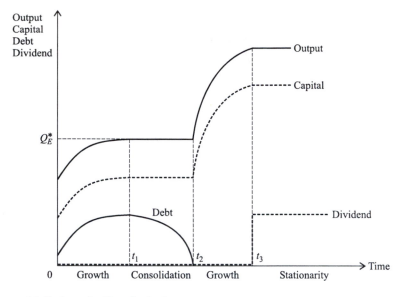

Figure 6.2 Trajectories if equity is cheap.

When equity is cheap ($i < r$) then, assuming that the owner-manager has at least some equity at start-up, the firm will increase its borrowing to start with (until t_1) (cf. Figure 6.2), because the marginal revenue of sales exceeds the marginal cost of debt finance, or $S' > c_{EB}$. Or, each additional unit of capital which is bought with debt finance generates a greater increment in sales than the increment in cost of debt incurred. Once $S' = c_{EB}$ debt will start to be paid back out of retained earnings (during the consolidation phase), until it is completely paid back (t_2), at which stage further growth occurs (after t_2) because $S' > c_E$ where c_E is the marginal cost of capital goods which are financed entirely by equity. This will cease (in the stationary phase) once marginal returns from sales fall to i. The optimal output (Q_E^*) will then have been reached, only replacement investment will occur, and the remaining dividend will go to shareholders. This develops the model sufficiently for present purposes, though further extensions are possible (cf. Hilten *et al.*, 1993, Parts C and D).[5]

6.5   Some illustrative examples from the literature

A number of papers in the literature closely follow the methodology expounded in this chapter, of integrating finance into the theory of the small firm. The first such example is Schütte (1996). In that paper, to illustrate, the author uses methods of dynamic optimisation to investigate the relationship between a bank and a firm, both of which function in an economic system undergoing financial liberalisation.

Examples of such transition have occurred since the 1980s in Hungary, Poland and Czechoslovakia (the Czech Republic and Slovakia). Schütte asks what a bank should do when faced with a non-performing part of its portfolio that is attributable to small firms with profitability prospects that may not be good. The key conclusion is that the banks should support small firms willing to undergo credit restructuring, but should initiate bankruptcy proceedings against those that are not. However, Schütte has assumed that small firms truthfully reveal information about themselves while seeking loans.

This may be appropriate to transition economies, but in free market contexts, it may not be so. This may be because of problems such as adverse selection. In Schütte's context of an economy in transition, the assumption of accurate information being in the hands of banks is more acceptable, as under the previous planning regime (typically Eastern European) banks had worked closely with small business enterprises (SBEs). But, in the second illustrative case given subsequently, that of Binks and Ennew (1996), this harmony may be absent.

Binks and Ennew summarised theoretical arguments explaining how, in those financial markets to which small businesses have access, impediments to their efficient functioning can arise. These are the classical problems of adverse selection and moral hazard, which arise when firms and banks each have access to private information which is not fully shared. Thus, entrepreneurs may over-report the soundness of a business proposition to secure funding (adverse selection); and then, having secured funding, thus diminishing risk, they may reduce effort (moral hazard). Binks and Ennew (1996) suggest that the problems of information asymmetry that thereby arise are particularly acute for small compared to large firms, especially if they are growing. Whilst the availability of collateral can attenuate adverse selection (thus, banks may require it, to secure their loan), growing small firms may be prone to inadequate collateral positions, and as a consequence may be vulnerable to constraints being put on credit. Binks and Ennew used a perceived credit constraint variable [cf. equations (5.1) and (6.2)] derived from a large body of data provided by the Forum of Private Business. They explain the perceived credit constraint by: financing arrangements; banking relationships; and firm specific effects (e.g. age, size and profitability). In an ordered probit model it was found that the greater was the growth rate of the small firm, the greater was the probability of a perceived credit constraint. The interest rate premium on loans and, indeed, the use of overdrafts, experience of financial difficulties, and the requirement of full information provision were also all found to be positively associated with the probability of perceiving a credit constraint. Age, profitability and indices of trust and bank approachability, were all negatively associated with the probability of perceiving a credit constraint. Thus experience (proxied by age), performance (proxied by profitability) and devices for reducing information asymmetry (to ameliorate moral hazard and adverse selection), like trust and approachability, all reduced perceived credit constraints. But overdrafts, interest burdens and increased monitoring all increased perceived credit constraints.

These results all support the view that financial markets are imperfect from the standpoint of small firms. Surprisingly, in view of its potential importance as a signalling and bonding device, the collateral ratio (measured in relation to overdraft limits) was found to have had no significant effect on the perception of a credit constraint, whereas specifically *personal* collateral had a positive effect. The latter finding may be explained by the greater risk associated with personal guarantees.

The third illustrative example is that of Robson's (1996) empirical paper which takes as its starting point the study by Black *et al.* (1992). The latter suggested that the real value of new housing wealth is a significant determinant of the rate of small firm formation. Housing assets are thought to be an important source of collateral to individuals contemplating the 'entrepreneurial event' of starting up a business. In earlier work Robson (1993) had apparently discovered, confirming evidence of Black *et al.* (1992), that real net housing wealth had a significant positive effect on the rate of new VAT registrations in the United Kingdom. However, Robson (1996) took a more sophisticated look at the dynamics of small business creation, casting doubt on the validity of earlier results. Therefore, established small businesses can gain access to additional lines of credit, to an extent determined by housing wealth, as opposed to new small business founders overcoming the capital barrier to entrepreneurship because of their housing wealth.

The core of Robson's work is a re-appraisal of the detailed statistical procedures of Black *et al.* (1992). Concerning variables, Robson criticised the dependent variable they used for its neglect of variations between regions of the incubator population from which new small firms emerge. Also, the measure of housing wealth adopted by Black *et al.* (1992) was found to be unsatisfactory in that it neglected outstanding mortgage debt. Turning to equation specification, Robson (1996) noted that the latter authors neglected dynamics, which would bias standard errors. Correcting the variables in the way suggested, and using an 'error correction' specification to deal with autocorrelations, Robson himself failed to find any evidence of a positive relationship between housing wealth and new small firm formation at the regional level. Apart from regional and time-specific fixed effects, only population density and the ratio of unemployment to vacancies appear to have significant effects on regional rates of new small firm formation. If housing wealth is included as an explanatory variable, it has a perverse (negative) sign. The only partial support for the hypothesis that housing wealth acts as collateral comes from the association of higher housing wealth regionally with lower rates of VAT deregistration. Robson's results are consistent with the view that housing wealth is associated with the greater longevity of firms rather than their greater inception rates.

The fourth illustrative paper, that of Cressy (1996), had a similar concern with start-up and its determinants, and also was important as an exercise in falsification, in that it refuted the famed Jovanovic (1982) model in its original form (namely because pre-entrepreneurial income and growth rates are found to be positively correlated, rather than uncorrelated, according to Jovanovic). Cressy sought to develop a new model that preserved the important insight of Jovanovic's model, that entrepreneurs learn as they run small firms, but added new features. These included: differential start-up sizes and outside opportunities; satisficing by the entrepreneur (in terms of seeking a 'target income'); stochastic income; and human capital (proxied by the entrepreneur's age at start-up). The model developed does not have a thorough-going temporal analysis behind it, as in Hilton *et al.* (1993), for example, but Cressy's 'no-fat' modelling allowed him to develop crisp predictive results, in the form of hypotheses that are capable of falsification by real-world data. To illustrate, growth of the small business cash flow is predicted to rise with pre-entrepreneurial income, and with entrepreneurial age. Cressy used a random sample of small firms who had opened their accounts with one of the big UK clearing banks in 1988. Nearly 80 per cent of these were new starts. Cressy used debt turnover as his cash-flow growth variable in a quadratic approximation to his non-linear growth rate equation. He found that the more viable new small firms were, the larger were the start-ups *per se*, and also the larger were start-ups which were run by more mature owner-managers. The estimation procedure was careful, and involved tests for 'sample selection bias', along lines made familiar by Heckman (1976, 1979), though Cressy found no evidence of its existence (as has typically been the case with the author of this book).

Surprisingly, in view of relevant organisational theories of the firm, Cressy found that limited companies do not grow any faster or slower than sole traders or partnerships. However, differences between this finding and that of Reid (1993) may be accounted for by the very different concept of growth used by Cressy (i.e. cash-flow growth, as distinct from employment, sales or asset growth). His satisficing model, in which the entrepreneur aims to create an income for himself ('target income') to replace that obtained in previous employment, has intuitive appeal and presents a unified, sharp hypothesis to be confronted with the evidence.

On turning to evidence, Cressy confirmed that small firms run by owner-managers who have had higher pre-entrepreneurial incomes grow faster than other start-ups. However, they have no better survival prospects. But, a paradox remains: small firms run by older owner-managers have greater longevity than those run by younger owner-managers. Whilst this, in itself, explained survival well, the addition of pre-start income did not help further to explain survival. This is surprising, as pre-start income and age of owner-manager are positively correlated, both with each other and with growth.

A final illustration to be used in this chapter is the paper of Chittenden *et al.* (1996). Its focus was on growth and finance: but no unique hypothesis, along lines adopted by Cressy (1996), for example, was adopted. Rather, a whole range of theories in the extant literature was appealed to: a common procedure with applied econometricians, but a slightly methodologically dangerous one, as it is sometimes difficult to determine which sub-hypotheses are joint and which are rivalrous, or alternative. The broad concern of Chittenden *et al.* (1996) was to examine factors which affected the financial structure of small firms using 5 years of data on about 3500 companies chosen from the 'UK Private +' database. Economic (neoclassical), pecking-order, and agency theories were the sub-hypotheses explored for the light they cast on the stage of the small firms development and its financial structure. The account given by Chittenden *et al.*, of various theories of small firm growth and finance, can be related to the more general framework of Section 6.4.

For example, in their analysis of the life-cycle approach, the small firm is described as growing rapidly at a pace determined by debt finance and volume of undistributed earnings. Particularly interesting is their reference to the 'pecking-order' theory of Myers (1984), which has been thought to be largely of relevance to large corporations, but is seen also to be of obvious applicability to small firms.

The third theoretical approach explored, agency theory, takes Chittenden *et al.* (1996) into similar territory to that explored by Binks and Ennew (1996). It may be that this theory is not independent of the pecking-order theory, and in itself it is difficult to test by econometric (as opposed to case study) methods [cf. Reid (1998) on investor–investee relations]. The authors explain components of financial structure (e.g. debt, liquidity) by variables suggested by the three theories being explored (profitability, sales growth, asset ratio, size, age, stock market access, etc.). This empirical paper concludes that the Modigliani-Miller (MM) (1958) view of financial structure is irrelevant to small firms. Access to capital markets is not frictionless and it influences capital structure. The empirics provide strong support for a pecking-order view of financial structure, explaining well the tendency of small firms to rely heavily on internal funds. Aspects of agency theory that could be tested (e.g. the use of collateral) were well supported in this work. A note of caution, inspired by the analysis of Section 6.4, would be that the authors too readily assume non-optimality, if relatively unbalanced financial structures arise. As the analysis of Section 6.4 indicates, it may be optimal to have quite different financial structures at different phases of the growth trajectory of the small business enterprise.

6.6   Conclusion

This chapter is intended to argue the case for appropriate methods of analysing small firm financing and growth. Whilst it is clear that no consensus has emerged, the chapter argues the case for the use of both rigorous theoretical and empirical methods. On an empirical level, the importance of collateral, human capital and financial structure for early growth of the small firm have been noted. But probably more important, this chapter suggests a whole range of *dynamic* theoretical perspectives which aim to provide the starting point for a new vein of research into small firm financing and growth in the chapters that follow.

Endnotes

1 The constraint in (6.4) differs from that in the previous chapter (5.1), in that in (5.1) *all* finance capital (*M*) is denoted, whereas in (6.4) only equity (*E*) finance is used (for simplicity). Another difference is that in Chapter 5 factors were specifically identified as part-time and full-time workers, whereas in Chapter 6 they are generic.

2 For example, it required that the discount rate be equal to the borrowing rate, but yet that there was a decreasing efficiency of debt compared to a constant efficiency of retained earnings.

3 Hence, also, the rate of change of capital assets equals the rate of change of equity plus the rate of change of debt.

4 Note that the restriction $\pi \geq 0$ is, as Reid (1991) points out, a survival criterion for 'staying in business'. This criterion must be met by firms which remain in the panel. Furthermore, note that only seven out of 150 firms lacked cash to put into the business at start-up, the average sum committed being £13,014. Of those who did not put in their own cash, most will have had outside financial support, possibly (though rarely) of equity form.

5 For example, if adjustment costs are present, arising from re-organisation and training as the firm grows, with its consequential strains on managerial and administrative capabilities (cf. Richardson, 1964; Slater, 1980; Reid, 1995), the above framework can be appropriately extended. In the simplest scenario, shorn of financial considerations, the investment rate is constant and there is no stationary value for capital stock. If employment is explicitly considered, basic trajectories similar to the above, for (i) cheap debt and (ii) cheap equity, occur, with: (i) growth then stationarity; and (ii) growth, consolidation, then stationarity. Employment tracks output and capital in each case. If business cycle effects are incorporated, the analysis hinges on the severity of the recession. Optimal conditions again resemble those displayed in Figures 6.1 and 6.2 of the main text. Zero investment may occur not just during, but both before and after the recession. An important new feature of this extended model is that a severe recession may induce an accounting cash-flow problem which the firm deals with by borrowing - but this may lead to bankruptcy, even after the recession has ended (Hilten *et al.*, 1993).

7 Capital structure at inception and the short-run performance of micro-firms

7.1 Introduction

This chapter focusses on financial structure and performance in the early stage of the life-cycle of the young micro-firm. For the section of the database used (see Chapter 2), the firms examined have an average time from financial inception of just one and a half years. As regards size, their average number of employees is only three full-time, and two part-time workers. They are, indeed, 'nascent' firms (Reynolds *et al.*, 2004). Short-run performance is measured quite simply over a 1-year period, in terms of ability of the micro-firm to continue trading. A more detailed consideration of performance, building on this, is undertaken in the next major section of the book, Part 4. While this chapter retains a focus on financial structure, the theme of Part 3, as a whole, also provides consideration of performance issues, preparing the ground for the discussions of Chapters 9 and 10.

The key issue explored here is the extent to which financial structure close to inception has a bearing on early performance of the micro-firm. It has been seen (Chapter 6) that, in a neoclassical theory of the small firm, generalised to incorporate money capital (cf. Vickers, 1987), the conditions for maximising profit will determine an optimal asset structure for the small firm, along with the familiar marginal conditions for production optimality. It requires that the full marginal cost of debt should equal the full marginal cost of equity, which in turn should equal the discount factor on the marginal income stream. Thus optimal amounts of debt and equity (and hence gearing) are determined, along with optimal hiring of factors of production. Previous evidence (cf. Reid, 1991) has suggested that this optimality requirement has been reflected in a strong measured association between gearing and survival of the small firm. In particular, lower gearing significantly raised survival prospects for the small firm over a 3-year time horizon. It is likely that this arises because of both the lower risk exposure and the lower debt servicing associated with lower gearing. In this chapter, a principal goal is to look at asset structures much closer to inception, and to see which forms of structure best promote survival.

An additional goal is to ask whether an unequal distribution of entrepreneurial ability has implications for even the youngest of small firms. Specifically, this research goal can be related to the small firms' model of Oi (1983), in which the size distribution of small firms is generated by entrepreneurial ability. Therein, higher ability entrepreneurs raise the marginal productivities of their workers by more successfully coordinating all factor inputs, and by more effectively monitoring labour inputs. Thus they enjoy better performance and, in doing so, create larger firms than do lower ability entrepreneurs. Furthermore, Oi (1983) shows that this implies that, if there is also a distribution of efficiency of workers, the more productive workers will be paired with the higher ability entrepreneurs. This conclusion is reinforced by other notable small firm theories, including the influential theory of Jovanovic (1982), which predicts a positive association between firm size and entrepreneurial ability.

In focussing on the small firm's early life-cycle, this chapter provides a particularly detailed picture of financial structure: an area in which (given reporting conventions) the state of current knowledge is generally poor.[1] In doing so, the key information utilised from the database (Chapter 2) relates to sales, profits, debt, equity, gearing, credit, assets and financial history (e.g. on personal financial injections, loans and grants).

The general finding of this chapter is that financial structure is not a major determinant of performance in this, the very earliest, phase of the life-cycle of the micro-firm. Whilst it is possible to identify specific financial features which may favour survival (e.g. the availability of trade credit) or may threaten survival (e.g. the use of extended purchase commitments), conventional features of financial structure (e.g. assets, gearing) do not play a significant role. However, other (non-financial) explanations of early stage survival are available, including the use of advertising and business planning, and the avoidance of precipitate product innovation. The latter effect, which takes us into real options reasoning, has been explored further by Power and Reid (2003). Elements of this approach are incorporated into the latter part of Chapter 18.

Overall, the findings of this chapter suggest that market features (cf. Brouthers and Nakos, 2005) and internal organisation (Chaston *et al.*, 1999; Chaston, 1997) of the micro-firm may dominate financial structure (cf. Michaelas *et al.*, 1999) as determinants of survival in the very earliest phase of the life-cycle. A subsidiary finding of this chapter supports the view that high ability entrepreneurs tend to form larger firms, in turn attracting higher efficiency (and higher paid) labour. This finding supports an 'efficiency wage' view of micro-firm labour hiring policy.

7.2 Continuing or ceasing to trade

This section focusses on detailing statistical differences, such as they are, between two types of micro-firms, those which went out of business within a year of the first interview, and those that remained in business. Explicit econometric analysis will not be undertaken until the next section. However, the treatment in this section is explicitly inferential, unlike in Chapter 3, where it is largely descriptive. The general finding here is that, over a surprisingly wide range of attributes, these two types of micro-firms differ very little. For that reason, when differences in attributes are observed, given the dichotomous outcome (namely continuing or ceasing to trade) such attributes are especially worthy of further attention.

One such set of differences relates to size and the wage rate. Again, relevant to these differences is the small firm model of Oi (1983). According to this theory, entrepreneurs allocate efforts optimally over coordinating and monitoring activities. A small firm will be larger, the greater is the ability of the entrepreneur to use time efficiently to coordinate production, and hence to increase the size of the business. The better the deployment of entrepreneurial skill, the higher the marginal productivities of factors used in the more efficient small firms. Thus it is the distribution of entrepreneurial ability which generates the size distribution of small firms, with the larger ones being associated with higher ability. Furthermore, the larger, more efficient small firms reward factors of production, including labour, relatively highly, because their superior efficiency at coordination shifts marginal productivity schedules upwards.[2]

Consider, first, Table 7.1, which deals with the general characteristics of these young micro-firms. It is apparent that firms that continue to trade are larger than those which do not. This is especially true of size, measured by gross profits (*Grprof*) and sales (*Grsales*), but also true, in some measure, of size measured by employment (*Ftime, Ptime*). Furthermore, micro-firms which continue to trade tend to pay premium wages (*Wagerate*). That is, their wages are generally higher (indeed 16 per cent higher, on average) than in firms that ceased to trade. A 95 per cent confidence interval for the difference between these mean (μ)

Table 7.1 General characteristics

Variable	Continued trading $N_1 = 122$			Ceased trading $N_2 = 28$		
	n_1	Mean	SD	n_2	Mean	SD
Grprof	100	56,442	88,044	24	31,082	53,242
Netprof	106	13,329	29,890	25	14,514	24,651
Grsales	119	0.26047×10^6	0.9351×10^6	27	0.11468×10^6	(0.2418×10^6)
Ftime	122	2.9754	6.8544	28	2.0357	4.1498
Ptime	122	2.0082	12.781	28	0.71429	1.3569
Wagerate	61	919.16	462.01	12	790.00	312.24
Hrswk	122	58.123	19.332	28	56.679	13.676
Secschl	122	4.7623	1.1787	28	4.6786	0.9833
Impact	121	16.442	20.427	27	11.093	9.1673

Notes:
a For the convenience of the reader, definitions of variables are given in the appendix to this chapter. A fuller account of these data is given in Part 1 of this book.
b There were 122 (N_1) firms which continued trading, and 28 (N_2) firms which ceased trading, in the sample as a whole. However, data are incomplete for some variables, for some firms. Hence n_1 and n_2 indicate the relevant sample sizes for each category of firm, for which means and standard deviations (SDs) were computed.

wage rates is given by $Pr(15.688 < \mu_1 - \mu_2 < 242.632) = 0.95$ which does not contain the origin, rejecting the hypothesis of equal mean wage rates. This finding is consistent with the small firms model of Oi (1983) which suggests that more productive workers (with higher efficiency and hence higher wages) will tend to be matched to more able entrepreneurs (with better performance).[3] It is also consistent with an 'efficiency wage' view of employment, of the sort discussed by Yellen (1984). According to this view, firms which operate in the non-unionised sector, which is typical of micro-firms, have a tendency to pay an 'efficiency wage' which is at a slight premium on the going wage rate for similar work. This may increase efficiency by reducing labour turnover, making workers feel more committed, etc. Surprisingly, given its emphasis in the informal literature,[4] there is very little difference in terms of hours worked between firms which cease and firms which continue to trade. Furthermore, years of secondary schooling (*Secschl*) differ little between the two groups though, as human capital arguments suggest, schooling may be important for some aspects of performance.[5]

The last variable listed in Table 7.1 measures how many months the entrepreneur looks ahead in decision-making within the firm (*Impact*). It suggests that, on an average, entrepreneurs who continue trading have a 48 per cent longer time horizon than those who do not. A 95 per cent confidence interval for the difference between mean time horizons is provided by $Pr(0.3320 < \mu_1 - \mu_2 < 7.3659) = 0.95$ which does not contain the origin, so we reject the hypothesis that the means are the same. This is an interesting result, and certainly works against a widespread myth of extreme short-termism in micro-business decision-making. The exact question asked was: 'How far ahead do you look when evaluating the impact that planned decisions may have?' (See AQ1, Q.4.2 in Section 4 on Business Strategy, appendix to this book). The mean response was 15.466 months; and this response was itself set in the context of other questions on business strategy. Despite contrary evidence by the likes of Storey (1994), the evidence reported here makes sense in a business strategy context.[6] For example, 89 per cent of respondents had a business plan, and it was a formal, written plan for the great majority (79 per cent).[7] This plan was reviewed on average every 5 months. Thus, the average impact planning time horizon would involve about three business plan revisions, which is a convincingly coherent picture, and one which accords well with fieldwork perception of small business planning.

The next body of evidence to be considered is presented in Table 7.2, and concerns key financial variables, like net profit (*Netprof*) and net assets (*Netfixas*) as well as various financial ratios, like the gearing (debt/equity) ratio at start-up or financial inception (*Gearst*), and the ratio of stocks to net assets (*Stkass*). The evidence on size, as measured by the net and gross fixed assets variables, and the amount of cash (*Owncash*) entrepreneurs put into their businesses at launch, is that firms which continued trading were, on an average, much larger (about twice the size) of those that did not. This is consistent with the evidence on gross profits and sales in Table 7.1. Again, of note, is the lower net profit of those continuing to trade. This was explained earlier by the higher wage bills of such firms. This observation is now reinforced by evidence of their lower net profitability (measured by *Nprass* = *Netprof* ÷ *Netfixas*). Indeed, for the firms which continued to trade, average net profitability was negative (−4.0 per cent), compared to the positive net profitability of those which ceased to trade (+3.5 per cent). It must be borne in mind that many well-specified business plans do operate on the assumption of unprofitable trading for a considerable part of the early life-cycle of the small firm, so these results should not be interpreted as being surprising, but rather as being in accordance with entrepreneurs' plans. It may be that the types of markets in which these firms which have ceased to trade do have rather different features from those of firms which continued to trade, like a shorter product life-cycle, and a shorter time to harvest. Indeed, this is suggested by the significantly shorter impact planning horizon of those firms which ceased trading, noted in Table 7.1.

The gearing (i.e. debt/equity) ratios at financial inception (*Gearst*) and at the time of interview (*Gearnow*), typically measured by the ratio of bank indebtedness to owner-manager's personal financial injections, appear to be unrevealing. There is a slight tendency for gearing to rise after inception, and a slight indication that firms which continued trading redeemed debt more quickly (starting higher geared, and ending lower geared), but this difference is not statistically significant. Whilst apparently unremarkable, this bland feature of the gearing evidence contravenes earlier evidence (e.g. Reid, 1993, Ch. 9) that gearing is a major predictor of staying in business, and that highly geared small firms, being both relatively risk-exposed and prone to debt servicing crises, have significantly inferior survival prospects than lower geared firms.

However, the earlier evidence related to firms which were on average 3 years old at the time of initial interview, and were investigated 3 years later to see whether

Table 7.2 Financial variables and ratios

Variable	n_1	Continued trading $N_1 = 122$ Mean	SD	n_2	Ceased trading $N_2 = 28$ Mean	SD
Netprof	106	13,329	29,890	25	14,514	24,651
Netfixas	120	20,957	45,957	27	9,072	23,467
Grfixass	120	27,227	47,915	27	12,264	31,185
Nprass	122	−3.984	27.718	25	3.4628	71.246
Gearst	119	158.69	341.46	24	136.88	294.99
Gearnow	118	165.68	377.96	24	172.38	444.33
Stkass	120	97.963	278.82	25	421.88	1486.0
Owncash	117	14,331	32,768	24	7008	6,187

Notes:
a Definitions of variables are given in the appendix to this chapter.
b There were 122 (N_1) firms which continued trading, and 28 (N_2) firms which ceased trading, in the sample as a whole. However, data are incomplete for some variables, for some firms. Hence n_1 and n_2 indicate the relevant sample sizes for each category of firm, for which means and standard deviations (SDs) were computed.

they were still in business (cf. Reid, 1991). In contrast, the micro-firms in the present sample were never more than 3 years old at the time of the first interview (and indeed had an average age of just 1.5 years) and the time frame for examining whether they were still in business was just one further year. Thus the evidence appears to indicate that gearing, as a crucial feature of financial structure, has an effect on survival which is highly sensitive to the stage of the life-cycle of the micro-firm. This observation is the key to the development of a full analysis of the trajectories of financial structures in Chapter 8, that follows the current chapter. In the analysis of this chapter, where all firms are close to inception, financial structure appears to be unimportant to performance. In contrast, for the small firms in the study of Reid (1991), which were 6 or more years from inception, financial structure is crucial. The dynamics of such effects are explored in detail in Chapter 8, and indeed the writing of Chapter 8 was inspired by the observed discrepancy between capital structure at inception and a few years further along in the life-cycle of the small firm.

The final feature to be remarked upon in Table 7.2 is the financial ratio *Stkass*, which measures the ratio of the value of stocks to the net value of fixed assets (n.b. after depreciation, which was typically set at something like 25 per cent $-33\frac{1}{3}$ per cent p.a.). For the sample as a whole, this ratio was 160 per cent, but as Table 7.2 indicates the micro-firms which continued to trade had a much lower ratio (98 per cent) of stocks to net assets than did those which ceased to trade (422 per cent). This might be caused by a difference in sectoral composition of the micro-firms. This may perhaps be the case, as the following evidence suggests. If the samples are dichotomised by SIC code, according to whether the micro-firm is, broadly speaking, in manufacturing ($01 \leq SIC \leq 59$) or in services ($60 \leq SIC \leq 99$), the results are as follows: the minority of firms (44 per cent) which continued trading were in services; whilst the majority (56 per cent) of firms which ceased to trade were in manufactures. Thus micro-firms which ceased to trade were more predominantly in manufactures, where circulating capital requirements are typically much higher than in services. Arguably, micro-firms which have to tie up far greater capital in circulating form are at a survival disadvantage compared to firms which can more immediately put their capital to work.

To conclude this section, Table 7.3 reports on further variables which may impinge on whether a micro-firm continues, or ceases, to trade. They are all qualitative variables, being based on binary responses (Yes/No) to questions. From a macroeconomic perspective, grants and terms of credit may be directly influenced by policy makers, and it is of interest to observe whether variables which capture such influence had a different effect on micro-firms which continued to trade, as opposed to those which ceased trading. The *Grant* dummy variable measures whether a firm had received a grant or subsidy when it was launched. This was evidently very common, with firms that stayed in business being less likely (78 per cent) to have received much support than those that did not (84 per cent). There is evidence that micro-firms can be heavily driven by grant/subsidy regimes and tax breaks, to the extent that a variety of so-called

Table 7.3 Qualitative financial variables

Variable	Continued trading $N_1 = 122$			Ceased trading $N_2 = 28$		
	n_1	Mean	SD	n_2	Mean	SD
Trcredit	122	0.8032	0.3991	25	0.6000	0.5000
Debt	122	0.5082	0.3992	25	0.4400	0.5066
Outeq	121	0.0578	0.2344	25	0.0400	0.2000
Bankloan	121	0.3141	0.4661	25	0.3200	0.4761
Grant	121	0.7769	0.4181	25	0.8400	0.3742
Extpur	122	0.0410	0.1991	25	0.1200	0.3317
Hirpur	122	0.2869	0.4542	25	0.1600	0.3742
Leaspur	122	0.0492	0.2171	25	0.0000	0.0000
Finown	122	0.9098	0.2876	25	0.9200	0.2769
Finbank	122	0.5082	0.5020	25	0.3200	0.4761

Notes:

a Definitions of variables are given in the appendix to this chapter.

b There were 122 (N_1) firms which continued trading, and 28 (N_2) firms which ceased trading, in the sample as a whole. However, data are incomplete for some variables, for some firms. Hence n_1 and n_2 indicate the relevant sample sizes for each category of firm, for which means and standard deviations (SDs) were computed.

'paper entrepreneurship' has been identified, which depends more on bureaucratic than market opportunity.[8] This view is consistent with these figures, though they do not provide incontrovertible supporting evidence.

Table 7.3 indicates that the use of outside equity (*Outeq*), extended purchase (*Extpur*) and lease purchase (*Leasepur*) was slight for both classes of firm. According to the pecking-order theory of finance (cf. Chapter 6), of Donaldson (1961) and Myers (1984), these – being amongst the most expensive – are amongst the least desired forms of finance. Hire purchase (*Hirpur*) was more common, especially amongst the firms that remained trading (29 per cent compared to 16 per cent). Both types of firm had been equally likely to use a bank loan to launch the business (just under 50 per cent in each case), and both had been equally likely to have been financed by the owner-manager (about 90 per cent in each case). The proportions in which these forms of finance were used are consistent with a pecking order of finance,[9] which would put inside equity first (e.g. *Finown*), debt finance next (e.g. *Debt*), and outside equity last (e.g. *Outeq*). Whether micro-firms continue or cease to trade, they appear, on average, to conform to the predictions of this theory.

These observations having been made, emphasising the neutrality of financial structure across the continued/ceased trading divide, two salient features which differ are worthy of further examination. First, whilst 80 per cent of firms which continued trading had trade credit arrangements, just 60 per cent of the firms which ceased trading had such facilities. A 95 per cent confidence interval for the difference between these proportions is given by 0.2 ± 0.02 which does not contain the origin, so the difference between these proportions is statistically significant.

Thus it seems that at, and close to, inception, the use of trade credit arrangements is of great importance to the relatively fragile, nascent micro-firm. It often cannot implement more formal devices for cash-flow management so 'time to pay' (usually 30 days, but occasionally up to 90) can be important for survival. Second, whilst just over one-half (51 per cent) of the micro-firms which had continued to trade had previously been financed by bank loans (*Finbank*), just less that one-third (32 per cent) of those who had ceased to trade had enjoyed this form of outside finance. A 90 per cent confidence interval for the difference between these proportions is 0.19 ± 0.17 suggesting a statistically significant difference between them.

In financial markets where information asymmetries arise (e.g. between lender and borrower), an inability to raise loan finance may be signalling a business which is perceived to be unworthy of support (e.g. because of inadequate collateral or excessive risk) (cf. Lund and Wright, 1999). The pattern of bank loan support suggested by the variable *Finbank* is consistent with the evidence of Table 7.2, which indicated that firms which continued trading had on an average over twice the assets of firms which ceased trading, and their owner-managers had put in over twice the equity at launch.[10]

Before proceeding to the formal inferential methods of Section 7.3, it is useful to summarise what the evidence has indicated so far.

(a) The firms which continued trading were on an average about twice the size of those which ceased trading, as measured by sales, cash invested in the business and assets.

(b) By many other attributes, these firms looked similar: employment, hours worked, years of high school education of owner-manager, gearing (past and present), use of financial instruments (e.g. bank loans, debt, hire purchase, lease purchase, outside equity) and access to grants or subsidies.

(c) Financial structures were similar whether firms continued trading or not, and indicated a preference for finance-capital which conformed with that predicted by the pecking-order theory of finance (cf. Chittenden *et al.*, 1996), namely: inside equity, debt, outside equity, in decreasing order of importance.

(d) There is little difference in net profit between the firms which continued trading and those that did not, but net profitability was negative, on an average, for the former, and positive, on average, for the latter, possibly due to the significantly higher (by 16 per cent) wages paid in the former firms.

(e) The finding of greater size and greater wages within surviving, compared to non-surviving, firms supports theories of entrepreneurship which suggest abilities of economic agents are unequally distributed (e.g. Lucas, 1978; Oi, 1983), and that the better ability agents receive greater rewards and seek employment with larger firms.[11]

(f) Important distinct features of micro-firms which continued trading, compared to those which did not, were: significantly longer (by 48 per cent) impact planning time horizons; and significantly greater (by 33 per cent) access to trade credit arrangements.

7.3   Econometric estimates

In earlier work, as in Reid (1991), it was possible to think of the decision to stay in business as being based on a rational calculation which hinged on positive net economic profitability. In the current context, where, as we have seen in the previous section, the average net profitability of micro-firms which remained trading was negative, this line of reasoning is probably inappropriate, even if one would want to put aside the possibility that accounting and economic profitability may differ. With these micro-firms being so close to financial inception, the use of what is in reality a *long-run* net profitability criterion is not relevant. Indeed, given start-up costs, the need to build up a customer base, and the progression up learning curves by both entrepreneur and workers alike, one would naturally expect an early phase of negative profitability. However, it is still of great interest to know how micro-firms survive this early stage of the life-cycle. The purpose of this section is to provide an econometric model of survival over a 1-year period (cf. Keasey and Watson, 1991; Mata and Portugal, 2004).

If the micro-firm were still trading 1-year after the entrepreneur was interviewed, then a dependent variable y (which was called *Inbusin*) was coded as unity. If the micro-firm had ceased trading, y was coded as zero. Then the econometric model adopted was that of binary probit analysis, with $y = x'\beta$ where x is a vector of independent control variables (like current gearing, *Gearnow*; and net fixed assets, *Netfixas*) and β is a corresponding vector of coefficients. Assuming that an error term can be added to this model, which is independent normal, the value of β may be estimated by the method of maximum likelihood (cf. Manly, 1986). Furthermore, a variety of statistical tests may be applied to the estimated model and its coefficients.[12]

Table 7.4 reports on a large set of control variables which may provide a statistical explanation of the probability that a young micro-firm will continue trading a further year. As well as using all the financial variables already discussed in Section 7.2, it introduces some more variables (like whether the firm advertises, *Advert*; how important is rapid occupation of a market niche, *Rapidocc*; and the extent of product innovation, *Prodinn*). Variables, estimated coefficients, asymptotic t-ratios, and Hencher–Johnson weighted elasticities are given in the four columns of this, and the following table. On a likelihood ratio test the model has a 1 per cent probability level, and the Cragg–Uhler R^2 of 0.516 is very high for this sort of cross-sectional model. There is also a high percentage (86 per cent) of correct predictions. But reference, specifically, to the statistical significance of the coefficients of over twenty financial structure variables, of the sort discussed above in Section 7.2, does not present a strong picture of their predictive importance.

For example, outside equity (*Outeq*), and gearing at inception (*Gearst*) have coefficients which are not significant. However, the coefficient on *Trcredit* is statistically significant ($\alpha = 0.025$). Access to trade credit (*Trcredit*) is obviously important to continued trading as it keeps cash-flow healthy – probably a more important consideration, shortly after launch, than is profitability. The holding

Table 7.4 Binary probit with large set of control variables

Variable	Coefficient	t-ratio	Weighted elasticity
Advert	1.311	3.120***	0.125
Trcredit	0.902	2.070**	0.089
Debt	−1.365	−2.065**	−0.103
Outeq	3.974	0.063	0.185×10^{-5}
Bankloan	−0.467	−0.500	−0.028
Grant	0.489	0.461	0.073
Gearst	-0.458×10^{-4}	−0.059	−0.001
Gearnow	-0.855×10^{-4}	−0.142	−0.003
Extpur	−1.826	−2.493***	−0.023
Hirpur	0.757	1.352+	−0.025
Leasepur	5.304	0.089	0.104×10^{-5}
Grfixass	-0.17×10^{-4}	−0.851	−0.031
Netfixas	0.707×10^{-5}	0.526	−0.015
Impact	0.787×10^{-4}	0.518	0.002
Sicdum	−0.184	−0.439	−0.017
Owncash	0.248×10^{-4}	0.943	0.030
Rapidocc	0.291	−1.037	−0.077
Stkass	−0.017	−1.831*	−0.027
Othbus	1.517	1.754*	0.016
Procinn	−0.249	−1.348+	−0.062
Prodinn	−0.456	−2.332**	−0.095
Prodgrp	0.023	0.361	0.015
Timplan	0.076	1.850*	0.088
Timdeal	−0.023	−0.710	−0.021
Hrswk	0.748×10^{-3}	0.066	0.007
Secschl	−0.026	−0.131	−0.021
Runbef	0.148	0.373	0.014
Finown	−0.610	−0.721	−0.101
Finbank	2.009	1.959*	0.142
Fingrnt	−0.169	−0.181	−0.023
Nprass	0.006	1.210	−0.008
Constant	0.491	0.323	0.087

Note:
Likelihood ratio test:

$$\chi^2 = 51.7 > \chi^2_{0.01}(31) = 50.9$$

Cragg–Uhler $R^2 = 0.516$; Binomial estimate $= 0.815$.
Sample size $(n) = 135$; Percent correct predictions $= 86\%$.
Critical t-values: $^{+}t_{0.10} = 1.289$, $^{*}t_{0.05} = 1.658$, $^{**}t_{0.025} = 1.980$, $^{***}t_{0.010} = 2.358$.

of business debt (*Debt*) is also significant ($\alpha = 0.025$) and affects adversely the
probability of the micro-firm continuing to trade. The weighted elasticity for this
variable is also relatively high. Although debt is shown to be important, this is not
true of the two ratios of debt to equity (i.e. gearing ratios), *Gearst* and *Gearnow*,
gearing at inception and gearing at the time of the interview. This finding is an

important qualification to earlier evidence (Reid, 1991) based on considerably older small firms, suggesting gearing was a significant determinant of performance. The use of an extended purchase facility (*Extpur*) to buy plant and equipment has a highly statistically significant ($\alpha = 0.010$) negative coefficient, although the elasticity is not high (-0.023). The use of hire purchase (*Hirpur*) has a marginally significant positive coefficient ($\alpha = 0.10$), but again a low elasticity (-0.025).

The *Stkass* variable which measures the ratio of stocks to net assets, and which has been analysed in detail earlier, has the expected negative effect. A higher value of *Stkass* lowers the probability of continuing to trade. Its coefficient is statistically significant at the usual level ($\alpha = 0.05$), but again the elasticity is low (-0.027). The *Finbank* variable, which measures whether a firm has been financed by a bank loan, has also received earlier discussion, and appears here with a significant coefficient ($\alpha = 0.05$) and, most importantly, a relatively high elasticity (0.142). Indeed this is the highest estimated elasticity for this probit, suggesting that being in receipt of a bank loan is a major determinant of whether a micro-firm will continue to trade. This in turn suggests that banks were rather effective monitors of small firm performance and potential. All other financial variables perform badly in this probit equation, including net profitability (*Nprass*), assets (*Grfixass*, *Netfixas*), gearing (*Gearst*, *Gearnow*), use of a bank loan at launch (*Bankloan*), outside equity (*Outeq*) and raising finance from personal financial injections (*Finown*).

Thus it is clear from this probit that non-financial, rather than financial factors appear to play a large part in determining whether a micro-firm will continue to trade 1 year down the line. The shape and form of these variables are too diverse to explore fully here, so what has been attempted is to indicate what non-financial factors may be important. Heading the list is whether or not the micro-firm advertises (*Advert*). The coefficient of this variable is highly statistically significant ($\alpha = 0.010$) and the elasticity is the second largest (0.125), next to that of *Finbank* (0.142). This evidence is contrary to earlier evidence (cf. Reid, 1993) suggesting the relative unimportance of advertising for older micro-firms. For the younger firms being examined here, clearly advertising is more important, as it is effective in establishing the initial market, after which it may become less important as firms depend more on repeat purchases, and the spreading of information by 'word of mouth'. Running another business, *Othbus*, arguably a sign of superior business acumen, and certainly a way of diversifying away risk, has a significant positive coefficient ($\alpha = 0.05$), but a small elasticity. It is that firms can attempt to innovate too early: process and product innovation (*Procinn*, *Prodinn*) are both negatively associated with continuing to trade. It seems likely that early innovation imposes too high resource and adjustment costs, and may be indicative of an ill-judged initial target market niche.[13] Chapter 18 explores such ill-judged steps, in a flexibility framework that points towards the use of real options reasoning. In view of what was said earlier about time horizons for judging the impact of plans, it is of note that the proportion of time in a week spent planning (*Timplan*) has a significant ($\alpha = 0.05$) positive coefficient. To summarise the picture of the significant coefficients in Table 7.4, it is notable that just five are for financial variables.

However, it is also clear that some non-financial variables do not have the expected effect in the very early stages of the life-cycle of micro-firms. For example, Ungern-Sternberg (1990) has argued that diversification into several products is a tactic used by small firms in an attempt to cope with fluctuations in the demand for individual products. This implies that the number of product groups (*Prodgrp*) should be positively associated with continued trading. However, here this variable's coefficient is statistically insignificant. This does not rule out the validity of this argument at a later stage in the life-cycle, but it does not seem to apply at this earlier stage. Given the many insignificant coefficients in the probit of Table 7.4, it is of importance to seek a more parsimonious model in a statistical sense. This is presented in Table 7.5.

In going to the parsimonious model of Table 7.5, the process innovation variable (*Procinn*) has been dropped. The sample size has increased for this estimated probit, because fewer missing observations have to be dealt with, when fewer variables are present. All the variables in this probit have coefficients which are statistically significant, and as a matter of robustness it is reassuring to note that the signs of coefficients are stable (i.e. unchanged) across estimates. Naturally, the Cragg–Uhler R^2 has fallen, but still remains relatively high. Using a likelihood ratio test, the model has a very small probability level of 0.1 per cent. The percentage of correct predictions is high at 83 per cent. Comparing the models of Table 7.4 and Table 7.5 using a likelihood ratio test, one gets a χ^2 value of 26.16 which is less than the $\chi^2_{0.05}(21)$ critical value of 32.7. Thus the data do not accept the extra restrictions of the probit in Table 7.4, compared to the probit in Table 7.5.

Table 7.5 Parsimonious binary probit

Variable	Coefficient	t-ratio	Weighted elasticity
Advert	0.853	2.774***	0.111
Trcredit	0.848	2.609***	0.118
Debt	−0.580	−1.483+	−0.060
Extpur	−1.238	−2.165**	−0.024
Hirpur	0.492	1.302+	0.019
Stkass	$−0.805 \times 10^{-3}$	−1.719*	−0.023
Othbus	0.983	1.520+	0.012
Prodinn	−0.254	−2.039**	−0.069
Timplan	−0.048	2.033**	0.080
Finbank	0.845	2.051**	0.073
Constant	−0.347	−0.920	−0.080

Note:
Likelihood ratio test:

$$\chi^2 = 36.4 > \chi^2_{.001}(10) = 29.6$$

Cragg–Uhler R^2 = 0.357; Binomial estimate = 0.816.
Sample size (n) = 147; Percent correct predictions = 83%.
Critical t-values: $^+t_{0.10} = 1.289$, $^*t_{0.05} = 1.658$, $^{**}t_{0.025} = 1.980$, $^{***}t_{0.010} = 2.358$.

The parsimonious model of Table 7.5 is therefore the preferred one, at least on statistical grounds.

7.4   Conclusion

This chapter has examined empirically the potential financial determinants of the nascent micro-firm's decision to continue trading one further year. It is found that many financial features do not change across firms which continue to trade, compared to firms which cease to trade. For example, both classes of firms follow a pecking-order financial format (Donaldson, 1961; Myers, 1984). Traditionally important financial features, like gearing and assets, appear to be unimportant in the early life-cycle. At this stage, other financial features appear to be more important to continued trading, notably the existence of trade credit arrangements, and the avoidance of extended purchase commitments.

To obtain a satisfactorily parsimonious probit model, which also predicts well whether young micro-firms will continue to trade, non-financial variables need to be introduced. It is found that the use of advertising and business planning is important to a micro-firm's continued market activity in the early stage of its life-cycle, and that the more able entrepreneurs tend to run larger firms and to hire more able employees. The overall lesson suggested from this chapter's empirical work is that purely microeconomic factors may not provide a complete account of the propensity of micro-firms to continue trading. In some measure, one may also need to look at macroeconomic effects for further illumination, such as the impact of the phase of the business cycle on pricing, production, employment and innovation. Such macroeconomic effects, specifically the variations in the bank lending rate, are given explicit consideration in Chapter 8.

APPENDIX

Definitions of Variables used in Text and Tables

Advert	=1 if firm advertised, otherwise 0
Bankloan	=1 if a bank loan was used to launch the business, otherwise 0
Debt	=1 if business had debt, otherwise 0
Extpur	=1 if firm had extended purchase commitment, otherwise 0
Finbank	=1 if firm had previously been financed by a bank loan, otherwise 0
Fingrnt	=1 if firm had previously been financed by grant/subsidy, otherwise 0
Finown	=1 if firm had previously been financed by the owner-manager, otherwise 0
Ftime	= number of full-time employees
Gearnow	= gearing (i.e. debt/equity) ratio at the time of interview
Gearst	= gearing ratio at the launch of business
Grant	=1 if grant or subsidy was received at launch, otherwise 0

Continued

Definitions of Variables used in Text and Tables—cont'd

Grfixass	= gross value (£) of fixed assets
Grprof	= gross profits (£) for last financial year
Grsales	= gross sales (£) for last financial year
Hirpur	=1 if firm had hire purchase commitments, otherwise 0
Hrswk	= number of hours per week devoted to the business
Impact	= number of months entrepreneur looked ahead in evaluating impact of decisions
Inbus	= number of months firm had been in business
Leasepur	=1 if business had any lease purchase commitments, otherwise 0
Loan	= size of bank loan (£) at launch of business
Netfixas	= net value (£) (after depreciation) of fixed assets
Netprof	= net profits (£) for last financial year
Nprass	= *Netprof* ÷ *Netfixas*
Othbus	=1 if respondent runs any other business, otherwise 0
Outeq	=1 if business had any outside equity, otherwise 0
Owncash	= cash (£) put in by inside equity holder(s) at launch
Procinn	=0 (no change), =1 (slight change), =2 (significant change), =3 (important change) in process innovation since starting business
Prodgrp	= number of product groups produced
Prodinn	=0 (none), =1 (1–5), =2 (6–10), =3 (11–20), =4 (>20) new products since starting business
Ptime	= number of part-time employees
Rapidocc	=0 (not at all), =1 (moderately), =2 (very) important to rapidly occupy a market niche
Runbef	=1 if entrepreneur had run a business before, otherwise 0
Secschl	= number of years spent at high school
Sicdum	=1 if firm was in manufacturing ($01 \leq SIC \leq 59$) and 0 if it was in services
Stkass	= ratio of value of stocks to net fixed assets
Timdeal	= proportion of time spent doing deals in a week
Timplan	= proportion of time spent planning in a week
Trcredit	=1 if business has trade credit arrangements, otherwise 0
Wagerate	= wage-rate (£) for best skilled full-time workers per month

Endnotes

1 See the comments made by van der Wijst and Thurik (1993, pp. 55–56) in introducing their study of small firm debt ratios.
2 Though this is partially offset by monitoring costs.
3 Empirically, it is also consistent with a widely confirmed size–wage effect, which is more generally associated with wider size dispersion than is present in this study. See Brown and Medoff (1989) for six alternative explanations.
4 See Barrow's (1986, p. 16) analysis of 'total commitment' in his *Routes to Success*, where he writes 'You will need single-mindedness, energy and a lot of hard work ...

working 18-hour days is not uncommon'. In contrast, Dunkelberg and Cooper (1990), see following note, find that the more able the entrepreneur, the fewer the hours worked.

5 See Dunkelberg and Cooper (1990) who argue, using US National Federation of Independent Business data, that human capital (more widely measured than here) is of greater significance than finance-capital early in the life-cycle of the small firm.

6 Compare presentation by Smith (1997a), University of Abertay Dundee, 'Small Business Strategy in New Scottish Firms'.

7 However, firms that plan do not necessarily perform better. For a Ghanaian example, (Yusuf and Saffu, 2005).

8 'Paper entrepreneurship' has been defined by Kent (1984, p. 117) as 'meeting standards of political conduct associated with taxation and regulation that may be of dubious value. Such activities may neither increase national income, produce any new products, nor generate additional jobs'.

9 See Chittenden *et al.* (1996) for support of this theory in a small firms' context.

10 Compare the evidence presented by Storey (1994), using his Cleveland (England) data, which suggests that bank lending is unrelated to those characteristics of founders which are thought to be conducive to small firm performance, but is clearly positively related to the use of personal savings in financing the firm at start-up.

11 For another (but related) approach, see the work of Sadler-Smith *et al.* (2003) on the links between managerial and entrepreneurial ability and performance (in terms of sales growth).

12 See Reid (1993, Appendix to Chapter 9) for a detailed mathematical treatment of the applications of this methods to models of small firm survival. The technique has already been used in this book in the preliminary analysis of Chapter 5 above (especially Section 5.4). Here, treatment is slightly more thorough, as the model now bears a greater weight of interpretation as a technique for survivor analysis.

13 Again, this is suggestive of the recent findings of Power and Reid (2003), which emphasise the merit of waiting, and being able to step back relatively costlessly from a within-firm investment.

8 Trajectories of financial structure

8.1 Introduction

This chapter expounds and tests a theory of the financial structure of the new SBE. Its approach is evolutionary in that it focusses on how, in theory and practice, the key variables which characterise the small firm's financial structure evolve over several time periods after inception. The variables emphasised are sales, profits, debt, equity, interest rates and gearing (i.e. debt ÷ equity). Each of these variables is considered to be functionally dependent on time, and therefore is discussed in terms of a time path or *trajectory*.

The characteristic of the theory expounded here (which builds on the development in Chapter 6 above, Section 6.3), is that it is dynamic, and conceives of small firms as lying in risk classes. It considers a small firm which is run by an owner-manager or entrepreneur who aims to maximise the firm's value over a finite time horizon. Value is expressed as the present value of the dividend stream plus the present value of the terminal equity. The body of evidence to which this theory (cf. Chapter 6) is applied is as described in Chapter 2: an unbalanced panel of observations on 150 entrepreneurial firms. These were tracked over a 4-year period (1993–97), gathering data by intensive face-to-face interviews (using an administered questionnaire of the form AQ1 in the appendix to this book). In this sense, these firms are several stages beyond the nascent firms which were examined in Chapter 7.

The starting point of all discussion of capital structure must be Modigliani and Miller (1958, 1963) who initially favoured the view that capital structure was irrelevant, subsequently modifying this to the view that financing by debt alone was optimal. Whilst suggestive, and indeed correct, within the strict theoretical framework adopted, their predictions are considerably at variance with the evidence. Certainly in a small firms context, these views are an unreliable guide to reality. Developments of the literature, since then, have revolved around the issue of the consequences for financial structure of constraints on external finance. The key elements of this literature are the agency, pecking order and signalling views. The agency approach is exemplified by the work of Jensen and Meckling (1976); the pecking-order approach by the work of Donaldson (1961) and Myers (1984); and the signalling approach by the work of Myers and Majluf (1984).

According to the agency approach, information asymmetry can lead to inefficient contracting. If this is extended to the principal-agent approach, differing attitudes to risk [e.g. between entrepreneur and venture capitalist (Reid, 1998)] also frustrate optimal contracting. The empirical implications of this have been explored in a small firms context by the likes of Binks *et al.* (1988). According to the pecking-order approach of Donaldson (1961) and Myers (1984), firms self finance first, access borrowing next and last of all seek (outside) equity. At root the motivation for this is cost, but this goes beyond the direct cost of finance to considerations of autonomy and control (Coase, 1937). An example of this approach applied to the small firm is the work of Chittenden *et al.* (1996), and Hamilton and Fox (1998). Some evidence for this theory has also been detected in the empirical analysis of Chapter 7. Finally, there is the signalling approach of Ross (1977) and Myers and Majluf (1984). According to this approach, which leads to similar conclusions to the pecking-order approach, inside equity signals most value, as its extent measures the confidence the entrepreneur has in the firm's prospects.

There follows debt, which signals the desire of the entrepreneur to appropriate the anticipated extra value, rather than to share it with other investors, and finally there follows outside equity, which signals that the inside equity holders are willing to dilute their interest. Evidence of this sort of conduct in a small firms context is contained in the work of Lopez-Gracia and Aybar-Arias (2000) and Guidici and Paleari (2000).

This chapter proceeds by reviewing briefly the theoretical background, then summarises the evidence, expounds the results (including the graphing of trajectories – the empirical equivalents of Figures 6.1 and 6.2 in Chapter 6), and then moves to conclusions.

8.2   The dynamic approach

The theoretical analysis of this chapter differs from that widely adopted in the small firms literature, in that it is explicitly dynamic.[1] Another novelty, in terms of standard small business analysis, is that it looks at small firms as being in risk classes, which set a limit on the gearing ratio. The treatment given later suggests that two broad scenarios are important, the one relating to cheap equity and the other to cheap debt [see Hamilton and Fox (1998) for an empirical setting]. If debt is cheap, then the predicted trajectories for output, capital and debt are always rising until they reach a stationary level (see Figure 6.1 of Chapter 6). If equity is cheap, then the predicted trajectories for output and capital are initially rising, becoming constant during a period of consolidation, but then start rising again until a final and higher stationary level is reached (see Figure 6.2 of Chapter 6). During this process, debt *is* initially acquired, even though equity is cheap, but it is phased out in the consolidation stage before final growth and then stationarity is achieved.

The empirical analysis of this chapter constructs and examines the trajectories suggested by this theory. This test methodology provides an alternative to procedures that emphasise testing the optimality conditions. Here, optimality is assumed, and it is the implications of optimality which are examined.

It is shown that the theoretical model of Chapter 6 (Section 6.4) casts considerable light on small firm financial practice. Debt and equity (and as a corollary, gearing or leverage) are highly time-dependent. The fact that debt, in practice, even if it is initially readily acquired, is then rapidly retired, suggests a cheap equity regime. However, as the interest rate on long-term debt falls over the sample period, reflecting general macro-economic conditions, a greater willingness to hold debt again is observed. One obvious interpretation is that some small firms are switching from a cheap equity to a cheap debt regime. Another is that a later cohort of small firms is experiencing the same effect, but at a later point in time. This is less plausible as the 'birth dates' of the small firms in the sample are close together, so the cohort effect should be slight.

Without explicit reference to the mathematics of Chapter 6, the nature of the time dependence of key financial variables is readily sketched. A number of master trajectories can be identified. Here, the reader may find it helpful to refer back to Figures 6.1 and 6.2 of Section 6.4 (*The Dynamic Model*) of Chapter 6. In the most obvious case, illustrated by Figure 6.1, debt finance is relatively cheap.[2] The firm will expand output provided marginal revenue exceeds marginal cost, and will eventually cease to grow (beyond time t_1), that is, will achieve stationarity, once diminishing returns eliminate this inequality (at t_1). Until time t_1, growth proceeds at a maximal rate, with no dividend being paid, as all earnings are used for expansion. This is because, during the growth phase, the marginal return on equity exceeds shareholders' time preference. They, therefore, desire to convert all earnings into equity by reinvestment in the firm. Once stationarity is achieved at time t_1 (because of diminishing returns), all variables achieve their optimal levels. Maximum profit is earned, and the dividend pay-out is maximised by allocating retentions only to maintaining the capital stock at its optimal level (i.e. only investment to cover depreciation is undertaken). This picture of maximum borrowing in the early stages of growth is not unfamiliar in a small firms' context. The concavity of the growth trajectory is uncontroversial, as much empirical literature suggests it should be concave (i.e. 'smaller' small firms grow faster than 'larger' small firms).

Turning now to the case of cheap equity,[3] the picture becomes more complex as illustrated in Figure 6.2 of Chapter 6. The optimal financial structure changes between phases of the growth trajectory. This sort of trajectory is encouraged by small initial amounts of equity: a common feature of the small business start-up. In the first growth phase the firm again starts with maximum borrowing, as in Figure 6.1 of Chapter 6. This occurs, despite debt being more expensive than equity, because marginal revenue exceeds the marginal cost of debt finance; thus debt finance, which is used to augment capital stock, generates increases in income and raises the growth rate. At the same time, shareholders will be willing to forgo all dividend payouts and will want all earnings reinvested in the firm, as equity is cheaper than debt.

In the consolidation phase that follows (after t_1), earnings are used to pay back debt. The debt servicing rent therefore falls, raising earnings and hence accelerating the rate at which debt is repaid. His consolidation phase is completed at time t_2. Once consolidation has been completed, the firm faces a lower cost of capital and it is then profitable to engage in a further phase of maximal growth, this time with no debt and fully financed by retentions. This growth rate is initially faster than that experienced at the end of the first growth phase, and continues to rise until stationarity is achieved at t_3. Again, diminishing returns put an end to this growth phase, as in Figure 6.1 of Chapter 6, and profit is maximised, with just enough earnings diverted to keep capital stock at its optimal level, but all remaining earnings being distributed as dividends to the shareholders.

This type of analysis, as developed by Hilten *et al.* (1993), can be extended in a number of further directions, to embrace adjustment costs, active tax and subsidy regimes, intensive investment, business cycles, and uncertainty. This illustrates, with just a few examples, how powerful this approach can be. However, rather than pursuing these extensions, the aim here has been to provide a non-technical account of a complex literature that provides the theoretical backdrop to many considerations of dynamics and financing. It is hoped this will help the reader to approach this issue with a common, general frame of reference.

8.3   Evidence

There is a relative paucity of empirical work on the financial structure of small firms, compared to large firms. Of the small firms literature, noteworthy are the contributions of Ang (1992), Chittenden *et al.* (1996), Hamilton and Fox (1998), Winker (1999), Lopez-Gracia and Aybar-Arias (2000), and Guidici and Paleari (2000). Some of this literature has a specialised focus relevant to this chapter, such as the analysis of debt ratios by Wijst and Thurik (1993), of debt versus equity preference by Hamilton and Fox (1998) and of financing constraints by Winker (1999) and Jeffersen (1997). The earliest papers on credit rationing, by Evans and Jovanovic (1989) and Fazzari *et al.* (1988) provide an alternative starting point to the kind of approach used in this chapter. However, in the former case, the test methodology has been questioned. For example, Cressy (1999, p. 296), argues that we merely 'cannot conclude that credit rationing does *not* exist'. In the latter case, criticism has focussed on the use of inappropriate proxies for financial constraints in econometric models. Other approaches to financial structure, and in particular to its common feature of the limited use of debt in the small firms case, include effects like bankruptcy, insolvency or closure (Cressy, 1996a, 1996b) and control aversion (Cressy, 1995). Broadly speaking, the credit rationing approach still has considerable currency amongst expert opinion, although influential contrary views, which seem well founded both theoretically and empirically, have also been expressed, e.g. Cressy (1996c).

The alternative approach used in this chapter, appeals to a 'limit on risk exposure' argument, rather than a credit rationing argument. The underlying assumption is that a small firm lies in a specific *risk class*. This will determine, for example, the premium of the interest rate set on debt, by advancers of debt finance (typically clearing banks in this case), over the base rate set by the Central Bank. It will therefore also determine the maximum leverage (i.e. gearing or debt/equity ratio) for a small firm which has been identified as being in a particular risk class.

The data used to test the theory (as expounded in the next section) were all gathered by the fieldwork methods described in Chapter 2. Contacts in the field were obtained through directors of enterprise stimulating units,[4] who provided representative samples of owner-managers from their client lists. Nineteen distinct areas within Scotland were sampled, and the initial sample in the first year contained 150 firms. These firms have been re-contacted in successive years and subjected to similar forms of examination.[5]

Owner-managers were interviewed using an administered questionnaire (see AQ1 of the appendix to this book) which covered seven themes: markets, finance, costs, business strategy, human capital, organisation and technical change. This chapter largely draws on the finance section, which looked at: profits and sales; debt and equity; loans and interest rates; grants and subsidies; actual and predicted gearing; trade creditors and trade debtors; extended purchase, hire purchase and lease purchase commitments; assets and stocks (inventories); share capital and loan finance (see Questions 2.1 to 2.2 in Section 2, *Finance*, of the AQ1 in the appendix to this book).

The firms in the sample were close to financial inception, being just 1.5 years old, on average, in the first year's cross section of data. They are therefore particularly suitable for examining the early life-cycle of the small firm. To illustrate, data like this minimise the cohort effect that can emerge if the small firms have very varied start-up points. Business services were the best represented group in the sample, and the overall split between services (SIC codes 50-99) and extractive/manufactures (SIC codes 01-49) was two-thirds and one-third, respectively. Thus the data are those of a modern, largely service-based economy, subject to quite strong competitive forces, and embedded in a commercial and financial culture of long standing.

The database had, in principle, 450 observations, but this number was reduced by missing observations, making the effective maximum about 330 observations (Chapter 2). For the subset of data considered here, the financial variables alone are emphasised, of which there were about 35 real variables and four text variables, drawn from a database composed of over 600 real variables, and about 50 text variables. The overall statistical characteristics of the financial data for a small firm, in an average sense, were as follows. Gross sales were £273,530 and gross profits were £70,053. Net profits were £15,814 after deductions of all costs, taxes and directors' remunerations. Only about half (52 per cent) of firms had any debt at all (including the business overdraft form) which strongly supports the appropriateness of regarding the general financial background as being other than that of cheap debt. Outside equity (e.g. financial injections from a local 'business angel' who had invested money into the business) was uncommon (6 per cent). However, when held, it was usually a significant holding (58 per cent) but one which attracted little or no dividend payment (see Note 3).

Unfortunately, the data do not provide good estimates of dividend payments, because of the simplicity of the financial structure of most small firms in the sample. Clearly, owner-managers derive income from their activities, and in that sense their equity is working for them, but it is difficult to identify a numerical estimate of dividend payment in the general absence of a formal share capital arrangement. Outside equity was rarely used (by just 5 per cent) to launch a business. The most important source of equity was inside equity. At launch, this was given by the owner-manager's personal cash injection. This had an average value of £13,014.

For a significant minority of firms (32 per cent) a bank loan was used to launch the business, and the average size of loan was £29,979. As the panel progresses through time, it is found that survivors are more likely to have used a bank loan at inception than non-survivors. For example, by the third year 51 per cent of the survivors had used a bank loan in the process of launching the business. This suggests that those owner-managers who can attract loan finance at start-up have, on an average, better quality businesses than those who do not; but in fact the picture is not at all clear cut when one uses a relatively sophisticated analysis of business performance (cf. Reid and Smith, 1996).

When a bank loan was granted, the rate of interest charged was typically well above base rate. For the sample period as a whole, the average rate of interest on long-term debt was 9.9 per cent, whilst the base rate was between 8.2 per cent (start of period) and 5.9 per cent (end of period). Furthermore, the *range* on loan interest rates was considerable, being 6–19 per cent; 6–13 per cent; and 6–12 per cent in each of the three successive years. Whilst the spread of interest rates charged on small-firm debt fell considerably over the sample period, some firms were clearly paying a large premium over the base rate. Certainly, it seems reasonable to say that the early and middle part of the sample period was *not* characterised by cheap debt, though by the latter part of the period, probably a significant number of small firms were enjoying cheap debt.

A large proportion of firms (78 per cent) had received a grant or subsidy in starting up, with an average of £4256 being awarded. In subsequent years, the proportion receiving grants or subsidies fell drastically (to 15–20 per cent) although the average level of grant or subsidy awarded went up, to £7532 and then £12,011 in the second and third years, respectively. Although this clearly suggests that grants were available on a 'picking numbers' basis, there is no evidence that the award of grants enhances business performance, and indeed some little evidence that it does not (cf. Reid and Smith, 2000a,b). This finding is reinforced by the fact that owner-managers of small firms ranked grants as merely 'helpful' (43 per cent) as a modal response, on a four-point scale of importance from 'unimportant', through 'helpful', 'important', to 'crucial'.

Entrepreneurs provided figures for the gearing ratio at the launch of the business (i.e. debt divided by equity, typically bank loan divided by personal financial injections). This was done at the time of initial interview, at which time the current gearing ratio was also provided. Owner-managers were also asked 'What level do you aim to get your gearing ratio to, in the next three years?', and were requested to provide a brief explanation for their answers. The average launch, current, and future gearing ratios had values of 157, 169 and 73 per cent, respectively, in the first year of data, and average gearing for the 3 years as a whole was 107 per cent, just slightly above the level at which debt is fully collateralised. The average expected gearing 3 years ahead was 47 per cent, and as the fuller analysis of Section 8.4 on '*Evidence*' (below) indicates, the general trend of both actual and expected gearing was downwards.

The financial structures of the small firms were relatively primitive. Less than one-third (29 per cent) had share capital, and only a very small percentage (2 per cent) used debenture finance. Considered in conjunction with the fact that only a small proportion (5–6 per cent) had any outside equity, this limits the extent to which all aspects of the formal analysis of Chapter 6 can be related to the empirical outcomes of the next Section 8.4, on '*Results*'. Most notably, it makes detailed commentary about dividend policy somewhat speculative.[6] However, this still leaves much to be discussed, notably output, capital and gearing.

8.4   Results

An advantage of the theory developed in Chapter 6, is that the variables used can be closely related to evidence. It is not necessary, therefore, to adopt a complex test methodology to circumvent shortcomings of the data, or to remedy a lack of correspondence between theoretical constructs and their empirical counterparts. Thus, in this chapter, testing is direct, and simply involves examining the empirical trajectories of key variables suggested by the theory, from inception, on through the time periods which pertain to the early life-cycle of the small firm. Unlike typical econometric data, which has firms moving in and out of the data-set at any point in time, the sample used for the work of this chapter is tightly controlled. All firms in it were start-ups and they were close together, in the sense of time of launch. This attenuates cohort and age effects in the sample. What is proffered here as evidence is not econometric in form, but more like calibration. The data have considerable dispersion, so curves were fitted through mean values to describe the data in a parsimonious way. In this sense the curve fitting is a descriptive, rather than statistical device. The empirical trajectories constructed in this way are then compared with the theoretical predictions. Reference is made below to a number of diagrams which, by contrast to Figures 6.1 and 6.2 of Chapter 6, plot real world data through real time.

For clarity, trajectories were mapped using a curve fitting routine which interpolates between average values of three successive years of data after inception, for the time periods 1994–95, 1995–96, 1996–97. These will be referred to as the first, second and third years, respectively. To illustrate the method, Figures 8.1 and 8.2 will be compared, and then the method will be used freely thereafter. For the case of the gearing or leverage ratio (i.e. debt/equity ratio), Figure 8.1 displays several hundred data points for the time interval 1994–97. Whilst some very high levels of gearing were occasionally observed, the frequency of low gearing was much greater. Indeed, the modal or typical level for the gearing ratio was zero (i.e. no debt held at all). Figure 8.1 visually understates the frequency of occurrence of this zero gearing because of multiple observations lying one on top of another. The solid line of Figure 8.2 displays the gearing trajectory derived by interpolating between group averages of the data in Figure 8.1. It is readily related to the

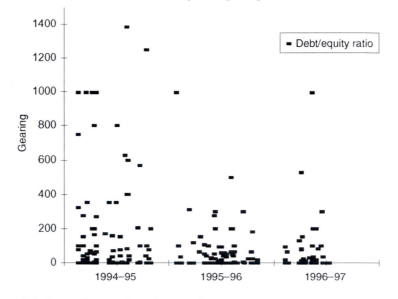

Figure 8.1 Scatter diagram of gearing over time.
Note: Three high gearing ratios are omitted for presentational purposes, but were used to compute averages.

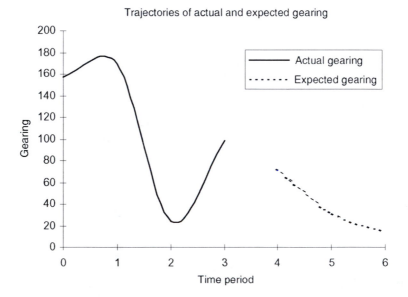

Figure 8.2 Trajectories of actual and expected gearing.

general profile of data in Figure 8.1. The diagram also displays, by a dotted line constructed by interpolation between group averages, data provided in response to a question which asked owner-managers what they expected their gearing ratios to be 3 years ahead of the time of interview (see Q.2.11 of Section 2, *Finance*, of the AQ1 in the appendix to this book). They were also asked to provide brief comments about their forecasts.

Figure 8.2 indicates an average gearing at financial inception of 158 per cent, rising to an average of 169 per cent in the first year, falling to 24 per cent in the second year, and rising to 99 per cent in the third year. That is, there was an initial rise in gearing, followed by a rapid fall, and then a rise again. This pattern can be further explored by reference to Figures 8.3 and 8.4, which graph the debt and equity trajectories, respectively, along with the trajectories of the base lending

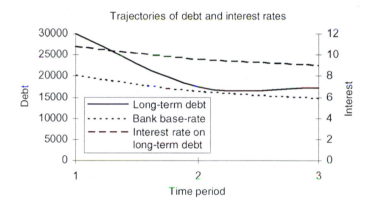

Figure 8.3 Trajectories of debt and interest rates.

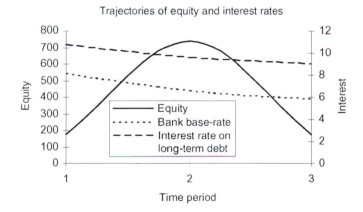

Figure 8.4 Trajectories of equity and interest rates.

rate and the interest rate on long-term debt. Figure 8.3 shows debt falling from an average level of £30k at the start of the sample period to an average of about £16k in the middle and end of the period. This reduction of debt is a feature of the theoretical analysis of Chapter 6, Section 6.4, earlier. The base rate was generally falling throughout the sample period, as were the interest rates offered on loans to small businesses. So it may be that indebtedness would have been reduced even more than it was, had there not been a downward drift in interest rates. In Figure 8.4, the trajectory of equity shows a rapid rise from an average value of £17.8k at the start of the sample period to a mid-period value of £73.8k, falling to £16.2k by the end of the period. Thus owner-managers were typically injecting considerable funds into the business early in the sample period, and taking funds out of the business later in the sample period.

Considering Figures 8.3 and 8.4 together, the fall in debt and rise in equity in the first half of the sample period explain the early fall in gearing. Likewise, the levelling out of debt, and fall in equity, explain the rise in gearing at the end of the sample period. At a deeper level, the relative costs of debt and equity are playing a role here, as are the optimality calculations of the owner-manager. The presumption has been that a period of cheap equity encourages the owner-manager to acquire only debt early on, so as to take immediate advantage of market opportunity, subsequently reducing debt as rapidly as possible. However, it looks as though the relatively low interest rate regime at the end of the sample period has encouraged owner managers to hold more debt and less equity than their earlier calculations would have led them to expect. The trajectory on expected gearing for the years 4, 5 and 6 in Figure 8.2 suggests that, given the interest rates prevailing at the start of the sample period, the intention is to reduce gearing significantly. The average three-period ahead forecasts of gearing for these 3 years were 73, 31 and 19 per cent, respectively. This evidently involves an intention to implement a major reduction in debt, to judge by the comments made by owner-managers. A frequently expressed view early in the sample period was that debt was too expensive. A sample of the typical views expressed by owner-managers is as follows.

A: "I don't like finance costs";
B: "Because of interest rates";
C: "The more we pay back, the less we make ourselves. At 2½ per cent above base rate, we could have money in the bank – could be our own bank, in effect";
D: "I don't want any debt, but if the bank rates drop I might think about it";
E: "I will probably get venture capital funding, or something. It seems the best way to go";

It has been observed that the retirement of what is here called long-term debt[7] initially proceeds rapidly. But then it starts to rise as the interest rate on long-term debt continues to fall. However, in the theoretically based trajectory of Figure 6.2 in Chapter 6, debt is retired entirely by the end of the second period, whereas in the practically based trajectories of Figures 8.2 and 8.3 there is another rise in debt (and gearing) at the end of the sample period. This outcome should be considered in the light of the above comments, and the observed steady fall in the interest on long-term debt. Depending on how interest elastic is the demand for debt finance, it may be that for at least some small firms a switch from a cheap equity to a cheap debt regime had occurred by the end of the sample period.

A premium of something like 1.5 per cent is paid, on an average,[8] on the base rate, in determining the interest rate on long-term debt advanced to small firms. The base rate fell from an average value of 8.16 per cent at the start of the sample to 6.60 per cent at the middle and finally to 5.94 per cent by the end. The actual rate charged to small firms was an average of 10.85 per cent at the start of the sample period, 9.66 per cent by the middle and 9.07 per cent by the end. These are low levels, historically speaking, which may partly account for the greater enthusiasm for debt. This having been said, the general trend on gearing, taking account of expectations as well as outcomes, is downwards.

Whilst the relative prices of debt and equity clearly have played a part in explaining the shape of the trajectories for key variables of the small firm, the dominant role of value maximizing behaviour should not be ignored. The general import of Section 8.3 has been that the small firm takes steps to gain what it can from the market opportunity with which it is presented. This involves output and capital growth under both cheap debt and cheap equity scenarios. From Figure 8.5, it will be seen that average sales were steady at about £250k for the start and middle of the sample period, and rose considerably to £373k by its end. The behaviour of profit was somewhat similar, with net profit remaining steady at an average figure

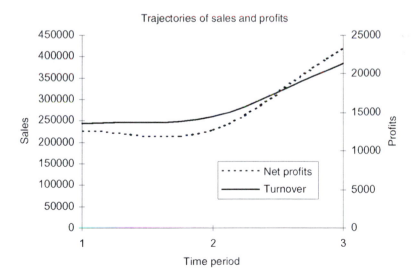

Figure 8.5 Trajectories of sales and profits.

of around £14k for the early and middle parts of the sample period, rising to an average of £20k by the end of it. This growth in the output and profit of the small firm was accompanied by growth in both working and fixed capital.

Of the various methods of acquiring assets by instalments, only hire purchase was widely used (27 per cent), with extended purchase (6 per cent) and lease purchase (11 per cent) being relatively uncommon. Owner-managers were asked to estimate the value of their stocks (inventories) in relation to their net assets, in percentage terms. The average value for the sample period was 199 per cent, suggesting a rather high level of stockholding, given that only a minority of firms were in extractive, agricultural and manufacturing sectors (Figure 8.6).

Owner-managers were also asked whether they had any trade credit arrangements (this was true in about 80 per cent of cases), and if so, what forms they took. The average current balance on trade creditors over the sample period was £21k and, typically, suppliers allowed about 1.5 months to pay. The average current balance on trade debtors was £32k and, typically, customers were given one month to pay (Figure 8.7). Thus trade credit was a significant repository of working capital, and owner-managers typically negotiated superior terms of payment. These aspects are treated in greater detail in Section 8.4.

For the sample period as a whole, gross fixed assets stood at an average of £38,456 and net fixed assets at £26,540 (Figure 8.8). Finally, the trajectory of fixed capital over time needs to be considered. The general theoretical finding is a rising trajectory of capital for both regimes (cf. Figures 6.1 and 6.2 of Chapter 6). In Figure 8.8, fixed assets are seen to rise from an average figure at inception of £24.4k to £44.3k by the middle of the sample period, finishing up at £54.2k by the end of the period. The net book value of fixed assets tracks this trajectory from below with an implied average depreciation rate over the sample of about

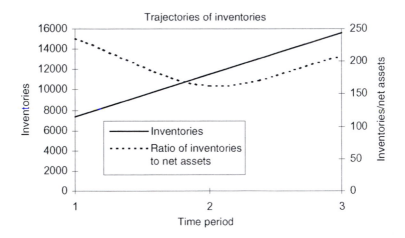

Figure 8.6 Trajectories of inventories.

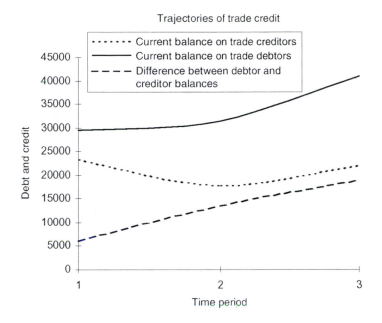

Figure 8.7 Trajectories of trade credit.

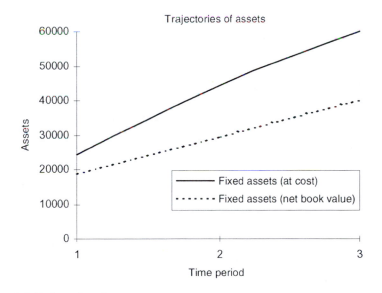

Figure 8.8 Trajectories of assets.

30 per cent. Net assets start from an average value of £18.8k at inception, rising to £29.5k by mid-sample, and ending up at a value of £36.1k.

8.5   Conclusion

Although the small firms sector is quantitatively important, with some 3 million firms accounting for about one-third of UK employment (Daly and McCann, 1992) during the fieldwork period, the state of our scientific knowledge of what makes individual firms function is still limited. This chapter has attempted to remedy this deficiency by using a dynamic theory of the value-maximising small firm to confront a body of new evidence in panel form.

This theory generates clear qualitative predictions about key financial features of the small firm. If debt is relatively cheap, it will be used comprehensively, and the trajectories of debt, capital and output will rise over time after financial inception until a stationarity level is achieved. Only then will dividend be paid. If equity is relatively cheap, debt will still be acquired in the early stage after financial inception, and output and capital will also grow rapidly. Then a consolidation phase is reached when capital and output level out, and debt is rapidly retired. A further phase of growth in output and capital then occurs until a stationary level is achieved. Again, it is only at this stage that any dividend will be paid.

The evidence illuminated by this theory is based on observations of 35 key financial variables for 150 new small business starts over a 3-year period after inception. It has been found that predictions of the theory enjoy some support in terms of the shape of average trajectories of key financial variables. Specifically, evidence is found of:

(a) Steady growth of output (sales), including some phases of consolidation.
(b) Steady growth of capital, as measured by fixed assets.
(c) Sensitivity of debt (observable also through gearing) to the interest rate on long-term debt.
(d) Absence or deferral of dividend payments.
(e) Retiral of debt when sales are consolidated. This could be attributed to a cheap equity regime.
(f) Increase in debt when sales are rising. This could be attributed to a cheap debt regime.
(g) Arguably a sensitivity of equity (observable also through gearing) to the relative costs of debt and equity.

The methods used to obtain these results (namely calibration) are not yet widely adopted in the small firms literature. Unfortunately, the extant literature lacks a dynamic financial theory of the small firm. The testing of financial hypotheses has therefore typically lacked an analytical underpinning. Furthermore, financial hypotheses have been expressed in general terms, lacking the fine detail which has been used here. The aim of this chapter has been to attempt to redress some of these weaknesses and to take a first step in testing detailed hypotheses about the financial structure of small firms.

Endnotes

1 But note a number of empirical papers espouse a dynamic analysis of small firms, including Furrukh and Urata (2002) on East Asia, Kleindl (2000) on the virtual marketplace, Liedholm (2002) on Africa and Latin America, and Li Kuo (2003) on FDI. However, all these papers lack rigorous theoretical foundations.
2 That is, cost of equity (i) exceeds the rate of interest on debt (r) net of corporation tax (c): $i > (1 - c)r$. Note that in this figure, and also in Figure 6.2 earlier, only capital and debt are measured in the same units (money). Dividend and output are measured in different units, being money per unit of time and units of output per unit of time, respectively. Thus only debt and capital are directly comparable in this figure. However, if one thinks of the vertical axis being re-scaled to illustrate the trajectories of output and dividend as well, the time-phasing of behaviour of these variables is worth noting on a combined graph, even though the *relative* position of the curves is arbitrary.
3 That is, $i < (1 - c)r$ where i is cost of equity, c is the corporation tax rate and r is the rate of interest on debt.
4 Called Enterprise Trusts in Scotland. See Reid and Jacobsen (1988, Ch. 5) for further details on this type of institution.
5 Failure rates are low, with 81 per cent remaining in business by the second year, and 78 per cent by the third year.
6 Seven firms had the capacity to pay dividends in the first year, but no payment was made; five could in the second year, and paid an average of 1.6 per cent (with a range of 0–8 per cent); and just three could in the third year, and paid an average of 0.8 per cent (with a range of 0–2.5 per cent). In effect, dividend payment was largely in abeyance, a feature typical of the model's prediction about the growth phase.
7 Essentially bank loans, which may be contrasted with short-term indebtedness arising from trade credit arrangements.
8 However, some firms paid substantially more than this for debt finance. For the sample period as a whole, the rate was 9.93 per cent on average, with a standard deviation of 2.56 per cent and a range of 6–19 per cent. To illustrate, owner-manager C (of the main text) reported paying 2.5 per cent on base rate.

Part 4

Performance

9 Performance rankings and cluster analysis

(with Julia A. Smith)

9.1 Introduction

This chapter seeks a good measure of new business performance (e.g. Zimmerman *et al.*, 2002), and then explains this measure by various dimensions of business strategy.[1] Three criteria are used to create a one-dimensional ordinal ranking of high, medium and low performance for new business starts-ups: employment growth; return on capital employed and labour productivity. It is shown that statistical cluster analysis provides a convincing separation of a sample of new business start-ups into high, medium and low performance categories, using a minimum distance criterion for clustering.[2] The technique of cluster analysis introduced here will also be relevant to the use of cluster analysis in Chapter 14, where a morphology of firm types is developed.

9.2 The data

The data used in this chapter are a subset of the larger database created on the life-cycle experience of 150 new business starts over a 4-year period (Chapter 2). As is now familiar, data were collected by face-to-face interviews with owner-managers of small entrepreneurial firms. All were contacted through Directors of Enterprise Trusts in Scotland, and representative samples of contacts were provided from client lists in eighteen areas.[3] Interviews were conducted using an administered questionnaire (AQ1) that covered the agenda of markets, finance, costs, business strategy, human capital, organisation and technical change. This chapter largely draws on the market and financial sections for the cluster analysis (see appendix to this book, AQ1, Sections 1–7).

It is worth emphasising, briefly, the extent to which the sample is representative of Scottish firms in general, and the level of confidence that can be had in the statistical inferences made throughout this chapter. First of all, 150 firms are certainly a sufficient number to constitute a statistically 'large' sample, as defined, for example, by small sample distribution theory.[4]

Second, as explored earlier, figures available from Scottish Enterprise (1996) for the relevant comparison period suggest that the sample corresponds closely to the larger picture of new Scottish firms in the 1990s. For example, by legal form, the 1993–94 sample of 150 firms used in this study comprised 26 per cent sole traders working from home, 29 per cent sole traders operating from business premises, 19 per cent partnerships and 27 per cent private limited companies. The Scottish Enterprise figures for 23,000 new firms in 1996 give sole proprietorships at 48 per cent, partnerships at 21 per cent and limited companies at 30 per cent.[5] The categories, although slightly different, show clearly that there is a marked similarity of breakdown by legal form between the two samples.

The division by sector is a slightly more contentious issue, but is nonetheless still worth addressing. Scottish Enterprise states that 68 per cent of new businesses in Scotland in 1996 were in services, which compares with the 64 per cent in this study (Smith, 1997, Ch. 4).[6] Figures from the Department for Education and Employment suggest that, for the United Kingdom as a whole, 'service sector firms represent just over 70 per cent of all small firms in the economy' [*Labour Market Quarterly Report* (1996, p. 11)].[7] However, it is often very difficult to classify firms by sector, as it is the product, and not the business, to which the SIC applies. Some firms, offering different products or services, may be identified by two or more sectors, and it is not uncommon for firms to fall into both the services and manufacturing divisions.

In terms of legal form and industrial classification, there can be considerable confidence that the sample is representative of Scottish firms, although admittedly there may be slight bias towards firms with greater start-up support. For example, the evidence on which this study is based uses the ETs for the sampling frame. Furthermore, the Scottish Enterprise (SE) figures are based on bank records. Both sources indicate that the firms in question had either advice or financial support available to them from an early stage. However, it may be that the enterprise regime in Scotland was not very supportive of new businesses generally (Reid, 1999b) over the sample period, so it is cheering to note the similarities, given the difference in sample size (namely 150 compared to 23,000). It is with some confidence, therefore, that the sample is used to provide a representation of new micro-firms in Scotland in the early 1990s.

Turning to the performance variables utilised in the cluster analysis, the relevant variables for constructing various ratios were: total number of employees[8] or 'head count' (*Employ*); net profit (net of taxes, VAT, etc.) (*Netprof*); the owner-manager's personal cash injection at start-up (*Owncash*); and the gross annual sales, based on the latest estimates (typically the last tax year) (*Sales1*). Two of the performance variables were constructed using data from a second round of interviews with entrepreneurs, which took place a year after the first round (using the AQ2). There was a high survival rate of new starts, with 81 per cent staying in business until the second year. The issue of sample selection bias therefore arises in the estimation of the ordered logits of the following chapter, and the ways of handling this problem are discussed and applied.

9.3 Performance ranking

There is no unique way in which the performance of a small business (or any other business) can be evaluated. One approach to performance evaluation is entirely relativist. It asks what goals a firm has set, and then enquires into the extent to which these goals have been achieved. The problem with this approach is that it neglects the important fact that performance evaluation can never be divorced from the market nexus. It is true that a variety of utility-based views of the firm, embracing various types of managerialism, for example, can be construed as underpinning this relativist view of performance.[9] However, ultimately, the firm has to pass the long-run test of economic survival; and bundles of relatively mobile combinations of finance-capital and labour will tend to seek best alternatives. Both of these considerations undermine a more self-referring or relativist view of performance. Even if a life-style based firm fully met its life-style performance goals (e.g. in terms of hours worked, hiring of family members, or adherence to traditional production methods), economic failure of the firm, especially if it should involve financial distress or insolvency, would nullify the performance significance of its having fulfilled life-style targets.

For this reason, this chapter uses what may be termed 'objective' measures of performance, selecting a trio of measures that are widely used for performance evaluation, namely employment growth, rate of return, and productivity. This method may be contrasted not only with the earlier relativist method, but also with the subjectivist method (Sapienza, Smith and Gannon, 1988). The latter is based on skilled judgements of performance, with those making the judgements being allowed to appeal to any such evidence, qualitative or quantitative, that they may have at their disposal. This approach is often applied when data are incomplete or subject to considerable measurement error, and are part of a complex and dynamic setting which limits the efficacy of simple numerical indices of performance, because they are unavailable, irrelevant or unimportant. An example of the application of this method is the performance evaluation of joint ventures between Greek and Eastern European partners reported upon by Salavrakos (1996). In this case, subjective evaluations of performance on a five-point scale were made by joint venturers during interviews because, amongst other things, incomplete, missing or highly imperfect markets in these territories ruled out using conventional financial ratio measures of performance, which hinge upon the existence of complete markets which are highly competitive. Chapter 18 will return to this theme, where circumstances dictate that subjective performance measures have a distinct advantage over so-called objective measures.

For the purposes of this chapter, there were many potential performance indicators available; but the problem confronted is not only of paucity of data, but rather of separating the wheat from the chaff (Foreman-Peck, 1985). Here, a measure of performance is sought, after business start-up, which is: *objective*, in that it appeals to well-defined measures of performance; *parsimonious*, in that it provides an efficient aggregation of a variety of measures into a simple ordinal rank; and *plausible*, in that the ranking thereby derived bears a credible relationship to the wider body of evidence one gathers by fieldwork methods. Some of the latter evidence is objective, but not reducible to indices, and some is subjective (like perceptions of the morale of the workforce, or the drive of the entrepreneur). Both are, nevertheless, potentially important in reaching a sound judgement about business performance.

9.4   Cluster analysis

The technique used in this chapter (and, indeed, later in Chapter 14) for developing an ordinal ranking of small firms into low, medium and high performance was hierarchical cluster analysis.[10] The data for clustering may be considered to be an $N \times K$ matrix of measurements X with typical element x_{ij}, which is the magnitude of the j-th measurement ($j = 1, \ldots, K$), like profitability, on the i-th firm ($i = 1, \ldots, N$). The measure of distance d_{ij} between observations i and j is the Euclidean metric:

$$d_{ij} = \left\{ \sum_{k=1}^{K} (x_{ik} - x_{jk})^2 \right\}^{\frac{1}{2}}$$

where x_{ik} is the value of the k-th variable for the i-th firm. As Euclidean distances are very sensitive to scales of measurement, variables are standardised[11] before using the Euclidean distance. The clustering method due to Ward (1963) was adopted, which merges clusters which contribute the least to the overall sum of the squared within-cluster distances. Clustering proceeds by finding the closest pair of clusters, combining them into a new larger cluster, and then computing the distance between this and the other remaining clusters. The process starts with every firm treated as a single cluster, so the first new cluster will be a two-firm cluster, and the next may be a two-firm or a three-firm cluster, and so on. Clustering ceases when the final two clusters have been combined, so all the data are in one cluster.

A variety of performance measures were used in the exploratory cluster analysis,[12] and the finally adopted set of three were: employment growth (*Employ-mentGrowth*); profitability (*Profitability*); and productivity (*Productivity*). These three measures of performance were available for all 150 firms in the sample. *EmploymentGrowth* shows the percentage change in total employment from year 1 to 2, which serves to give an indication of the investment by each firm into the means by which it carries on its trade (namely its workforce). A negative figure for *EmploymentGrowth* would indicate that staff cut-backs had been made, possibly because business was slack; whereas a positive figure would suggest that business was going well, and more people were required to accomplish the increased workload.[13] A positive result for this variable therefore suggests good performance because an increase in expenditure on staff generally follows an increase in business (i.e. sales), leading to further expected future growth. Storey (1994, p. 112) points out that small firms that 'plan to and achieve rapid growth in employment [are] of interest [because] they are the major providers of new employment within the small firms sector, ... they are likely to purchase a wide range of financial services, ... [and] they are much more likely to be seeking a wide range of advisory services than is the case for firms experiencing modest growth or no growth at all'.

A further indication of business performance, and one that will be of interest to many small business owner-managers, is one that can assist those who hold a stake in the business in assessing the value and quality of the investment they have made. Ansoff (1965, p. 42), for example, suggests that 'rate of return on investment is a common and widely accepted yardstick for measuring business success ... [and] for comparison of business prospects in different industries'. An accounting ratio that measures such a return is the Return on Capital Employed (ROCE). The variable *Profitability* is an approximation to this ratio, and measures the net profit earned by the business divided by the amount of financial capital injected by the owner-manager at the start of trading. A high figure here would represent a high return on the owner-manager's investment, and therefore is taken to be an indication of good performance.

The third and final variable upon which the clusters are based is *Productivity*. It is similar to *Profitability*, in that it represents a return on inputs to the production function. *Productivity* measures the amount of turnover in year 1 that can be attributed to each employee. In other words, it is turnover in year 1 divided by total employment in year 1. *Productivity* is an indicator of the efficiency of the business in converting effort (in cooperation with other of the firm's resources) into sales. The higher the value of this variable, the greater are the sales attributable to each employee, which may be interpreted as a measure of greater productivity within the business. With the exception of *Productivity*, which is based only on year 1 data, the other two performance indicators are only defined for surviving firms. Thus *Profitability* and *EmploymentGrowth* are set equal to zero for non-survivors; so *Productivity* is the prime performance indicator for non-survivors.

Small firms are very distinct from other economic organisations. For example, the owner-manager is very personally involved and often has committed a personal investment or has family employed. Therefore, his aims are varied and multiple, rather than following the traditional idea of a profit-maximising organisation with one sole objective. So the performance measure adopted here was chosen to reflect the (observed) aims or goals of the owner-managers of these firms, namely, growth in employment (e.g. for family or fulfilment), return on their personal investment, and high productivity per member of staff. It must also be stressed that the performance index was developed subsequent to the data gathering, in order to see how behaviour was reflected in performance.

Other performance measures which were used in trial clusters included staying in business,[14] employment growth, asset growth and the profit to sales ratio. These generally picked out a similar set of high-performing firms, which varied only very slightly as a proportion of the sample (about 7 per cent). There was greater (but still not extensive) variation in the composition of medium and low performing clusters.

Perhaps the main difficulty is in deciding whether or not the clusters obtained do actually describe the relationships desired. Everitt (1980, p. 45) describes clusters as 'continuous regions of . . . space containing a relatively high density of points, separated from other such regions containing a relatively low density of points'. For the firms under investigation in this work, a three-dimensional scatter plot of the clusters (Figure 9.1) showed that the high performers stood out quite clearly from the rest.

Another problem lies with the choice of variables. As was mentioned previously, many different combinations were tried, but the three variables settled upon gave the best and clearest results. For one thing, data were available for each of the 150 cases. For another it was felt that the variables selected gave as good an indication of performance and measurement of growth as it would be possible to obtain using such methods.

Finally, as regards clustering, a simple analysis of the figures is sometimes not enough to assure the investigators of the validity of the clusters. Some element of subjective judgement must also be applied to decide which of the three clusters is indeed the high, medium or low performance group. Firms from each cluster were identified by name, and it was checked that the two main fieldworkers who had first-hand knowledge of the businesses through face-to-face meetings, were agreed that the firms could legitimately be grouped into the three categories given, with no apparent anomalies.

Thus in viewing the rankings generated by the various cluster runs[15] reference was also made to the wider body of fieldwork evidence and experience of the fieldworkers themselves (e.g. in face-to-face interview), for checking that statistical procedures were not at variance with fieldwork judgement.[16]

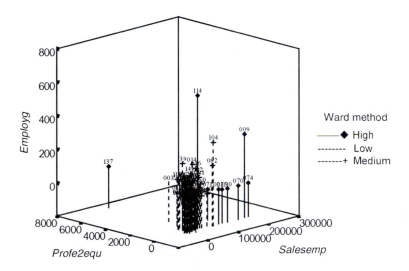

Figure 9.1 Three-dimensional scatter plot of performance clusters.

The conclusion reached was that the clusters which were generated accorded well with more general judgements of performance of the sampled small firms in their start-up phase of the life-cycle. The final set of clusters adopted can be displayed by a dendrogram (Norusis, 1994, pp. 91–3), where the top three levels of clusters can be identified as high, medium and low performance firms (see Figure 9.2, where the small print of cases need not be read). It was found that the primary split was between high performers and the rest. The rest were then split into medium and low performers. Individual case numbers were then used to refer back to schedules, field notes and other evidence gathered during interviews, for the purpose of confirming the general plausibility of the clusters generated by the dendrogram from the standpoint of richer data.

There were 91 (61 per cent) firms in the low performance category, 49 (33 per cent) in the medium performance category, and 10 (7 per cent) in the high performance category. It is of interest to examine the performances of each firm group (low, medium, high) for the three underlying measures, employment growth (*EmploymentGrowth*), return on capital employed (*Profitability*) and labour productivity (*Productivity*), from which the ranking was produced by cluster analysis.

The clustering was deliberately stopped at three groups for several reasons. First, to leave enough observations in each performance category to allow statistical inferences to be made.[17] Second, because a categorical measure was required for the technique employed – it was necessary to sift out the 'gazelles' (Birch, 1996) from the pack; and to identify better performers (i.e. medium performers here) as distinct from the 'average' or lower performers (the majority). These findings too are consistent with other literature that has examined the percentage of very high performers in any sample of small firms (e.g. Storey, 1994). Finally, the focus of the chapter is primarily on the higher performers, and these are clearly distinct from the rest.

The relevant means and standard deviations for each variable are related to performance rank in Table 9.1. On average, the low performers experienced employment contraction. Whilst the shedding of labour might be a sign of searching for efficiency, with a view, for example, to raising labour productivity, this seems not to have been the case here,[18] in that low performing firms also had the lowest labour productivity in terms of sales generated per employee (just £15,000, as compared to £32,000 and £128,000). Viewing the table overall, for each performance measure the magnitudes are ranked according to the general performance ranking generated by cluster analysis. It is to be noted that the high performers are especially impressive in terms of the measure of labour productivity. Here, their performance advantage over both medium and low performers was particularly marked. This accords well with observations made by Birch (1996)[19] that there is a strong tendency for the bulk of small firms to generate similar levels of sales per employee, with a much smaller percentage (<10 per cent), which he called the 'gazelles', generating very much higher sales per employee. It should be noted that the return on the capital employed variable was rather narrowly defined, though certainly in a way that appeals to entrepreneurs. It related

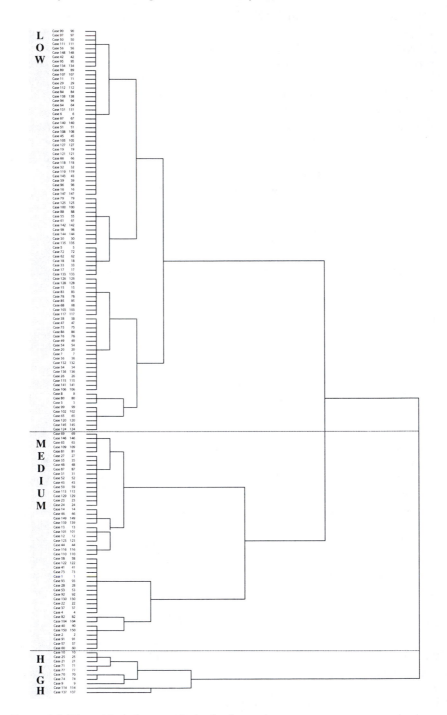

Figure 9.2 Hierarchical cluster analysis: dendrogram.

Table 9.1 Mean values for performance variables used in cluster analysis, cross classified by performance rank

		Low performers n = 91 (=61%)	Medium performers n = 49 (=33%)	High performers n = 10 (=7%)
EmploymentGrowth	Mean	−6.04	76.72	97.92
	(SD)	(18.10)	(63.65)	(199.49)
Profitability	Mean	117.47	136.88	1,036.14
	(SD)	(349.93)	(262.79)	(2,236.01)
Productivity	Mean	15,120.70	32,007.52	127,550.30
	(SD)	(9,989.40)	(23,950.07)	(59,272.27)

Note: There are some small rounding errors in percentages. The standard deviation (SD) is given in brackets.

the second year's net profit to the entrepreneur's financial injection in the first year.[20] Whilst there is a slight average performance advantage of the medium over the low performers, the high performers do remarkably better on this yard-stick. In interpreting the evidence on this performance variable (*Profitability*), all of which looks favourable, it should be borne in mind that entrepreneurs' financial injections are not the only source of finance-capital for the small firm (e.g. other sources, like bank finance, are common, and outside equity is not unknown).

In Table 9.2, a wider body of evidence is brought to bear on the performance rankings. It should be made clear that the variables in Table 9.2 were not used to construct the performance rankings by cluster analysis *but that nevertheless, using a variety of measures, the performance ranking is consistent. Inbusin* is unity if the firm stays in business or zero otherwise (see appendix to Chapter 9 for this and other definitions). If survival is to be regarded as a measure of performance, then the 25 per cent failure rate of low performers, 10 per cent failure rate of medium performers and zero per cent failure rate of high performers is strong corroborative evidence for the performance rankings adopted.

However, merely surviving is not necessarily an indicator of good performance, nor is non-surviving necessarily an indicator of poor performance (e.g. if firms had always intended to rapidly exploit a small niche profitably, and then to liq-uidate, having harvested the niche). Nevertheless, *on average*, the non-survivors are low performers on other measures such as profitability. The ages of the low, medium and high performers differ by no more that 9 months. Low performers and medium performers have almost identical ages on average (20 months), and though the average age of high performers at 8.13 months above medium per-formers is statistically significantly[21] higher, this effect has doubtful economic significance, certainly not enough to explain the markedly better performance on sales, for example, of high performers.

Table 9.2 Mean values for additional descriptive variables, cross classified by performance rank

		Low performers n = 91 (=61%)	Medium performers n = 49 (=33%)	High performers n = 10 (=7%)
Inbusin	Mean	0.75	0.90	1.00
	(SD)	(0.44)	(0.31)	(0.00)
Age	Mean	20.18	20.37	28.50
	(SD)	(17.83)	(10.68)	(19.15)
Assets1	Mean	17,154.73	13,891.25	66,017.88
	(SD)	(32,470.95)	(20,636.60)	(135,564.05)
Assets2[a]	Mean	23,135.19	37,047.56	31,400.75
	(SD)	(46,014.64)	(86,403.83)	(36,172.94)
Employ1	Mean	5.20	8.06	9.20
	(SD)	(6.90)	(23.28)	(13.18)
Employ2[a]	Mean	3.27	12.63	4.80
	(SD)	(6.20)	(44.34)	(3.61)
Sales1	Mean	94,729.05	192,599.43	1,556,075.00
	(SD)	(180,129.44)	(371,865.10)	(2,892,615.86)
Sales2[a]	Mean	130,902.85	256,321.02	760,475.38
	(SD)	(228,614.09)	(520,141.26)	(721,130.70)
Netprof1	Mean	7,873.29	21,695.11	23,000.00
	(SD)	(15,613.83)	(39,583.89)	(44,774.43)
Netprof2[a]	Mean	12,802.54	8,559.92	53,050.50
	(SD)	(41,024.27)	(17,832.35)	(50,607.31)
Owncash	Mean	10,817.30	15,309.46	24,250.00
	(SD)	(24,475.76)	(37,650.43)	(34,602.85)
OutsideEquity	Mean	0.04	0.06	0.11
	(SD)	(0.21)	(0.24)	(0.33)
Bankloan	Mean	0.27	0.39	0.44
	(SD)	(0.45)	(0.49)	(0.53)
Grant	Mean	0.78	0.82	0.67
	(SD)	(0.42)	(0.39)	(0.50)
Gearst	Mean	165.92	136.13	188.78
	(SD)	(359.83)	(290.27)	(322.54)
Gearnow	Mean	182.46	167.40	43.33
	(SD)	(371.95)	(450.28)	(77.87)

Notes:
There are some small rounding errors in percentages. Standard deviation (SD) in brackets.
a Computed on smaller sample size of 122.

In the first year, ranking by assets did not quite accord with the performance ranking, though it did in the second year. Size by employment accorded with performance rank in the first year, but not in the second. The second year saw both low and high-performers down-sizing, though presumably for quite different reasons; in the first case to avoid failure, and in the second case to promote efficiency. Sales in the first and second years are ranked according to the performance ranking, with the superiority of the high performers being particularly evident.

Turning to the financial variables at the bottom of Table 9.2, in the first year net profit averages accorded with the performance ranking, though these figures differed little. By the second year, the medium performers appeared to have a lower net profit than low performers, though high performers did very much better than both, on average.[22] It may be that there is a measurement problem here, with regard to net profit, arising because medium performers are more likely than low performers to net out salaries (including managerial salaries) from profit.[23]

If a performance ranking cross classification (not shown) is undertaken, it is found that the better the performance, the greater the cash committed by the owner-manager at inception, and further the greater is the access to outside equity, and the greater is the access to bank loans. These findings accord well with financial theories of the firm.[24] The greater the prospective value of the enterprise, the more willing is the entrepreneur to commit cash at inception. Furthermore, the greater the availability of cash to commit in this way, the higher is likely to be the human capital embodied in the entrepreneur. A signalling of the quality of new start-ups in this way is more likely to attract outside finance-capital in both debt and equity form. Thus, for example, the high performers have 11 per cent outside equity and 44 per cent bank loan involvements, whereas the low performers have just 4 per cent and 27 per cent, respectively.

The interpretation of gearing (i.e. debt/equity) ratios is more troublesome. Whilst gearing is regarded as essentially arbitrary in some traditional areas of large firm finance,[25] in small firm finance, where bankruptcy considerations are non-trivial, higher gearing is associated with risk exposure and a tendency to debt-servicing crises, especially during downswings of the business cycle. At start-up, low, medium and high performers were all highly geared (*Gearst*), with the highest geared on average (at 189 per cent) being the high performers. However, by the time of the first year interview, gearing (*Gearnow*) had fallen drastically for the high performing group (to an average of just 43 per cent) and had also risen for both the medium and low performing group. For *Gearnow* the magnitudes accord with a small firms view of financial performance, with lower gearing being associated with better performance (cf. Reid, 1991). The fact that, for initial gearing, *Gearst*, all ratios are well above unity (suggesting debt is not fully collateralised) is indicative of a generally perceived high quality of business start-up on the part of lenders. At inception, their willingness to permit very high gearing is both rational and encouraging, in view of previously held opinions to the effect that banks are excessively (indeed irrationally) cautious in their approach to small business financing.

Finally, the *Grant* variable denotes whether or not a firm received a financial grant or subsidy at inception. How grants are awarded, and their aims, do not necessarily tally with the dictates of the market, or the imperatives of business strategy. However, the assumption is that they provide, in some sense, a positive instrument for the social market economy. The evidence here is that the high performers had the least involvement with grant support, on average, though the level of support involved was generally high, across the board.

9.5   Conclusion

To conclude this chapter, it is apparent that the cluster method employed, which used just three performance measures (thus satisfying the principle of parsimony), has produced a ranking of businesses which accords well with diverse other attributes of the same businesses but which, however, were not themselves used in the cluster analysis itself (thus satisfying the principle of efficacy). Furthermore, the rankings accord well with collateral evidence of both the qualitative and quantitative variety, gathered both during fieldwork and in interviews with entrepreneurs. Overall, therefore, considerable confidence may be placed on the performance classification, and on the method by which it was derived. The next and most important task remains of explaining the ranking of performance by the business strategies deployed by owner-managers. It is to this task that the analysis of Chapter 10 is directed.

Endnotes

1 See, Yusuf and Saffu (2005) for the deploying of cluster analysis in their examination of the performance of small firms in Ghana.
2 See, for example, the linking of strategic choices and small business performance in the work on Ankara, Turkey by Acar (1993).
3 Inverurie, Aberdeen, Dundee, Crossgates, Cupar, Edinburgh, Midlothian, Alloa, Grangemouth, Stirling, Glasgow, Strathkelvin, Govan, Cumnock & Doon, Perth, Hamilton, Lanark and Brechin.
4 From the perspective of the student t-distribution sample sizes above 70 are effectively 'large' samples.
5 Storey (1994) reports on the findings of Bannock and Partners, who calculated that, in 1986, for the United Kingdom as a whole, 55 per cent of small firms were sole proprietorships, 26 per cent partnerships and 19 per cent limited companies. By 1989, Daly and McCann (1992) found a similar breakdown of United Kingdom firms by legal form.
6 Again, the Scottish Enterprise categories vary slightly in definition from those used in this study.
7 See Reid (1993, Ch. 1) for detailed comparisons of the Scottish small firms sector with that of the United Kingdom.
8 Measured as Directors + Managers + Full-time employees + Part-time employees + Trainees, this being the total 'head count' for the business.
9 This includes well-known theories due to Baumol (1962) and Williamson (1967), (cf. Reid, 1987, Ch. 9), but also the satisficing approach of Simon (1957), which has obvious relevance to 'life-style' small firms which, provided they reach satisfactory levels of profit (which may be no more than enough to ensure survival), will not be managed to seek greater profit, but rather to pursue other goals.
10 A procedure that was accomplished using *SPSS* (*Professional Statistics*), as described in Norusis (1994). See Manly (1986, Ch. 8) for technical details. See also Smith (1997) for application in a business strategy context, and Everitt's (1980) useful text on the subject, *Cluster Analysis*.
11 Data values are standardised to unit range from −1 to +1. Each value for the item being standardised is divided by the range of the values. If the range is zero, all values are set to zero (Norusis, 1994, p. 107).
12 Everitt (1980) suggests trying several cluster techniques, based on different assumptions, or using different variables, on the same set of data. Then only clusters which are produced by all or the majority of these methods should be accepted.

13 In the long term, a strategy might be to shed inefficient labour, or to 'downsize' the workforce in order to cut costs or because of technological innovations. This would make sense if the retained workforce were enhancing their skills, perhaps through training. However, here, short-term effects amongst very young firms are being observed, so the argument stands.

14 An element of the 'staying in business' variable (*Inbusin*) was retained in the three measures finally used to create the clusters in that, by their construction, second-year net profit and second year head-count were set equal to zero if the firm did not survive.

15 See Norusis (1994, p. 98) for details on how these runs are performed on *SPSS*.

16 This is possible because the case numbers (just visible) in Table 9.1 provide access to field notes, and other forms of evidence (e.g. brochures, price lists, accounts, advertising material).

17 Note that clustering only groups together those cases with similar characteristics, and that subjective judgement (based partly on personal knowledge/contact with the firms) had to be used to decide which of the groups were high, medium and low performers.

18 The effect is partly attributable to the procedure of assigning a zero employment level for the second year if the firm had gone out of business.

19 At the Jönköping International Business School Conference on 'Entrepreneurship, SMEs and the Macro Economy', 13–14 June 1996, when he reported on general features of his vast database.

20 If the firm had gone out of business in the second year, net profit was assigned to zero for this year.

21 A 99 per cent confidence interval for the difference in average age between medium and high performers is Prob $(-12.25 < \mu_1 - \mu_2 < -4.01) = 0.99$ which does not contain the origin, thus rejecting the hypothesis of equality of ages.

22 It should be noted that the figures for *Profitability* of Table 9.1 cannot be derived from ratios of mean values of *Netprof2Equ* and *Owncash* in Table 9.2, as the figure in Table 9.2 is the mean of the ratios for all firms, which is not the same as the ratio of the means.

23 It should be noted that the numerator in the variable *Profitability* is net profit in year two, and the denominator is *Owncash* (as in next line of Table 9.2).

24 Which emphasises the ability of the entrepreneur to signal the quality of his firm e.g. by a willingness to commit personal equity to the business. Such a positive signal can encourage bankers to advance loans, and business angels to take an equity stake in the business.

25 In particular, those dominated by the Modigliani–Miller theorem. See Hay and Morris (1991, Ch. 12).

10 Performance and business strategy

(with Julia A. Smith)

10.1 Introduction

In this chapter, an ordinal logit model (with selection) is used to explain the small firms performance ranking obtained in Chapter 9. The results indicate that many widely discussed features of small business strategy have little, or even negative, impact on performance (cf. Acar, 1993; Crick *et al.*, 2003). Of the numerous aims that owner-managers may adopt (survival, growth, etc.), only one appears to have a major impact on performance; the pursuit of the highest rate of return on investment. Many of the perceptions that entrepreneurs have of their own capabilities appear false or unimportant,[1] with the exception of organisational features and systems.

To help understand this chapter fully, it is helpful to review briefly the content and methods of the previous chapter. Chapter 9 asked how best to measure, in a simple fashion, the performance of new business starts. It then enquired into those dimensions of business strategy that best explain this performance. It examined ways of gauging the performance of new starts using multiple criteria that were then mapped into a one-dimensional ordinal ranking of high, low and medium performance. These multiple criteria were: employment growth; return on capital employed; and labour productivity. It then demonstrated that statistical cluster analysis provides a convincing separation of a sample of new business starts into high, medium and low performing categories, using a minimum distance criterion for clustering.

An ordered logit model (with selection) will now be considered in this chapter and then estimated to explain this performance ranking, using data on small business strategies. The results of this estimation indicate that many widely discussed features of small business strategy (see Section 4, *Business strategy*, of AQ1, appendix to this book) have little, or even negative, impact on performance. For example, neither the construction of a business plan, nor having been financed by a grant or subsidy, appear to enhance performance.[2] Of the numerous aims that an owner-manager may adopt (survival, growth, long-term/short-term profit, etc.) only one appears to have a major positive impact upon performance, namely the narrowly economic one of the pursuit of the best rate of return on investment. Owner-managers' perceptions of their relative strengths (see Questions 4.16–4.18

of AQ1, appendix to this book) seem to indicate an immaturity of judgement, suggesting entrepreneurial learning is indeed important, close to business inception. The most realistic entrepreneurial perception seems to be of the organisational features and systems that have been created in the start-up business.

The overall empirical picture that emerges is that it is certainly possible to provide a coherent one-dimensional yardstick of 'business performance' despite its underlying multi-attribute qualities. However, few of the business strategies discussed in the literature were found to have a positive impact upon performance. In contrast, the economist's narrow criterion of seeking the best return on investment had a positive and significant impact on performance. This chapter develops these conclusions by: (a) discussing (briefly) the primary source data upon which the analysis is based; (b) considering how cluster analysis can be used to reduce a multi-attribute view of small business performance to a one-dimensional ordinal scale or ranking and (c) reporting on an ordered logit model (with selection adjustment) which is estimated to explain this derived ranking of businesses by performance.

10.2 The data

The questionnaire section on business strategy (see Section 4 of AQ1, this book's appendix on instrumentation) included planning, aims, decision-making, strategy formulation, financing, customer relations, trade intelligence, information technology and quality. A 'strengths, weaknesses, opportunities and threats' (SWOT) analysis, over dimensions like adaptability, foresight, product quality, specialist know-how and innovativeness, was undertaken using entrepreneurial responses (see Questions 4.16–4.18 of AQ1, appendix to this book). In the terminology of Sadler-Smith *et al.* (2003) these explore features like management behaviour and entrepreneurial style. Answers to questions were generally coded as real, binary $(0,1)$ or categorical $(1, 2, 3, \ldots)$ variables. This chapter largely uses the business strategy section for the construction of the ordered logit estimates, and Table 10.1 provides a listing of all the variables used in this chapter. Most of the variables' names are self-explanatory, but detailed definitions are given in the appendix to this chapter. The table provides means, standard deviations and the range (min, max) for attributes of the 150 firms in the sample. Some of the variables are binary or categorical variables. If the former, the mean can be taken as a percentage representative of this sample. Thus 70 per cent of the firms advertised (*Advert*), 32 per cent had a bank loan or overdraft (*Bankloan*), 73 per cent had received financial support in terms of a grant or subsidy (*FinGrnt*) at start-up and 5 per cent had outside equity participation (*OutsideEquity*). Most of the continuous real variables had distributions with a positive skew. This was true, for example, of size variables, like net fixed assets in year 1 (*Assets1*), and sales in year 1 (*Sales1*). Thus whilst mean net assets in year 1 were £18.8 thousand, the maximum value was £400 thousand; and whilst average sales in year 1 were £23.4 thousand, maximum sales were £9.6 million.

Table 10.1 Mean, standard deviation (SD) and range of each variable

Variable	Mean	SD (σ)	Min	Max
Advert	0.7	0.46	0	1
Age	20.79	15.97	0	132
Assets1	18759.24	42485.99	0	400000
Bankloan	0.32	0.47	0	1
Busplan	0.89	0.31	0	1
Employ1	6.4	14.70	1	157
Faith	2.69	0.59	0	3
FinGrnt	0.73	0.45	0	1
Ftime	2.8	6.44	0	46
Gearnow	168.94	388.27	0	2667
Gearst	157.53	334.50	0	1875
Grant	0.79	0.41	0	1
Grfixass	24478.7	45588.2	0	400000
Hrswk	57.85	18.38	0	126
Impact	15.47	18.97	0	120
AltUnemploy	0.26	0.44	0	1
GetRich	0.07	0.25	0	1
FamilyBus	0	0	0	0
ProfitHobby	0.09	0.28	0	1
BeOwnBoss	0.19	0.39	0	1
NeedAchieve	0.26	0.44	0	1
Inbusin	0.81	0.39	0	1
Innovativeness	2.25	0.86	0	3
ITemail	0.12	0.32	0	1
ITCell	0.42	0.50	0	1
AimSurvive	0.17	0.37	0	1
AimHighROR	0.09	0.28	0	1
Managers	1.19	1.27	0	3
Netprof1	13554.98	28879.37	−50000	151000
Organisation	1.59	1.06	0	3
OutsideEquity	0.05	0.23	0	1
Owncash	13013.81	29855.38	0	250000
Plant	1.79	1.01	0	3
Quality	2.79	0.57	0	3
Range	2.37	0.91	0	3
Sales1	233513.4	851644.3	0	9600000
SecondarySchool	4.75	1.14	2	7
SmallerProfits	0.89	0.31	0	1

In terms of general features[3] of the database (cf. Chapters 2 and 3), the firms examined were young (1.5 years), small (3 full-time employees), and operated in a local market. The full range of sectors by SIC was represented, running through from domestic services (99) to agriculture and horticulture (01). The best represented SICs were: 49, other manufacturing industries (9 per cent); 50, construction (9 per cent); 64–65, retail distribution (9 per cent); 83, business services

(15 per cent); and 96, other services provided to the general public (7 per cent). Thus the modal firm supplied a business service. In terms of the overall split between services (SIC 61-99) and extractive/manufacturers (SIC 01-50) the split is 55 per cent for the former and 45 per cent for the latter, which reflects the balance of services over manufactures in the macroeconomy.

The focus of this chapter is not on identifying individual strategies associated with the many varied sectors into which small firms fall. Indeed, such a task would be time-consuming and arguably futile. Instead, it aims to identify generic strategies which may be applied equally to any young micro-firm. This should prove more useful to policy makers, for example, who cannot afford the time or money required to create policies for each class and type of small firm but, instead, are looking to devise incentives and assistance that can apply to any new young business.

10.3   Explaining performance rank by business strategy

There are two alternatives one can take to explain performance rankings. The first is to devise some numerical measure which assigns a firm to a particular performance class, and then to seek to explain this measure (i.e. the position of a firm within a rank class) by a set of exogenous variables. The second is to seek to explain the rank class alone, implying a categorical dependent variable of the form $(0, 1, 2, \ldots)$.[4] The latter approach is preferred, and it is on this that the latter sections of the chapter are based. Whilst the split between high performing and medium/low performing firms is quite sharp and stable using cluster analysis, this is less so of the split between medium and low performers. The composition of firms within these bottom classes does vary slightly, given different cluster methods (e.g. by choice of metric) or different performance variables (e.g. ceasing/continuing trading). Furthermore, the ordering of cases (firms) given in the dendrogram of Table 9.1 (Chapter 9) is not necessarily directly mapped into a performance index.

For these reasons, the path of 'data reduction', pruning sample information for salience, is the preferred method of obtaining a better explanation of performance. An advantage of doing so is that the subsequent statistical analysis has a much stronger bearing on policy issues. In a policy context, a simple trichotomy of low, medium and high performance, which has evidently close links to other features of the firm's behaviour (as is evident from Table 9.2 of the previous chapter), and is robust under within-cluster ordering, is understandable, appealing, and non-controversial. It immediately invites the question: what explains which new start-up will become a low, medium or high performer? This chapter concludes by offering an answer to this question in terms of the business strategy adopted by the entrepreneur.

It is apparent that two of the performance measures, return on capital employed (*Profitability*) and employment growth (*EmploymentGrowth*) link time together in a meaningful way. This is a desirable property of a performance measure, introducing as it does a dynamic element. However, as it limits the potential sample size to those that survived into the second period,[5] the base period measure of performance, labour productivity (*Productivity*) allows us, with some adjustment, to construct performance ranks for all 150 firms. In performance evaluation it is also necessary to take into account the problem of selection bias (or, strictly speaking, statistical inconsistency) arising from the fact that the second period survivors are, in at least some senses, the better performers. This will be done in the next section.

10.3.1   Ordered logit model with sample selection

The statistical model appropriate to this combined set of problems, of an ordered dependent variable (performance) and selection bias (caused by survivor superiority), is the ordered logit model with sample selection.[6] Fundamental contributions to selectivity bias are Lee (1982, 1983); and influential papers on ordered logits are Beggs *et al.* (1981) and Becker and Kennedy (1992). This model has the following form: $z = \beta'x + \varepsilon$, where ε is unit normal, and z is not observed but rather y, which assumes the values 0, 1, 2 according to threshold intervals (determined by a parameter vector μ) within which the values of z lie. In the current context, the x are control variables measuring features of small business strategy (like the use of a business plan, and the decision-making time horizon); z ('true' performance) is unobserved, and y is our performance variable, *Perform*, which takes on values 0 for low performance, 1 for medium performance and 2 for high performance. This variable was derived in Chapter 9, using cluster analysis. Figure 9.1 and Table 9.1 show the separation of data that enabled the *Perform* variable to be constructed. As only some firms survive, and they may be better performers, to this is added a selection mechanism of the form $w_i^* = \alpha'x_{i2} + u_i$ where the cumulative distribution of u_i is logistical and $w_i = 1$ if $w_i^* > 0$, and zero otherwise, this being a univariate logit model. To complete the statistical specification, y_i is assumed to be observed if, and only if, $w_i = 1$; that is, only the performance rank is known of the survivors. The joint distribution of ε and u is assumed to be bivariate standard logistic (mean 0, standard deviation 1.81 approx.) with correlation coefficient ρ. The model is estimated by starting with a first-stage logit model, to estimate and hold a correction term, and then the ordered logit is estimated with the selectivity correction included. Final round estimation is by full information maximum likelihood (FIML) using the Davidon–Fletcher–Powell algorithm.[7] The selection model is estimated first by ordinary least squares and then by maximum likelihood. The ordered logit is estimated first as though there were no selection, to generate initialising values, and then by full information maximum likelihood, jointly estimating α, β, ρ and the threshold parameter μ. Examples of such estimates are given in Tables 10.2 and 10.3. The coefficients are reported along with standard errors, standard normal values, and probability values. As the dependent variable *Perform* is defined as $y = 0, 1, 2$ and the lowest threshold value μ_0 is defined as zero, only one threshold parameter (μ) is to be estimated. The log likelihood for the full model is reported in each table, as is the error correlation.

Table 10.2 Ordered logit model with selection (*n* = 150)

Variable	Coeff. (b)	Std. Error (se)	b/se	Prob.
Ordered Logit				
Constant	0.41368E-01	1.5086	0.027	0.97812
Busplan	−0.82729	0.40280	−2.054	0.03999
Impact	0.96481E-02	0.45009E-02	2.144	0.03206
AltUnemploy	−1.3081	0.40940	−3.195	0.00140
GetRich	0.22035	0.47235	0.467	0.64085
ProfitHobby	−1.6967	0.59333	−2.860	0.00424
BeOwnBoss	−1.9715	0.46816	−4.211	0.00003
NeedAchieve	−1.3539	0.39373	−3.439	0.00058
AimSurvive	−1.1290	0.42561	−2.653	0.00798
AimHighROR	1.2705	0.34945	3.636	0.00028
Fingrnt	0.36754	0.32914	1.117	0.26414
SmallerProfits	0.98041	0.69650	1.408	0.15925
ITemail	−0.15094	0.20665	−0.730	0.46513
ITcell	0.15086	0.20661	0.730	0.46530
Faith	0.39466	0.31192	1.265	0.20578
Plant	−0.36002	0.12260	−2.937	0.00332
Managers	0.80463E-02	0.11829	0.068	0.94577
Quality	0.18678	0.26305	0.710	0.47768
Range	−0.13955	0.12835	−1.087	0.27692
Organisation	0.29753	0.11829	2.515	0.01189
Innovativeness	−0.36497	0.15692	−2.326	0.02003
MU(1)	2.7273	0.30181	9.036	0.00000
Selection Equation				
Constant	0.45135	1.0637	0.424	0.67133
Impact	0.13260E-02	0.70614E-03	1.878	0.06040
AltUnemploy	−0.50580	0.34614	−1.461	0.14395
NeedAchieve	−0.52743	0.40211	−1.312	0.18963
Ftime	−0.16465E-01	0.71123E-01	−0.231	0.81693
Grsales	0.39356E-06	0.17394E-05	0.226	0.82100
Advert	0.78525	0.31897	2.462	0.01382
Bankloan	−0.37208	0.39021	−0.954	0.34032
Grant	−0.26904	0.41145	−0.654	0.51319
Gearnow	−0.14561E-03	0.34190E-03	−0.426	0.67019
Grfixass	0.10805E-04	0.98901E-05	1.092	0.27463
SecondarySchool	0.77153E-01	0.15526	0.497	0.61923
Hrswk	0.57155E-03	0.12570E-01	0.045	0.96373
Rho(1,2)	−0.15090E-06	0.92539	0.000	0.00000

Note: Log likelihood function = −165.5986.

10.3.2   The performance-strategy relationship

Turning now to the substantive content of the model, the main body of evidence drawn upon for explaining performance was the business strategy section (Section 4) of the administered questionnaire (AQ1) discussed in Section 10.2. This part of the questionnaire aimed to take the earlier approach to small business

Table 10.3 Parsimonious ordered logit model with selection ($n = 150$)

Variable	Coeff. (b)	Std. Error (se)	b/se	Prob.
Ordered Logit				
Constant	2.4267	0.76156	3.186	0.00144
Busplan	−0.66290	0.35691	−1.857	0.06327
Impact	0.99201E-02	0.42364E-02	2.342	0.01920
AltUnemploy	−1.3208	0.32734	−4.035	0.00005
ProfitHobby	−1.7575	0.43364	−4.053	0.00005
BeOwnBoss	−2.0150	0.37167	−5.422	0.00000
NeedAchieve	−1.2842	0.34368	−3.737	0.00019
AimSurvive	−1.1881	0.34517	−3.442	0.00058
AimHighROR	1.2002	0.30482	3.938	0.00008
Plant	−0.38198	0.10073	−3.792	0.00015
Range	−0.14674	0.11766	−1.247	0.21235
Organisation	0.34625	0.11485	3.015	0.00257
Innovativeness	−0.24169	0.13201	−1.831	0.06713
MU(1)	2.6676	0.23862	11.179	0.00000
Selection Equation				
Constant	0.45135	1.0552	0.428	0.66883
Impact	0.13260E-02	0.70595E-03	1.878	0.06033
AltUnemploy	−0.50580	0.34270	−1.476	0.13996
NeedAchieve	−0.52743	0.39720	−1.328	0.18422
Ftime	−0.16465E-01	0.70601E-01	−0.233	0.81560
Grsales	0.39125E-06	0.16894E-05	0.232	0.81685
Advert	0.78528	0.31500	2.493	0.01267
Bankloan	−0.37208	0.38009	−0.979	0.32762
Grant	−0.26904	0.40172	−0.670	0.50304
Gearnow	0.14561E-03	0.33954E-03	−0.429	0.66803
Grfixass	0.10803E-04	0.90861E-05	1.189	0.23447
SecondarySchool	0.77153E-01	0.15462	0.499	0.61780
Hrswk	0.57155E-03	0.12354E-01	0.046	0.96310
Rho(1,2)	−0.12697E-08	0.81618	0.000	0.00000

Note: Log likelihood function = −168.7156.

strategy in Reid *et al.* (1993) a stage further, as reflected, for example, in the work of Smith (1998). In general, data were available for all of the 150 firms in the base period for explaining subsequent performance over the next period. The method adopted is explicitly econometric, but has its roots in the three rules about 'necessary connection' [see Hume (1739) *A Treatise of Human Nature*]. These are that: cause and effect must be contiguous in time and space; cause must be prior to effect; and there must be a constant conjunction between cause and effect.

A first interest was in the role of business plans. The owner-managers had been asked whether they had a business plan (*BusPlan*). It was found that 89 per cent did have, and that, of these, 79 per cent had a formal, written plan. However, business plans are no longer a filter of ability [see Yusuf and Saffu (2005), for example], as perhaps they were in an earlier policy era of enterprise stimulation, and their construction now often assumes merely ritual status. Furthermore, modern theories of business strategy (cf. Mintzberg, 1987, 1994) emphasise factors like flair, imagination, drive and leadership just as much as formal plans, so this is a variable of interest. More important than the plan itself is the impact it may have in the future. Entrepreneurs were asked how far they looked ahead in evaluating the impact that planned decisions might have (see Q.4.2 in AQ1 of appendix to this book). It was found that this *Impact* variable had a surprisingly long mean value of 15.5 months; a much longer time than is suggested by some academic work,[8] and by policy critiques of independent businessmen, emphasising their supposed tendency to 'short-termism'. Why this *Impact* variable should be longer than expected intrigued us, and led us to seek and determine its consequences for performance. Furthermore, it led to the interest in long-lived small firms, reflected in the content of Chapter 18.

Formal theories of entrepreneurship like Blanchflower and Oswald (1990), emphasise rational goals for establishing a new business, which may go beyond pecuniary considerations to a desire for autonomy or control. Therefore an *Involve* variable was created in the questionnaire (see Q.4.3 in Section 4, *Business Strategy*, of the AQ1 in the appendix to this book), which was based on responses to a question which asked the entrepreneur for his or her *main* reason for becoming involved in the business, as follows: (a) as an alternative to unemployment; (b) to get rich; (c) to take over the family business; (d) to profit from a hobby; (e) to be your own boss; (f) to satisfy the need for achievement; (g) to exploit a new market opportunity; and (h) something else. Unfortunately, only 11 per cent said to exploit a new market opportunity and just 6 per cent said to get rich, so the variables *NewOpportunity* and *GetRich* had limited statistical leverage in the sample. The modal choices were as an alternative to unemployment (25 per cent) (*AltUnemploy*) and to satisfy the need for achievement (25 per cent) (*NeedAchieve*). These are commonly expressed, and widely discussed reasons for small business involvement, especially in a relative performance framework. Here, enquiry into the consequences of these motives is now pursued with an objective, absolute performance framework.

In a similar fashion, the entrepreneur was asked for the main single aim of his or her business (see Q.4.4 in the AQ1 of this book's appendix) from the following list: (a) survival; (b) short-term profit; (c) long-term profit; (d) growth; (e) increased sales; (f) increased market share; (g) high rate of return; and (h) other. The modal response for this *Mainaim* variable, which was intended to cast light on managerial theories of the firm as applied to small business enterprises, was long-term profit (30 per cent) (*LongTermProfit*), followed by growth (20 per cent) (*Growth*). Short-term profit (*ShortTermProfit*) was rarely nominated (1 per cent), perhaps not surprisingly, given the doubt already cast on a short-termist view of small business management; but one wonders why high rate of return (*AimHighROR*) was infrequently nominated (8 per cent), and sought to determine just how important this strictly pecuniary aim might be for performance. The results of this enquiry are recorded in Tables 10.2 and 10.3 above.

Given the finding in Table 9.2 of the previous chapter, that high performers apparently had lower grant involvement at inception than lower performers, interest was aroused in more formally testing the significance of the *FinGrnt* variable, which was based on a question which asked whether the firm had previously been financed by a grant or subsidy.[9] As evidence for a growth/profitability trade-off exists, even for small firms,[10] entrepreneurs were asked whether they were willing to accept smaller profits for a while, in order to expand the business (*SmallerProfits* variable). In view of a number of research initiatives into the role of IT in small business management (e.g. Buick, 2003), interest focussed on whether or not its use had led to objective, absolute performance enhancement. Given the emerging importance of the Internet, it was important to examine the impact of email (*ITemail*); and the abundant evidence on increasing use of the cellular telephone (not all of it edifying) led to questions about what performance advantage, if any, it was bestowing on owner-managers (*ITCell*).

Finally, in the context of a SWOT analysis (cf. Johnson and Scholes, 1993, Ch. 4), the questionnaire (AQ1) enquired into the impact that certain self-rated attributes of the business had on performance, including: faith in the business (*Faith*); plant and resources (*Plant*); managers (*Managers*); product quality (*Quality*); product range (*Range*); organisational structure/systems (*Organisation*); and innovativeness/new ideas (*Innovativeness*). It is apparent from theories of entrepreneurship that emphasise the role of market-place experience (cf. Jovanovic, 1982; Frank, 1988), especially shortly after inception, that it should not necessarily be assumed that self-rating by entrepreneurs were accurate or insightful in the early stages of the life-cycle [cf. Hamilton and Fox (1998) on misperceptions of capital structure by entrepreneurs in New Zealand].

10.4   The estimates

Above 20 or so variables have been considered for inclusion as control variables in an ordered probit. They were chosen because of their interest from a theoretical or empirical standpoint. However, they are but a small subset of the business strategy variables available to this study, so the approach here is selective, rather than comprehensive. The specification of the selection equation was based partly on the familiarity with these strategy variables [see Verhees and Meulenberg (2004), Sadler-Smith *et al.* (2003), Zimmerman *et al.* (2002), Hankinson (2000), Chaston (1997) and Acar (1993)], but also on previous experience (Reid, 1999a) in estimating models of small firm survival.

Consider now Table 10.2 which provides estimates, based on an ordered logit model with selection, of the impact of business strategy variables of the sort discussed earlier on the performance variables (*Perform*). The model is run on a sample size of 150 firms. Typically, all 122 surviving firms made complete returns on data, and at least a partial performance indicator is available for the rest. For specific models which were run, sample sizes varied just slightly because of omissions in a small number of responses. The ordered logit is the key relationship here, being a type of performance equation. It has a first pass R^2 of 0.21, with a probability value of 0.04.

As in previous work (cf. Reid, 1999a) it was found in the selection equation that advertising and forward planning had a major positive impact on small business survival. As regards the ordered logit itself, the use of a business plan (*BusPlan*) seems associated with poor performance, but forward planning (*Impact*) appears to enhance performance, reinforcing the conclusion suggested by the selection equation. The latter is related to the result of Chapter 7 (Table 7.4) which finds that time spent on planning (*Timplan*) correlates highly with business survival. The result also reinforces the finding of Chapter 7 (Table 7.1) that those small firms that continued training had much longer forward planning horizons (16.4 months) than those that did not (11.1 months). The clear conclusion is that merely writing a business plan now has little implication for performance. What counts is how you use that plan to look ahead, which may involve modifying actions.[11]

Most of the reasons, largely not market-driven, for getting involved in business have negative impacts on performance, and those that are likely to have a positive effect, like *GetRich* (to get rich), turn out to have too few sample observations and, for lack of degrees of freedom, seem not to be statistically significant. If the entrepreneur aims merely to survive (*AimSurvive*), this has a negative effect upon performance, whereas if he aims to make a high rate of return (*AimHighROR*), this has a significant and positive effect upon his performance. The financial grant (*FinGrnt*) and profit trade-off (*SmallerProfits*) variables are insignificant, as are the IT variables (*Itemail*, *ITCell*). The self-assessed capabilities variables were insignificant in four out of seven cases, *Faith*, *Managers*, *Quality*, *Range*. The next results suggest that hubris plays a role in forming the judgements that entrepreneurs make about their own plant and resources (*Plant*), and their innovativeness (*Innovativeness*). Thus very positive self-appraisals do not seem to translate into performance advantage, with the coefficients of these variables being *negative* and significant. However, entrepreneurs have a more accurate sense of the value of their organisation and system (*Organisation*) in delivering good performance, and this variable's coefficient is positive and highly significant (Prob. = 0.01).

Table 10.3 presents a more parsimonious ordered logit model that does not modify any of the empirical conclusions drawn from Table 10.2, but does slightly sharpen up the picture as regards statistical significance. The selection equation is very close to that in Table 10.2, and bears the same interpretation. In both sets of results the performance and selection equations appear to have uncorrelated errors. Whilst this suggests caution in the use of a selection equation to correct possible bias, it was thought to be useful to report results in this form, as a reassurance that potential biases have been taken care of, allowing a confident interpretation of the performance equation. A likelihood ratio test applied to a comparison of the model in Table 10.2 with that in Table 10.3 produces a χ^2 statistic of 6.234, which is considerably less than the relevant $\chi^2_{0.05}(8)$ significance point of 15.5. By implication, the preferred specification is the parsimonious model of Table 10.3.

10.5   Conclusion

To use a classical phrase of Binks and Coynes (1983), the general concern of this chapter is with 'the birth of enterprise'. Its principal aim was to estimate a model that explains the contribution that is made to performance after start-up by various elements of business strategy.

The use of cluster analysis in Chapter 9 enabled the investigation to use three performance indicators to rank firms into low, medium and high performance categories. A statistical explanation of the ranking categories was then undertaken in this chapter, using an ordered logit model with sample selection. The estimates suggested the importance of two factors, in particular, for performance: long-range planning (rather than plan formalism); and the pursuit of pecuniary goals (rather than lifestyle goals). With the exception of one operational area (namely organisation and systems), estimates cast doubt on the quality of the inexperienced entrepreneur's judgements about the efficacy of his or her own small firm. Estimates suggest that entrepreneurs may adopt 'wrong' reasons for starting up in business, and can be prone to poor self-appraisal. The better performing entrepreneurs are those who initially make realistic appraisals of their abilities. They do not exaggerate their strengths and opportunities, nor do they underestimate their threats and weaknesses (Smith, 1998).

APPENDIX

Definition of variables

Advert	=1 if the firm advertises, =0 otherwise
Age	age of the firm at first interview, in months
Assets1	value (£) of net fixed assets in year 1
Assets2	value (£) of net fixed assets in year 2
Bankloan	=1 if firm has a bank loan or overdraft, =0 otherwise
Busplan	=1 if the firm has a business plan, =0 otherwise
Employ1	total number of employees in year 1
Employ2	total number of employees in year 2
Faith	how respondent rates firm in terms of faith in the business; =0 (not applicable); =1 (could be better); =2 (fair); =3 (good)
FinGrnt	=1 if grant or subsidy has been received, =0 otherwise
Ftime	number of full-time employees
Gearnow	=gearing (debt/equity × 100 per cent) at time of first interview
Gearst	=gearing (debt/equity × 100 per cent) at start-up
Grant	=1 if firm received a grant at start-up, =0 otherwise
Grfixass	gross value of fixed assets
Hrswk	number of hours a week entrepreneur devotes to the business
Impact	number of months firm looks ahead when evaluating impact of decisions

Continued

Definition of variables—cont'd

AltUnemploy	=1 if involved in business as alternative to unemployment, =0 otherwise
GetRich	=1 if involved in business to get rich, =0 otherwise
FamilyBus	=1 if respondent took over family business, =0 otherwise
ProfitHobby	=1 if involved in business to profit from hobby, =0 otherwise
BeOwnBoss	=1 if involved in business to be own boss, =0 otherwise
NeedAchieve	=1 if involved in business to satisfy need for achievement, =0 otherwise
NewOpportunity	=1 if involved in business to exploit a new market opportunity, =0 otherwise
Inbusin	=1 if the firm is in business in year 2, =0 otherwise
Innovativeness	how respondent rates the firm's innovativeness/ new ideas; =0 (not applicable); =1 (could be better); =2 (fair); =3 (good)
ITemail	=1 if firm uses electronic mail, =0 otherwise
ITCell	=1 if firm uses cellular/mobile phone, =0 otherwise
AimSurvive	=1 if main aim of the business is survival, =0 otherwise
AimHighROR	=1 if main aim of the business is high rate of return, =0 otherwise
Managers	how respondent rates managers in the firm; =0 (not applicable); =1 (could be better); =2 (fair); =3 (good)
Netprof1	net profit (£) in year 1
Netprof2	net profit (£) in year 2
Organisation	how respondent rates the organisation's structure and/or systems; =0 (not applicable); =1 (could be better); =2 (fair); =3 (good)
OutsideEquity	=1 if firm has outside equity investment, =0 otherwise
Owncash	value (£) of owner-manager's cash injection at start
Plant	how respondent rates the firm's plant and resources; =0 (not applicable); =1 (could be better); =2 (fair); =3 (good)
Quality	how respondent rates firm's quality of product/service; =0 (not applicable); =1 (could be better); =2 (fair); =3 (good)
Range	how firm rates firm's product/service range; =0 (not applicable); =1 (could be better); =2 (fair); =3 (good)
Sales1	value (£) of turnover in year 1
Sales2	value (£) of turnover in year 2
SecondarySchool	number of years respondent spent at secondary school
SmallerProfits	=1 if respondent willing to accept smaller profits to help business expand, =0 otherwise

Endnotes

1 See, Hamilton and Fox (1998) who point to unrealistic expectations of deals involving financial structure in New Zealand small firms.
2 These points have already been observed in earlier chapters, e.g. Chapter 3 (Table 3.2) and Chapter 7 (Table 7.3) on insignificant (or ineffective) role of grants.
3 Averages are given in brackets.
4 The aim in these two cases is to get an explicit statistical measure of rank, based on a set of determining qualitative judgements by entrepreneurs, possibly against benchmark cases, as in Zimmerman *et al.* (2002). Chapter 18 moves more towards this position.
5 This is not true of the data reported in Section 10.3, for which nominal second period values (e.g. employment of zero) were imputed to non-survivors for the second year, in order to have complete performance measures for all the 150 firms that initially started.
6 These problems are discussed, separately, in Chapters 21 and 22 respectively of Greene (1993). So far as is known, there is no theoretical discussion in the extant journal literature of the combined occurrence of these problems, although the appropriate software for undertaking this is discussed in the Limdep manual.
7 Estimation was undertaken using *Limdep7* software. The 'ordered probit' command is used (Greene, 1992, pp. 527–9). This is run in the logit variant by adding the 'logit' command. Sample selection is achieved with the 'select' command (Greene, 1992, Ch. 45).
8 For example, the paper presented by Cressy (1995) to the 'Risk in Organisational Settings' conference at the White House, London, 16–17 May 1995. Based on a bank loans database, it was suggested that planning time horizons were typically as short as 1 month.
9 Evidence on grants has so far been equivocal. See, for example, Table 3.2 of Chapter 3, *Grant* variable. Also see Table 7.4, where *Grant* is insignificant in a binary probit.
10 See Reid (1993), based on an earlier sample of Scottish firms.
11 See Johnson and Scholes (1993, Ch. 3) on ways of understanding and dealing with the future in a business strategy context.

11 Actions and outcomes

11.1 Introduction

In this chapter, the entrepreneur within the new small firm is regarded as taking complex rather than simple actions, which determine whether he or she will remain in business. Thus instead of simply choosing output, as in the standard analysis of the competitive firm, the entrepreneur may take actions which involve choices about markets, finance, organisation, innovation and much else besides (cf. Acar, 1993; Chaston, 1997; Verhees and Meulenberg, 2004; Yusuf and Saffu, 2005; Sadler-Smith *et al.*, 2003; Hankinson, 2000). To explore this approach, very detailed information on actions within the small firm is required. This chapter shows how this was deployed.

A rich statistical picture is created of actions within the new small firm (Hankinson, 2000; Acar, 1993). In turn, this permits econometric analysis of actions that help a new small firm to stay in business; in this case, over a 3-year period. The evidence indicates that the crucial actions which enable a small firm to stay in business are: rapid retiral of debt (cf. Chapter 8); and a willingness to sacrifice short-run profit for growth. There is also evidence that staying in business is fostered by tight control of the wage bill, especially by substituting other labour inputs for full-time employees (cf. Chapter 5).

When Alfred Lord Tennyson wrote[1] 'It surely was my profit had I known', he was describing in poetry what the market achieves quite naturally. Whether or not entrepreneurs are conscious of it, by the actions they undertake to make their small firms more competitive, they participate in a selection process which favours the survival of those firms which achieve superior performance. Conventionally, economists have tended to think of such entrepreneurs as having few actions at their disposal to achieve good competitive performance. In fact, the competitive firm faces many action possibilities, extending well beyond output, location, advertising, etc. For example, it has many possible actions which can be taken as regards both financial structure (e.g. Chapters 7 and 8), and the composition of its workforce (e.g. Chapter 5 and this chapter).

This chapter examines evidence on the complex set of actions which entrepreneurs may undertake. These complex actions are classified under the headings of markets, costs, strategy, finance, organisation, human capital and innovation (see AQ1 in appendix to this book). The outcome of these complex actions is simple; the new start-up either folds or remains in business. An econometric analysis of the probability of staying in business over a 3-year period, depending on the actions of entrepreneurs, was undertaken. This produced three results of particular note. First, using a bank loan or overdraft was detrimental to staying in business. This accords with theoretical views of small firm financial structure which emphasise the importance of rapid debt retiral (Hilten *et al.*, 1993), and low gearing (Reid, 1991), for staying in business. Second, the attitudes adopted towards running the business are important. If the entrepreneur treats the business as simply an alternative to unemployment, or uses it to fulfil personal dreams, like getting rich quick, being one's own boss, etc., survival prospects are diminished. However, if the entrepreneur is willing to sacrifice profit initially in order to 'grow' the firm, it is much more likely to stay in business. Third, the structure of employment within the new small firm is important. On a headcount basis, larger small firms have better survival prospects than smaller small firms, which is associated with a reduction in full-time employees and tighter control of the wage bill (see also results in Chapter 5, Table 5.4, emphasising control of the wage bill for survival of the small firm). There is also a hint that early innovation is generally not important in the inception stage of the lifecycle of the new small firm. Arguably the firm is itself 'the innovative event'; and precipitate further innovation reduces prospects for staying in business.

11.2   Background

Small, competitive enterprises are the lifeblood of any economy with a significant market mediated sector. According to figures supplied by the Department of Trade and Industry (DTI) over the relevant sample period, 99 per cent of businesses in the UK economy (barring the sector for electricity, gas and water) were small to medium-sized enterprises (SMEs), defined as businesses which employed 250 or fewer employees. Of these, many were very small. Indeed, in the United Kingdom during the sample period, of the 3.7 million active businesses, over 2.5 million were sole traders or partners without employees. As well as being the embodiment of competitiveness (cf. Newbert, 2005; Reynolds *et al.*, 2004; Mitra, 2003; Furrukh and Urata, 2002 for a range of national contexts) – through their lack of market power and exposure to rivalry – these small firms are important as vectors of change and innovation, according to the 'new learning' of industrial organisation (Acs and Audretsch, 1993). Yet knowledge of their functioning, especially at the bottom or 'micro-firm' end of the size distribution of firms, is rather scant, particularly if a broad theoretical perspective is taken of their *modus operandi*.

An insightful view of the entrepreneur's actions within the small firm, in general, is that he or she can be taken to engage in a variety of *activities* which generate private benefits and costs. In analysing the literature which distinguishes the entrepreneur from a mere small business manager, Rispas (1998, p. 113) concludes that the key question is: 'What kinds of activities does the entrepreneur perform?' Unfortunately, if such activity were viewed only in the most traditional framework, it would involve no more than the selection of outputs. But, departing from this traditional perspective and viewing the small firm more generally, the activities of entrepreneurs involve a complex of choices: of location (in both physical and characteristics space), production, inventory, hiring, advertising, business strategy, innovation, financial structure and so on. If actions a_i define a vector of actions $\mathbf{a}$ which are chosen from a wide action set $\mathbf{A}$, $\mathbf{a} \in \mathbf{A}$, and the corresponding revenues and costs are $R(\mathbf{a})$ and $C(\mathbf{a})$, then in a static setting the small firm can be thought of as maximising the concave profit (π) function

$$\pi(\mathbf{a}) = R(\mathbf{a}) - C(\mathbf{a}) \tag{11.1}$$

over $\mathbf{a} \in \mathbf{A}$ (Varian, 1992). From optimality theory, this implies a set of Kuhn–Tucker conditions

$$R'(\mathbf{a}) - C'(\mathbf{a}) \leq 0 \quad \text{for all } a_i \geq 0 \tag{11.2}$$

which have both familiar and less familiar interpretations. Familiar conditions include setting the marginal cost of a positive output equal to its corresponding marginal revenue or setting the ratio of marginal physical products to the factor price ratio (see Chapter 6, Section 6.2); and less familiar conditions, extending the purview to a financial theory of the firm, include setting the marginal value productivity of money capital equal to the capitalised value of the full marginal cost of borrowing (Vickers, 1987, Ch. 4). As indicated in Chapter 6 (Section 6.3), this approach can be extended to a dynamic framework for which the maximand is an integral over an intertemporal profit function, subject to side constraints. This defines best *trajectories* of actions rather than best *points* of action, as in Hilten *et al.* (1993). Despite the scope for thus creating an increasingly general view of the small competitive enterprise, an abiding consideration for long-term survival is that $\pi(\mathbf{a}^*) \geq 0$, i.e. the non-negativity of profits, generated by whatever set of chosen actions $\mathbf{a}^*$, no matter how complex their form.

This chapter combines a view of the complex of actions that an entrepreneur within a small firm can take, embracing markets, costs, finance, strategy, human capital, organisation and technical change, with this simple criterion of long-run survival, $\pi \geq 0$. This complex view of the small firm's operations is possible because of the close empirical detail available on 150 new small businesses using fieldwork methods (Chapter 2). These firms were then tracked over a period of 3 years (Chapter 3), and their withdrawal from the market was noted as a violation of the simple condition $\pi \geq 0$. In this way, mapping from profit to the binary outcome of survival or non-survival, an econometric model of the consequences of a complex of actions on survival probability can be estimated. What is being done here is to examine survival itself, as the key focus, rather than using (as in Chapter 10) the survival estimates as statistical corrections for a performance equation.

Table 11.1 provides summary statistics on that part of the database used in this chapter. The variables represented in this table are those that figure prominently in the econometric analysis of this chapter. Variables are defined in the appendix to this chapter, but are often self-explanatory. To illustrate what kind of detail Table 11.1 is conveying by reference to financial data, only one-third of the firms

Table 11.1 Summary statistics for key variables

Variable[a]	N	$\bar{x}$	σ	(min, max)
Bankloan	149	0.322	0.467	(0,1)
Busplan	150	0.893	0.310	(0,1)
Colluni	149	0.752	0.434	(0,1)
Debt	150	0.507	0.502	(0,1)
Employ[b]	150	6.400	14.70	(1,157)
Ftime	150	2.800	6.435	(0,46)
Hrswk	150	57.85	18.38	(0,126)
Impact	148	15.47	18.97	(0,120)
Inbus	150	20.79	15.97	(0,132)
InvolveA	150	0.260	0.440	(0,1)
InvolveB	150	0.067	0.250	(0,1)
InvolveE	150	0.187	0.391	(0,1)
InvolveF	150	0.260	0.440	(0,1)
LegbusA	150	0.26	0.440	(0,1)
LegbusB	150	0.29	0.454	(0,1)
LegbusC	150	0.187	0.391	(0,1)
MainaimA	150	0.167	0.374	(0,1)
MainaimG	150	0.087	0.282	(0,1)
NewtechA	150	0.533	0.501	(0,1)
NewtechD	150	0.373	0.485	(0,1)
Owncash	150	13014	29860	$(0, 0.25 \times 10^6)$
Prodgrp	150	4.313	3.890	(1,30)
Product[c]	150	46.57	88.08	(0,999)
Procinn	150	1.387	1.110	(0,3)
Prodinn	150	1.0733	1.118	(0,4)
PtFt	150	1.114	1.267	(0.021,9)
Secschl	150	4.747	1.142	(2,7)
SmlProf	149	0.893	0.311	(0,1)
Timman	150	15.54	16.667	(0,100)
Timprod	150	40.69	31.16	(0,100)
Wages	148	24.91	24.58	(0,90)

Notes:
a Each row gives the variable name used for analysis in the text, along with its mean, standard deviation, and minimum and maximum values. Variables are fully defined in the appendix.
b Just one firm accounts for the large maximum on the employment variable. This was a cleansing firm that coordinated a large number of unskilled workers, who were listed as available for work, to undertake daily contract cleaning in commercial premises like shops and factories. The mean employment size was just six.
c The upper range on product variety, if this was described as 'very large' or 'huge', etc. was set at 999.

had used bank loans to launch the business, and the typical entrepreneur had put in as much as £13k at launch. These figures tend to suggest a good quality of business start, in that typically entrepreneurs are sufficiently confident in their project qualities to allocate considerable personal resources to their success, and do not wish to increase risk exposure, or to incur debt servicing costs, by taking on loans too early in the life-cycle of the small firm. Most entrepreneurs (89 per cent) were willing to foster growth (*Smlprof*) at the expense of short-run profit.

There were twice as many entrepreneurs (17 per cent) who just aimed to survive (*MainaimA*), rather than to maximise their rate of return (*MainaimG*) (9 per cent). That is, the achieving of the condition $\pi \geq 0$ was more important than the maximisation of π/K, where the latter is equivalent to maximising π if K (capital), is constant in the short run. The preference for the former motive is also emphasised by the willingness of entrepreneurs to sacrifice some profits for the sake of growth (cf. Chapter 4 on the small firm's growth-profitability trade-off). However, none of this is inconsistent with long-run profit maximisation. Indeed, long-run profit (*MainaimC*), not shown in Table 11.1, was the most commonly nominated business aim (30 per cent), though it did not prove significant in the econometric analysis.

In terms of technical change, most firms had typically not adopted new technologies since start-up (*NewtechA* = 53 per cent), though a significant minority had done so successfully (*NewtechD* = 37 per cent). Product and process innovation (*Prodinn*, *Procinn*) were not undertaken to a great extent. This should not be taken to suggest that innovation is unimportant to small firms, for this would fly in the face of evidence previously cited, like Acs and Audretsch (1993). Rather, it suggests that the innovation, if such it be, occurred *at or in the launch* of the business itself; and that, for these very young small firms, with an average age in business of 21 months, no further scope for innovation was subsequently perceived to exist in the period shortly after inception. In this sense, the so-called 'entrepreneurial event' of business inception should also be regarded as a cardinal 'innovative event'.

In terms of human capital, both as regards its quality and application, Table 11.1 provides some insight into its role in small firm activity. Most entrepreneurs (75 per cent) had college, or university qualifications (*College*); and the average number of years of high school education was nearly five (*School*). However, the hours worked were long, at 58 hours per week. Furthermore, much of this time (41 h) was devoted to the product (*Timprod*) rather than to management (*Timman*) (just 16 h). Thus the entrepreneurs, whilst being relatively well educated, displayed attributes of what are sometimes called 'artisan entrepreneurs'. Such entrepreneurs, by their actions, tend to give primacy to supply of the commodity rather than to its fitness to fulfil a customer need. They tend to spend long days at the workplace, and devote more attention to process than to purpose. One would expect learning in the market place to modify this aspect of entrepreneurial behaviour, along lines suggested by Jovanovic (1982), Frank (1988) and others.

11.3 Determinants of survival

Previous analysis (e.g. Chapter 3) has shown how many features of small businesses are subject to change, even marked change, over short periods like three years. However, the interpretation of such features as part of the complex of actions which entrepreneurs may undertake, and the consideration of their consequences for staying in business, have yet to be considered. This section aims to remedy this deficiency by giving more formal expression to the relationship between the complex of actions an entrepreneur may take in a new small business and its probability of staying in business over a period of 3 years. The data on actions open to the entrepreneur relate to 1994–95, and were acquired in the first year of the study. The data on survival relate to the period 1996–97, the third year of the study.

For estimation purposes, a probit model is used (cf. Chapters 5 and 7), of the form $I = \mathbf{X}\boldsymbol{\beta}$, where I is an index of survival, equal to unity if the firm stays in business and to zero if the firm goes out of business (cf. the selection equation of Table 10.2 in the previous chapter). Statistically, the set of actions which entrepreneurs may take, $\mathbf{X}$, is a set of control variables, and $\boldsymbol{\beta}$ a set of estimated parameters. Estimation is by maximum likelihood and was performed using *Shazam* software. For the estimation method, which makes use of the Newton–Raphson iterative method, see Greene (1993, pp. 643–647). The coding used in the *Shazam* routine is due to John Cragg. For a tolerance limit of 0.001, convergence usually occurs in five or so iterations. The estimates are reported in a form which provides summary statistics, estimated coefficients, asymptotic t-ratios and weighted aggregate elasticities. For the computation of weighted elasticities, see Hencher and Johnson (1981, pp. 59–63). The Hencher–Johnson elasticities, rather than the estimated coefficients, or even elasticities at the mean, give the appropriate measure of the responsiveness of the survival probability to exogenous variation in any of the control variables. For example, if the headcount of the workforce (*Employ*) had a significant positive effect on the probability of survival of small business over a 3-year period, and the associated weighted aggregate elasticity were +0.2, this would mean that a 10 per cent increase in headcount, *ceteris paribus*, would increase the survival probability by 2 per cent.

Table 11.2 reports on a probit model for a wide set of control variables, 31 in number, including those concerned with financial structure, wages and employment, markets, motivation, business form and innovation. The overall fit of the probit is satisfactory, as judged by the Cragg–Uhler R^2 of 0.51, which is high for cross section models of this sort. A likelihood ratio test of the null hypothesis that all the elements of the $\boldsymbol{\beta}$ vector are zero produces a test statistic of 54.8, which exceeds the $\chi^2_{0.01}(31)$ critical value of 50.9, thus rejecting the null hypothesis. It is therefore appropriate to proceed to discuss the estimated coefficients.

A number of the variables in $\mathbf{X}$ have been examined earlier, in Chapter 3, which explores how attributes of the sample of small firms have varied over a 3-year time period. Of note in the estimates reported in Table 11.2 are the following. Having had a bank loan (*Bankloan*) has a significant negative effect upon the probability of survival. This is a result which Storey's (1994) notable analysis of new firm growth and bank financing was unable to derive from such data as were at his disposal. The reasons for this different result here appear to be that, on the one hand, a bank loan requires debt servicing, which entails both cost and risk; and on the other hand relatively inferior projects which fail to attract equity (e.g. from an informal investor or 'business angel'), because they lack promise as investment propositions, may end up being financed by a bank loan. However, the effect, whilst significant, has a relatively small elasticity (of just −0.09). Considering other financial variables, neither the use of debt finance (*Debt*) nor the level of

Table 11.2 Probit for full set of control variables

Variable	Coefficient	t-ratio	Weighted elasticity
Bankloan	-1.119	-2.301**	-0.946×10^{-1}
Inbus	0.330×10^{-1}	1.821*	0.133
Ptft	-0.816×10^{-1}	-0.307	-0.186×10^{-1}
InvolveA	-2.033	-3.031***	-0.135
InvolveB	0.150	0.137	0.948×10^{-3}
InvolveE	-1.229	-2.007**	-0.658×10^{-1}
InvolveF	-1.431	-2.580***	-0.115
Smlprof	1.236	1.999**	0.233
Employ	0.170	1.084	0.194
Ftime	-0.291	-1.561^{+}	-0.181
Wages	-0.220×10^{-1}	-2.447***	-0.137
Busplan	-0.843	-1.148	-0.175
Debt	0.562	1.224	0.572×10^{-1}
Owncash	0.190×10^{-4}	0.911	0.318×10^{-1}
Prodgrp	0.249×10^{-1}	0.435	0.213×10^{-1}
Product	0.130×10^{-3}	0.723×10^{-1}	0.146×10^{-2}
Impact	0.870×10^{-2}	0.877	0.299×10^{-1}
MainaimA	0.250×10^{-1}	0.490×10^{-1}	0.111×10^{-2}
MainaimG	5.481	0.217	0.723×10^{-5}
Secschl	0.160	0.885	0.166
Hrswk	0.658×10^{-2}	0.559	0.818×10^{-1}
Colluni	0.287	0.688	0.453×10^{-1}
TimProd	0.499×10^{-2}	0.715	0.496×10^{-1}
TimMan	0.140×10^{-1}	0.817	0.411×10^{-1}
LegbusA	-1.011	-1.5969^{+}	-0.736×10^{-1}
LegbusB	-0.901	-1.490^{+}	-0.520×10^{-1}
LegbusC	-0.901	-1.237	-0.381×10^{-1}
ProcInn	-0.182	-0.950	-0.55840×10^{-1}
ProdInn	-0.377	-1.869*	-0.849×10^{-1}
NewtechA	-2.702	-2.042**	-0.340
NewtechD	-2.956	-2.141**	-0.257
Constant	3.737	1.751*	0.824

Note:
Likelihood Ratio test:

$$\chi^2 = 54.8 > \chi^2_{.005}(31) = 53.7.$$

Cragg–Uhler $R^2 = 0.510$; binomial estimate $= 0.790$.
Sample size $(n) = 138$; percent of correct predictions $= 82\%$.
Critical t-values: $t_{0.10} = 1.289^{+}, t_{0.05} = 1.658$*, $t_{0.025} = 1.980$**, $t_{0.010} = 2.358$***.

the entrepreneur's personal financial injection into the business (*Owncash*) have significant effects upon survival.

The number of months a firm has been in business (*Inbus*) has a positive and significant effect upon survival (cf. Evans, 1987), and a relatively high elasticity (0.13). The time a firm is in business provides a measure of the opportunity afforded to the entrepreneur for market place learning (cf. Jovanovic, 1982; Frank, 1988). The best way to learn about business is to run a business, and in the process of learning in this practical fashion, the entrepreneur's human capital is enhanced. The mean age of the business at first interview was 21 months. These features of the age variable, *Inbus*, indicate varied experience of entrepreneurial learning and also help to estimate the coefficient of this variable with some precision.

The ratio of part-time to full-time workers (*PtFt*) is measured as (*Ptime* + 1) ÷ (*Ftime* + 1) where *Ptime* and *Ftime* refer to numbers of part-time and full-time workers, respectively. This ratio apparently has an insignificant effect upon survival probability (cf. more significant finding reported earlier in Chapter 5, Note 8). This variable is a measure of the casualisation of the small business workforce, it being the larger the more predominantly is the workforce of a part-time form, with a smaller body of 'core' full-time workers. The longer-term evidence of Chapter 5 suggests casualisation of the workforce raises the probability of survival, through lowering unit labour costs[2] and increasing task flexibility within the enterprise. However, over the relatively short period considered here, the *PtFt* variable does not pick up this effect, though further evidence, reported upon later, suggests the structure of the workforce already has at least some bearing on survival probability, even at the early stage of the young firm's life-cycle.

Three widely mentioned reasons for getting involved in running a small business – to provide an alternative to unemployment (*InvolveA*); to be one's own boss (*InvolveE*); and to satisfy the need for achievement (*InvolveF*) – are considered, and all have significant negative effects upon the probability of survival (see Q.4.3 of AQ1 in this book's appendix). Using a broader based measure of performance than mere survival, Reid and Smith (1996) show that only the most economically driven reasons for business involvement tend to convert into good performance. However, if they are vaguely specified (e.g. 'to get rich', as for *InvolveB*) they tend to have no bearing on survival (cf. Results in Table 10.2. Note the coefficient of this variable is insignificant in Table 11.2).

Aims of the business can be important for performance, but are not of measurable importance here for mere survival. *MainaimA* (survival) and *MainaimG* (high rate of return) have insignificant coefficients. From evidence elsewhere (cf. Reid and Smith, 1996), aiming to make a high rate of return certainly fosters small business performance, measured by weighting profitability, productivity and growth. But here, in this chapter's evidence, it does not seem to influence brute survival. Even running a firm with the limited aim of survival in mind (*MainaimA*) does not prove effective. As is common in the early stages of the small firm's life-cycle, entrepreneurs are still learning what best to do for their businesses.

If they are willing to sacrifice some short-run profit to promote growth (*Smlprof*), this has a positive and significant effect upon survival, and also a high elasticity (0.23). In commenting further on this variable, observe that if an entrepreneur is seeking only short-run profit and then an early exit, the business will *by design* only be short-lived. But beyond this, the avoidance of a short-run view (e.g. looking relatively far ahead in terms of business planning) has been shown to enhance business performance (see the *Impact* variable in Chapter 10,

Table 10.3). Here, however, it has no measurable effect on mere survival, as the coefficient on the *Impact* variable is insignificant, this being a measure of how many months ahead an entrepreneur looks when evaluating the impact of decisions. Merely having formulated a business plan (*Busplan*) does not promote survival, emphasising that a formulaic approach to business planning is ineffectual as compared to a strategic approach.

Earlier work (Reid, Jacobsen and Anderson, 1993) has suggested that the wage bill is often a principal 'cost driver'[3] of small firms, and that tight control of the wage bill is a prerequisite to survival, and indeed, more broadly, to performance. In the probit of Table 11.2, the variable *Wages* measures the percentage of total costs that are attributable to wages, salaries and directors' remuneration. We have seen earlier that the average for this variable is 25 per cent, with the figure being below a quarter for survivors and approaching one-third for non-survivors. Not surprisingly, the coefficient on *Wages* is negative and highly statistically significant. A 10 per cent reduction in the proportion of costs allocated to labour will raise the survival probability by nearly 1.5 per cent. The related variables, head-count employment[4] (*Employg*) and full-time employment (*Ftime*) are of marginal significance in this 'encompassing' probit probably because of some collinearity with the *Wages* variable. However, their interpretation is important, and more detailed consideration will be given to them in Section 11.4 , when reporting upon a more parsimonious probit equation (cf. Table 11.2).

Previous work (Reid, 1991) with older firms has shown that especially the number of product groups (*Prodgrp*) and even the number of products (*Product*) produced by the small firm have a bearing on survival. The product range enables a small firm to exploit economies of scope and to attenuate risk by adopting a portfolio balance approach to product placement across different market segments (cf. Ungern–Sternberg, 1990). However, here these variables have coefficients which are insignificant, suggesting that such considerations are unimportant with these very young small firms. They may be too busy trying to find and exploit niches in the first place, before even coming to consider finer matters like risk spreading.

Human capital aspects are thought to be important in any productive process, of which running a small entrepreneurial firm is an example (cf. Bates, 1990; Townroe and Mallalieu, 1993). However, two of the human capital variables, years of secondary schooling (*School*) and having done a college or university degree (*College*) prove to be insignificant determinants of survival. The marketplace experience, and the learning it implies over time, appear to be more important than academic credentials for survival through the early stages after business inception.

Other aspects of the production function of a small firm are inputs like hours of effort, and hours devoted to various tasks (cf. Oi, 1983). In fact, both hours per week spent in the business (*Hrswk*) and the proportion of effort allocated to production (*TimProd*) or management (*TimMan*) have insignificant effects upon the probability of survival. The evidence elsewhere (see Chapter 3) is that of the various allocations of effort by the owner-manager, only time spent planning has a significant positive effect upon survival.

Although a more detailed analysis of business structure, for example based on transactions' costs consideration (Coase, 1937), suggests certain business types have superior properties to others, both in terms of survival, and of more general measures of performance (e.g. profitability, growth), the basic legal structure of a small firm appears unimportant for survival, at least in the short term.[5] Thus the coefficients are all insignificant for the variables which measure business form: sole proprietorship working from home (*LegBusA*); sole proprietorship working from business premises (*LegBusB*); and partnership (*LegBusC*).

An important characteristic of small firms is their capacity to be innovative (cf. Acs and Audretsch, 1993). However, for the micro-firms under examination here, once the innovation of launch itself had passed, process innovation (*ProcInn*) had an insignificant effect on survival, and indeed the main consequence of product innovation (*ProdInn*) was generally to lower survival probability, presumably because of premature introduction of new products (cf. Verhees and Muelenberg (2004) and their findings on 'weak' innovation). Either not using new technology at all (*NewTechA*) or even perceiving one's capability to implement new technology to be good (*NewTechD*) had significant and negative effects upon new business survival. Indeed, the elasticities of these last two control variables were the highest of the set, at −0.34 and −0.26, respectively.

However, the results may be indicating that the performance of small firms that innovate early are more variable than those that do not. As a consequence, from the pool of early innovators there may be a higher exit rate. The *ex ante* profit on early innovation may even be positive. Very often, the launch of the firm is itself the major technological leap, either in terms of production, or of organisation. There is evidence that it is not just specific technological advances that are important for survival and performance, but rather the assemblage of collective new technical capabilities (cf. Smith, 1997). For example, in the use of new IT it is not so much whether or not you use a fax, phone, or PC on an individual basis, but rather whether you use *clusters* of fax, phone and PC together. These clusters effectively coordinate IT functions, and positively influence performance and survival (cf. Morikawa, 2004; Lin *et al.*, 1993).

11.4   A parsimonious model of survival

We turn now from the encompassing model of Table 11.2 to a more parsimonious model in Table 11.3. The reported Cragg–Uhler R^2 of 0.25 is satisfactory, and a likelihood ratio test that all elements of the β vector are zero rejects this hypothesis at the 1 per cent level. This model has advantage over that of Table 11.2 in terms of both economy, in a methodological sense, and of better displaying how employment structure influences survival.

We note, first of all, that the signs and significance of the coefficients of the variables *Bankloan*, *Inbus* and *Involve(A,E,F)* are all much as before, and the earlier interpretations are sustained (see Q.4.8.3 of the AQ1 in the appendix to this book). The stability of the behaviour of these variables between both sets of estimates is also a measure of the robustness of the empirical regularities they represent.

Table 11.3 Parsimonious probit for subset of control variables

Variable	Coefficient	t-ratio	Weighted elasticity
Bankloan	-0.638	-2.168**	-0.736×10^{-1}
Inbus	0.198×10^{-1}	1.868*	0.105
Ptft	-0.353×10^{-1}	-0.186	-0.107×10^{-1}
InvolveA	-1.184	-2.930***	-0.109
InvolveE	-0.957	-2.365***	-0.682×10^{-1}
InvolveF	-0.907	-2.372***	-0.886×10^{-1}
Smlprof	0.839	1.947*	0.221
Employ	0.200	1.938*	0.283
Ftime	-0.235	-1.956*	-0.175
Wages	-0.102×10^{-1}	-1.907*	-0.820×10^{-1}
Constant	0.635	1.144	0.192

Note:
Likelihood ratio test:

$$\chi^2 = 25.7 > \chi^2_{.01}(10) = 23.2.$$

Cragg–Uhler $R^2 = 0.250$; binomial estimate $= 0.788$.
Sample size $(n) = 146$; percent of correct predictions $= 77\%$.
Critical t-values: $t_{0.10} = 1.289^+$, $t_{0.05} = 1.658^*$, $t_{0.025} = 1.980^{**}$, $t_{0.010} = 2.358^{***}$.

The benefits to survival of sacrificing some short-term profit for growth (*SmlProf*) are again indicated.

This parsimonious model now displays more sharply what is happening in the area of employment within the small firm.[6] 'Larger' small firms, as measured by headcount (*Employ*), have superior survival prospects to 'smaller' small firms, and the associated elasticity is relatively large (0.28). Thus a 10 per cent increase in headcount will raise survival probability by nearly 3 per cent. However, the composition of the headcount is important. Particularly in the 'larger' small firms, where they are the typical employee type, full-time employees (*Ftime*), some-times called the 'core employment' of the business, can create pressure on the wage bill. Indeed, as before, the *Wages* variable, which represents the proportion of costs accounted for by wage and salary payments, has a coefficient which is highly significant and negative. That the number of full-time employees is strongly negatively associated with survival (*Ftime*) should therefore come as no surprise. The elasticity is relatively large, and suggests a 10 per cent shedding of full-time employees would raise the probability of survival over 3 years by nearly 2 per cent. Though this in itself does not prove that casualisation of the workforce, even in this early stage of the life-cycle,[7] enhances survival, as once again the coefficient of the *PtFt* variable (the ratio of part-time to full-time workers) is insignificant, it hints at such a possibility. This possibility is further strengthened by the already known fact that the more are senior, skilled personnel deployed within the nascent busi-ness early on, the better are its survival prospects (cf. Atkinson and Meager, 1994). This suggests that most modification of employment structure to promote survival will occur further down the hierarchy of the small firm. Employment structure within the firm can be characterised as follows (cf. Williamson, 1967). Suppose w_i is the wage rate at the i-th hierarchical level; and l_i is the headcount at this level. Then total headcount is $L = \sum l_i$ and the wage bill is $W = \sum w_i l_i$. If employees can be moved between hierarchical level, the question to be posed is: Can headcount (L) rise at the same time as the wage bill (W) falls?

To approach this point by illustration, consider average figures for both wages and salaries and employment, at different hierarchical levels within the firm. These figures are based on Chapter 3, Table 3.6. Average employment levels from the top down are: 1.9, 1.8, 3.3 and 2.0. The levels can be thought of as: owner-managers, senior full-timers, junior full-timers and casual or part-time workers. The evidence is that the last category of worker provides an effort which is a considerable proportion (certainly much greater than 50 per cent) of the effort of full-timers. This is reflected in remuneration. If the bottom level of worker has a remuneration which is standardised at unity (1), then the remunerations as you go up the hierarchical level are, on average, 1.4, 2.1 and 3.6 (the data source is again Chapter 3, Table 3.6). This average firm has a headcount (*Employ*) of $(1.9 + 1.8 + 3.3 + 2.0) = 9$ and a wage bill of $(1.9 \times 3.6) + (1.8 \times 2.1) + (3.3 \times 1.4) + (2.0 \times 1.1) = 17.44$. At the top level of the hierarchy are the owner-managers, who are effectively fixed, and presumably earning what is just sufficient to retain them in the entrepreneurial role.

Suppose they restructure employment to control the wage bill, casualising all junior employees and one senior employee, and hiring a further casual employee to boost labour effort. Then the average headcount becomes $(1.9 + 0.8 + 0.0 + 7.3) = 10.0$ which has gone up, but the wage bill becomes $(1.9 \times 3.6) + (0.8 \times 2.1) + (7.3 \times 1.1) = 16.55$ which has gone down. These figures are illustrative, but certainly they make a point: casualising the workforce can powerfully control the wage bill without reducing employment in terms of headcount. Indeed, it *is* true that surviving firms have higher levels of employment at the bottom level of the hierarchy than non-surviving firms. Furthermore, the numerical example presented illustrates how the headcount can even rise, and yet the wage bill fall, by selective restructuring of the composition of employment within the small firm. It may be that re-structuring of the workforce more readily allocates workers according to marginal productivity. That is, at inception workers may not be optimally allocated, for example, because their productivity levels have not yet been observed.[8] However, in the early phase of the life-cycle, such evidence emerges, and the profit maximising allocation is then better approached.

These findings are consistent with large sample findings elsewhere, suggesting an increase in part-time employment as a proportion of total employment, especially in the small firm sector. The global observation that there is more rapid job creation amongst small firms, based on headcounts, may in part reflect an increase in part-time employment. This appears to be associated with an increased wage gap between large and small firms, see, for example, the study of Picot and Dupuy (1998), which explores these effects in detail for the case of the Canadian economy.

Finally, one needs to compare the probit models of Tables 11.2 and 11.3 from a statistical point of view. Although the first model, in Table 11.2, is of interest in many of its features, a large number of its coefficients are not significantly different from zero. A likelihood ratio test of the extra restrictions imposed in the second model produces a χ^2 statistic of 34.158, which is less than the critical value of $\chi^2_{0.01}(21) = 37.57$, so we just accept the hypothesis that the restrictions imposed by the second model are valid at the 1 per cent level, and thus the parsimonious probit of Table 11.3 is the preferred specification. This model has 77 per cent of predictions correct, which is somewhat less than the 82 per cent of the first model, but acceptable, given its relative simplicity, as an explanation of the survival probability of small firms.[9]

An additional matter which needs to be considered concerns possible effects on the model of industrial sector. Table 11.4 presents results for the parsimonious model, with the addition of dummy variables for nine industrial sectors. The model is of marginal significance overall at the 1 per cent level in terms of a

Table 11.4 Parsimonious probit with sectoral dummies

Variable	Coefficient	t-Ratio	Weighted Elasticity
Bankloan	-0.638	-2.079**	-0.704×10^{-1}
Inbus	0.245×10^{-1}	1.925*	0.120
Ptft	-0.230×10^{-1}	0.102	-0.631×10^{-2}
InvolveA	-1.250	-2.805***	-0.103
InvolveE	-1.106	-2.395***	-0.658×10^{-1}
InvolveF	-1.080	-2.643***	-0.102
Smlprof	1.096	2.247**	0.263
Employ	0.208	1.815*	0.271
Ftime	-0.244	-1.855*	-0.167
Wages	-0.731×10^{-2}	-1.142*	-0.533×10^{-1}
SIC0	-0.247	-0.253	-0.175×10^{-2}
SIC1	-1.435	-1.755*	-0.157×10^{-1}
SIC2	4.670	0.187×10^{-2}	0.410×10^{-9}
SIC3	-0.514	-0.804	-0.106×10^{-1}
SIC4	-0.763	-1.585^+	0.548×10^{-1}
SIC5	0.287×10^{-3}	0.488×10^{-3}	0.883×10^{-5}
SIC6	-0.345	-0.711	-0.169×10^{-1}
SIC7	5.898	0.187×10^{-2}	0.323×10^{-9}
SIC8	-0.552	-1.061	-0.269×10^{-1}
Constant	0.684	1.057	0.190

Note:
Likelihood ratio test:

$$\chi^2 = 35.84 \cong \chi^2_{.001}(10) = 36.2$$

Cragg–Uhler $R^2 = 0.339$; binomial estimate $= 0.786$.
Sample size (n) $= 145$; percent of correct predictions $= 81\%$.
Critical t-values: $t_{0.10} = 1.289^+$, $t_{0.05} = 1.658$*, $t_{0.025} = 1.980$**, $t_{0.010} = 2.358$***.

likelihood ratio test of the model with a constant term only, against the model with all variables, including sectoral dummies. Thus (as elsewhere in this book, e.g. Chapter 5) the dummy variables appear to add little to the statistical picture. More precisely, if a likelihood ratio test of the model of Table 11.3 against the model of Table 11.4 is performed, a test statistic of just 10.66 is obtained, which is considerably less than the $\chi^2_{0.01}(9)$ value of 21.7. The model of Table 11.3 is therefore much preferred using this test methodology. Turning now to individual SIC dummies, it will be observed that not one is significant at the 1 per cent level. Although there are marginally significant effects for sector 1 (heavy manufactures: met als, minerals, chemicals, etc.) and sector 4 (light manufactures: food, textiles, footwear, furniture, etc.), these effects are not robust under alternative specifications, when non-significance is usually observed. Furthermore, the effect of sectoral dummies in this model is slight, as judged by the low absolute values of the weighted elasticities, which are typically smaller by a factor of ten or more than the weighted elasticities for the other included variables. It therefore is concluded that the consequences of sectoral effects for staying in business are slight.

11.5   Conclusion

This chapter starts from a view of the new small firm that emphasises the wide variety of actions open to the entrepreneur (e.g. in terms of financing, business strategy, organisation, etc.), (cf. Rispas, 1998). This is in contrast to a traditional view, which emphasises merely control of output by a passive manager. The proposed approach was used to construct and test a model showing how entrepreneurial actions affected the probability of new small firms remaining in business over a 3-year time horizon. The data used were for the period 1994–97 (i.e. the data detailed in Sections 1.3–1.5 of Chapter 1).

Using a probit model to estimate the effects of entrepreneurial actions on new small business survival, it was found that many actions do indeed influence future business viability. It was also found that certain actions and situations did not favourably influence business viability, even though there might be a *prima facie* case that they should (e.g. innovation, sector). These cases are worthy of attention first. Thus it was found that especially product and, in some measure, process innovation soon after business birth had negative consequences for staying in business. It is known that small firms are often 'early adopters' of product innovations, see Karlsson and Olsson (1998), which may suggest that adoption is best done at inception itself, rather than shortly afterwards. It is also possible that early innovators have a higher performance variability, with better performance on average, but relatively higher exit rates.

Turning now to industrial sector, an emerging trend in small firms economic policy is towards an explicitly sectoral view. This is no doubt partly the result of more successful sectorally based small business lobby groups, e.g. those operating through trade associations. However, if the entrepreneur is a profit seeking businessman, rather than an artisan, and is not therefore wedded to one sector, and key factors like finance-capital and unskilled labour are mobile across sectors, one would not expect sectoral effects to be significant. It must also be borne in mind that even very small firms can, and frequently do, produce products across several industrial sectors.[10] Despite the policy penchant for a sector specific view, it should therefore come as no surprise that the econometric evidence did not support the view that sectoral effects were important.

The literature on financial structure of small competitive firms (and, indeed, the analysis of Chapters 6–8) suggests that even if debt finance is useful for launching a business, and might fuel the initial growth burst after inception, it is generally desirable to retire debt as the firm's position is consolidated (cf. Hilten *et al.*, 1993). It is also known that for firms which are 3 or more years old, high gearing (i.e. high debt in relation to equity) tends to reduce the chances of staying in business, partly because debt is costly in itself, but also because uncertainty about interest rates increases risk (cf. Reid, 1993). These insights are reflected in the econometric evidence which indicated that a bank loan or overdraft in the previous year typically reduced the probability of survival.

Whilst economists have sometimes been reluctant to use attitudinal variables in their empirical work, an emerging literature, like that of Rispas (1998) in the small firms area, suggests they can play an important role.[11] Here, this was indeed the case and it was found that 'lifestyle' based attitudes to running a business (e.g. control-driven motives) were inimical to survival. On the other hand, a willingness to sacrifice profit for growth (arguably a willingness to subordinate short-run profit seeking to long-run profit seeking) was significantly linked to staying in business.

Finally, it was suggested that the organisational structure of the small firm was important. Casualising the workforce can sharpen incentives across hierarchical levels, and it offers opportunities for controlling, and even lowering, the wage bill. Whilst the headcount of total employment, *Employ*, was found to have the strongest positive consequences for survival, with a 10 per cent increase in headcount raising survival probability by 3 per cent, it was also found that a 10 per cent decrease in full-time employees raised the survival probability by nearly 2 per cent. Given that the members of the firm who typically have highest human capital, and enjoy the greatest remuneration, the entrepreneurs, are effectively fixed specialised factors of production, these findings suggest that a casualisation of the workforce within these new small firms helps them to stay in business. This may reflect the better approximation to the marginal productivity conditions necessary for profit maximisation achieved by small firms after inception, having started with an initial workforce of relatively unknown productivity. This process essentially involves broadening the base of the employment pyramid, especially at the bottom, where non-core labour is employed.

Thus it is felt that this attention to a more realistic view of the complex actions that an entrepreneur may take in a small firm, has been rewarding in producing insights that are both theoretically compelling, and empirically well founded.

APPENDIX

Definitions of Variables

Variable Name	Definition
Bankloan	=1 firm has used bank loan or overdraft in previous year, =0 otherwise
Busplan	=1 firm has a business plan, =0 otherwise
College	=1 respondent went to college or university, =0 otherwise
Debt	=1 firm has debt, =0 otherwise
Employ	total headcount (directors + managers + full-time and part-time employees + trainees)
Ftime	no. of full-time employees
Hrswk	no. of hours a week spent by the owner-manager in the business
Impact	planning horizon of the firm (months)
Inbus	time since business inception at first interview (months)
InvolveA	=1 respondent became involved in the business as an alternative to unemployment, =0 otherwise
InvolveB	=1 respondent became involved in the business 'to get rich', =0 otherwise
InvolveE	=1 respondent became involved in the business to be own boss, =0 otherwise
InvolveF	=1 respondent became involved in the business to satisfy the need for achievement, =0 otherwise
LegbusA	=1 firm is sole trader (operating from home), =0 otherwise
LegbusB	=1 firm is sole trader (operating from business premises), =0 otherwise
LegbusC	=1 firm is partnership, =0 otherwise
MainaimA	=1 main aim of business is survival, =0 otherwise
MainaimG	=1 main aim of business is high rate of return, =0 otherwise
NewtechA	=1 firm has not used new production technologies, =0 otherwise
NewtechD	=1 firm has generally been successful in implementing new production technologies, =0 otherwise
Owncash	cash injection by owner-manager at business inception (£)
ProcInn	level of process innovation undertaken by firm (=0 none, =1 a little, =2 a lot)
Prodgrp	number of product groups or categories firm offers
ProdInn	number of new products introduced by firm (=0 none, =1 '1–5', =2 '6–10', =3 '11–20', =4 'more than twenty')
Product	number of products firm offers
PtFt	=(part-time employees + 1) ÷ (full-time employees + 1)
School	time respondent spent at secondary school (years)
Smlprof	=1 respondent is willing to accept smaller profits for a while to facilitate growth, =0 otherwise

Continued

Definitions of Variables—cont'd

Variable Name	Definition
TimMan	percentage of respondent's time spent on management
TimProd	percentage of respondent's time spent on production
Wages	percentage of total costs attributable to wages, salaries and directors' remuneration

Endnotes

1 Guinevere 1652.
2 In a variety of forms: lower wages, lower pension and insurance costs, lower costs of hiring and firing, etc.
3 A term due to Porter (1985) meaning a grouping of costs which dominate cost trends.
4 Headcount of all in business, managers, directors, full-time, part-time workers and trainees.
5 In the longer term, this is unlikely to be true. Both theoretical and empirical analysis suggest the organisational form of a firm has a significant bearing on growth and profitability (cf. Reid 1997; Dobson and Gerrard, 1989; Harrison, 2004; Atkinson and Meager, 1994). Furthermore, the work of Storey (1994) suggests that limited companies are more likely to acquire debt, and to start up with more employees, than sole proprietorships.
6 This view might be confronted with that of Matlay (1999), who emphasises personalised and mostly informal management styles in small firms. This may be true, but it does not mean hierarchy is abandoned. It remains, but with much selective intervention.
7 Though this may well be so in the late stage (cf. Reid, 1996a, b) for mature firms – in this case on average 14 years old.
8 This is an issue of adverse selection. It is to be confronted with the approach in Chapter 5, where allocation is off the (capital saturated) expansion path (where factor price ratios equal marginal rates of substitution), because the money capital constraint is binding.
9 The parsimonious model predicts survival in 82 per cent of cases which did survive and 34 per cent of failures. The encompassing model had corresponding figures of 87 per cent and 50 per cent. The latter is therefore a better predictor of failure than the former. However, as our focus is on factors determining success, the parsimonious model seems to perform comparatively well.
10 When this occurs, the relevant sector used for labelling the firm is that in which most sales are generated by a product group.
11 The validity of this approach is accepted, and the implied agenda moved forward, in Chapter 18.

Part 5

Information and contingency

12 Information and performance

12.1 Introduction

This chapter progresses the research agenda of this book by probing further issues broached earlier, like the role of hierarchy (Williamson, 1967, 1975, 1985), examined in Chapters 5 and (in more detail) in Chapter 11. It is part of a new concern with the internal organisation of the firm, but, as over the performance perspective (especially that of Part 4), is always in evidence. Crucial to the internal workings of the small firm is the information system (IS) (Caldeira and Ward, 2003; de Guinea *et al.*, 2005). It is this, for example, which allows the entrepreneur to monitor and control his firm with a view to performance enhancement (Teece, 1998; Hartman *et al.*, 1994; Daake *et al.*, 2004).

This chapter provides a critical analysis of selected theoretical and empirical literature on IS development in the small firms. It does so under five headings: (1) the information needs of the small firm; (2) the use of information to guide decisions; (3) the management accounting perspective; (4) the performance of the small firm and its link to IS development (Caldeira and Ward, 2003) and (5) the statistical analysis of IS development and small firm performance. In challenging the standard economic assumption of economic agents being fully informed, it considers information as being a precious resource which can be more, or less, effectively utilised to the end of enhancing small firm performance. In doing so, it hopes to open the door to a new and important research agenda.

12.2 Information needs

Small firms need to make accurate decisions under competitive pressure. Such decision-making depends upon the available information set. Contrary to the standard economic theory of the firm, such information cannot be taken for granted. Casson (1994, p. 136) captured the essence of the problem when he said 'accurate and relevant information is a resource'. Furthermore, as Chang and Lee (1992) have suggested, information use is a constituent element of business strategy itself. This section aims to consider the key dimensions of information use within the small firm, including the roles of user involvement, technology, cost effectiveness and externalities [see Hunter (2004) for a survey of a broad range of research issues, as they relate to small firms and IS].

Successful IS development within the small firm has three prerequisites. First, the information created should be reliable, extensive and timely. Second, the skills shortages which typically limit the capacity of the small firm to develop a system best suited to its purposes, must be broken. This must be done without losing sight of its bespoke character. Third, meeting such needs may require the setting of deliberate limits to the complexity of the IS being adopted, to ensure its cost effectiveness.

In the past, the information needs of small firms for successful performance were largely ignored (Trindade, 1990). Symptomatic of this was the fact that there was no database methodology available (Jones, 1985), to address the information needs of the small firm. This had made it hard to form a rational view on how best to enhance their potential by more effective information use. Fortunately, some principles for successful IS development in small firms are emerging. The prime one is that the user should be involved as early as possible (cf. de Guinea *et al.*, 2005). In this way, experience is tapped in developing a new IS. This encourages an internally consistent and operationally effective approach to IS development. It encourages relatively rapid progress up the learning curve by the user, and more effectively integrates users' operational know-how into the IS development process.

Also important to the development of ISs has been the advance of computing technology, especially as embodied in workstations and personal computers. The use of computers has been encouraged by rapid decreasing unit costs over time and increasing sophistication, coupled with greater user friendliness. At the same time, new software and network infrastructure have been developed. Though complex, they have been increasingly better adapted to user needs, with the aim of making them more easy to utilise, with a skills set that is more rapidly learnt. Of particular note, from the standpoint of trends, was the role of distributed database management systems (DDBMS) for enhancing small firm information acquisition and handling (Ganzhorn and Faustoferri, 1990).[1] There are two key features of DDBMS (Daudpota, 1998). First, they provide rich access to local sites. Second, they allow privileged access to all sites. In this way, they permit the complex concatenation of disparate data files. Thus there is a role for serendipity; and previously unknown, but productive, data links can be discovered and utilised. Systems like this have important implications for small firm performance and development. Currently, most small firms do not have access to multiple sites for internal information retrieval (as distinct from public internet access). However, the use of DDBMS is likely to become increasingly important to information use and management within the small firm. An early indication of the importance of this approach to small firms and the stimulus it provides to productive accounting information system (AIS) development is given in Jorrisen *et al.* (1997a).

Although much IS development will fall short of ambitious arrangements like those discussed earlier, some clear requirements emerge. For example, the information to be retrieved should be directed to the needs of the user, and should satisfy quality thresholds. As user needs change, so should information provision. This provision itself should interface increasingly effectively with the user, making access more open, and interaction more productive.[2] Finally, cost-effectiveness principles should govern IS development. A cost which has often been neglected, but which can tip the cost-effectiveness balance, is that of maintaining the IS once it is up and running. Significant costs of this nature are incurred in updating, expanding and developing the system.

Two brief examples illustrate how principles like the above have been implemented. First, in Gall (1990), it is shown how ISs were used to stimulate innovation within German small firms. The system aimed to help small firms which did not have R&D facilities. It combined Chambers of Commerce data on innovations with distributed database support. The latter provided internet access and translation facilities. Second, in Fang (1990), an IS developed for over a thousand enterprises in Shanghai, most of which were small firms, was described. Although few firms had been involved in formal IS development, their information needs were considerable. To meet these needs in a cost-effective way, an information network was set up, geared specifically to local conditions. Because personal computers were scarce, but telephones were common, it was based on fax machines. They were used to send data which were highly time-dependent, e.g. data on the supply of raw materials.[3] This is a model which could be imitated in other countries or regions not well endowed with computer systems.

These two examples emphasise the exploitation of positive network externalities. The role of externalities, in terms of ISs, rather than economies of agglomeration, and related effects (e.g. industrial districts) has not had the attention it deserves in the extant literature. There has been an unnecessarily close focus on IS development within the small firm itself. However, networks to which the small firm has access should not be treated as a distinct issue. Here, one is not just thinking of the neglect of the impact of the internet (cf. Levenburg *et al.*, 2001). The point made in Reid and Jacobsen (1988, Ch. 5) for Scottish small firms remains valid, that the small firm is embedded in a rich institutional network.[4] Though this cannot be navigated by the internet alone, as person-to-person contact remains important, it is a potentially nurturing external information resource. Thus further ways of exploiting synergies between internal and external information sources need to be explored (cf. Reid and Smith, 2004, on coevolutionary systems). To illustrate further, Jorrisen *et al.* (1997a) have argued that small firms can benefit from access to external networks for information on matters such as industry trends and new technologies. These can be combined usefully with internally generated information for the formulation of small business strategy, for example. Trends in information management of this sort are characteristic of the 'weightless economy' first discussed by Quah (1997), and the significance of this view for small firm and their information management has been analysed by Swartz and Boaden (1997).

12.3   Guiding decisions

Informal decision-making within the small firm, perhaps based on a hunch, or intuition, may be too prone to systematic bias. These are sometimes known as 'heuristic biases'. Thus the frame of reference within which an intuitive decision is made will affect its form (cf. Hogarth (ed.), 1990). As Slovic *et al.* (1990) have illustrated, judging the value of a company depends on what data on company rankings one can access.

If the decision-making involves risk appraisal, a preference may be displayed by the entrepreneur for qualitative, rather than quantitative, risk appraisal. Thus assigning events to risk classes (e.g. high, low) may be preferable to assigning numerical probabilities, based on a hunch. Both Knight (1921) and Keynes (1921) argued that some forms of uncertainty could not be appraised by reference to a known probability law. In the case of Knight, a type of pattern recognition had to be used to appraise one-off situations which were uncertain. In the case of Keynes, types of events, on a spectrum of vagueness, were recognised.

By admitting to vagueness in probability assignment, a form of cost-effectiveness approach to risk can be adopted. Soft risk assessment blunts precision of decision-making and sacrifices the capacity to calculate compound, conditional and marginal probabilities. These are the costs, but the positive effects are that decision-making is more realistic. It is also under control, in the sense that no more is read into an uncertain situation than is warranted by the evidence to hand. That such benefits will materialise was first encouraged by the work of Wallsten (1990), which suggested that human subjects can handle vague uncertainty quite reliably. Ways in which score-carding systems, or even expert systems, can be developed for decision support in this area have been considered by Hardman and Ayton (1997).

There are two features of decision-making which are particularly relevant to new, growing small firms. The first is that time is involved in an essential way. The second is that the locus of decisions is genuine clock time. Briefly, decision-making is dynamic and embedded in real time. Thus Brehmer (1990) and Levy and Powell (1998) have compared small firm decision-making to fire-fighting. Independent decisions must be made seriatim, in the face of both endogenous and exogenous environmental change. As with the fire-fighter, the entrepreneur may not be fully in control, and some decisions are forced upon her. She is dealing more with the control of a process than with the choice of an action.

Two control approaches are available: feedforward or feedback control. The more familiar feedback control bases actions on the system's contemporaneous configuration. But also important is the less familiar feedforward control, which bases actions on predicted states of the system. Both control types help to solve real time dynamic decision problems. However, feedforward control is less effective, the greater is the environmental instability. On the other hand, feedback control is less effective, the greater are the reporting delays in the system.

Feedback controls, being simpler, tend to be more popular than feedforward controls. However, they are unreliable when information for control does not feedback sufficiently rapidly. Information which feedbacks too slowly will lack salience. Although feedforward control is potentially powerful, its efficiency is contingent on good data, strong modelling and a stable environment. Below, it will be argued that an information system (IS), especially when used for environmental scanning, can help to make feedforward control more effective. In support of this view it has been argued that feedback controls are ineffective without good feedforward controls, as performance measures and budget variances, of the sort that are used in an IS, are unreliable without them (cf. Emmanuel and Otley, 1986).

12.4   Using information systems

Higher productivity and greater profitability are important goals of small business strategy. However, alas, traditional accounting tools, like annual accounts, provide no more than an historical record of the small firm's position, e.g. as regards profit or loss. Though necessary for statutory requirements, like tax assessment, they do not foster superior monitoring and control, though they remain an important information source for small firms (Baliga, 1995). Before the development of fast desktop personal computers and associated user-friendly software, management accounting methods were laborious to apply, and could readily be misused. Currently, such methods are utilised more readily. Gone are the days when an office full of clerks to perform simple chores was necessary, even in small firms. Modern software means quite ambitious programmes of positive management control can be contemplated.[5]

Admittedly, this control remains largely internally focussed, though it was recognised early (Perry, 1968) that superior knowledge of external events could foster better internal control [see also, more recently, Hunter (2004)]. Examples of such external events include the business cycle and currency stability.[6] With the use of modern software, feedback functions can be put in place to direct the entrepreneur's attention to performance gains and losses. If performance is linked to responsibility within the small firm it becomes responsive to any variance between target and outcome. Thus poor performance can be detected, and remedy can be sought. To the latter end, a feedforward function may be utilised. Thus, specifically, a management accounting system (MAS), as implemented in small firms, should display both feedback and feedforward functions.

There are clear principles of monitoring and control (e.g. as embodied in MASs) to be applied to small and medium sized enterprises (SMEs), involving both feedback and feedforward functions. The most important of these are: to set a profit target; to select a budget period; to connect profit with cost control; to form budget centres; and to value time. The feedforward system then focuses on matters like variances: that is to say, the difference between estimated and actual expenses at their designated cost centres. Thus, to illustrate, the use of a MAS takes on a prescriptive function, enabling the entrepreneur to enhance control, with a view to increasing profit.

Important work by Jarvis *et al.* (1996) on financial control of the small firm, in an IT intensive environment, focused on cash-flow management and performance measurement. It found that the main aims of the entrepreneur are to survive, and to achieve an adequate standard of living. Certainly, cash flow was important to them, but only as a means of survival. These findings are disappointing, in that the small firm's owner-manager looks limited in outlook. However, it should be emphasised that they are not inconsistent with the seeking of profit by enhanced control. Indeed survival in the long run may be regarded as equivalent to maximising profit, as only profit maximisers will withstand continuous competitive pressure, see Chapter 11 above. Thus enhanced monitoring and control, in fostering survival, with thereby foster the pursuit of profit. While profit is the ultimate performance measure, it is usually treated in multidimensional terms (cf. Chapter 9 above). These various dimensions, and their relation to IS development will now be considered.

12.5   Performance and IS development

Starting from inception, the growth stages of a small firm can be split up into start-up growth and mature growth (Romano and Ratnatunga, 1994). As growth proceeds, planning and control are found to become increasingly important, extending from no more than operational oversight to internal, external and managerial issues. The implementing of a formal system, like an accounting information system (AIS), is found to be important to the successful evolution of the small firm through the stages of start-up and growth.

At start-up, many entrepreneurs eschew formal planning and control, and emphasise the use of personal authority. As has been seen (e.g. Chapters 3, 5 and 11) this is often exercised through the use of hierarchy. However, if renewed growth after a successful launch is to be sustained, a strategy for planning and control needs to be developed. This should embrace a range of considerations, including employment, technical change, finance, marketing and production. Without such a strategy, renewed growth is improbable.

The evidence on small firms analysed by Romano and Ratnatunga (1994) suggests that, for successful mature growth, formal systems are invariably adopted. These involve complex planning and control. Such planning is far from routine. It emphasises resource development and management of innovation, not just the maintenance of operations. This work, which is based on case study evidence, suggests that a commitment to IS complexity predates subsequent growth. Thus causality is from IS development to superior performance in the small firm. It is desirable, in future work, that this conclusion should be put on a more secure basis, using formal statistical methods.

Figure 12.1 helps to display the relationship between performance and IS, in a way that will provide the basis for a subsequent more formal treatment, in

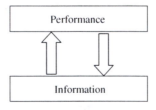

Figure 12.1 Mutual causality in the performance–information relationship.

terms of algebra and geometry. The suggested causality, from information to performance, is depicted by the left-hand arrow of Figure 12.1. It may be captured in a relationship like

$$\pi_t = f(r_{t-\tau}) \tag{12.1}$$

where π_t is a performance measure at time period t, like profit, and $r_{t-\tau}$ is an information measure τ periods earlier, like frequency of *reporting*, and $f' > 0$. The function f may be described as the 'performance function'.

Reversing the argument of the previous paragraph, Holmes *et al.* (1991) have examined how the growing small firm generates a demand for IS development. Thus performance feeds forward to IS development as depicted in the right arrow of Figure 12.1. This is in contrast to the discussion earlier, in which Equation (12.1) only looked at causality from the reverse direction. There, it considered how IS development 'fed forward' to higher growth. Both effects are now combined, and IS development both determines, and is determined by, growth.

The formal statement of the system can be extended by considering how performance in the past (say $\pi_{t-\tau'}$) determines the current IS, measured by r_t. This function can be written

$$r_t = F(\pi_{t-\tau'}) \tag{12.2}$$

where it may be assumed that $\tau' < \tau$ (e.g. profit changes feed forward more rapidly to IS changes than IS changes feed forward to profit changes). This equation is now combined with the earlier $\pi_t = f(r_{t-\tau'})$ relationship. Let us now examine these functions F and f in greater detail.

In considering Equations (12.1) and (12.2), and the function f, note that the causality is from developments in planning and control to superior small firm performance, as noted earlier by Jorrisen *et al.* (1997a, b). A similar view was expressed in Reid (1998a, b). The latter work examined how complex monitoring and control systems could be installed in small firms, at the behest of outside investors, before they would agree to invest in the form of an injection of equity finance. Typically, the frequency and scope of monitoring were increased at the time of committing more funds. Such modifications of ISs are known to enhance the post-investment performance of the small firm.

Consider now the function F of Equation (12.2). While it is true that successful small firms generate a demand for IS development, it is also true, as Jorrisen *et al.* (1997a), that struggling small firms actually generate more demands for IS development than do successful small firms. A related effect, pointed out by Nayak and Greenfield (1994) was that younger, smaller and less well performing small firms were often what they called 'less knowledgeable' than their larger counterparts. They therefore generated greater information demands, for example, in determining their pricing policy.

This is all to suggest that the function F may have special properties. Let F be denoted the 'control equation'. Its potential forms will now be examined. Studies have suggested (as noted in the previous paragraph) that r is convex in π, that is to say $F'' > 0$, but not every where monotonically increasing or decreasing.

Rather, the function $r_t = F(\pi_{t-\tau'})$ is actually U-shaped. Thus either relatively low or relatively high profits generate high values of r (where r might be stylised as frequency of reporting, for example). So, for π less than some π^*, $F' < 0$ and for π greater than or equal to π^*, we have $F' > 0$. To simplify matters further, let us suppose that adjustments all occur within τ time periods. Then the performance and control equations may be written simply as:

$$\pi = f(r) \quad f' > 0 \quad \text{for all } r \qquad \text{and} \qquad (12.3)$$

$$r = F(\pi) \quad F' < 0 \text{ for } \pi \text{ less than some critical value, } \pi^* \qquad (12.4)$$

$$F' > 0 \text{ for } \pi \text{ greater than or equal to critical value } \pi^*$$

These equations may be drawn as in Figure 12.2.

It is to be noted that the system has two equilibria, at A and B. The equilibrium at B is preferred on economic grounds. It is the high profit, high information equilibrium. It has desirable properties over the equilibrium at A. Suppose the efficiency of monitoring improves, so the whole function F shifts down from F to F_1. That is to say, efficiency has improved in the sense that, for a given level of profit, less frequent monitoring is now required. This might correspond to the implementation and use of new software within the small firm. Equilibrium A is pushed to a lower profit, lower information position, whereas equilibrium B is pushed to a higher profit, higher information position. One can conceive of the goal of the struggling small firm being to move from an equilibrium like A to one like B (or from A_1 to B_1). That is, the high profit, high information equilibrium is preferred to the low profit, low information equilibrium for high or low efficiency settings.

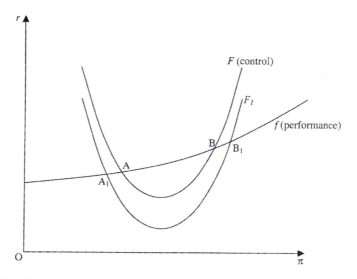

Figure 12.2 The performance and control equations.

12.6   Statistical analyses of IS and performance

This final substantive section considers the explicit use of statistical methods, especially econometric methods, to test hypotheses about the link between small firm performance and information use. One of the earliest studies in this area was by Raymond and Magnenat-Thalmann (1982). They considered the relationship between decision problems in the small firm and information use. The importance of decision problems was ranked by owner-managers, with a view to assessing what role information played in solving them. Given the era during which this work was conducted, in terms of IT development, it is no surprise that information use was considered only in terms of the use of electronic data processing (EDP). For almost all uses of EDP there was found to be no statistically significant link with solving the owner-manager's decision problems. The sole exception was the link between preparing financial statements and problem solving. Not surprisingly, the authors were rather negative about the implications of computer based ISs. In that sense, they echo the disenchantment of Note 1.

However, the result must also be considered in the context of more recent IT development. Owner-managers were found to be negative about using computers for decision support. Rather, they emphasised the use of computers as labour saving devices. This allowed capital to be substituted for labour, and hence permitted a tighter control of the wage bill (cf. Chapters 5 and 11). This attenuation of cost led to improved performance. Furthermore, although extensive use of software packages was observed, this was largely to displace laborious clerical accounting tasks, e.g. accounts receivable and payable, payroll, sales, etc. Packages were mechanical in their application and were not oriented towards monitoring and control functions. Accounting information systems were still in their infancy in the 1980s, with applications to management accounting systems (MASs) being scarcely contemplated.

The situation has since changed materially. A decade later, for example, Gul (1991) focussed specifically on the use of a MAS within the small firm for enhancing owner-managers' performance. A positive link between MAS and small firm performance was posited, and this itself was postulated to depend upon perceived environmental uncertainty (PEU). In other works, the information-performance link was set within a contingency theory framework (Burns and Stalker, 1961; cf. Chapter 13, to follow). The methodology adopted had several refinements. For instance, the MAS was measured multidimensionally. Its information characteristics were measured in terms of scope, interaction, speed and decision support.

Second, a specific linear hypothesis was tested, of the form:

$$Y = \alpha + \beta(\text{MAS}) + \gamma(\text{PEU}) + \delta(\text{MAS} \times \text{PEU}) + u \qquad (12.5)$$

where Y is performance, MAS is management accounting system complexity, and PEU is perceived environmental uncertainty. A third refinement is the introduction of MAS $\times$ PEU as an interaction term. u is a disturbance term. Given a high perceived risk, it was found that the greater the complexity of MAS, the better was small firm performance. But, given a low perceived risk, the relationship was reversed, with MAS complexity and performance being inversely related.

These results are important, both for their refinement and for the new light they cast on the link between MAS use and small firm performance.[7] A high risk environment, one might say a typically entrepreneurial environment, encourages the use of a more complex MAS. Trouble shooting is thereby facilitated, but to also to permit a more refined approach to monitoring and control. New contingencies can be better handled because the MAS provides information which is timely, frequent and of high quality. However, in a low risk environment, a complex MAS is 'over specification'. This can encourage dysfunctional behaviour within the small firm. For example, complex software might be mastered just for the sake of it (a classical 'activity trap'), rather than for enhancing performance.

Libby and Waterhouse (1996) tested a related hypothesis, that more competitive environments stimulated greater MAS development. Though they did not confine their analysis to small firms, such firms were a major part of their sample, and few very large firms were included. A multiple regression model was estimated to explain MAS development by regressors which measured decentralisation, size, competition and organisational capacity. They found organisational capacity to be the best predictor of MAS development. An additional regression was estimated to explain change in attributes of the MAS, like directing, decision-making, controlling, costing and planning. This measures the quality of the MAS. Organisational capacity was found to be a significant predictor of MAS quality in this sense. This focus on organisational form is a theme that will be developed in detail in Chapters 13, 14 and 18 to follow.

Yet more ambitious is the work of Lybaert (1998). It adopted a linear structural relations modelling (LISREL) approach.[8] This is a type of regression method which both measures and analyses relations between components of the system being examined. It was found that greater information use in small firms was associated with better performance. Information use was found to be positively associated with factors like strategic awareness, growth orientation and delegation. In their approach, causality was from performance to information use. Thus Gul (1991) can be considered to have estimated a 'performance equation' and Lybaert (1998) a 'control equation'. It is apparent that econometric work in this area requires yet further refinement. An obvious development to contemplate is the estimation of a simultaneous system, as represented by Equations (12.3) and (12.4) of $f(\cdot)$ and $F(\cdot)$, respectively, as defined in Section 12.5.

12.7   Conclusion

The purpose of this chapter has been to explore the prospects of a new research agenda for small firms. This involves abandoning the assumption that economic agents are fully informed in their running of small firms operating under competitive conditions. In fact, the entrepreneur of the small firm is ignorant both of his/her own firm's information characteristics and of information relating to the environment in which it functions. Information needs of the small firm were identified, and methods of using that information to guide decisions were considered, with an emphasis on feedback and feedforward mechanisms. It was argued that MASs were particularly compatible with this perspective.

The argument then moved on to ways of formalising the performance-information nexus. A distinction was made between the monotonically increasing performance equation and the U-shaped control equation. Both functions are required for a complete system but, of the two equilibria generated, only one is desirable, the high profit/high information equilibrium. It was shown that extant studies only attempted to estimate econometrically one equation or another. For the simultaneous system involved, both equations should be estimated together in any further empirical work. Such work will need to be alert to matters of sectoral composition and sensitive to the possibility that different relationships may prevail in different countries, at different points in time. A preliminary work in this area is that of Power and Reid (2003).

To conclude, this chapter has laid the foundations of an agenda that explicitly links information and performance. But both are multidimensional concepts, generalising the simple functions of Equation (12.3) and (12.4). In the remaining chapters of Part 5, these multidimensional issues will be broached and suitable calibrations suggested, which will then be used in the explicit estimation of econometric performance relationships.

Endnotes

1 Relevant background to this is the paper by Liansheng (2000) on document database construction in China in the 1990s. See also Jones (1985) for general principles of database construction.

2 For example, de Guinea *et al.* (2005) find that both management and member support are essential for IS effectiveness in the small firm, in their comparative study of Singapore and Canada.

3 For further work on IS development in Shanghai, see Vaughan and Tague-Sutcliffe (1997).

4 An example of such networks, at the industry level, is given by the analysis of Human and Provan (1997) of the US wood products industry.

5 This having been said, some entrepreneurs are themselves only slight users of computers. They are often heavily engaged in person to person contact, and use 'fast and dirty' methods. As one Californian information guru said, flicking through his well thumbed personal (paper) diary: 'This is still the most cost effective information system ever devised – cheap, light, portable, rapid access, multi-mode'.

6 At the extreme end of the spectrum, micro-computer based IS can be used by small firms for 'disaster preparedness', as Vijayaraman and Ramakrishna (1993) have put it. They had in mind computer-based information systems (CBIS) disaster preparedness (e.g. irretrievable system crash) but the methodology is transferable to other disaster types.

7 These insights have been extended by Lang *et al.* (1997), who argue small firms seek information in response to environmental threats and opportunities. They found a positive relationship between perceived threats and information seeking, and between perceived opportunities and information seeking.

8 See also the work of Vaughan and Tague-Sutcliffe (197), determining the impact of information on small manufacturing business in Shanghai, PR China, using LISREL techniques.

13 Contingency and information system development

(with Julia A. Smith)

13.1 Introduction

The focus of this chapter, and the subsequent Chapter 14, is on testing those aspects of contingency theory which lend themselves to statistical analysis. The central hypothesis is that IS development is determined by contingencies (Anderson and Lanen, 1999; Brignall, 1997; Burns and Stalker, 1961; Chandler, 1962; Lawrence and Lorch, 1967). Put briefly, this hypothesis is that organisational form (e.g. of the small firm) is determined by adaptation to the environment, technology, strategy etc). The data used here relate to the period 1994–98 for the sample of new Scottish small firms, described in Chapters 2 and 3. Contingency theory is tested by correlation methods in this chapter, and by cluster and regression analysis in Chapter 14.

Here, correlation analysis is applied to the timing of IS development and the timing of contingencies, like: severe cash-flow crises; severe shortfalls of finance which seriously restrict strategic investment; and significant innovations. The data used relate, first, to the base sample of small firms described in Chapter 2 and, second, to augmented sample information specifically oriented towards an investigation of contingency theory, using the administered questionnaire of the fourth year (see Section 8. *Development of MAS*, in the AQ4 of the appendix on *Instrumentation* of this book).

As is well known, the general argument of contingency theory is that there is no ideal or universal form for an organisation, or of its representation by an information system (IS). Rather, particular circumstances, or contingencies, dictate the best choice of system in each particular circumstance. These contingencies are usually classified as the environment, organisational structure and technology (Emmanuel *et al.*, 1990).

While this approach has, for some time, found favour in analysing best practice in large firms, its relevance to small firms has remained largely unexplored. The objective of this chapter is to remedy this neglect of contingency research. In this chapter, the approach focusses on the evolution of a specific IS, namely the management accounting system (MAS), in the dynamic phase of inception and early growth of the small firm.

The structure of this chapter is as follows. First, the elements of contingency theory are outlined. Here, the emphasis is on drawing on those aspects of contingency theory that lend themselves to statistical testing. Second, the appropriate use of sections of the small firms' database is briefly examined. Third, contingency theory is tested, using time-phased correlation analysis. This relates the occurrence of contingencies to contemporaneous subsequent IS development.

The general conclusion reached is that the occurrence of specific contingent events leads, with a time lag, to adaptation in a small firm's IS, as represented here by its management accounting system (MAS). The time-phasing of the correlations suggests this causality is indeed from contingencies to organisational adoption. This confirms contingency theory, from the standpoint of the IS as a characterisation of organisational form.

13.2   Contingency theory

Contingency theory was developed to explain the differences that were observed in the structure of organisations. There are many ways in which such organisations can be represented. Of particular interest to entrepreneurship studies is the way one approaches 'the personification of the organisation'.

This chapter suggests one useful way, which is both plausible and readily calibrated, in terms of the firm's IS. In essence, the theory says that the appropriate form of an organisation is entirely circumstantial, or 'contingent'. It is a set of 'contingencies' which governs the configuration of a particular organisational form. As such contingencies may vary greatly, the implication is that there is no ideal organisational form. Rather, organisational form reflects contingencies and will adapt to change in contingencies (cf. Harrison, 2004).

It is useful, in seeking to understand the development of contingency theory, to analyse its intellectual development over time, by various authors.[1] The earliest work on the subject, by Burns and Stalker (1961), emphasised the influence of environmental conditions, such as technological uncertainty, on organisational form. Around the same time, Woodward (1958, 1965) emphasised the technology employed by the firm as a key contingent variable. An example of such a contingency would be the type of production system used in the firm. In the literature that followed, the list of contingencies was extended: to corporate strategy by Chandler (1962); and to market environment by Lawrence and Lorch (1967). The scope of the contingency theory framework continues to be expanded. The work of Anderson and Lanen (1999) emphasises both national culture and competitive strategy as having a major effect on the MAS, as a key feature of organisational form; and Brignall (1997) has also used a contingency theory framework to focus on the design of cost systems. Recent work by the author, with several co-workers, extends contingency to issues of co-evolution (Reid and Smith, 2004), flexibility (Power and Reid, 2003) and high risk environments (Reid and Stewart, 2005).

The authoritative survey of what might be called the classical contingency literature is by Donaldson (1995, pp. xvi–xvii). He observes that 'the contingency theory of organizations can be rated as a success...[which] remains the mainstay of almost all serious textbooks on organizational structure and design'. He also observes that part of this success may be attributed to steady attempts by its advocates to extend its scope. This chapter is itself an attempt to contribute to that growing literature. Its particular contribution is to consider whether contingency theory is applicable to small firms, thus extending its scope from the large firms for which it was originally developed.

For the purposes of this chapter, the MAS will be regarded as the personification of the small firm's organisational form. This interpretation finds support in the extant literature. Thus Burns and Waterhouse (1975) discovered budgeting practice to be governed by organisational autonomy, management centralisation and business uncertainty. These were thought to depend on how the principal activities were structured within the firm. In the work of Hayes (1977), the way in which management accounting practices varied across organisational subunits was discussed. He concluded that three contingent variables were the main determinants of the MAS. These were: subunit interdependence (e.g. R & D intensity); dynamism of environment (e.g. marketing intensity); and work method specification (e.g. production intensity).

With the work of Waterhouse and Tiessen (1978), contingency theory was refined by their providing an explanation of subtle differences in MAS across organisational forms. They held that contingent variables would have different effects, depending on which part of the firm was being considered. A further extension of the framework was by Kloot (1997). She coined the term 'contingency planning'. She argued that strategic planning should embrace contingency planning. This would improve organisational flexibility, and in particular would make the firm more adaptive to unanticipated external shocks (cf. Power and Reid, 2003, 2005).

Gordon and Miller (1976) view the determination of the form of the MAS in normative terms, emphasising decision-making style, and organisational and environmental factors. This work suggests how contingent variables tend to cluster. As a consequence, three different types of firm can be recognised. The first is described as *adaptive*. It functions in a dynamic environment, which requires decision-making itself to be dynamic, and it operates in a decentralised fashion. The second is described as *running blind*. This type of firm also functions in a dynamic environment, but is run on a more intuitive basis. Its decision-making is entrepreneurial in character, and its organisational structure is centralised. The third is described as *stagnant*. Its environment is stable and its decision-making is conservative, involving little analysis. Its organisational structure is strongly centralised. Further works relevant to this include Otley (1980) and Alum (1997). Chapters 13 and 14 have been significantly influenced by this classification of firms suggested by contingency theorists. For the first time it is given statistical content, in the cluster analysis which is reported in the subsequent chapter, Chapter 14.

The later literature extends the boundaries of contingency theory yet further. For example, another contingent variable has been proposed by Jones (1985) for situations in which a takeover has occurred. He emphasises the influence of the parent company on the subsidiary in determining the form of the latter's MAS. A further refinement by Chapman (1997) is to recognise uncertainty as a so-called intervening variable. This brand of uncertainty arises through the formulation of objectives and actions. It influences the way in which the MAS will adapt to external contingencies. Chapman claims that his approach helps to explain some inconsistencies in previous studies. Amplifying this point, the work of Langfield-Smith (1997) reviews much previous work, drawing out the way in which a firm's strategy affects its control system in a contingent fashion. Other recent developments include the impact on MAS of: IT (Xiao *et al.*, 1996; Kinder, 2000; Buick, 2003); international competition (Anderson and Lanen, 1999) and societal differences (Bhimani, 1999).

13.3   Methodology

Here, the methods used to construct the data set for the work of Chapters 16 and 17 are briefly reviewed. First, an explanation is provided of how the administered questionnaire was designed and utilised for use in face-to-face interviews with entrepreneurs. Second, a statistical picture is presented of the main features of the MAS in the sampled firms.

The sampling procedure adopted has been reported in detail in Chapter 2. Briefly, 150 new small firms were selected in 1994–95. As reported later, a subset of these firms, which were interviewed 3 years later, provides the sampling frame for this chapter. Geographically, the major population centres in Scotland were covered by the sample, from Inverurie in the Northeast, to Stirling and Falkirk in the central belt, and extending to Midlothian in the East, and Cumnock & Doon in the West.

In the initial period of a year (between April 1994 and May 1995) of the wider study, upon which this book is based, 150 micro-firms were examined by on-site interviews (Chapter 2). The data from these interviews define the initial sampling frame. Surviving firms were then interviewed every year until 1997–98. For this chapter, the relevant sample was that collected over the period 1997–98. For that phase of fieldwork, additional questions on IS development were incorporated into the questionnaire (AQ4 of the appendix to this book). Essentially, data collected on this basis were from small firms from the initial sample which had survived another 3 years. There were a total of 105 such firms. Of these, data were obtained on 84 during the period 1997–98. This is the basic sample size for this chapter. The investigation of IS development in this sample of 1997–98 depended on a specific section of the questionnaire (see AQ4, Section 8, in appendix to this book). This instrument also covered eight other topics: market data, finance, costs, business strategy, human capital, organisation and technical change.

As an illustration of how the database was used, consider testing the effect of contingencies on the MAS. The longitudinal aspect of the database was used to identify the nature and timing of specific contingencies. This was possible because the database contains considerable detail on each firm's characteristics over time. Features of the available data which are relevant to the testing of contingency theory include: the strength and nature of the firm's competitors; and the impact of technological change on both the industry and the firm. Other ways in which the data are valuable, in terms of testing contingency theory, include: the tracing of structural change within the organisation; and the evolution of aims and strategies, as the developing firm grapples with problems of growth. By using the database in this fashion, it is possible to identify the point in time at which a specific contingency occurs.

The section in the questionnaire on the development of the MAS involved a detailed enquiry into how the firm managed its business information (see Section 8 of AQ4 in appendix of this book). The first part of it asked who prepared accounting information. Further enquiry was then made into its intensity and scope. For example, as regards scope, questions were asked about profit and loss account, balance sheet and cash flow (see Q.8.2). This part of the questionnaire then moved on to look at: capital investment (Q.8.3), cost management (Q.8.4), information flows (Q.8.5), software usage (Q.8.5.3), accounting information (Q.8.6) and the temporal development of information (Q.8.7).

To illustrate, when questions were asked about accounting information, interest focussed on its regularity and its use for measuring performance or setting budget targets. The last issue examined in this part of the administered questionnaire concerned the complexity of accounting information. Here, our concern was with effective planning and analysis, the activation and direction of daily operations, and with problem solving and decision-making. Summary statistics on the MAS of the typical firm within the sample are provided in the following two paragraphs. Statistics reported are either mean or modal values. This brief descriptive presentation is a prelude to the later, more detailed, inferential work to be reported upon in Section 13.4.

Over a quarter of firms (27%) were split up into groups or divisions, rather than being of unitary form. In terms of time scale, the organisational split usually happened about 2 years (25 months) down the line after inception. Furthermore, in over half of the firms (59%), information was decomposed by product or product group. Nearly a half (49%) also decomposed information by customer, or customer type. Over a quarter (26%) divided their information according to subunits in the firm like departments, divisions or workgroups. A minority of these small firms (15%) was interested in the breakdown of their information according to geographical area.

Within the small firms which had experienced evolution in their information provision over time, several factors had typically been at work in bringing this about. A prime case was growth in sales, which over three quarters (76%) of respondents identified as the major force for change. Nearly a half (49%) thought such change was precipitated by performance problems. Less important, though still influential as vectors of change in IS development over time were: growth in product lines (43%), growth in employees (37%), increase in the complexity of operations (35%), change in organisational structure (33%) and the injection of outside finance (14%).

13.4   Timing of contingencies and IS development

This section presents the results of the empirical analysis. They involve different applications of time-phased correlations. These relate to the contingencies of cash flow, innovation and funding shortfall. The section examines the association between specific contingencies of this type and the inception of modifications to ISs within firms.

The focus of this section is on the *timing* of specific contingencies, and the subsequent development of ISs. The structure of the data, by conscious design, permits the dating of specific occurrences after a small firm's inception. The specific occurrences examined (e.g. innovation) can be interpreted as contingencies.

Three important events in the life of a new small firm have been chosen for their natural interpretations as contingencies. They are as follows:

1. The point at which the small firm experienced its most severe cash-flow crisis.
2. The point at which a severe shortfall of finance most seriously restricted strategic investment in the small firm.
3. The point at which the most significant innovation was made in the small firm.

The next three tables of this section report on correlations between the above three contingencies and IS development. The timing of each of these specific events is correlated with the timing of the introduction into the firm's IS of a number of standard monitoring techniques. To illustrate how this method works, consider the contingency of a cash-flow crisis. Entrepreneurs were asked (Q.2.6.3 in AQ4 of appendix to this book), 'When did you have your most severe cash-flow crisis (m/y)?'. This required them to identify the year and month of their most severe cash flow crisis. It is in this sense that this chapter refers to the 'timing' or 'occurrence' of a contingency. Using this datum, the timing figure was converted into a duration figure from the point of inception of the firm. For example, if a firm had experienced its most severe cash-flow crisis in December 1996, and had been launched in March 1993, this duration figure would be 45 months.

An example of a variable with which this duration figure would be correlated may be illustrated by this extract from the questionnaire (see Q.8.4 from AQ4 in appendix to this book):

8.4 I shall describe some methods for managing costs. For those methods that you do use, could you tell me when they were first implemented (m/y)?

	Used?	When?
(e) Strategic pricing	☐	_____
e.g. product life-cycle pricing, price discrimination		

The answer to this question indicates the 'timing' or 'occurrence' of a new implementation of a feature of the small firm's monitoring and control system. It too can be converted into a duration variable, as illustrated before. Thus, if for this firm which was launched in March 1993, which had experienced the contingency of a cash-flow crisis in December 1996, there followed an adaptation of the monitoring and control system to accommodate to strategic pricing in March 1997, the duration figure for this accommodation would be 48 months. In this sense, there is a lag of 3 months between the occurrence or timing of the contingent event and the occurrence or timing of the subsequent adaptation of the monitoring and control system. For the cross section of firms in the sample, the correlations of duration variables such as these were computed, producing the results reported on later.

Expressed algebraically, if the i-th firm's duration variable for a contingency has a value of x_t^i, and the duration variable for the subsequent accommodation in the MAS is x_τ^i, the correlation computed is $\rho(x_t, x_\tau)$, for the sample size $i = 1, \ldots, n$. Here, the adaptation of the monitoring and control system to the contingency occurs with lag $\tau - t$. This time lag between appearance of a contingency (e.g. a cash-flow crisis) and the adaptation of a small firm's monitoring and control system (e.g. the adoption of activity based costing), provides a necessary if not sufficient condition for the causality going from the contingency to the adaptation. Because not all firms encountered the same contingencies, and not all firms adapted their monitoring and control system in the same way, the effective sample sizes (n) for these correlations were typically well below the full sample size. For these smaller sample sizes, one depends, in the usual way, on small sample distribution theory for the inferences made.

In Table 13.1, the correlations and the variables to which they relate are identified under the headings of project appraisal, managing costs and computer applications. Table 13.1 displays the Pearson product moment correlation coefficients (r) between the timing of cash-flow crises and the timing of the introduction of new procedures (e.g. pricing, financial modelling). In terms of the statistical methodology behind such coefficients, to assert that the hypothesis of zero population correlation ($\rho = 0$) is false, is to assert dependence of the variables being correlated. Further if the variables being correlated (in this case, the timing of variables) follow a bivariate normal law, then if they are uncorrelated, they are independent. Though this second statement depends on normality, it is robust under considerable departures from it. Furthermore, for large samples, r is itself approximately normal. To test the hypothesis $\rho = 0$, the usual Fisher statistic $\sqrt{(N - 2)}r/\sqrt{(1 - r^2)}$ is referred to the Student t-table with $N - 2$ degrees of freedom. Significance levels for two-tailed tests of the null hypothesis are given in the second column of Table 13.1. The sample size N relevant to this test is given in the third column. N assumes a variety of values, depending on the response rates of respondents and the filter structure of the questionnaire. That is, some questions are only answered if a sequence of conditions is satisfied.

Turning first to the usual methods of project appraisal, one finds that none of the techniques (return on investment, residual income, internal rate of return, payback methods) showed any significant correlation with IS development. This is perhaps to be expected, as we would not normally assume cash-flow to have a strong impact upon the nature or outcome of strategic capital investment decisions.

The time at which any of the methods for managing costs were implemented, on the other hand, was highly correlated with the time at which cash-flow crises

Table 13.1 Correlation of information system development with cash-flow crisis

	Pearson correlation (r)	Significance (p)	Sample size[a] (N)
Methods of project appraisal			
Return on Investment	−0.138	0.598	17
Residual Income	0.594	0.159	7
Internal Rate of Return	−0.088	0.912	4
Payback	−0.065	0.819	15
Methods of cost management			
Just-in-Time	0.738**	0.000	18
Activity-Based Costing	0.832**	0.000	14
Quantitative Research Analysis	0.768	0.232	4
Value Analysis	0.577**	0.004	23
Strategic Pricing	0.078	0.736	21
Transfer Pricing	–	–	4
Computer applications			
Storing Information	0.379*	0.030	33
Project Appraisal	0.549	0.101	10
Financial Modelling	0.375	0.187	14

Notes:
** Correlation is significant at the 0.01 level (two-tailed).
* Correlation is significant at the 0.05 level (two-tailed).
  The r and p values for *Transfer Pricing* cannot be computed because of insufficient sample variation.
a Sample sizes vary, depending on responses to a variety of questionnaire filters.

were experienced. Recall that respondents were asked if, and when, they had experienced a major cash-flow crisis. Specifically, when these crises occurred in their severest form, it was found that firms were also likely subsequently to put in place modern production practices, such as just-in-time methods of management or automated manufacture($r = 0.738**$), to implement modern accounting techniques, such as activity-based costing or throughput accounting($r = 0.832**$), and to use value analysis to identify products or activities that were not adding value ($r = 0.577**$). In addition to these new methods of managing costs within the business, it is also interesting to note that the first use of a computer to store information in the firm is also significantly correlated ($r = 0.379*$) with the worst experience of a cash-flow crisis.

Respondents were also asked whether, in a strategic sense, they had sometimes wished they had access to more finance for the business. We refer now to the correlation results in Table 13.2. When it comes to assessing the link between IS development and the experience of an acute shortfall in finance for strategic purposes, again the methods of managing costs were all positively correlated with the timing of this financial crisis (Table 13.2). Just-in-time methods of management ($r = 0.633*$), activity-based costing ($r = 0.826**$) and value analysis ($r = 0.514*$) were all implemented at a time which corresponded to the firm's experiencing financial budgetary pressure. Furthermore, computers were first used to store information at

Table 13.2 Correlation of information system development with shortfall of finance for strategic purposes

	Pearson correlation (r)	Significance (p)	Sample size[a] (N)
Methods of project appraisal			
Return on Investment	0.058	0.831	16
Residual Income	0.475	0.281	7
Internal Rate of Return	−0.272	0.659	5
Payback	−0.165	0.500	19
Methods of cost management			
Just-in-Time	0.633*	0.011	15
Activity-Based Costing	0.826**	0.000	14
Quantitative Research Analysis	0.917	0.083	4
Value Analysis	0.514*	0.014	22
Strategic Pricing	0.030	0.898	21
Transfer Pricing	–	–	5
Computer applications			
Storing Information	0.389*	0.037	29
Project Appraisal	0.664	0.051	9
Financial Modelling	0.395	0.182	13

Notes:
** Correlation is significant at the 0.01 level (two-tailed).
 * Correlation is significant at the 0.05 level (two-tailed).
   The *r* and *p* values for *Transfer Pricing* cannot be computed because of insufficient sample variation.
 a Sample sizes vary, depending on responses to a variety of questionnaire filters.

a time correlated to this event ($r = 0.389^*$). While we might have expected to see here some evidence of a correlation between financial crises, in investment terms, and methods of appraising capital investment decisions (e.g. return on investment, net present value, internal rate of return, payback period), none is apparent for the samples available. Presumably this is because some firms, even if they are finance-capital constrained (cf. Chapters 5, 6 and 8) still take the going cost of capital as their reference point when using techniques of investment appraisal.

The final contingency of interest here is the implementation of the firm's best innovation or new technology, as perceived by the entrepreneur, who was asked specifically when he thought the firm's best innovation or major improvement had occurred. This suggests, therefore, turning to the results in Table 13.3. The timing of the introduction of techniques for managing costs (JIT, ABC, etc.) is significantly correlated with the timing of best innovations. Thus we find just-in-time ($r = 0.749^{**}$), activity-based costing ($r = 0.777^{**}$) and value analysis ($r = 0.720^{**}$) techniques all having highly significant positive correlations with innovation. Especially noteworthy in the results of Table 13.3, are the significant correlations for implementation of a 'best' or 'new' technology and computer applications. At a more detailed level, the timing of the use of a computer, to store

Table 13.3 Correlation of information system development with implementation of best innovation

	Pearson correlation (r)	Significance (p)	Sample size[a] (N)
Methods of project appraisal			
Return on Investment	−0.163	0.479	21
Residual Income	−0.048	0.929	6
Internal Rate of Return	−0.771	0.127	5
Payback	−0.115	0.552	29
Methods of cost management			
Just-in-Time	0.749*	0.000	22
Activity-Based Costing	0.777**	0.000	16
Quantitative Research Analysis	0.355	0.769	3
Value Analysis	0.720**	0.000	26
Strategic Pricing	−0.065	0.733	30
Transfer Pricing	−0.802	0.055	6
Computer applications			
PC used to Store Information	0.516**	0.000	43
PC used for Project Appraisal	0.706**	0.007	13
PC used for Financial Modelling	0.610**	0.003	22

Notes:
** Correlation is significant at the 0.01 level (two-tailed).
 * Correlation is significant at the 0.05 level (two-tailed).
 a Sample sizes vary, depending on responses to a variety of questionnaire filters.

information ($r = 0.516^{**}$), for project appraisal ($r = 0.706^{**}$) and for financial modelling ($r = 0.610^{**}$), are all significantly positively correlated with the timing of best innovation. These latter results might even be interpreted as suggesting that the best innovation *per se* was the introduction of a personal computer itself to the business. However, probably a more subtle interpretation is appropriate, namely that the best innovation which respondents were referring to were the first use of methods such as project appraisal and financial modelling, which as it happened, were most efficiently introduced through computer implementation.

This section on correlation concludes by asking what has been learned from the results of Tables 13.1–13.3. First, it is notable that the adoption of standard methods of project evaluation does not seem to be precipitated by contingencies like short-term crises (e.g. poor cash flow), long-term crises (e.g. lack of finance for investment), or new innovative steps taken within the firm. Rather, it is methods for managing costs which, above all, seem responsive to these contingencies. It is they which seem to assume the greatest importance in times of change, whether those changes be for the better or for the worse (e.g. a shortfall in finance). The next salient point to notice is that the implementation of computer applications tends to occur when new contingencies arise. Such implementations are generally embraced for information storage, whatever the contingency.

But in particular, their intensity of use is greatest when the contingency impacting on the firm involves the implementation of best innovation. Then, computer applications extend beyond data storage to more analytical purposes; specifically, to project appraisal and to financial modelling. Thus although specific methods of project appraisal (e.g. IRR) do not correlate with innovation, the generic use of such methods does.

Reaching conclusions about cause and effect is notoriously difficult, but the correlation analysis earlier is not entirely silent on such issues. The significant correlations obtained do relate, unequivocally, to situations in which cause (here contingency) is *prior to* effect (small firm adaptation). However, nuances of interpretation remain. It might be asked, for example, whether the shortfall in financial capital for strategic investment came to light only following detailed analysis of a proposed project, say, in terms of value analysis or computerised financial modelling. Or did the need for more finance for long-term investment give rise to a subsequent need for more detailed and rigorous financial analysis and reporting? On issues like this, further work should be done. But certainly the above correlations highlight significant and noteworthy associations between the timing of events, or contingencies, and the timing of changes in the small firm's procedures and practices. This, in itself, is a significant finding, particularly as regards the identification of specific contingencies and the associated specific adaptations in ISs. More sophisticated analysis must now be used to elaborate the treatment of causality, and the following chapter aims to address such issues.

13.5   Conclusion

This chapter reports upon tests of hypotheses which arise from contingency theory. These tests were applied to a body of small firms' data which was rich in its representation of the IS within the small firm. This may be specifically interpreted as the MAS or, more analytically, as its monitoring and control system. The key hypothesis was that cash-flow crisis, funding shortage and innovation all had timings which corresponded with IS development. This hypothesis was sustained under comprehensive time-phased correlation analysis. It was found to be particularly well supported in the cases of cost management and computer applications.

Endnote

1 An alternative representation, which runs in terms of an analytical cross-tabulation of authors' contributions to the subject is provided in Emmanuel *et al.* (1990, Ch. 2).

14 Small firm type, organisational form and contingency

(with Julia A. Smith)

14.1 Introduction

In many ways, Chapters 13 and 14 go together. They are based on the same subset of data, from the larger database of Chapter 2, and they both focus on contingency theory. Finally, they both use an IS to characterise the organisational form of the small firm. However, these chapters do differ. Most significantly, they differ in the techniques of analysis used. Thus, in this chapter, new techniques are utilised to investigate the properties of contingency. First, cluster analysis (cf. its use in Chapter 9 above) is used to identify three classes of firm types, which are shaped by contingencies (Section 14.2) (Gordon and Miller, 1976); and, second, regression analysis is used to show how organisational form is influenced by contingencies (see Section 14.3).

Cluster analysis is used to test the hypothesis that contingencies cluster to form three configurations of small firms, adaptive, running blind and stagnant. The cluster analysis which is performed identifies three classes of firm types, which are shaped by contingencies. These types can be related to the empirical analysis of three firm archetypes, first undertaken by Miller (1975). This new typology of firms is useful for further empirical analysis, for enterprise policy frameworks and for enriching the vocabulary and prescriptive content of small business strategy.

A central tenet of contingency theory is that technological uncertainty (Woodward, 1958, 1965), production systems (Brignall, 1997), strategy (Chandler, 1962) and the market are key determinants of organisational form. It is found, for example, in Chapter 13, that most aspects of the theory are well supported by empirical evidence. An exception is that, for the relatively new micro-firms of the sample (cf. Chapter 2), technological uncertainty seems unimportant as a determinant of organisational form. Furthermore, a specific hypothesis is tested about the determinants of the form of small firm ISs. These are identified in the literature as subunit interdependence, market dynamics and work methods (Hayes, 1977). Some support is found for this hypothesis, particularly in terms of the effects of subunit interdependence on small firm information system (IS) complexity.

The general conclusions reached are that:

(a) cluster analysis successfully separates the data into three firm types that can be related directly to the adaptive, stagnant and running blind categories identified in contingency theory; and

(b) the organisational form of the small firm, as measured by a type of weighted headcount, is successfully explained by generic categories of contingencies under the headings of technological uncertainty, production systems, business strategy and market environment. Thus the evidence is found to be generally supportive of contingency theory, suitably adapted to a small firms context.

14.2   Cluster analysis of small firm types

The works of Gordon and Miller (1976), Otley (1980) and Alum (1997) all suggest that the effects of contingencies on the form of IS adopted within a firm lead to distinct firm types. This subsection aims to identify empirically, for the first time, these firm types suggested by the above authors, using statistical cluster analysis. Next, firm structure is explained by contingency variables like strategy, markets and production systems. The form of the IS and, specifically, the accounting information system (AIS) is then explained by subunit interdependence, market dynamics and work method specification, as suggested by the work of Hayes (1977).

The work of Gordon and Miller (1976) is an exemplar of the view that the firm's IS is determined by its environment, its organisational form and by its decision-making style. This argument can be interpreted as suggesting that these contingent variables tend to 'cluster'. Objective empirical content is given to this, in a statistical sense, below. It will be recalled that their work suggests that the clustering of contingencies leads to three types of firm, the adaptive, the 'running blind' and the stagnant. The purpose of this subsection is to take the notion of a cluster a step further than its informal use in Gordon and Miller (1976). Statistical cluster analysis involves four steps: (1) selection of classes or types of firms, which here is determined by existing analysis, like that of Gordon and Miller (1976); (2) determination of measures of similarity between firm types; (3) grouping of firms into firm types and (4) the interpretation and description of the results of grouping. The data reduction which arises from grouping data into firm types is both useful in suggesting further forms of analysis, and in identifying underlying theoretical structures in the data.

The statistical procedure for identifying clusters was undertaken using SPSS software. The Euclidean distance metric was adopted. Thus if the attributes of a first set of measured characteristics are given by the vector $(x_{11}.........x_{1k})$ and, of a second set, are given by the vector $(x_{21}.........x_{2k})$, then the dissimilarity between these vectors will be is measured by the Euclidean squared distance $(x_{11} - x_{21})^2 + \cdots\cdots\cdots + (x_{1k} - x_{2k})^2$. The technique utilised aims to minimise *within* cluster variation, and to maximise *between* cluster variation. In the latter case, the distance between clusters is measured from their respective centroids.[1]

A cluster analysis was undertaken, using the following four variables: (1) growth in sales (*Sales*); (2) change in size of the firm's market share (*Market*); (3) 'discretionary time', in the sense of the proportion of time left available, during a typical week, for the owner-manager to make decisions (in terms of planning, strategy, etc.) within the business (*Time*) and (4) the use of informal, rather than formal planning methods (*Informal*). These variables were chosen because they capture key aspects of the evidence used to characterise firm types by contingency dynamics, flexibility, decision making and formality.

By reference to Table 14.1, it can be seen that the clustering technique adopted was indeed able to separate the data successfully into three types of firms. Their quantitative features are given in Table 14.1. In terms of clustering, Type 1 firms are 'most' separated from Types 2 and 3. The latter, while separated, are 'closer' to one another than to Type 1 firms.

Type 3 small firms are similar to, but not identical with, Gordon and Miller's (1976) 'adaptive firms'. They have the following characteristics: high sales growth; high market share increase; high discretion and low informality. Their high sales growth suggests dynamic small firms. Furthermore, such firms are flexible in the sense of enjoying success in expanding market share (cf. Chapters 15 and 17). In this firm type, the entrepreneur has a lot of discretionary time, in the sense of time for decision-making, rather than time allocated to creating the goods or services. Arguably, this is a characteristic of a high quality small firm.

The Type 2 small firm experiences considerably lower sales growth; 176% over 4 years, compared to 315% over 4 years for Type 3 firms. It also has less market share penetration: just +6 per cent compared to +9 per cent for Type 3 firms. Thus this small firm type is less dynamic, but displays some adaptiveness. It is far less attuned to formal planning than other firm types, suggesting it is more intuitively run. It approximates best, in this sense, to the 'running blind' type of firm which Gordon and Miller (1976) have identified and discussed. As compared to other firm types, Type 2 small firms spend proportionately more time on production than on more strategic activities. Their emphasis on the process of providing goods or services for customers squeezes out activities like planning, managing and strategic thinking. Thus the 'running blind' title seems to be fittingly applied to Type 2 small firms.

Table 14.1 Statistical evidence on firm types using cluster analysis

	Sales	*Market*	*Time*	*Informal*	*n*
Type 1 firms	142 (49)	−0.4 (3)	79 (11)	0.29 (0.18)	8
Type 2 firms	176 (71)	6 (3)	57 (15)	0.33 (0.33)	17
Type 3 firms	315 (86)	9 (11)	89 (5)	0.18 (0.12)	23

Note:
In this table, the main figures are rounded mean values. Standard errors are given in brackets. Mean values were stable under 5% trimming. Forty-eight firms were available for the cluster analysis, using the Euclidean metric (see Chapter 9).

By consideration of the statistics in Table 14.1, it is now possible to analyse Type 1 small firms. They clearly perform unimpressively. Sales growth was only moderate, being less than half that of Type 3 small firms. A 95% confidence interval for the difference between mean (μ) sales growth for Type 3 and Type 1 small firms is $(224 \leq \mu_3 - \mu_1 \leq 122) = 0.95$ for a critical value of $t_{0.025}$ (with 29 d.f.) of 2.045. This does not contain the origin, so the hypothesis of equal growth rates of sales is rejected. Adaption was poor, in terms of market share. Indeed, on an average, Type 1 small firms had lost market share. A 95% confidence interval for the difference between mean market shares for Type 3 and Type 1 small firms is $(14.6 \leq \mu_3 - \mu_1 \leq 4.2) = 0.95$ which does not contain the origin, so the hypothesis of equal market shares is rejected. Type 1 small firms are more informal in their running of business than Type 3 small firms, and also have less discretionary time for planning and decision-making. Although Type 1 and Type 3 firms have very different performances, the first group being poor, and the second being high performers, both groups have relatively active discretionary policies. In their emphasis on planning and management, they tend to generate an increased demand for IS use and development. This confirms the insight of Jorrisen, Laveren and Devinck (1997a, b) to the effect that it is either poorly performing small firms or very successful small firms that generate the greatest IS needs. For Type 1 small firms, the stagnant ones, they act in this way to attempt to counteract poor market dynamics and inflexibility. For Type 3 small firms, the adaptive ones, IS development is stimulated by the desire to continue to exploit successfully the dynamics of their markets.

The above argument can be summarised by reference to Table 14.2. Essentially it captures the sense of the statistics in Table 14.1, and translates that evidence into the terminology of contingency theorists like Gordon and Miller (1976), Otley (1980) and Alum (1997). Thus the work of these authors is supported, in the sense that a non-judgmental technique for grouping firms, namely statistical cluster analysis, singles out three distinct small firm types which relate closely to the stagnant, running blind and adaptive categories. The stagnant small firm is inflexible, lacks formal planning, and has poor market dynamics. To compensate, indeed to survive, it is activist in its management of the business. 'Running blind' small firms also lack formal planning. They are less challenged, performance wise, than stagnant small firms, so they do not use activist management. Yet they lack flexibility, and have unexciting market dynamics. The successful small firms are more formal in their

Table 14.2 Categories of firm types identified by cluster analysis

Attribute	Firm type		
	Stagnant	Running blind	Adaptive
Dynamics	Low	Moderate	High
Flexibility	Poor	Moderate	High
Discretion	Active	Moderate	Active
Informality	High	High	Moderate

planning and management than the stagnant and 'running blind' small firms. They enjoy far superior performance, benefiting from lively market dynamics, to which they accommodate with flexibility. Because of their good performance, they pursue an activist management style.

14.3 Regression analysis of organisational form and contingency

This empirical section adopts more formal methods of statistical inference to test contingency theory, as compared to those utilised in Chapter 3. The key contingencies to be considered are technological uncertainty, production system complexity, business strategy and the market environment. In the empirical analysis, these are to be treated as independent variables. The dependent variable is organisational form. As this is a multidimensional attribute, the main first task is to create an index of, or proxy for, organisational form. A new measure is proposed for this purpose, which is, at root, a measure of organisational scale. The variable suggested is a type of weighted headcount, in which full-time workers are weighted at 100 per cent, part-time workers at 50 per cent, and trainees at 25 per cent. The strength of this index or proxy is that worker types play an explicit role in calibrating organisational form within the small firm. Furthermore, the weighting scheme at least partially captures their relative significance within the organisation. This dependent variable will be defined as the weighted headcount (*HeadCount*). Contingency variables, as generic categories of independent variables, were considered under the headings of technological uncertainty, production systems, strategy and markets. Within these generic categories, there were three independent variables in each. Table 14.3 lists these independent variables in the left-hand column. The table also reports upon a linear regression with *HeadCount* as the dependent variable and 13 independent variables, including the constant term.

The statistical model used is a pure cross section model, estimated by ordinary least squares. The coefficient of multiple determination, adjusted for degrees of freedom $(\overline{R}^2)$ is 0.295, which is high for cross section models. Concerning goodness-of-fit, the F statistic for the whole model is highly statistically significant, having the small probability level of 0.001. As usual this statistic provides a test of the null hypothesis that all the coefficients in the regression are zero. Thus it tests whether the regression equation as a whole is insignificant. Given the high F value, this null hypothesis is clearly rejected. Consider now the independent variables listed under the four generic headings.

14.3.1 Technological uncertainty

There are three independent variables to be considered under the heading of technological uncertainty. *ProcessInvention* is a measure of the competitive threat which rivals' process inventions impose on the small firm. *ProductInvention* is defined in a similar way, but with 'product' inserted for 'process'. Here the usual definition is adopted, that process invention involves improving an existing productive

Table 14.3 Regression of contingencies on head count

Contingencies	Independent variables	Coefficients
Technological uncertainty	*ProcessInvention*	−0.617 (−0.298)
	ProductInvention	2.934 (1.404)
	TechnicalChange	−2.473 (−0.960)
Production systems	*AttributableCost*	1.537 (1.811*)
	WagesShare	5.932×10^{-2} (1.146)
	CostCut	0.513 (0.193)
Strategy	*ImpactHorizon*	0.177 (2.926**)
	SacrificeControl	1.007 (0.423)
	SacrificeProfit	−0.411 (0.128)
Market	*MarketShare*	7.645×10^{-2} (1.603)
	MajorRivals	0.152 (2.416**)
	Competition	1.954 (1.258)
	Constant	−11.359 (−1.836)

Notes:
Defined variable is *HeadCount*.
$\bar{R}^2 = 0.295$; $F = 3.369$**; t-values are in brackets under coefficients.
**Highly statistically significant; *statistically significant.

activity (see Q.7.1 in Section 7, *Technical Change*, in AQ1 of appendix to this book), whereas product invention involves discovering an entirely new good (see Q.7.2 in appendix to this book). Process and product invention are not mechanically achieved, but are shrouded in uncertainty, as is all invention. Technical change relates not just to the firm, but to its industry as a whole. These two variables measure the owner-manager's perceived strength of competition, in terms of rivals' process and product invention or innovation, on a Likert scale, where a higher number means stronger competition. In that sense it is a measure of the technological environment. Again, the scale of technological change in the firm's industry is as perceived by the owner-manager. It is of note that none of the independent variables that lie under the generic contingency of technological uncertainty are significant. This seems to be an important and interesting result. It suggests that the operational domain of contingency theory does not necessarily extend from large firms, for which it was developed, to small firms, which are being investigated for the first time, here, in this context.

14.3.2   Production systems

Consider now the next three variables, grouped under the generic heading of production systems. *AttributableCost* is a categorical variable (see Q.3.6 in AQ1) which measures the degree to which components of cost may be directly attributed to products. So, for example, the more costs (such as direct materials, labour, production overheads, selling costs, etc.) that can be attributed to individual units of production, the higher the value for this variable. *WageShare* measures the proportion which the cost of wages bears to total cost (see Q.3.7 in AQ1). *CostCut* is a binary variable which measures whether or not the small firm has something to gain in a competitive sense if it cuts costs to a marked degree, according to the owner-manager's estimation (see Q.3.13 in AQ1). Although these three variables appear to have a positive effect on *HeadCount*, only the *AttributableCost* variable has a coefficient which is statistically significant, in this case, with a probability level of 0.075. This suggests that an aspect of production systems, as a contingency, does indeed appear to affect organisational form, as measured by weighted headcount. The use of an attributable cost system, which attributes elements of costs to products, like material and labour, tends to encourage larger small firms in an organisational sense.

14.3.3   Strategy

The next generic contingency is strategy (see Section 4, *Business Strategy*, in AQ1). Three independent variables are listed under this heading. *ImpactHorizon* is a real variable (see Q.4.2 in AQ1). It measures, in months, the time or planning horizon of the entrepreneur when the impact of a decision upon the business is being contemplated. It is, in a sense, a measure of the far-sightedness or the strategic inclination of the entrepreneur (see Q.4.9 in AQ1). *SacrificeControl* is a binary variable (i.e. 1 = 'yes', 0 = 'no') which asks whether the owner-manager is willing to sacrifice some control over the firm, for example by permitting outside equity holding, to enhance the performance of the business (see Q.4.10 in AQ1). *SacrificeProfit* is another binary variable, which shows whether the owner-manager might be willing to sacrifice short-run profit in order to promote the growth of the business. The sacrifice of control, and of profit, have an insignificant effect upon organisational form. However, the effect of *ImpactHorizon* (see Q.4.2 in AQ1) upon the dependent variable is positive, and highly statistically significant with a probability level of 0.005. This indicates that forward planning by the small firm, which involves following through the consequences of current decisions to their future impact, has a strong positive effect on organisational change, measured by weighted headcount.

14.3.4   The market

The last generic contingency is the market. Under this heading there are three specific contingency variables. *MarketShare* is a real variable, measuring the market share of the principal product group by sales volume (see Q.1.8 in AQ1). *MajorRivals* is an integer variable, counting the number of major rivals of the small firm, as estimated by the owner-manager (see Q.1.9 in AQ1). *Competition* is an attitudinal categorical variable, which measures on a Likert scale the perceived strength of competition in the small firm's main market, where a higher figure represents stronger competition (see Sheet 1.11 in AQ1). It is evident from Table 6 that *MarketShare* and *Competition* do not have statistically significant effects upon *HeadCount*. However, the influence of *MajorRivals* on *HeadCount* is positive and highly statistically significant. That is to say, strong competitive pressure, here calibrated by number of major rivals, is an important stimulus to organisational change, proxied here by weighted *HeadCount*.

The regression in Table 14.3 is of interest in both a statistical and a theoretical sense. It demonstrates that, within the small firm, organisational development, as proxied by a weighted *HeadCount* measure, can indeed be explained in a statistical sense by a range of contingent variables, which fall within generic contingency categories which are familiar from the extant literature on contingency theory. These generic categories are production systems, business strategy and market environment. It is of note that, for the case of small firms, no contingent variables under the generic contingency heading of technological uncertainty, were significant. Concerning specific contingent variables, complex costing systems, far-sighted decision-making, and competitive pressure from major rivals, all seem to be important influences on the organisational form of the small firm.

In Reid and Smith (1999, Table 6) this set of results is further highlighted in a parsimonious regression model which drops insignificant variables. The effect is dramatic, raising $\bar{R}^2$ to 0.325 and the F statistic to 8.213, which has a probability level of less than 0.001. By removing 'noisy' variables from the regression (in Table 6 of Reid and Smith, 1999), the overall significance of the regression is improved, and all the contingent variables used, *AttributableCost, ImpactHorizon, MarketShare, MajorRivals* and *Competition* are statistically, or highly statistically significant.[2]

14.3.5   The applicability of contingency theory to small firms

This evidence leads to sharp conclusions about the applicability of contingency theory to small firms. Technological uncertainty is viewed as a key contingency in the extant literature. It was identified as being potentially important in the earliest works on the subject by Burns and Stalker (1961). However, it should be pointed out that this early work related to the very large, technologically intensive firms. However, most micro-firms do not approach to this technological intensity. The only innovative step relevant to most micro-firms is business inception itself. Such micro-firms have little formal research and development capability. They take just small innovative steps, by such means as being the firm which is 'first to market'.

In the work of Reid and Smith (1999), reported on briefly above and in footnote 2, generic contingencies of production systems and strategy do have one contingency variable each, which appears to be important. The *AtttibutableCost* variable has a positive coefficient with a probability level of 0.072. The *ImpactHorizon* variable has a positive coefficient which is highly statistically significant, with a probability level of just 0.002. Even more important than these contingency variables are the three that come under the generic contingency of the market. These three contingency variables are *MarketShare, MajorRivals* and *Competition*. The coefficients of all three are positive and highly statistically significant, having probability levels of 0.052, 0.003 and 0.048, respectively. In summary, the evidence on contingencies, as they apply to small firms is that technological uncertainty seems unimportant, as compared to its impact on larger firms. Rivalry and competition are the main contingent variables to have an impact on organisational form, from the market category. Aspects of production systems, specifically the ability to attribute cost, and of Strategy, specifically the ability to plan ahead, are also important.

14.3.6   The management accounting system

The focus of discussion will now be narrowed by looking specifically at the management accounting system (MAS) within a small firm, and its determinants, in terms of contingencies. Of particular relevance is the work of Hayes (1977). His hypothesis is that the form which an MAS takes depends on three contingent variables, namely, subunit interdependence, market dynamics and work methods. Related to this is the work of Libby and Waterhouse (1996), which develops this approach by seeking to predict the development of MAS by contingencies like decentralisation, competition and organisational practices. These theoretical approaches provide the basis for the empirical analysis which follows.

The first step is to develop a measure of MAS complexity. This is accomplished by measuring MAS complexity (*Complex*) by a type of count variable. The basis for its construction is the use of all types of accounting information within the small firm. These are grouped into planning, activation and decision-making categories (see Q.8.8 of AQ4 in appendix to this book). For each category, several measures are utilised. So, for example, under planning and analysis, the owner-manager might say that he uses accounting information to identify cost-cutting opportunities, or to reach specific levels of output. Under activation and direction of daily operations, he might use such information to assess and manage stock levels, or to measure the use of work time. And under problem-solving and decision-making, he might find accounting information helpful in assessing a new project or investment, or in analysing the riskiness of a new idea. The more uses to which he puts accounting information, the higher will be the figure which measures the complexity of his MAS (*Complex*).

Next we take four measures of subunit interdependence, three measures of market dynamics and three measures of workplace methods to try to explain this MAS complexity. To illustrate, one way in which subunit interdependence can be measured is by the way the information flow is divided up within the business. The variable *Divide* is a binary variable, indicating whether or not information is split up in reporting (i.e. divisional or segmental reporting) (see Q.8.5 in AQ4). For example, information may be split up by customers or by geographic areas. Other variables under this heading of subunit interdependence are concerned with the splitting up of tasks within the small firm. They are all binary variables. *Define* measures whether or not employees' tasks are well defined within the business; in other words, is there a clear job description (see Q.6.11 in AQ4). *KnowTasks* measures whether personnel within the firm are familiar with tasks other than their own, and so whether there is flexibility and transferability between employees (see Q.6.12 in AQ4). *TakeOnTasks* measures whether, in certain circumstances, personnel within the firm take on each others tasks (see Q.6.13 in AQ4).

Market dynamics were measured by three variables: change in market share from one year to the next (*Market*) (see Q.1.8 in AQ4); the extent of the market covered by the firm (*MarketExtent*) in terms of its regionality, internationality etc., again on a Likert scale, where a higher figure represents a wider geographical market (see Q.1.7 in AQ4); and the growth of sales from 1 year to the next (*Sales*) (see Q.1.4 in AQ4).

Work methods were measured by three variables. *Discretion* measures the amount of discretion a superior has over a subordinate, where a higher figure represents more control (see Q.6.6 in AQ4). *Authority* measures the extent to which there is flexibility in the exercise of authority at any level. For example, might superiors intervene selectively in exercising authority over subordinates, or is a simple hierarchical structure in place, whereby authority is only exercised at the level directly below, by immediate superiors (see Q.6.4 in AQ4)? *Standard-Procedures* measures the extent to which monitoring is standard (i.e. at regular, known intervals) or discretionary (i.e. as and when required) (see Q.6.8 in AQ4). In Table 14.4 a linear regression tests the theories of Hayes (1977) and Libby and Waterhouse (1996). The complexity of the MAS within the small firm is the dependent variable (*Complex*). Estimation is by ordinary least squares. Variable types are grouped under the headings of subunit interdependence, market dynamics, and work methods.

Given the scope and complexity of questions asked, there are many missing values. This restricts degrees of freedom for estimation, and only 32 firms were available to run this regression. The R^2 is satisfactory, though the F statistic is not significant. Two of the variables have coefficients which are significant. The first is *Divide* which is a variable in the subunit interdependence category.

Table 14.4 Regression of determinants of MAS complexity

Category	Variable	Coefficient
Subunit interdependence	*Define*	0.437 (0.195)
	KnowTasks	1.497 (0.226)
	TakeOnTasks	5.407 (1.209)
	Divide	5.690 (1.807*)
Market dynamics	*Sales*	-4.31×10^{-3} (-0.530)
	MarketShare	0.253 (0.193)
	Market	-4.45×10^{-2} (-0.741)
Work methods	*Discretion*	4.499 (2.269**)
	Authority	-3.247 (-0.826)
	StandardProcedures	3.873 (-0.981)
	Constant	-9.776 (-0.841)

Notes:
$R^2 = 0.348$; $F = 1.176$; *t*-values are in brackets (after) coefficients.
**Highly statistically significant; *statistically significant.

It has a probability level of 0.084. The second is *Discretion* which is in the work methods category. It has a probability level of 0.033.

In Reid and Smith (1999, Table 8) a parsimonious variant of the above regression is estimated. It uses only the variables under the heading of subunit interdependence. Both *Define* and *Divide* had coefficients which were statistically significant (and positive) and the overall regression was significant ($F = 2.27$). The explanations of MAS deriving from Hayes (1977), Libby and Waterhouse (1996) has some measure of support in this small firms context. Subunit interdependence and work methods provide significant explanations of MAS complexity. The former effect seems more important. In particular, well-defined task definition within the small firm, and the splitting up of business functions, in terms of information handling, have clear positive effects on MAS complexity.

14.4 Conclusion

The purpose of this chapter has been to see whether contingencies can explain or predict IS form, and in particular the form of the MAS. The general conclusion is in the affirmative. However, it is clear that going down from large firm applications to small firm applications limits the scope and emphasis of contingency theory. Most notably, at this new micro-firm level, there is a lesser influence of technological uncertainty. However, even at this fine micro level, subunit interdependence plays an important role in shaping the MAS.

The first hypothesis was that contingencies clustered to identify three firm types, adaptive, stagnant and running blind. Using a Euclidean distance measure, a good separation of the sample into these firm types was achieved, with each type bearing a close resemblance to one of the three recognised categories. Furthermore, over key dimensions like sales growth and market shares, differences between attributes of groups were statistically significant.

The second hypothesis tested was that features of technological uncertainty, production systems, strategy and the market determine the organisational form of the small firm, expressed in terms of an index measure, the weighted headcount. This hypothesis was tested using linear regression analysis. It was supported in most aspects, except that, for these new micro-firms, technological uncertainty was unimportant as a determinant of this specific measure of organisational form.

The third hypothesis was that the complexity of the MAS adopted within the small firm was determined by subunit interdependence, market dynamics and work methods. The measure of MAS complexity used was a high count variable over the dimensions planning, activation and decision-making. This hypothesis was tested using linear regression analysis, and some support was found for it, particularly in terms of subunit interdependence affecting MAS complexity.

The different ways of approaching the testing of contingency theory, both in this chapter and in Chapter 13, are each, in their ways, supportive of the theory. Through their different methods of approach, they also provide a kind of triangulation on the strength of the theory, as well as a test of its robustness. In sum, they sustain the case for the application of contingency theory in a small firms contexts, be it all subject to certain modifications.

The four different hypotheses tested in Chapters 13 and 14 take different approaches to testing aspects of contingency theory. As restricted assumptions needed to be made, in order to test aspects of this theory, the coverage is by no means complete. Within the limits set by the methods used, the outcomes of the four tests of hypotheses are each, in their own ways, supportive of these aspects of the theory. The main limitation suggested is that the scope of the contingency theory, in which the IS is treated as a set of management accounts, may be somewhat reduced when one moves from a large firm to (as here) a small firms context.

APPENDIX

Definitions of Variables

Variable	Definition
AttributableCost	The degree to which components of total cost may be directly attributed to products
Authority	The extent to which there is flexibility in the exercise of authority at any level, i.e. it is exercised at next level down ($=0$) or at discretion ($=1$)
Competition	Strength of competition overall ($=0$, 1, 2, 3), where a higher figure represents stronger competition
Complex	The complexity of the firm's MAS, in terms of its use in planning and analysis, activation and direction of daily operations, and problem-solving and decision-making
CostCut	Whether firm gains advantage by extreme cost-cutting [$=0$, 'no', $=1$, 'yes']
Define	Precision of definition of areas of specialisation, in terms of clarity of job description
Discretion	Amount of discretion superior has over subordinates [$=0$, 1, 2, 3, 4, 5], where a higher figure represents more discretion or control
Divide	Whether or not information is reported by segment or division [$=0$, 'no', $=1$, 'yes']
Headcount	Weighted measure of total employment, giving a measure of organisational form
ImpactHorizon	Number of months owner-manager looks or plans ahead, when considering impact of decisions
Informal	Whether or not planning is conducted formally or informally
KnowTasks	Whether different specialists in the firm are knowledgeable about others' skills [$=0$, 'no', $=1$, 'yes']

Continued

Definitions of Variables—cont'd

Variable	Definition
MajorRivals	Number of major rivals, as estimated by owner-manager ($n \leq 100$)
Market	Change in percentage share of market held from one year to the next
MarketShare	Share of the market held for firm's major product group
ProcessInvention	Strength of competitive pressure put on by rivals' process innovation
ProductInvention	Strength of competitive pressure put on firm by rivals' new products
SacrificeControl	Whether respondent willing to sacrifice proportion of stake held in order to promote growth [=0, 'no', =1, 'yes']
SacrificeProfit	Whether respondent willing to accept smaller profits to expand the business [=0, 'no', =1, 'yes']
Sales	Increase in sales from one year to the next
StandardProcedures	Whether monitoring is standard (=0) or discretionary (=1)
TakeOnTasks	Whether different specialists take on each others' tasks [=0, 'no', =1, 'yes']
TechnicalChange	Whether there has been a lot of technical change in firm's industry [=0, 'no', =1, 'yes']
Time	Discretionary time (as a proportion of total time spent in the business) available in a typical week for making decisions
WagesShare	Percentage of total costs that are attributed to wages

Endnotes

1 The centroid is the point of means for a cluster. See Cooper and Weekes (1983, Ch. 13).
2 Table 6 of Reid and Smith (1999) is

Contingencies	Variables	Coefficients	t-statistics
Production	*AttributableCost*	1.297	1.825*
Strategy	*ImpactHorizon*	0.180	3.297**
Market	*MarketShare*	7.811×10^{-2}	1.980*
	MajorRivals	0.160	3.046**
	Competition	2.520	2.009**
	Constant	10.161	2.267**

Notes:
$\overline{R}^2 = 0.325; F = 8.213**$
**Highly statistically significant; *statistically significant.
These results are discussed further in the main text. See also Mitchell, Reid and Smith (2000).

Part 6

Flexibility

15 Flexibility, growth and survival

(with Bernadette Power)

15.1 Introduction

Part 6 of this book, of which this is the first chapter, is concerned with the flexibility of the small firm. Flexibility has already been looked at, especially in terms of control of the wage bill, e.g. by changing the ratio of part-time to full-time workers, in Chapters 4, 5, 7 and 11. Supporting literature, confirming this flexibility for small firms, includes Simmons (2001) and Ndimande (2000). This flexibility, if it exists, is not considered as a virtue in itself, but rather as a useful attribute, which should have positive implications for growth and performance (of which survival is one aspect). The three following chapters consider flexibility from three standpoints. First (Chapter 16), flexibility is looked at in terms of the ability to increase or decrease firm size towards an optimal small firm size (in relation to factors of production, technology and market opportunities). Second (Chapter 17), flexibility is looked at in terms of the market extent that the small firm is able to exploit, be it local, national or international. Third (Chapter 18) flexibility is looked at in terms of speed of adaptation to the turbulent conditions (Beesley and Hamilton, 1984; Markusen and Teitz, 1985), which a small firm may encounter. This chapter is a peparatory, in that it considers key concepts and definitions, and introduces the basis of analysis in each of the three subsequent chapters.

15.2 Growth and viability

The flexibility of small firms explains their growth and viability, see Brock and Evans (1989), Piore and Sabel (1984) and Acs *et al.* (1990). Thus small firms survive and prosper, alongside larger firms, because of their relative flexibility. For example, smaller firms are more flexible because they have proportionately fewer impediments to organisational change. To illustrate, they have a lesser need to employ hierarchy to control their operation (Reid, 1998a, b).

Another argument, as in the introduction to this chapter, would be that small firms are relatively more flexible because they offer opportunities for the greater intensity of utilisation of variable factors of production. An illustration of this would be their tendency to the casualisation of labour to enhance performance (Reid, 1999a–c), as discussed earlier.

A further argument, due to Carlsson (1989) is convincing, in that the development of theoretical ideas about flexibility has been to the detriment of improving our knowledge about its empirical dimensions. Carlsson (1989) identified three important aspects of flexibility in his empirical examination of larger firms. These were operational, tactical and strategic flexibility. This approach of Carlsson must be modified in the present SME context, in two respects: first the focus must shift to the small firm, away from the large firm; and second, more attention must be given to that aspect of flexibility that has been under-explored in the extant literature, merely because it is the most difficult to calibrate, namely strategic flexibility.

15.3   Flexibility and performance

This section aims to achieve three things. First, it discusses concepts of flexibility and firm-specific turbulence (the latter being particularly relevant to Chapter 18). Second, it discusses conceptual problems of the measurement of performance, leaving to Section 15.4 the explicit consideration of how to calibrate performance. Third, it discusses briefly the effects that flexibility, and firm-specific turbulence, are expected to have on performance.

Early evidence on the relationship between flexibility and performance was provided by Smallbone *et al.* (1992). It was found that firms which had been active in making adjustments were the most successful, in terms of growth in real turnover, employment change and survival. These authors used data from mature manufacturing firms in the United Kingdom. However, they did not examine the process, or speed, by which adjustments were made, nor did they look at performance implications of such adjustments. Part 6 of this book, of which this is the first chapter, aims to remedy these shortcomings of earlier work. For example, speed of adjustment, period by period, is considered explicitly in Chapter 16 and 17. Furthermore, a related flexibility, speed of response, in an organisational or decision-making sense, is considered in Chapter 18.

According to Stigler (1939), a firm's choice of cost structure determines its degree of flexibility. The shape of the cost curve determines how responsive output decisions are to price changes. Flexibility is greater with flat-bottomed average cost curves, and flat or gently inclined marginal cost curves, in the context of U-shaped cost curves. Central to Stigler's notion of flexibility is the idea that expected profit will increase with greater flexibility. Thus, the more flexible a firm is, the higher its expected performance. The marginal gain is greater, the greater is environmental uncertainty. Thus greater flexibility is preferred to lesser flexibility, when the environment is uncertain.[1]

The work of Mills and Schumann (1985) is notable in that it explicitly associated the notion of greater flexibility with smaller, rather than larger firms. They have argued that small firms achieve greater flexibility through their ability to alter variable factors of production more readily.[2] This source of flexibility enables small firms to thrive in uncertain environments. Mills and Schumann (1985) have relied on Stigler's (1939) view that flexibility should be inversely related to the convexity of the cost function. This can be measured by the elasticity of supply at the mean price, where it is assumed that price equates supply and demand, when the environment is uncertain. Empirically, the Mills and Schuman (1985) measure of flexibility was approximated by an index of firm sales variability or employment variability.[3] Other measures adopted include those of Acs *et al.* (1990). They explained flexibility in terms of increases in small firm presence, and decreases in mean plant size, using measures of change in production technology.

In examining flexibility in the theory of the firm, Carlsson (1989) argued that flexibility is not necessarily inherent in small firms. Rather, it arises from the ability of small firms to use variable factors of production as their source of flexibility. This occurs because the existence of few organisational barriers allows small firms to mount a quick response to detected changes in their environment. Relevant to this perspective is Ghemawat's (1991) view on the source of flexibility. He would hold that flexibility arises from the expected value-added which the firm can generate from revising its strategy. It does so by adopting alternative courses of action, as the outcomes of uncertain events unfold.

Although Ghemawat (1991) developed the idea in a corporate context, it is also entirely applicable to the small firms' case. Thus, it is as true for small firms as for large firms that the value-added created by flexibility arises in some sense from 'the degree of preparedness'. Specifically, this refers to the ability of the firm to commit the necessary resources to pursuing different courses of action. Flexibility in this sense is not the optimisation of strategy, but rather the selection of strategies that can be adapted to a range of critical outcomes.

Ghemawat's (1991) conception of flexibility, adapted in the case of this book to the small firm's context, has been influential in the formulation of dimensions of flexibility in Chapter 12. In that chapter, reference is made to them in terms of *Agility* and *Speed*. *Agility* arises from the ability of the small firm to use variable factors of production to assist in achieving adaptations to its internal organisational structure. Thus, the agile small firm is responsive to change or prepared for change. *Speed* is measured by the ability of the small firm to act expeditiously in the face of both precipitating influences (arising from its environment), and consequential adjustments (arising from its own organizational change). Thus, the speedy small firm acts quickly before and after internal organizational change. The lower the reaction-time needed by the small firm to detect changes in the environment, the more flexible is this small firm. Thus, the specific interpretation of *Speed* used throughout Chapter 18 is that of 'elapsed time'. The shorter is elapsed time, the greater is 'speed' in the conventional sense. This elapsed time interpretation of *Speed* should be kept in mind throughout that chapter.

As well as acting on precipitating influences and consequential adjustments, the small firm needs to be able to detect that circumstances have changed *per se*. To illustrate, Mata (1993) has found that detecting precipitating influences can be a source of flexibility in small firms, and this ability differs across entrepreneurs. He found that if entrepreneurs within the small firms' sector were not alert to detecting environmental changes, the presence of small firms would not grow.

There is some deviation in this book's treatment of firm-specific turbulence from that used in other parts of the literature of industrial organisation. A common approach is that of Beesley and Hamilton (1984) who approximated firm-specific turbulence by accounting for flows in the birth and death of firms in particular industries. However, their measure is industry-specific rather than firm-specific. Closer to the approach of this book is the case-study evidence of Markusen and Teitz (1985). In their work, which concerned the underlying dynamics of the competitive environment in which mature small firms operated, they found that the markets of such small firms were turbulent. Thus, all firms in the sample were expecting some change, whether in the form of a crisis or of a growth opportunity. The approach of Chapter 18, following Markusen and Teitz (1985), as opposed to Beesley and Hamilton (1984), is to measure turbulence at the firm level. In that chapter, firm-specific turbulence (*FSTurbulence*) is estimated by a count of the number of changes undertaken by the mature small firm, *qua* organization, over its lifetime. Thus, a relatively high number of changes signals that the mature small firm is operating in a turbulent environment.

15.4   Measuring performance

Several approaches to measuring performance in small firms are possible. For example Reid and Smith (2000a) identify three. In particular, they contrast an objective measure (e.g. quantitative measures like profitability and rate of return) with a subjective measure (e.g. a judgmental evaluation of performance, drawing on both quantitative and qualitative evidence). In this part (Section 7) of the book, the latter approach is adopted. It is both more comprehensive and more compatible with the evidence base that is being used. The requirement for a comprehensive measure of performance is consistent with the literature on entrepreneurship and management accounting as applied to the small firm (e.g. Wickham, 2001, Ch. 20). Essentially, it recognises that the proper control of the firm requires a comparison of current performance to a predetermined plan or objective.

As regards the compatibility of the evidence base, the subjective measure of performance evaluation in Chapter 18 facilitates new forms of modelling which otherwise would be denied with the sample available. In adopting a subjective performance measure, it may be noted that so-called objective performance measures themselves do have subjective elements to them. Not the least of these is that the so-called 'objective data' were recorded and manipulated by human subjects. They themselves are prone to error and are likely to exercise judgment inconsistently on matters like incomplete or inaccurate returns of data. In the small firms context, such weaknesses in so-called objective measures arise from a variety of courses. These include: failure to value intangible assets; difficulty in distinguishing profit from income; and poor reliability of accounting records when ownership and control are not separated, see Keasy and Watson (1991), Sapienza *et al.* (1988) and Reid (1993). To illustrate, with the evidence used in this book, in Chapter 18 the sample is actually composed of three subsamples. Each subsample typically had a different range of objective performance measures gathered at different points in time. There was therefore an intrinsic lack of comparability of these measures over the lifetimes of the firms. Resorting to a new performance measurement approach (in this case, a subjective approach), which was common to the three subsamples, enabled the empirical work to be conducted on a common basis.

The firms to be examined in Chapter 18 have, in a sense, passed the long-run test of economic survival, and satisfied the aspirations of their founders. Thus, owner-managers have before them a body of qualitative and quantitative evidence from which they can evaluate their own performance. Naturally, there are many dimensions to this performance. To illustrate, over time they have learned how best to combine their factors of production to exploit market opportunities, and they have responded to threats in a way that has improved their performance and enhanced their survival. Given that owner-managers comfortably juggle these various performance measures in their own minds, it is a logical step to measure explicitly the subjective processes by which this juggling act is sustained. To the extent that this measuring exercise is successful, it provides a new form of empirical evidence which is useful in econometric estimation.

15.5   Performance, flexibility and firm-specific turbulence

This section briefly examines the expected causal relationship between flexibility and firm-specific turbulence (as independent variables) and performance (as dependent variable). In general greater flexibility is expected to have a positive effect on performance (Stigler, 1939; Ghemawat, 1991). Firm flexibility has been used to explain the relatively greater small firm presence in uncertain environments. This increased presence is therefore indicative of enhanced small firm performance.

The effect of firm-specific turbulence on performance is less clear. In general, a higher number of organisational changes would reflect a greater degree of firm-specific turbulence and vice versa. However, it does not automatically imply improved performance. Chapter 14 shows that both poorly performing ('stagnant') firms and high performing ('adaptive') firms have relatively active discretionary policies (see also Reid and Smith, 2000b). Whereas stagnant firms may often adopt organisational changes to counteract the consequences of inflexibility in terms of poor performance, adaptive firms frequently adopt organisational changes to facilitate greater growth and other aspects of improved performance.

In general, the greater the number of consequential adjustments, relative to the number of precipitating causes, the less agile is the firm. Here, agility is interpreted as one aspect of performance. The greater the agility of the small firm the better its performance should be. If speed is measured by the time taken to respond to both precipitating influences and consequential adjustments, it should be expected that speed (in this sense) will influence performance negatively.

15.6   Conclusion

This chapter may be summarised by saying that its concern is with 'scene setting' for the remaining chapters in Part 6 of this book. Chapter 16 focusses on scale flexibility by re-visiting the Gibrat Law first broached in Chapter 4. Chapter 17, which focuses on niche flexibility, uses the states of a Markov process to identify transition in such niches over time. Finally, Chapter 18 extends the vocabulary of flexibility to firm-specific turbulence, and adopts an approach to flexible decision-making, in the face of such turbulence, which is influenced by real options reasoning, and the contingency approach of Chapters 13 and 14.

All the three following chapters (namely Chapters 16, 17 and 18) are concerned with modelling adaptation and change. In that sense they are echoing the approaches of Parts 2 and 4 of this book, where the approach is intrinsically dynamic in nature. Although this is not the dynamics of time series analysis, it nevertheless provides a range of novel insights into dynamic processes of the small firm, including: (1) the quest for optimal size; (2) the choice of best market niche; and (3) the choice of best organisational adaptation to turbulence.

Endnotes

1 This focus on flexibility on the production side is echoed by an empirical literature on flexibility in manufacturing within the small business sector e.g. Collier (2003) on the use of automated guided vehicles (AGVs) and Petroni and Bevilaqua (2002) on best practice and manufacturing flexibility.
2 Mills and Schumann (1985) developed a model where the existence of available technologies affords a tradeoff between static efficiency and flexibility, so that in market environments with fluctuating demand it is possible for firms with higher minimum average cost also to survive, if they are sufficiently flexible. Technologically diverse firms are able to compete with each other by relying on offsetting cost advantages as a result of this tradeoff. This technological diversity was associated with smaller-sized firms because they use variable factors of production more rigorously than large firms.
3 This was taken as the standard error of regressions adjusted for serial correlation where the natural logarithm of annual sales (or employment) from 1970 to 1980 was regressed onto a constant and a linear time trend (see Mills and Schumann, 1985).

16 Scale flexibility

16.1 Introduction

The new business start ups that are typical of the evidence examined in this book often have entrepreneurs who are ambitious to see their firms grow rapidly. However, the growth process is fraught with uncertainty, and the possibility of re-trenching has also to be considered, as 'market experiments' may fail to be as successful as anticipated. In short, the entrepreneur must be adaptable, and has to be flexible in adapting the scale of operation of their small firm (either up or down) to changed economic conditions. This type of flexibility, to grow rapidly, but at possibly variable rates, or even to contract, depending on evolving opportunities, is the focus of this second chapter in the book's Part 6 on Flexibility. In essence, it builds on the existing evidence, as presented first in Chapter 4, and develops a number of new empirical insights. The approach extends the emerging body of evidence that tests Gibrat's Law (1931) for young small firms in specific national contexts, e.g. Almus (2000) for West Germany; Liu *et al.* (1999) for Taiwan; Weiss (1998) for Austria; Ganugi *et al.* (2005) for Italy and Chow and Fung (1996) for China.

The form of flexibility that is to be considered here might reasonably be regarded as being more general than the form of flexibility considered in Chapter 17 (on market niche flexibility). This is because flexibility in niche market choice, though of great analytical and policy interest, neglects much (e.g. workforce composition, calibrated by the ratio of full-time to part-time workers), that is readily accommodated within the concept of flexibility in scale of operation.

A number of measures of scale of operations could be used, but it has been found that the results are not particularly sensitive to this choice. The measure adopted here, for simplicity, is gross sales. The generic symbol used here for size is S_t, which denotes size in time period t. It is readily interpreted in terms of sales, and this will be done explicitly when empirical estimates are discussed.

16.2 Variants of Gibrat's Law

However, to start with, the general Gibrat's Law formulation, and its variants, will be briefly discussed (cf. Hart and Oulton, 1999), without any restriction on what is meant by size (S_t) – it could be sales revenue, output volume, capacity, headcount, assets, profit, whatever. Suppose markets expand at the rate γ and that all small firms share this common growth rate:

$$\frac{S_{t+1}}{S_t} = \gamma \tag{16.1}$$

This is the Gibrat's Law, or the Law of Proportionate Effects, to the effect that growth is independent of size, see Sutton (1988, pp. 242–243). If there is an endogenous effect of size on growth, one simple way of generalizing (16.1) is:

$$\frac{S_{t+1}}{S_t} = \gamma S_t^{(\beta-1)} \tag{16.2}$$

This is the most popular variant of Gibrat's Law, for which the Gibrat case falls out from (16.2)[1] when $\beta = 1$. When $\beta > 1$ larger small firms have higher growth rates than smaller ones, and when $\beta < 1$ smaller small firms have higher growth rates than larger small firms. There is much evidence to suggest that, whilst very large firms might approximate to Gibrat's Law ($\beta = 1$), smaller and younger firms depart from this prediction, in the sense of $\beta < 1$. A recent exploration (and confirmation) of this is Geroski and Gugler (2004).[2] Finally, the variant (16.2) can be extended by multiplying it by an independently distributed, positive random variable $\mu_t > 0$, giving:

$$\frac{S_{t+1}}{S_t} = \gamma S_t^{(\beta-1)} \mu_t \tag{16.3}$$

Equation (16.3) can be expressed in a form suitable for econometric estimation by casting it in log-linear form:

$$\ln S_{t+1} = \ln \gamma + \beta \ln S_t + \ln \mu_t \tag{16.4}$$

or

$$s_{t+1} = \alpha + \beta s_t + \varepsilon_t \tag{16.5}$$

where, in obvious change of notation, $\ln S_{t+1} = s_{t+1}$, $\ln \gamma = \alpha$, $\ln S_t = s_t$ and $\ln \mu_t = \varepsilon_t$. It is Equation (16.5) which is the focus of attention in this section. Once (16.5) is estimated, it may be written as:

$$s_{t+1}^e = a + b s_t \tag{16.6}$$

where e denotes expected value for the dependent variable, and (a, b) are regression estimates of (α, β). Equation (16.6) is an expression for a first-order linear difference equation, for which the stability condition is $0 < b < 1$. If this condition holds, then the sequence $\{s_t\}$ converges to an equilibrium value of s^*. Equilibrium is achieved when

$$s_{t+1}^e = s_t = s^* = a/(1-b) \tag{16.7}$$

Such an equilibrium typically has an interpretation of an *optimum* firm size, give that it is a scale of operation that is consciously sought by the entrepreneur [cf. Giordano (2003) on optimum firm size]. A useful way of representing the dynamics of (16.6) is by the use of a phase diagram, with s_{t+1} on the vertical axis and s_t on the horizontal axis, as in Chapter 4. The equilibrium set of points is then represented by those values of the size variable that are equal, period by period, that is for which $s_{t+1} = s_t$ $\forall t$. This is represented by a the 45° line in the phase diagram (see, for example, Figure 4.1 in earlier chapter, or Figure 16.1 below).

16.3   Regression estimates

Estimation of (16.5) by regression methods can proceed once variables have been expressed in constant prices. In this chapter, where 1994, 1995 and 1997 magnitudes are used, they are expressed in 1994 prices.[3] Estimates for a regression of log size on log one-period-lagged log size are reported in Table 16.1.

The linear regression of Table 16.1 may be written:

$$\text{lsales2}^e = 1.4730 + 0.8975\ \text{lsales1} \tag{16.8}$$

Table 16.1 Regression of log real sales 1995 on log sales 1994

102 OBSERVATIONS	DEPENDENT VARIABLE = LSALES2			
R-SQUARE = 0.8494	R-SQUARE ADJUSTED = 0.8479			

	ANALYSIS OF VARIANCE - FROM MEAN			
	SS	DF	MS	F
REGRESSION	184.85	1.	184.85	563.944
ERROR	32.779	100.	0.32779	p-VALUE
TOTAL	217.63	101.	2.1548	0.000

VARIABLE NAME	ESTIMATED COEFFICIENT	STANDARD ERROR	T-RATIO 100 DF	p-VALUE
LSALES1	0.89754	0.3780E-01	23.75	0.000
CONSTANT	1.4730	0.4162	3.539	0.001

test b=1

WALD CHI-SQUARE STATISTIC = 7.3490621 WITH 1 D.F.
                     p-VALUE= 0.00671

test b=0.79796

WALD CHI-SQUARE STATISTIC = 6.9418751 WITH 1 D.F.
                     p-VALUE= 0.00842

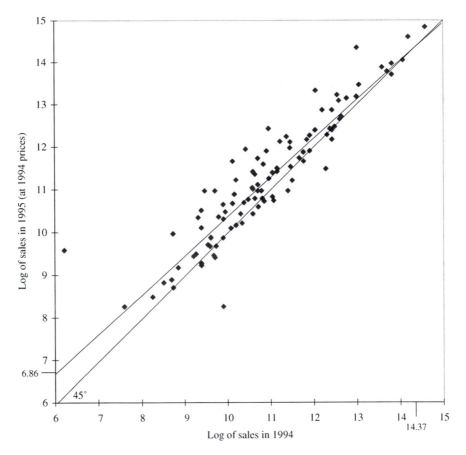

Figure 16.1 Regression of sales on lagged sales (1994–95).
Notes:
(a) Fitted line: lsales2= 1.4730 + 0.8975 lsales1.
(b) Superimposed on 45° line for which lsales1 = lsales2 (i.e. set of equilibrium values).
(c) One period lag.
(d) Sales are gross sales at 1994 prices.

Equation (16.8) is the estimated version of (16.5). Figure 16.1 provides a scatter diagram of the data used for the regression analysis that led to the estimated Equation (16.8). This equation has itself been superimposed on the scatter diagram.

The dependent variable is the natural log of real sales in 1995. The independent variable is the natural log of sales in the base period 1994. By reference to Table 16.1, it is seen that the adjusted R^2 is high at 0.85, and the F value (563.9), as a test of goodness-of-fit of the overall regression, is highly statistically significant ($p = 0.000$). On a Wald test, the null hypothesis of H_0: $b = 1$ is clearly rejected ($p = 0.0067$). That is, the slope coefficient of Equation (19.8) is highly significantly different from unity. This is an important finding, as it rejects Gibrat's Law, and further suggests a stable dynamic process of adjustment in small firm size. This rejection of Gibrat's Law ($b = 1$), in favour of the alternative $b < 1$ gives important status to small firms. In particular, it suggests that they will enjoy relatively greater growth prospects than large firms, and in this sense will display greater flexibility.[4]

16.4 Passage to equilibrium

The estimated regression Equation (16.8) will now be interpreted in the context of Figure 16.1, regarded as a phase diagram. Also shown on Figure 16.1 is a 45° line denoting equilibrium values. Visual inspection suggests that the regression line is a good fit to the set of data points. This is indeed confirmed by the explicit statistical testing in Section 16.3.

The slope of the regression line is low, at roughly 0.9. The equilibrium value for this process is, following the algebra of (16.10), $s^* = 1.4730 \div (1 - 0.8975) \cong 14.37$. This is indicated to the extreme right of Figure 16.1. It is immediately apparent from Figure 16.1 that most small firms in 1994–95 were well short of the equilibrium position of the dynamic adjustment process of which they were a part. This picture of adjustment is different from the one reported upon by the author in an earlier study of small firm dynamics in Scotland (Reid, 1993, Figure 11.3). In that study, there was more dispersion about both sides of the equilibrium. This is presumably because, therein, the small firms were considerably older than in this present study, allowing for greater adjustment about the equilibrium. In other words, in earlier work, as represented, for example, by Chapter 4, the more mature small firms of that sample included many firms which have overshot their equilibrium size, as well as those which had not yet reached their equilibrium size.

Discussion now turns to the adjustment process over the longer period 1994–97. Table 16.2 reports on a regression which runs the natural log of sales in 1997 (in 1994 prices) against the natural log of sales in 1994. Here, the OLS method has been modified by using White's (1980) heteroskedastic consistent covariance matrix estimator, see Greene (1993, p. 391). As regards goodness-of-fit, the adjusted R^2 of 0.7073 is high, and the F-test for overall significance of the regression gives a highly significant test value of 162.94 ($p = 0.000$). The estimated coefficients of the regression are also highly statistically significant ($p = 0.000$ for b; and $p = 0.008$ for a).

It is to be noted that the estimate of the slope coefficient (b) is less, at 0.79796, than in the previous regression (Table 16.1). By reference to Table 16.1, a Wald test can be constructed of the hypothesis that the slope coefficient (0.8975) of the first estimated equation (16.8) (Table 16.1) is not statistically significantly different from the slope of coefficient (0.79796) for the second estimated equation

Table 16.2 Regression of log real sales 1997 on log sales 1994

```
OLS ESTIMATION
       68 OBSERVATIONS            DEPENDENT VARIABLE = LSALES4

USING HETEROSKEDASTICITY-CONSISTENT COVARIANCE MATRIX
    R-SQUARE = 0.7117          R-SQUARE ADJUSTED = 0.7073

                    ANALYSIS OF VARIANCE - FROM MEAN
                       SS            DF            MS            F
REGRESSION          108.06          1.          108.06        162.940
ERROR                43.772        66.            0.66322     p-VALUE
TOTAL               151.84         67.            2.2662        0.000

VARIABLE          ESTIMATED       STANDARD      T-RATIO
NAME              COEFFICIENT     ERROR          66 DF        p-VALUE
LSALES1             0.79796      0.9550E-01      8.356         0.000
CONSTANT            3.0251        1.108          2.731         0.008

test b=1

WALD CHI-SQUARE STATISTIC = 4.4758942 WITH 1 D.F.
                          p-VALUE= 0.03438
```

(Table 16.2 or the representation of the regression therein in Equation 16.9). The hypothesis is strongly rejected ($p = 0.008$). Thus the adjustment processes over a one year period and over a three year period are quite distinct.

The estimated regression discussed above (of Table 16.2) is:

$$\text{lsales4}^e = 3.0251 + 0.79796 \, \text{lsales1} \tag{16.9}$$

This estimated equation is graphed upon the scatter diagram of Figure 16.2. The main difference between Equations (16.8) and (16.9) is in the slope coefficient. Furthermore, one notes that the dispersion of data points is greater in Figure 16.2, reflecting the longer histories of small firms for which data are displayed in that figure. For Equation (16.9), a Wald test (of $b = 1$) does indeed confirm that the slope coefficient is significantly different (at the 5% level) from unity ($p = 0.03438$), so again Gibrat's Law is refuted (Table 16.2).

In terms of the adjustment process, the equilibrium value implied by the dynamic Equation (16.6) is $s^* = 3.0251 \div (1 - 0.79796) \cong 14.97$. Measured in gross sales the implied equilibrium value is $\exp(14.97) = £3,181,227$ for estimated Equation (16.9). This is to be compared with the equilibrium value of $\exp(14.37) = £1,741,051$ in the case of the estimated Equation (16.8). In real terms this difference is considerable ($\cong 87\%$), although the use of logs of variables previously masked this feature of the results. Put briefly, the equilibrium position has risen considerably. A possible reason for this is the exit of firms from the sample between 1995 and 1997, thus selecting those firms which, on average,

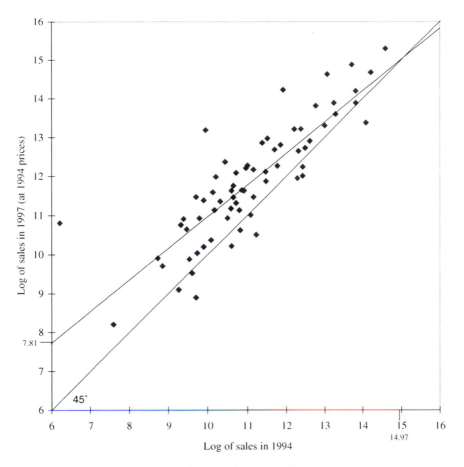

Figure 16.2 Regression of sales on lagged sales (1994–97).
        Notes:
        (a) Fitted line: lsales4= 3.025 + 0.7979lsales1.
        (b) Superimposed on 45° line for which lsales1 = lsales4 (i.e. set of
            equilibrium values).
        (c) Three period lag.
        (d) Sales are gross sales at 1994 prices.

have higher equilibrium firm sizes. However, this must be considered within the context of the general finding (see, for example, Chapters 10 and 18) of no sample selection bias.

It is notable that for both Figures 16.1 and 16.2, implied *equilibrium* values are generally considerably greater than the *average* size of the small firms in the sample. In 1995, the average gross sales figure for small firms in the sample was £226,000, whereas in 1997 it was £336,000 (both in 1994 prices). For Equation (16.8) small firms were approximately one-eighth (on an average) of their long period equilibrium values, and for Equation (16.9) they were approximately one-ninth (on an average) of their long-run equilibrium values, suggesting, indeed, that over the longer period 1994–97, a proportionally greater adjustment to long-run equilibrium has occurred. However, in ratio terms, these differences between Equations (16.8) and (16.9) are not great. What they do have in common is that both imply a lot of adjustment has yet to occur.[5] This evidence further illustrates the flexibility of adjustment that occurs in these small firms: indeed, such adjustments seem to be pervasive.

It is revealing to use Figures 16.1 and 16.2 to trace out explicitly the paths to equilibrium [see Reid (1996a, b, pp. 29–30) where this is done explicitly]. An illustration of this device has already been given in Chapter 4 (Figure 4.1, adjustment to equilibrium size). Using this device reveals that step lengths are shorter for Equation (16.8), compared to Equation (16.9), given any initial starting size. These difference in step length and paths to equilibrium are of course a direct reflection of the different speeds of adjustment of the dynamic processes implied by the different slope estimators reported in estimated Equations (16.8) and (16.9).[6]

16.5   Conclusion

The aim of this chapter, echoing themes developed elsewhere in this book, especially in Chapters 4 and 8, has been to explore a type of small firm dynamics (cf. Chow and Fung (1996) for a Chinese policy context, and Kawai and Urata (2002) for a Japanese policy context). Here, this has involved adjustment of scale of operations over time. Such changes in scale were calibrated by a size measure: in this case, sales. If growth rates are high, as indeed they typically are for small firms close to inception, considerable demands of flexibility are imposed on them, as they seek to move some distance to their implied equilibrium sizes.

The core technique of this chapter is a variant of a Gibrat's Law type of model. This examines the dependence (or otherwise) of growth on the scale of the firm. The model enables dynamic time paths, or trajectories, to be traced for small firms, towards a well-defined long-term equilibrium. Statements can also be made about the stability of the adjustment process. In the case of sales growth, considered in this chapter, Gibrat's Law was refuted. However, a stable adjustment process was nevertheless discovered, but one which required the elapse of many time periods before getting close to equilibrium. In the working out of this process, considerable scale adjustment was required of the small firm, and in that sense, it displayed flexibility over time. This focus on the flexibility requirement imposed on small firms by relatively high growth trajectories has organisational implications that have been explored in Chapters 4, 11 and 14. There is a natural link between three organisational approached and the Gibrat's Law, as echoed in work by Harrison (2004).

In the next chapter (Chapter 17, on market niche flexibility), the focus remains on flexibility, but now in a slightly different sense. The prime concern is with 'market re-positioning': that is to say, the moving to new niches for principal products, as a type of flexible response to changed market opportunities. The main technique utilised in Chapter 17 is that of Markov chain modelling. Such a model is estimated from data on changes in a small firm's main market. Again, as in the present chapter, small firm dynamics is the governing methodology.

Endnotes

1 See Aitchison and Brown (1969, Ch. 3) for further analysis.
2 Geroski and Guyler (2004) confirm the Gibrat's Law for large and mature firms, but refute it for smaller and younger firms, such as are modelled here.
3 The deflator for 1995 was 1.035, and the deflator for 1997 was 1.093. The retail price index was used for deflation.
4 It is also worth noting that 'smaller' small firms grow faster than 'larger' small firms. The original evidence in favour of Gibrat's Law, suggesting there was no size effect at all, is nicely summarised in Sutton (1998, Ch. 10). Contrary evidence for UK quoted companies (1948–60) is adduced in Singh and Whittington (1968) who find a positive relationship between size and growth ($b > 1$). However, this is *prima facie* implausible, implying as it does an unstable adjustment process. Kumar (1985), using a similar set of company data, relating to the next 16 years of evidence, found a negative relationship between size and growth. Since the 1970s, evidence has generally confirmed the result that $b < 1$, as summarised in the paper by Hart (2000, Table 1). A caution against complete generalisation of the result is contained in the work of Audretsch *et al.* (2004), where finely detailed sectoral analysis is carried out (in this case in the Dutch hospitality industry), showing the Gibrat's Law ($b = 1$) to be non-refuted in this specific case.
5 In this sense, the log scale of Figures 16.1 and 16.2 overstates the extent to which adjustment has been completed. However, as compared with the adjustment of market position alone (see Chapter 17), the scale adjustment considered here involves a great deal more modification of the small firm's operations e.g. workforce, capacity utilisation, debt, etc.
6 As Geroski and Gugler (2004) point out, these speeds of adjustment may drift over time. In their analysis of the Single Market Programme in 1992 in Europe, they found, using a Gibrat Process, that speed of convergence in corporate size had slowed post-1992.

17 Market niche flexibility

17.1 Introduction

The objective of this chapter is to show how another specific aspect of small firm flexibility can be modelled. Chapter 16 looked at flexibility in terms of the scale of operation of the small firm. The flexibility considered in this chapter involves the ability of the small firm to move into new markets. The model used is a Markovian model of shifts (see appendix to this chapter), period by period, in the market extent for the main product. Of particular interest, from a policy standpoint, is an extension of the small firm's market to the international. This has been extensively analysed in recent years (Brouthers and Nakos, 2005; Collinson and Houlden, 2005; Kalantaridis, 2004; Namiki, 2005; Lu and Beamish, 2004). Part of the policy interest is in whether such small firms, who are ambitious to internationalise early, are able to maintain their international position over subsequent years. The tools used in this chapter are well suited to answering this question.

This chapter demonstrates the following: (1) shifts in main markets are often substantial for new business start ups, yet have a distinctive pattern over time. (2) Furthermore, they show strong patterns of convergence over time, adapting towards the implied equilibrium position of the underlying dynamic process rather rapidly. (3) Finally, although small firms can be quite exploratory about their main markets in the periods shortly after launch, there is a strong tendency for them to retrench to local markets in the long run. (4) In conclusion, examining the dynamic processes described earlier, it is found that flexibility is relatively larger for market adjustment (as considered here), as compared to scale adjustment, as considered in Chapter 16.

The key technique of this chapter is the Markovian model (Parzen, 1960, Chapter 3). A summary, and self-contained treatment of key results and techniques, sufficient to the comprehension of this model, and associated techniques, is given in the appendix to this chapter. This dynamic model is estimated, and its implied adjustments to equilibrium are discussed. The general picture that emerges is of considerable flexibility of the small firm in its early life-cycle. Again, and somewhat unusually in a small firms' context, this chapter presents explicit trajectories of the adjustment processes by which this flexibility works itself out. This, again, echoes the agenda of small firm dynamics expounded in Chapters 4, 6, 7 and 8.

17.2   The Markovian model

The key aspect of flexibility to be considered in this chapter is that of ability of the small firm to change its principal market area. Entrepreneurs in the sample were asked early in the interview (when dealing with market data) the following question (see Q.1.7 of Section 1. *Market Data* in the AQ1 of the appendix to this book):

'1.7 Do you consider your *main* market to be:
Local   Regional   Scottish   British   or   International?'

In the first year of the study (1994), for example, firms replied: local (34 per cent), regional (28 per cent); Scottish (21 per cent); British (11 per cent); and international (6 per cent). This same question was asked in follow-up interviews for the next 3 years (1995–97). A frequency count was taken of these changes to estimate, by using the observed frequencies of moves, the probabilities of moving from one state to another.

These probabilities were then used to achieve four things. First, they were used to forecast future patterns of main markets, under the assumption that these probabilities were stable over time. Second, they were used to investigate the pattern of change in main markets, period by period, in effect looking at adjustment to equilibrium. Third, they were used to compute the long run equilibrium pattern of main markets for the small firms. Fourth, they were used to compare short-period adjustments to the ultimate long-run equilibrium, and thus to estimate the rate of convergence to equilibrium. To undertake these quantitative tasks, one requires recourse to the theory and techniques of Markov chain (also called 'process') analysis. Though the use of Markov chains has been only intermittent in industrial economics (including small business economics), a number of classical studies have used this technique, including Adelman (1958), Newman and Wolfe (1961), Hart (1962) and Prais (1974). More recent applications include the works of Gillespie and Fulton (2001) on hog production firms, Rosti and Chelli (2005) on transition to entrepreneurship and self-employment, and Mata and Portugal (2004) on post-entry performance of foreign-owned firms.

The principal theorems which are relevant to this type of modelling are presented as an appendix to this chapter.[1] Briefly, a Markov chain may be represented by a square matrix $\mathbf{P}$. This has the properties that all its *elements* are probabilities. As such, they are non-negative, and lie between zero and unity in value. Furthermore, the row sums of such a matrix are unity. A matrix such as $\mathbf{P}$ is said to be stochastic. Each row of it is a discrete distribution. This matrix $\mathbf{P}$ is called a *transition probability matrix*, because each row (or column) refers to the *state* of the *Markov process* (or *chain*), and each element of $\mathbf{P}$ defines the probability of moving from the i-th to the j-th state of the process in one step. Each such step is usually interpreted as taking place in one time period. This will be the interpretation used here.

Powers of the matrix $\mathbf{P}$ can be computed by post-multiplication. For example, $\mathbf{PP} = \mathbf{P}^2$ and $\mathbf{P}^2\mathbf{P} = \mathbf{P}^3$. In general, the m-th power of the matrix refers to the probability of moving from the i-th to the j-th state of the Markov process in *m* time periods. If the matrix **P** has the property of being *regular*, this implies that every state is ultimately accessible from any other state of the Markov process, if the process goes on long enough. Then powers of the matrix **P** tend to a limit, say, **P***. This limiting matrix has the property that its rows are identical. This property is sometimes expressed by saying that the Markov process 'has no memory'. The phrase is adopted because the ultimate state of the process is independent of its initial state. This chapter uses the notation that the *initial state* of the process is given by the distribution (or vector) $\mathbf{w}_0$ and the final state of the process is given by $\mathbf{w}^*$. The vector $\mathbf{w}^*$ is the common row of **P***. In the circumstances considered, the final distribution $\mathbf{w}^*$ is independent of the initial distribution $\mathbf{w}_0$. This is another way of expressing the idea noted earlier that a Markov process 'has no memory'. The determination of $\mathbf{w}^*$ is indirect, and involves use of the so-called 'fixed point property' (see appendix to this Chapter). This is why the terminology of a *fixed point vector* $\mathbf{w}^*$ will be used.

17.3   The transition matrix

Turning now to the data generated in the fieldwork, and using the previous notation, the initial vector of proportions of the sample in the classes local, regional, Scottish, British, international was given by

$$\mathbf{w}_0 = \begin{array}{ccccc} \text{LOC} & \text{REG} & \text{SCOT} & \text{UK} & \text{INT} \\ [0.340 & 0.280 & 0.210 & 0.110 & 0.600\text{E-}01] \end{array} \quad (17.1)$$

This shows that the Markov process has five states, each one of which corresponds to a market area (e.g. local, international, etc.). Using this same notation, the transition probability matrix **P** was estimated.[2] The basis of this estimation was the raw relative frequency for each of the 4 years of data (1994–97), on changes in main market areas. Proceeding in this way the estimate of the transition probability matrix was found to be:

P =

	LOC	REG	SCOT	UK	INT
LOC	[0.77	0.16	0.50E-01	0.90E-02	0.90E-02]
REG	0.23	0.65	0.11	0.00	0.20E-01
SCOT	0.14	0.16	0.63	0.60E-01	0.20E-01
UK	0.00	0.00	0.12	0.82	0.60E-01
INT	0.00	0.00	0.40	0.20	0.40

(17.2)

Three main points emerge from an inspection of the matrix in (17.2). The first is that the principal diagonal of **P** (i.e. those elements p_{ii}) contains the largest elements. Thus, if a small firm starts (the row aspect of **P**) with a main market that is regional (REG) there is a 0.65 probability that it will still be regional in the next period (the column aspect of **P**). The most 'absorbing' of the main market states is the UK market, with a 0.82 probability of a small firm which starts with that market remaining in that market to the next time period.

Second, there is still considerable flexibility in the selection of main market among periods. This is clearly displayed in the matrix diagonals which are parallel to the principal diagonal. In that attribute, they resemble the life-cycle-based Markov model of Newman and Wolfe (1961), in which small firms grew (or declined) rapidly, by quick movement to immediately adjacent states. This form of transition matrix was also characteristic of the empirical work of Adelman (1958). They tend to have the highest values next to those of the principal diagonal. Thus flexibility in main market is incremental, rather than radical. For example, there is a 0.23 probability that a small firm that starts with the region as its main market will have retrenched to a local market in the next period, and a 0.16 probability that a small firm which started locally will have become regional by the next period. Beyond these three diagonals, there is a little, but not much, action. For example, if the firm launched mainly in an international market, there is a zero probability that it will be in local or regional market in the next time period; and if a firm launched locally, it would have a tiny probability (0.009) of being mainly in an international market in the next period.

Third, the international market generally has rather little activity. There is a less than even chance (0.40) that if you launch internationally, you will remain international in the next period. If you do *not* launch internationally, there is only a slight probability that you will be international in the next period, irrespective of where you launched on the rest of the spectrum. For example, even if you launched with the United Kingdom as your principal market, there is only a 0.06 probability of this same business becoming international in the next period. This finding seems superficially to be consonant with past policy views on small firms in Scotland, to the effect that unless they start with marketing intentions which are aimed at the international, they will never make this their main market. However, this overlooks the incremental approach which small firms can adopt to an international marketing standing. Briefly, the argument is that the diagonals of the estimated **P** which are adjacent to the principal diagonal (sometimes called the sub- and super-diagonals) may give small firms access to states (i.e. main markets) which may be denied to them on a one-period basis. This argument will now be explored in more detail, as the evolution of the Markov process is considered. Finally, in this context, lessons are to be drawn from the work of Mata (2004). A preferred mode of entry into a foreign market may be to create a new firm, or to buy an already existing firm in the foreign country, rather than simply expanding a small firm to sell into the foreign market.

17.4 Passage to long-period equilibrium

Using the fixed-point property mentioned earlier (see appendix to this chapter for details), the long-run equilibrium distribution of the main market area for this Markov process, if it exists, is computed directly as:

$$\mathbf{w}^* = \quad [0.402 \quad 0.272 \quad 0.194 \quad 0.108 \quad 0.216\text{E}{-}01] \quad (17.3)$$

Comparing (17.1) to (17.3), which is to say the *initial* distribution across market areas ($\mathbf{w}_0$), the long-run or *final* equilibrium distribution ($\mathbf{w}^*$), it is observed that in long-run equilibrium the 'weight' of the distribution has shifted down, towards the local main market state. The international main market has become an almost rare state (down from 6 per cent to 2 per cent), and both Scotland and the United Kingdom as main markets have become less important. Above all, the local market has become the main (or modal) market (up to 40 per cent from 34 per cent).

It is of interest to observe too how this has come about, and to ask questions of the adjustment process to long-run equilibrium. For example, how rapidly does it proceed, and is its effect monotonic for all states? Table 17.1 displays second, third, fourth and fifth powers of the transition probability matrix $\mathbf{P}$.

It will be observed that the second-power $\mathbf{P}^2$ produces a matrix with all elements positive. Thus $\mathbf{P}$ is a regular, stochastic matrix. This provides quantitative confirmation of what theory predicts (namely that we should expect powers of the matrix to converge).[3]

This process of convergence is most evident in Table 17.1. Very rapidly, previously inaccessible states become accessible (after just one period). Also, transitions which once had very low probabilities quickly assume quite large probabilities. To illustrate, it was impossible (i.e. it was an event of probability zero) to go from an international main market to either a local or regional main market in just

Table 17.1 Second, third, fourth and fifth powers of estimated transition probability matrix $\mathbf{P}$

$\mathbf{P}^2$

0.63	0.23	0.92E-01	0.19E-01	0.15E-01
0.34	0.47	0.16	0.12E-01	0.25E-01
0.23	0.22	0.43	0.92E-01	0.28E-01
0.16E-01	0.19E-01	0.19	0.69	0.75E-01
0.56E-01	0.64E-01	0.43	0.26	0.18

$\mathbf{P}^3$

0.55	0.26	0.12	0.29E-01	0.19E-01
0.39	0.39	0.18	0.28E-01	0.26E-01
0.26	0.25	0.30	0.10	0.32E-01
0.45E-01	0.46E-01	0.24	0.59	0.76E-01
0.11	0.12	0.38	0.28	0.98E-01

$\mathbf{P}^4$

0.50	0.28	0.14	0.40E-01	0.22E-01
0.41	0.34	0.19	0.42E-01	0.27E-01
0.33	0.26	0.27	0.11	0.33E-01
0.79E-01	0.76E-01	0.26	0.51	0.72E-01
0.17	0.15	0.33	0.27	0.67E-01

$\mathbf{P}^5$

0.47	0.28	0.16	0.51E-01	0.24E-01
0.42	0.32	0.19	0.55E-01	0.28E-01
0.35	0.27	0.24	0.12	0.34E-01
0.11	0.10	0.26	0.45	0.67E-01
0.21	0.18	0.29	0.26	0.55E-01

Table 17.2 Distribution evolution of w_n year by year

	LOC	REG	SCOT	UK	INT
Initial distribution in 1994					
	0.340	0.280	0.210	0.110	0.600E-01
Distribution projections for years 1–5 ahead					
Year 1	0.355	0.270	0.217	0.117	0.434E-01
Year 2	0.366	0.267	0.215	0.121	0.374E-01
Year 3	0.373	0.266	0.213	0.123	0.352E-01
Year 4	0.379	0.267	0.211	0.124	0.344E-01
Year 5	0.382	0.268	0.210	0.124	0.342E-01
Long-run equilibrium distribution					
	0.402	0.272	0.194	0.108	0.216E-01

one period. However, there is a finite but small probability of doing either in the second period with probabilities 5.6 per cent and 6.4 per cent, respectively. In the third, fourth and fifth periods, these probabilities have risen to (11 per cent, 12 per cent), (17 per cent, 15 per cent) and (21 per cent, 18 per cent) respectively. In fact the rise in these probabilities is rapid, given that each period for which the power of P is computed is a year in the life of the small firm. Put another way, these small firms display considerable flexibility, in terms of adaptation of their main market, in the early years of their existence.

Another point to observe about Table 17.1 is that rows of the higher powers of P become increasingly similar quite rapidly. By period five, the difference between the first and second rows of P^5 is less than 5 per cent, whereas in the first and second periods, the difference was marked. It will be observed that rows of P have also come some distance to approximating to the long-run equilibrium, as represented by P^*, the matrix limit. This process is even more evident if attention is focused on the initial distribution w_0 and its successors.[4] The first five iterations of this are given in Table 17.2. Again one sees the relatively rapid convergence to the long-run equilibrium value. For example, the local state, which accounts for most of the small firm flexibility, has adjusted to within 95 per cent of its long-run equilibrium value by five iterations (i.e. within 5 years). The other probability weights in this vector are much closer, proportionally, to their long-run values than even this, after 5 years. One also notes that adjustment, whilst *typically* monotonic, is not *necessarily* monotonic. For example, the adjustment to the UK weight initially rises from 0.110 (indeed, rises for all the iterations shown to a value of 0.124) but must eventually fall, to reach the value of 0.108 in long-run equilibrium.

17.5 Conclusion

Overall, the evidence from the transition probability matrix analysis is that small firms exhibit considerable flexibility in switching between main markets.

Furthermore, the speed of adjustment towards long-run equilibrium is quite rapid, with a large proportion of adjustment occurring within just a few years. This lends further credence to the mode of analysis and its conclusions, in the sense that these periods of almost full adjustment are sufficiently short that it is not unreasonable to assume that estimates of transition probabilities are approximately stable over the time period concerned. What should be borne in mind is that the flexibility discovered, using Markovian methods, masks quite different patterns of underlying conduct. To illustrate, when Crick *et al.* (2003) looked at overseas market performance of UK high-technology firms, the UK-based and the indigenous firms, for a given level of performance, behave in very different ways. Therefore, one has to go, once more, into the 'black box' of the firm to learn more.

The next, and final, chapter (Chapter 18) takes the flexibility analysis of Chapters 16 and 17 several steps further, by combining elements of Parts 4 (on Performance) and 5 (on Contingency) with key concepts of Part 6 (on Flexibility). The resulting analysis is, in this sense, synthetic of much of the earlier material of this book.

Appendix: Principal theorems of Markov chains

The principal theorems which are relevant to this type of modelling are as follows.[5] Consider a square $(n \times n)$ *matrix* defined by $(p_{ij}) = \mathbf{P}$. It has the properties that for its *elements* p_{ij} it is true that $p_{ij} \geq 0$ $\forall ij$ and $\Sigma_j p_{ij} = 1$ $\forall i$. As each element of a row is non-negative, and row sums are unity, $\mathbf{P}$ is said to be *stochastic*, because, in effect, each row defines a discrete stochastic distribution. A matrix of the form $\mathbf{P}$ is defined as a *transition probability matrix*. The word transition is used, because each row (or column) is said to refer to the *state* of a *Markov process* (or *chain*), and the process evolves by movements between states. Each element p_{ij} defines the probability of moving from the i-th to the j-th state of the process in one step, where this step is usually interpreted as one time period. This is the interpretation used in this chapter.

Higher powers of this matrix are defined by simple matrix multiplication, giving powers like $\mathbf{PP} = \mathbf{P}^2$ and $\mathbf{PP}^2 = \mathbf{P}^3$. Elements of the m-th power of this matrix are denoted p_{ij}^m. In a similar way to the above, p_{ij}^m refers to the probability of moving from the i-th to the j-th state of the Markov process in m time periods. Then if $\exists m'$ such that for $\forall m > m'$ it is true that $p_{ij}^m > 0$ $\forall ij$ then the Markov process is described as *ergodic*. This property is sometimes said to imply that the matrix $\mathbf{P}$ is *regular*, the implication being that, if it holds, every state is ultimately (in the sense of for a sufficiently large m) accessible from any other state of the Markov process. The word 'ultimately' has the connotation of 'in a finite number of time periods'. A property of a regular transition probability matrix is that $\mathbf{P}^n \rightarrow \mathbf{P}^*$ as $n \rightarrow \infty$. For such a $\mathbf{P}^* = (p_{ij}^*)$ the property will hold that $p_{ij}^* = p_{kj}^*$ for any i, k. That is, the rows of $\mathbf{P}^*$ are identical.

This regularity property ensures that powers of $\mathbf{P}$ tend to a limiting matrix, which has the property that every row is identical. This means, whatever the row, that there is the same probability of getting to a specific column. Put another way, the Markov process 'has no memory' in the sense that the ultimate state is independent of the initial state. This notion is more clearly explained by considering an *initial state* vector $\mathbf{w}_0 = (w_i)$, where $\Sigma_i w_i = 1$ with $w_i \geq 0 \ \forall i$. This state will become $\mathbf{w}_1 = \mathbf{w}_0 \mathbf{P}$ after one time period and $\mathbf{w}_2 = \mathbf{w}_1 \mathbf{P} = \mathbf{w}_0 \mathbf{P}^2$ after two time periods, and so on. Given the properties of w_i, $\mathbf{w}$ is often referred to as a *distribution*.

The final state of the process is then given as $\mathbf{w}^*$ where this is determined by the *fixed point* relationship $\mathbf{w}^* = \mathbf{w}^* \mathbf{P}$. That is, the linear transformation $\mathbf{P}$ maps $\mathbf{w}^*$ into itself. Put another way, this is a way of finding the limiting $\mathbf{w}^*$, in the sense defined by $\mathbf{w}_n \rightarrow \mathbf{w}^*$ as $n \rightarrow \infty$, without having to compute higher powers of $\mathbf{w}$. The vector $\mathbf{w}^*$ is the common row of $\mathbf{P}^*$. The upshot of this discussion is that the final distribution $\mathbf{w}^*$ is independent of the initial distribution $\mathbf{w}_0$. This is another way of expressing the idea noted earlier that a Markov process 'has no memory'. Finally, a point that has to be borne in mind is that $\mathbf{w}^* = \mathbf{w}^* \mathbf{P}$ cannot be solved directly, as $\mathbf{P}$ is singular (because its rows are linearly dependent), implying $|(\mathbf{I} - \mathbf{P})| = 0$. So the property $\Sigma_i w_i^* = 1$ with $w_i^* \geq 0 \ \forall i$ has to be used as well, as an auxiliary condition, to determine the *fixed point vector* $\mathbf{w}^*$.

Endnotes

1 See, for example, the classical test book by Parzen (1960, Ch. 3) *Modern Probability Theory and its Applications*. A simpler account is available in Peston (1969). Advanced treatments are in Meyn and Tweedie (1993), Isaacson and Madsen (1976) and Chung (1967).
2 To save on notation, a hat has not been put over this $\mathbf{P}$ to denote 'estimate'. However, the $\mathbf{P}$ of (17.2) is indeed an estimate. It is estimated from all data over the period 1994–97 pertaining to all reported 'state to state' shifts of nominated main product markets over a 1 year period. The estimates for each cell are the normalised raw frequencies.
3 It also allows one to use the direct fixed-point method for computing the long-run equilibrium given in $\mathbf{w}^*$ of (17.3).
4 In the sequence generated by the algorithm $\mathbf{w}_n = \mathbf{w}_0 \mathbf{P}^n$.
5 See, again, Parzen (1960, Ch. 3) *Modern Probability Theory and its Applications*.

18 Flexibility, firm-specific turbulence and the performance of the long-lived small firm

(with Bernadette Power)

18.1 Introduction

The chapter is the last in this section on flexibility, and indeed marks the end of the substantive content of this book. It is linked closely to the rest of the book, and in a sense is the culmination of the scientific agenda pursued thought the book. It provides a link between evidence from the fieldwork of 1994–98 and that of 2001–02 (which involved re-contacting the same subsample of small firms); and a synthesis of the principal themes of the book so far, to wit, dynamics, performance and flexibility. It explains the performance of long-lived small firms in terms of firm-specific turbulence and flexibility (see Chapter 15 for terminology). The evidence presented suggests that (a) a trade-off exists between agility and speed (two measures of flexibility) in responding to external and internal changes; and (b) that firm-specific turbulence has a negative effect on performance. This chapter explores the relationship between firm-specific turbulence, flexibility and performance using data collected in face-to-face interviews with 63 long-lived small firms in Scotland. A long-lived small firm is defined as a business that has been trading for more than 10 years. The material below presents information on the database, the variables used in econometric estimation, the key hypotheses and instrument design, before turning finally to the estimates.

18.2 Data

The dataset was based on interviews with owner-managers of long-lived small firms in Scotland. The sampling frame of 86 long-lived small firms was derived from three 'parent' samples of Scottish small business enterprises.[1] One of these parent samples is that sample (Chapter 2) to which the greater part of the analysis in this book is directed. These parent samples relate to previous fieldwork studies undertaken in the 1980s and 1990s by the author. The parent samples were random samples from the population of small firms in Scotland at the time of the initial interviews.[2]

This approach to identifying long-lived small firms was found to be superior to that offered by the use of independent sources, such as Dun and Bradstreet. There are two reasons for this. First, proceeding in this way, data are available on non-survivors, which would not be the case with Dun and Bradstreet. This permits the analysis of the consequences of different strategies adopted by survivors, compared to non-survivors. Second, it permits the possibility of correcting for sample selection bias in estimating a performance equation, an important econometric refinement.

Of the 86 owner-managers of firms contained in the sampling frame, 63 were willing to be interviewed face-to-face between October 2001 and February 2002 (a 73 per cent response rate). The owner-managers were interviewed using an administered questionnaire. This examined the characteristics of the long-lived small firm, changes in its scale and scope, an analysis of pivotal changes in the running of the firm since start-up, factors which fostered the survival of the firm and the level of innovation and technical change within the firm. General features of the database and the variables used in the course of this analysis are described immediately.

The firms examined were mature (25.5 years on average; median age of 22). Almost all sectors by SIC were represented in the sample from agriculture (01) to domestic services (99). The main sectors represented were: 32, mechanical engineering (4.8 per cent); 43, textile industry (4.8 per cent); 61, wholesale distribution (4.8 per cent); 64, retail distribution (23 per cent); 66, hotels and catering (4.8 per cent), 67 repair of consumer goods and vehicles (6.3 per cent); and 83 business services (9.5 per cent). The modal firm was a retailer. The sample proportions between extractive/manufacturers (SIC 01–60) and services (SIC 61–99) were 37 per cent and 63 per cent, respectively. These proportions were similar across the 'parent' samples. Of the 219 firms in the three parent samples, 84 (38 per cent) were in manufacturing (SIC 01–60) and 135 (62 per cent) were in services (SIC 61–99). Figures from the Department of Trade and Industry, for all UK small firms over the fieldwork period, suggest that 27 per cent were in manufacturing and 73 per cent in services. The following regions were represented: Aberdeen, Argyll, Aryshire, Banff, Caithness, Cumnock, Dundee, Fife, Glasgow, Inverness, Isle of Skye, Lanarkshire, Lothian and Edinburgh, Midlothian, Moray, Orkney, Perth, Renfrewshire, Ross and Stirling.

Concerning age, evidence suggests that the sample is indeed of long-lived firms. The average age was about 26 years, (roughly one generation) and no firm was younger than 10 years old. The maximum age in the sample was 90 years (roughly two generations). Of the sample of 63 long-lived small firms, one (1.6 per cent) was a sole trader operating from home, 15 (23.8 per cent) were sole traders operating from business premises, 19 (30.2 per cent) were partnerships and 25 (44.4 per cent) were private limited companies. Eighteen (28.6 per cent) firms changed their legal form during the life of the business. There is general evidence of changes in organisational form, from the sole proprietorship form, to the partnership and private limited company forms, over the lifetimes of the firms (cf. Reid, 1998a, b). The number of full-time equivalent (FTEs) employees, which is one indicator of the size of these small business enterprises, varied from 1 to 130 with the average and mode being 13.55 and 6, respectively. The average size of firms (and, in brackets, the corresponding standard deviation) in terms of full-time equivalent employees were as follows: 5.94 (5.85), sole proprietorship; 7.91 (4.08), partnership; and 22.19 (27.69), private company. Size, measured by turnover for the last trading year, also varied widely by business type. Average turnover (and its standard deviation) was: £212,576 (£138,316) for sole proprietorships; £539,171 (£440,982) for partnerships; and £1,327,625 (£182,332) for private companies (all figures in 2001 prices).

18.3   Variables

This section provides statistics of key variables, and their definitions. It also explains the questionnaire design. Table 18.1 indicates the key variables that were used in the econometric modelling reported on in Section 18.5.

Firm-specific turbulence was calculated using a frequency count of the number of key organisational changes to which long-lived small firms were subject, over their lifetimes. Owner-managers were presented with a list of 18 such changes. This list was diverse, including features like ownership, legal form, technology, location, cashflow, line of business, capacity, investment, product range, market positioning, diversification and management. The occurrence of key organisational changes (and the year in which they occurred) was recorded.[3] Owner-managers were not limited to those listed; they were allowed to specify other main changes if they wished.

These key changes can be interpreted as critical decisions. Throughout the course of its life the mature small firm makes such decisions. Crucially, these critical decisions involve the commitment of resources (Ghemawat, 1991). Such changes can have a positive or negative impact. When performance is referred to, the implications of this will be drawn out. Essentially, the key changes are to be interpreted as 'pivotal points' or 'crossroads', rather than as crisis points. Typically, they are strategic in nature, and de-coupled from the more routinised decisions undertaken by the mature small firm on a day-to-day basis. Because of

Table 18.1 Mean, standard deviation (SD) and range of each variable

Variable	Mean	SD	Min.	Max.
Age	25.54	15.73	10	90
Employees (FTEs)	13.55	19.89	1	130
FSTurbulence	7.90	3.8	2	16
Agility	0.8737	0.4070	0.22	2.38
Speed	21.84	16.19	2.45	73.9
Precipitator	5.27	2.72	1	15.67
Adjust	7.31	3.33	1.67	16
PrecipitatorTime	75.60	62.28	0	260
AdjustTime	54.35	75.18	0	476.33
Perform	67.35	8.10	49.11	90.43

this, the consequences of these key changes are typically unpredictable: there is always a measure of uncertainty about the outcomes of such changes. They are treated as contingent events, which are driven by environmental forces.

In a technical sense, firm-specific turbulence (*FSTurbulence*) was calculated as ΣX_i where X_i is the occurrence of a change i. Emphasising the pivotal nature of key changes, it is observed that they occur, on an average, just eight times over the lifetime of the long-lived small firm (see Table 18.1). The range of key changes was 14 and the maximum number of changes was just 16. These key changes were not age dependent. Thus, owner-managers were clearly being very discriminating when they interpreted any change in their operations as being a key change.

Measures of agility and speed were obtained as follows. For the key changes identified by each long-lived small firm, the owner-manager was asked to select only those three changes which were most important to the running of their business, since inception. Just three changes were extracted for more detailed consideration, because pilot work had suggested that this was the best way of capturing salient information from the interviewing. A simple diagrammatic device (see Figure 18.1) was used in interviews with owner-managers to explain the focus of interest. They were told that we fieldworkers wanted to know what had pre-cipitated an organisational change, and what adjustments had been made after it had been achieved. The term 'precipitating influence' is used to describe those forces which led to organisational change. In a similar vein, the term 'consequen-tial adjustment' is used to describe those adaptations which followed on from organisational change.

An advantage of the figure used in interviews (Figure 18.1) was that it made quite explicit the pattern of causal relationships. This, in turn, made it easier to get owner-managers to estimate the intervals of time that occurred between precipitat-ing influences and organisational change, and between organisational change and consequential adjustments. Owner-managers were presented with a 'show-card' on which they could identify precipitating causes and consequential adjustments. This show-card contained a comprehensive list of 30 potential categories of pre-cipitating causes and consequential adjustments. An extract from this show-card is given in Figure 18.2.[4] This figure also indicates how responses were recorded. Figure 18.2 indicates some of the factors of interest to the work of this chapter. Others included credit policy, finance, trade intelligence and cash flow.

This line of inquiry was conducted for these three organisational changes, over the mature firm's lifetime, that the owner-manager had identified. Thus, the

Figure 18.1 Explanation of causation.

Time	Before	Factors		After	Time
		1. Headcount			
		2. Demand			
		3. New niches			
		4. Tax efficiency			

Figure 18.2 Response format for calibrating change.

sequence by which the data were elicited was as follows. First, the owner-manager was asked to identify the precipitating influences from the list of 30 factors (in the format displayed, in an abbreviated way), in Figure 18.2. Second, the owner-manager was asked to identify the number of months (*pt*, which stands for '*PrecipitatorTime*') which elapsed between identifying the precipitating cause and the undertaking of the organisational change within the small firm. Third, owner-managers were asked to identify the consequential adjustments which followed the change in organisational form. Fourth, the owner-managers were asked to identify the number of months (*at*, which stands for '*AdjustTime*') which had elapsed between the occurring of the organisational change and the appearance of the consequential adjustment.

Agility is the ratio of number of precipitating causes (P) to number of consequential adjustments (A). Agility was calculated for each of the three main changes identified by each respondent by counting the number of precipitating factors and adjustment factors for each change. A larger ratio implies that the firm is more agile and thus more flexible. Formally, agility is measured by the count of precipitating factors (P) divided by the count of adjustments (A) averaged over three main changes. Thus, agility is calculated as

$$\frac{\sum_{c=1}^{m} (P_c/A_c)}{\sum_{c=1}^{3} m_c} \tag{18.1}$$

where $A = \Sigma a_{jm}$ where a_{jm} is the occurrence of adjustment j for each change m and $P = \Sigma p_{jm}$ where p_{jm} is the occurrence of precipitating factor j for each change m where $\sum_{c=1}^{3} m_c$. The average value of the small firm's agility ratio was 0.8737. This ratio is less than 1, which implies that long-lived small firms found it difficult to limit the amount of trimming (i.e. the number of *adjustments*) they made as a consequence of organisational change. The average number of precipitating causes (*Precipitator*) was 5.27, whereas the average number of consequential adjustments (*Adjust*) was high at 7.31.[5]

The second measure, the overall speed of adjustment, was another important aspect of flexibility. Three measures of speed of adjustment can be obtained from the questionnaire structure, for each of the three main organisational changes identified by the owner-manager. These are: the length of time from the emergence of precipitating factors to the organisational change; the length of time from the organisational change to changes in adjustment factors; and the summation of the two. The shorter are these time periods, the more flexible is the long-lived small firm. The overall speed of adjustment was obtained by summing the average precipitating time and the average adjustment time. It was calculated here as

$$\frac{\sum_{c=1}^{3} (P_t + A_t)_c}{\sum_{c=1}^{3} m_c} \tag{18.2}$$

The average precipitating time is the sum of the number of months between detecting each precipitating factor (or 'driver') and making the organisational change, divided by the number of precipitating factors. Average precipitating time P_t was calculated as $\Sigma pt_{jm}/\Sigma p_{jm}$ where pt_{jm} is the length of time between each precipitating factor j and the occurrence of each main organisational change m. The average adjustment time was the sum of the number of months between making the organisational change and each consequential adjustment, divided by the number of adjustment factors. Average adjustment time A_t was calculated by $\Sigma at_{jm}/\Sigma a_{jm}$ where at_{jm} is the length of time between the occurrence of each main change m and each adjustment j. On average, the firm's overall adjustment speed was 22 months. The less is the time taken in adjustment, the more flexible is the small firm. The average total precipitating time (*PrecipitatorTime*) was 76 months whereas the average total adjustment time (*AdjustTime*) was 54 months.[6] As the average number of precipitating factors was less than the number of adjustments this suggests that small firms lingered until they were certain that change was required, and that then they responded quickly.

A quantitative index measure of overall performance was created, based on qualitative data. The data for creating this index came from the responses by entrepreneurs to questions about 28 dimensions of their firms' performance: strategy (9 questions); finance (4 questions); organisation (4 questions); and business environment (11 questions).[7] This approach is based on modern methods of performance appraisal in small entrepreneurial firms (Wickham, 2001), and the utilisation of scorecarding methods for performance appraisal, monitoring and control (cf. Epstein and Manzoni, eds., 2002) and, more generally, works emphasising the importance of multidimensional performance measures in the context of new and growing ventures, (Sandberg and Hofer, 1987; Chrisman *et al.*, 1998).

To judge how owner-managers evaluated their firm's ability to survive over the long haul, owner-managers were asked the following question: '*We'd like to know what has kept you in business down the years. Some things are good for business and some things are bad. What effect have the following had?*' Based on actual experience of running the business, they were asked to rate a wide range of dimensions of performance: suppliers, growth, competition, buyer's willingness to pay, customer loyalty, access to buyers, substitutes, new entrants, technology, rival's innovation, regulation, cash flow, debt, credit policy, capital requirements, market positioning, cost control, quality, market research, differentiation, advertising, product mix, diversification, operational efficiency, skills, filling product gaps.

4.1   We would like to know what has kept you in business down the years. Some things are good for business and some things are bad. What effect have the following had?

[Show with a cross whether the effect was good or bad.]

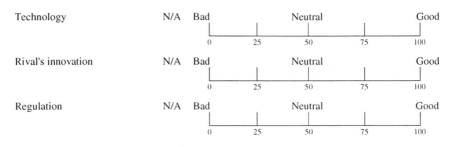

Figure 18.3 Response format for performance indicator.

Each dimension was scored by placing a cross on a continuum ranging from 0 to 100,[8] for its impact, bad or good, on performance, see the three examples (technology, rival's innovation, regulation) in Figure 18.3. If an item were not applicable, owner-managers were asked to say so. A score of zero denoted a very negative impact, 100 a very positive impact, and 50 a neutral impact on performance of a given dimension (e.g. quality, cash flow, operational efficiency).

The overall performance index was then created by summing the scores assigned to each performance dimension and normalising the aggregate figure obtained thereby, by the number of performance dimensions relevant to a given owner-manager's firm (i.e. the total score was divided by the number of items rated). Out of a maximum performance score of 100, the average long-lived small firm scored 67; the measure ranged from 49 to 90. Low performers had a performance rating between 49 and 62 (i.e. the lower quartile) and high performers had a performance rating of 73 to 90 (i.e. the upper quartile). This multidimensional approach has two main advantages over a single question approach. First, it produces detailed measurement across a wide spectrum performance-relevant variables, rather than a single variable. Second, by diluting variable specific effects, it produces a more comprehensive (and stable) measure of what we refer to as performance, allowing common influences to come through (DeVellis, 1991).

The reliability and validity of this new performance index were investigated by Power (2004) using methods proposed by Gerbing and Andersen (1998) and Hair *et al.* (1995). Reliability analysis assesses the internal consistency of the measure of performance (i.e. whether there are common features across these small firms which could have contributed to their becoming long-lived), whereas an analysis of correlations with objective measures of performance investigates its predictive validity (i.e. offers evidence in support of the utility of this index as a measure of the fitness of the small firm to survive over the long haul). Considerable agreement was found in the sample on those factors that contributed most to performance.

Cronbach's (1951) alpha coefficient was used to test for the reliability of the inclusions of influences in the performance index. Guidelines by Nunnally (1978) suggest a value of at least 0.7 is required to infer internal consistency. For the 28 influences on performance, Cronbach's alpha = 0.78, exceeded the recommended level of 0.7. High inter-item correlations also suggested that there were common features across these small firms which could have contributed to their becoming long-lived. Examples of relatively significant inter-item correlations include cost control and operational efficiency (0.584), credit policy and buyers' willingness to pay (0.521), monitoring and skills (0.497), capital requirements and market positioning (0.444), credit policy and customer loyalty (0.434), quality and product mix (0.414) and skills and operational efficiency (0.413). All of these were found to be significant at p-value <0.0001. Confirmatory factor analysis indicated that the data fitted well to the hypothesised multidimensional measurement model, using approaches proposed by Sandberg and Hofer (1987) and Chrisman *et al.* (1998) [$\chi^2(16) = 9.9762$; $p = 0.868$], see Power (2004). The former described new venture performance as a function of entrepreneurial attributes, strategy and industrial structure, whereas the latter extended analysis to include resources and organisational structure.

The long-run performance indicator was weakly positively correlated with net profits in 2001 (Pearson's $R = -0.165$, Prob. value <0.1). It was also negatively correlated with the level of indebtedness of the firm (Pearson's $R = -0.208$, Prob. value <0.05). Thus, in these cases, the long-run performance indicator is behaving as expected. For young small firms it is not expected, based on available evidence, that there will be a negative relationship between growth and performance early in the life-cycle. This is, indeed, part and parcel of why small firms (with the exception of a very small percentage of 'gazelles') typically stay small. There is evidence, however, of a growth/performance trade-off here, for these long-lived small firms, which is something to be treated in greater detail in a simultaneous equations framework (Power and Reid, 2003). This evidence for a trade-off supports the earlier evidence on small firms in Chapter 4, where the firms in the sample were typically beyond start-up (indeed, up to three years old).

For the purposes of this chapter, the above evidence acts as a kind of predictive validity check. For example, we note that asset growth and the performance indicator are negatively correlated (Pearson's $R = -0.298$, prob. value <0.05). In this, it parallels the relationship between accounting profit and asset growth (Pearson's $R = -0.747$, Prob. value <0.0001). This finding is robust with respect to the size measure used. Thus, both the performance index and headcount are negatively correlated (Pearson's $R = -0.210$, Prob. value < 0.1). In general, there is indeed a negative correlation between the index of long-run performance and size, further confirming the efficacy of the performance measure.

As regards what the index means, in terms of the diversity of views across entrepreneurs, the following data are revealing. Taking a mean rating of greater than 75 per cent as denoting good performance, the key influences on performance are judged to be quality (88 per cent, 12), customer loyalty (82 per cent, 15.8), product mix (81 per cent, 12.8), skills (80 per cent, 16.7), operational efficiency (78 per cent, 15.5) and diversification (76 per cent, 16.5) where the standard deviation is given after the mean percentage score. The high mean scores and low standard deviations suggest agreement amongst entrepreneurs on factors which foster long-run survival. Consider, in contrast, factors which are less important, or even detrimental, to long-run survival, like competition (54 per cent, 23.3), substitutes (50 per cent, 22.9), debt (48 per cent, 26.3), regulation (47 per cent, 22.7), rivals' innovations (45 per cent, 23.2) and new entrants (43 per cent, 21.5). These low mean score influences have higher standard deviations, indicating less agreement amongst entrepreneurs about their consequences for long-run survival. This is not surprising, for these specific low mean score influences. They relate to aspects of the small firm's environment (e.g. regulatory, competitive) over which the firm has little control; as compared to influences like quality, product differentiation, skills and operational efficiency, over which it has considerable control.

Although arguably not as familiar as an objective measure, it can be argued that the subjective measure adopted both acts as a good surrogate for objective measures of performance, and extends the compass (in a revealing way) of what we understand by the very word 'performance'. Thus, it seems that entrepreneurs 'act' on their own evaluations.

Table 18.2 examines measures of firm-specific turbulence, flexibility and performance, depending on firm type. Firm type, it should be noted, is highly correlated with firm size. Tests have been undertaken of differences between the mean values of these variables, across the sole proprietor, partnership and private company firm types, within our sample. It is found that there *is* indeed a significant difference in the mean sizes, whether measured by employment or sales. However, there are no

Table 18.2 Flexibility, firm size and performance

Variable	Sole proprietor (n =16)	Partnership (n =19)	Private company (n =28)
Sales*	219812 (143026)	557526 (455994)	1372821 (1855391)
Employees (FTEs)*	5.94 (5.85)	7.24 (4.15)	22.18 (27.18)
FSTurbulence	7.94 (3.07)	7.11 (3.31)	8.43 (4.46)
Agility	.8896 (.3431)	.8781 (.5316)	.8617 (.3554)
Speed	19.5478 (13.1333)	20.6476 (15.9629)	23.9555 (18.0923)
Perform	69.1519 (9.4962)	66.5217 (8.2249)	66.8754 (7.2764)
LabProd	55032 (45063)	72339 (3134)	64425 (76271)

*Significant difference in means using ANOVA at $\alpha = .05$ and $F_{(2, 60)}$.
The standard errors are in parentheses.

significant differences in the means of the measures of firm-specific turbulence, agility or speed, across firm types. This lends general support to Carlsson's (1989) theory that there are some aspects of flexibility which are not related to size. It is also found that there is no difference in the subjective measure of performance for different firm types (and therefore sizes). This is also true if a more 'objective' conventional measure of performance is used, like labour productivity (*LabProd*), here defined by sales divided by fulltime equivalent employees.[9] The central concern of this chapter is whether the dimensions of flexibility and firm-specific turbulence are helpful in explaining long-run differences in the performance of small firms, given that there are no significant differences in the performance and flexibility of these small firms by virtue of their type and size.

18.4   Estimates

To examine the degree to which the different measures of flexibility and firm-specific turbulence affect the performance of the long-lived small firms, use is made of Heckman's selection model (Lee, 1982, 1983; Heckman, 1976; Davidson and MacKinnon, 1993). Agility and speed measures are decomposed into their component parts to assist interpretation. The model adopted assumes that there exists an underlying relationship between the performance variable (*Perform*) and the measure of firm-specific turbulence (*FSTurbulence*), along with the measures of flexibility (e.g. *Adjust, AdjustTime*) for the sample of long-lived small firms.[10] This may be expressed as follows:

$$Perform = \beta_0 + \beta_1 FSTurbulence + \beta_2 Precipitating + \beta_3 Adjust$$

$$+ \beta_4 PrecipitatorTime + \beta_5 AdjustTime + u_{1i} \tag{18.3}$$

where $u_1 \sim N(0, \sigma)$. Sample selection bias is expected to exist, as the measures of performance, firm-specific turbulence and flexibility, are only observed for long-lived small firms, and not for all firms, including non-survivors. The first step of this procedure is to estimate a binary probit model of the survival of long-lived small firms.

This may be written as follows (see earlier Chapters 10 and 11 for this model):

$$S = X\beta + u_{2i} \tag{18.4}$$

where S is a binary variable, which is equal to unity if the firm has survived, but otherwise to zero. The matrix X contains observations on those factors thought to influence the long-run survival of small firms (e.g. number of full-time and part-time employees, gearing and number of product groups), the vector β contains the estimated parameter coefficients and $u_2 \sim N(0, 1)$. The correlation between u_1 and u_2 is given by ρ. From the binary probit estimation, one can calculate the so-called inverse Mills ratio (lambda). This inverse Mills ratio is then used as an additional regressor in the generalised least squares estimation of the performance equation (18.3). Heckman's (1979) two-step procedure provides consistent estimators, under certain regularity conditions.

Initially our model was run on a sample of 186 firms, which included sub-samples from each of the three parent samples (Table 18.4). This includes the 63 surviving long-lived small firms for which complete data sets are available to estimate the performance relationship (18.3), as well as the 123 non-surviving firms for which we have parsimonious (yet incomplete) data, but enough to estimate the selection relationship (18.4). In Heckman's two-step estimation for this sample of 186 firms, the selection equation (18.4) (containing largely size measures) was estimated using common data across the three subsamples: industrial sector (*Sector*); start year (*StYear*); sales in early years of trading (*StSales*); full-time employees (*FTEmployees*); and part-time employees (*PTEmployees*). Overall, this estimation aims to use the available data in the most comprehensive fashion.

For comparative purposes, Table 18.3 presents generalised least squares estimators for the performance relationship (18.3) without sample selection. Here the goal is to estimate, in a preliminary way, the impact of the flexibility and firm-specific turbulence measures on performance. An inspection of the graph of the residuals from an exploratory ordinary least squares regression, plotted against the predicted values, suggested that the residuals were increasing with values of the predictors. To correct for this, the ordinary least squares model was weighted by the reciprocal of *Sales*, as *Sales* were found to be proportional to the absolute value of the residuals, using the Glejser test for heteroskedasticity, Davidson and McKinnon (1993, Ch. 11). This procedure was found to remove the heteroskedasticity. The generalised least squares model presented in Table 18.3 had an R^2 of 0.99 with probability value of 0.000. Although this is highly significant, the results of Tables 18.4 and 18.5 will be the focus of the discussion, because these estimates have been corrected for selectivity bias. This is done on a precautionary basis, although it will be observed that the results in Tables 18.4 and 18.5, which use sample selection methods, are broadly similar to those in Table 18.3. Note that ρ, the correlation between the disturbances in the performance and selection equations is close to zero, suggesting selectivity bias is not a major problem. This echoes previous findings (e.g. in Tables 10.2 and 10.3, where ρ is also not significantly different from zero), that sample selectivity is

Table 18.3 Generalised least squares ($n = 63$)

Estimation	Coeff.	Std. error	Prob.	Elasticities at mean
GLS				
FSTurbulence	−1.701831	0.2878478	0.000	−0.2525534
Precipitator	1.852652	0.5263581	0.001	0.151157
Adjust	0.2762535	0.4601972	0.551	0.0306325
PrecipitatorTime	−0.0819913	0.0435265	0.065	−0.0648971
AdjustTime	0.1163448	0.0189599	0.000	0.0940773
Constant	67.7238	3.10898	0.000	1.041584

Note: R^2adjusted $= 0.99$; $F_{(6,\ 57)} = 67.6$, Prob. $> F = 0.0000$.

Table 18.4 Heckman sample selection model ($n = 186$)

Estimation	Coeff.	Std. error	Prob.	Elasticities at mean
GLS				
FSTurbulence	−1.679331	0.1928492	0.000	−0.2470291
Precipitator	1.886974	0.3946002	0.000	0.1526074
Adjust	0.2794347	0.3605423	0.438	0.0307136
PrecipitatorTime	−0.0883651	0.0254937	0.001	−0.0693288
AdjustTime	0.1156801	0.0114233	0.000	0.0927197
Constant	67.18461	1.975877	0.000	1.02423
Selection equation				
Sector	−0.0416648	0.2002715	0.835	−0.0727281
FTEmployee	−0.0040999	0.0120681	0.734	−0.0260707
PTEmployee	−0.013339	0.0171223	0.436	−0.0422587
StYear	−0.0030649	0.0111117	0.783	−0.2644557
StSales	5.00E-07	2.50E-07	0.045	0.1986496
Constant	−0.2515869	1.007342	0.803	
Mills (lambda)	814015	1065096	0.445	
Rho	0.12243			
Sigma	6649056			
Wald $\chi^2(6)$	10035.63			
Prob$>\chi^2$	0.0000			

not a pervasive, or even significant, problem for the modelling and estimation throughout this book. Therefore, what is true of the analysis in Tables 18.4 and 18.5 should also be true of the analysis of Table 18.3.

18.5   Selection equation

Here, discussion turns first to the selection equation of Table 18.4. This is computed with the largest sample size possible ($n = 186$), using data from all three of the parent samples. Observe that sales at first interview (*StSales*) are significant. That is, size early in the life-cycle has a positive effect on long run survival (cf. Tables 3.1 and 7.1, in earlier chapters, where sales amongst surviving small firms are about twice those of non-surviving small firms). This is a kind of effect one would expect to observe, in terms of fundamental modelling of the small firm's growth process. For example, if the time series of sales from inception is a random walk, terminating when the process hits the absorbing barrier of zero sales, the mean passage time to exit is higher, the greater are first period sales. The effect of size has quite a high positive elasticity (using elasticities computed at the means): a 1 per cent increase in mean sales at start-up increases the probability of survival by 0.2 per cent.

Table 18.5 Heckman sample selection model ($n = 89$)

Estimation	Coeff.	Std. error	Prob.	Elasticities at mean
GLS				
FSTurbulence	−1.793477	0.215148	0.000	−0.2727101
Precipitator	2.405389	0.5098721	0.000	0.2010891
Adjust	0.945891	0.4272299	0.027	0.1074695
PrecipitatorTime	−0.1539495	0.0378933	0.000	−0.1248546
AdjustTime	0.1029675	0.0132173	0.000	0.08531140
Constant	63.40325	2.460651	0.000	0.9991559
Selection equation				
Sector	0.2813531	0.319048	0.378	0.4416197
FTEmployee	−0.0038659	0.0208656	0.853	−0.0221049
PTEmployee	−0.0122082	0.01904	0.521	−0.0347784
StYear	−0.0160978	0.0272271	0.554	−1.249021
StSales	7.55E-07	4.43E-07	0.088	0.2697655
Gearing	−0.0002321	0.0005276	0.660	−0.0272064
ProdGroup	0.211399	0.1235461	0.087	0.5181847
Constant	−0.1704371	2.369223	0.943	
Mills (lambda)	284672.3	1754376	0.887	
Rho	0.03646			
Sigma	6820567			
Wald $\chi^2(6)$	7483			
Prob$>\chi^2$	0.0000			

Turning now to the sample selection equation in Table 18.5, it is to be noted that the sample size is now smaller ($n = 89$) and additional variables are included, on the gearing ratio (*Gearing*) and the number of product groups (*ProdGroup*). Here, additional variables for the selection equation have been gained, but at the cost of having access to only two of the three parent samples. Note that the number of product groups (*ProdGroup*) is significant at the 10 per cent level in Table 18.5. This variable also has a very high elasticity (0.52). The importance of product group size has been emphasised by others, including Reid (1993, Ch. 9). The work of Ungern-Sternberg (1990) provides an explanation of this effect in terms of diversification of the product portfolio, as an accommodation to fluctuating demand for individual products. In general, the selection equations of Tables 18.4 and 18.5 should be regarded as being statistical devices for guarding against sample selection bias, in the context of a Heckman two-step adjustment procedure, rather than as sophisticated models of small firm survival. The main focus of this chapter is, of course, on the performance equation.

18.6   Performance equations

Performance is examined using three estimators. First, generalised least squares estimators, without sample selection, using a sample size of $n = 63$ (Table 18.3).

Second, Heckman sample selection estimation, using a sample size of $n = 186$ (Table 18.4). Here, the selection equation uses all available sample data, but is restricted in the number of variables that can be used. Third, Heckman sample selection estimation, using a sample size of $n = 89$ (Table 18.5). In this case, a smaller sample size is used (accessing just two out of the three parent samples), but this is partially compensated by a wider range of variables (e.g. including gearing). The focus in the discussion to follow will be on the estimates with sample selection of Tables 18.4 and 18.5.

On referring to Table 18.4, it is found that firm-specific turbulence (*FSTurbulence*) has a negative impact on the count measure of qualitative performance (*Perform*). Judged by elasticities at the means, this variable has a larger impact than any other one on performance. Indeed, a 1 per cent increase in the mean count of organisational changes, has the effect of reducing performance by as much as 0.24 per cent. A similar effect, with an even higher elasticity, is found in Table 18.5. Excessive organisational change seems to be to the detriment of the long-lived small firm's performance. As a business journalist commented on an earlier draft of our chapter '*many a meddle may make a muddle of the business*' (Jamieson, 2002). There is an intuitive explanation for this, which supports the interpretation of Reid and Smith (2000b). It is that the relationship between firm-specific turbulence and firm performance tends to be U-shaped. Both poorly performing firms (or 'stagnant' firms in their terminology) *and* highly performing firms (or 'adaptive' firms in their terminology) tend to be relatively active in undertaking changes, compared to moderately performing firms. This echoes the findings of chapters in Part 5 on IS and performance. Thus, stagnant firms are relatively active in making organisational changes, just to survive, whereas adaptive firms are very active in making organisational changes, to improve performance and to promote growth. As expounded in Part 5, this implies heavier use of IS at these opposite ends of the performance spectrum. It may be that the presence of a number of these relatively 'stagnant' firms in the sample, doing really badly (sometimes called the 'living dead') is driving the negative relationship between *FSTurbulence* and *Performance*. If so, this suggests that there is another selection process here, besides the long-run test of economic survival. It may take the form of deciding whether or not the small firm grows to be a much larger firm – a 'gazelle' as described by Birch (1996). Part of the reason for the existence of gazelles may be that they are intrinsically designed to be of a relatively large scale, and that they very rapidly grow towards this target size after inception (i.e. that they are 'scaleable'). To illustrate, this may be true of the small number of firms which achieve international markets in the Markovian analysis of Chapter 17. Many of the small firms in the sample have succeeded in the first selection process but apparently very few are triumphant in the second.

A complex relationship exists between flexibility (as measured by our *Precipitator*, *Adjust*, *PrecipitatorTime* and *AdjustTime*) and performance, according to the evidence presented in Tables 18.4 and 18.5. Observe first that the number of factors which the owner-manager can identify as precipitating organisational change (*Precipitator*) has a highly significant and positive effect upon performance, and this effect is large, judged by the elasticity at the mean. Being aware of factors impinging on the small firm, by effective scanning of the business environment (e.g. Wickam, 2001, p. 324) is an aspect of entrepreneurial alertness which should be reflected in the count variable *Precipitator*. This capacity to identify precipitating factors that are potential drivers of performance enhancing change is an important aspect of successful small business strategy. Thus the owner-managers for whom the count variable *Precipitator* is high, are not just passively noting changes in the environment. Rather, they are actively seeking signs of environmental change, to which the business could be better adapted. In terms of options reasoning, the greater the array of factors embraced in the variable *Precipitator* the higher the potential option value generated (see McGrath, 1999, proposition 1). Furthermore, the *PrecipitatorTime* variable in Table 18.4 has a highly significant negative coefficient and a moderately large elasticity. This suggests that the more rapidly the mature small firm takes action, typically in the shape of organisational change in the face of critical changes in its environment, the better is its performance.

From Table 18.4, note that a 1 per cent increase in the *Precipitator* variable increases performance by 0.15 per cent; and a 1 per cent increase in the mean precipitating time (*PrecipitatorTime*) reduces performance by 0.07 per cent. In real option terms, this says that, for a larger number of detected drivers of change, the small firm has greater certainty that change is necessary to improving performance, including sheer survival. However, if a small firm is slow to respond to detected drivers of change, it risks being too late to achieve improvements in performance from instigating the organisational change, implying a trade-off relationship. The longer is the *PrecipitatorTime,* the greater is the number of *Precipitators* that are detected. The more *Precipitators* that are detected, the greater is the certainty surrounding the performance implications of change. But the longer the *PrecipitatorTime*, the greater the risk that the mature small firm will fail to capture some of the benefits of improved performance. Comparing the *Precipitator* and *PrecipitatorTime* variables of Table 18.4 with Table 18.5, we find a set of results whose implications are captured by the previous discussion. The significance level goes up, as do the magnitudes of both the elasticities [in the case of Table 18.5 ($n = 89$)]. Therefore the above analysis applies all the more so.

Organisational change forces small firms to make adjustments to headcount, stock levels, credit policy, etc. Note the differences between Tables 18.4 and 18.5 in the behaviour of the variable *Adjust*, which measures these effects. Specifically, the coefficient of *Adjust* is not significant in Table 18.4 (sample size $n = 186$), but has a positive and significant effect on performance (see *Perform*) [see the evidence in Table 18.5 (where $n = 89$) and the higher elasticity]. In the latter case, a 1 per cent increase in the mean count of adjustments (*Adjust*) increases performance by 0.10 per cent. Turning now to *AdjustTime,* this has a positive and significant impact on performance in both Tables 18.4 and 18.5, but a relatively small elasticity.

This suggests that the higher the number of adjustments (*Adjust*), other things being equal, following organisational change, the greater is the performance. A higher absolute number of adjustments also signals greater commitment by the firm to organisational change. Furthermore, a greater commitment by these firms indicates that the organisational change has significant implications for firm performance (including survival) (Ghemawat, 1991).

In Table 18.5, the number of consequential adjustments (*Adjust*) has a smaller impact on *Performance* than does the number of precipitating causes (*Precipitator*) (0.1 per cent *vs*. 0.2 per cent, respectively). Real options reasoning suggests that the certainty of the economic implications of an organisational change within the mature firm is more important than the number of adjustments made following the change. Faulty evaluations of the potential benefits of strategic change can have a negative impact on small firm performance (McGrath, 1999).

The variable *AdjustTime* refers to the lag between organisational change (instigated by some precipitating factors) and consequential adjustments (e.g. of headcount, of stock level, etc). A detailed definition is given in the appendix to this chapter. The statistical import of the variable *AdjustTime* is similar across Tables 18.3, 18.4 and 18.5. The coefficient of *AdjustTime* is positive and highly statistically significant and has a moderate elasticity. A 1 per cent increase in the mean adjustment time increases performance by 0.09 per cent. Although a mature small firm which is slow to adjust may be having difficulty in altering its factors of production (e.g. headcount), and in this sense lacks agility, the more plausible interpretation runs in terms of real options analysis (Bowman and Hurry, 1993; Luehrman, 1998; McGrath, 1999).[11] The statistical behaviour of the *Adjust-Time* variable seems to suggest the following argument. Extending *AdjustTime* can attenuate potential downsides by limiting fixed costs and irreversible investments. This should raise the bundled value of the portfolio of adjustments, typically investments, that might be labelled the mature small firm's 'strategy' in the light of organisational change (Luehrman, 1998; McGrath, 1999). By staging adjustments, a firm increases its option value to withdraw from change, or to continue to invest, having resolved uncertainties, thereby increasing its flexibility. However, the staging of adjustments may imply that it takes longer to receive payoffs from the organisational change. Thus, increases in the option value deriving from flexibility may come at a cost.

A brief case study illustrates this [as reported in newspaper coverage of this research in Judge (2002)]. The small firm from the sample was a corporate design and communications company. Its activities had a high creative content, and involved producing images and various forms of documentary reporting relating to its clients' business. The industry as a whole was subject to the impact of a major precipitating factor, namely the emergence of digital technology. The organisational change that was undertaken involved researching the market and determining the consequential needs of suppliers and trading partners. The entrepreneur who ran the small firm was aware of the potential for failing to adopt successfully the new technology. He invested in a pilot project for digital software, and then on the back of its success, a further investment was made in terms of employing a new team of people 'to deal specifically with that side of the business'. The entrepreneur in question said

> 'We forged close links with other companies, such as programming firms and internet service providers, so we could be sure that, if we went cold on the digital technology, those of our clients that were interested could still be serviced by someone else.'

Here one sees the entrepreneur taking actions, like staging commitments, and planning routes back from failed experiments. All of this is consistent with the real options interpretation adopted earlier.

The results in Tables 18.3–18.5 are broadly similar. Of these, Table 18.5 is arguably the most satisfactory in terms of overall significance, individual coefficient significance, magnitudes of elasticities, and specification of the selection equation. Regarding the latter, sample size is sacrificed in order to put market (*ProdGroup*) and financial variables (*Gearing*) into the selection equation. This seems to have paid off, statistically speaking, in that now more can be said, even with a smaller sample size. For this reason Table 18.5 contains the preferred specification.

If parsimony were the only goal of this research, the results of Table 18.3, on the smallest sample size ($n = 63$) would be recommended. However, they lack significance for the coefficient on *Adjust*, and leave one uneasy about possible consequences of sample selection bias being neglected. In fact, when the diagnostics relating to the Heckman two-step adjustment procedure in Tables 18.4 and 18.5 are examined, the Mills' lambda is not statistically significant in either case and the correlation between disturbances on the performance and selection equations is low. The results of Table 18.5 are preferred because they are careful about sample selection, and because, at the margin, any adjustment for it might have a marginal impact upon the performance equation (which seems to have been the case with the *Adjust* variable). Similar reasoning has related to the discussion in Chapter 10 (especially in Section 10.4).

18.7   Conclusion

This chapter has examined the effects of firm-specific turbulence and various dimensions of flexibility, on the performance of the long-lived small firm in Scotland. It identified the main factors that influenced the performance of long-lived small businesses positively. First, entrepreneurs must be alert (Kirzner, 1973). They must be good at recognising drivers of change. Second, they must be speedy. They should be quick to adapt their organisation in the light of these forces of change. Third, once organisational change has been implemented, the entrepreneur should follow through on *all* necessary adjustments. However, this should not be done impulsively. Such adjustments typically involve investments which are in the nature of exercising an option (McGrath, 1999; Luehrman, 1998). Fourth, delay on adjustment may have beneficial consequences for performance, if it reduces uncertainty and diminishes irreversibility. Acting in these ways, entrepreneurs can have a positive influence on performance. On the other hand, firm-specific turbulence has a negative effect on performance.

Performance is regarded as a multidimensional variable, as in Part 4. Here it was constructed from interview evidence with entrepreneurs, covering competitive environment, financial management, organisational structure and business strategy. The measures of performance, firm-specific turbulence and flexibility measures were all novel. Several performance models were estimated, using generalised least squares estimation (with heteroskedastic adjustment) with or without sample selection. When adjustment for sample selection bias was undertaken, two different specifications of selection equations were used, and the Heckman two-step procedure was adopted.

Whilst flexibility had a positive effect upon performance, this was not true of the firm-specific measure of turbulence (*FSTurbulence*). This is a count variable of the frequency of organisational change. It had a highly significant and strong negative effect on performance. This firm-specific turbulence refers to the total amount of 'trimming' of its activities that the firm undertakes. It was found that too much 'trimming' reduces performance. For example, it wastes resources, and suggests false or imprudent moves, which then require correction. The smart approach is to stage the commitment of resources allocated to a new strategy. This allows you to pull back if things do not pan out as you expected. Technically, it increases the 'option value' of the small firm.

APPENDIX

Definitions of variables

Age	Age of firm, in years.
Agility	Agility is the ratio of precipitating to adjustment factors averaged over three main changes.
Adjust	Count of adjustments averaged over three main changes = $\Sigma a_{jm}/3$ where a_{jm} is the occurrence of adjustment j for each main change m.
AdjustTime	Total adjustment time averaged over three main changes = $\Sigma at_{jm}/3$ where at_{jm} is the length of time between the occurrence of each main change m and each adjustment j.
Employees	Number of full-time equivalent employees in 2001.
FSTurbulence	Count of main changes over life of long-lived small firm = ΣX_i where X_i is the occurrence of a change i.
FtEmployee	Number of full-time employees at start-up.
Gearing	= Bank loan/personal injection.

Continued

Definitions of variables—cont'd

LabProd	= Sales/employees.
Perform	= $\Sigma f_i/n$ where f_i is the self-appraised score between 0 and 100 for each factor averaged overall factors 1 to n which were applicable.
Precipitator	Count of precipitating factors averaged over three main changes = $\Sigma p_{jm}/3$ where p_{jm} is the occurrence of precipitating factor j for each main change m.
PrecipitatorTime	Total precipitating time averaged over three main changes = $\Sigma pt_{jm}/3$ where pt_{jm} is the length of time between each precipitating factor j and the occurrence of each main change m.
ProdGroup	Number of product groups.
PtEmployee	Number of part-time employees at start-up.
Sales	Sales in 2001.
Sector	=0 services (SIC 61–99), 1 = manufacturing (SIC 01–60).
Speed	The overall speed of adjustment can be obtained by summing the average precipitating time and the average adjustment time and dividing by the number of main changes $\sum_{c=1}^{3} m_c$.
StSales	Sales at first interview (1985 for SBE, 1991 for telephone, 1994 for Leverhulme) at 2001 prices.
StYear	Year the business was established.
Survival	=1 survivor, 0 otherwise.

Endnotes

1 The sample is derived from three original samples. Data on the first parent sample of 86 SBEs in Scotland was collected between 1985 and 1988 using face-to-face interviews and examined in Jacobsen (1986), Reid and Jacobsen (1988), Reid et al. (1993) and Reid (1993). This study examined factors effecting the survival, growth, performance and competitive strategy of these small firms in their early years. Of these 86 firms 25 (29 per cent) survived. The 25 long-lived survivors from this sample are pooled with long-lived survivors from the other two parent samples of SBEs in Scotland. Data on the second sample was collected through telephone in 1991. These 113 firms were more mature at the time and examined in Reid (1996a, b). The administered questionnaire covered financial aspects of a very small firms existence, including funding shortages, forms of external finance, relations with banks and perceptions of the venture capital market. Fourty six out of the 113 firms are still in business (a survival rate of 41 per cent). Third, 20 long-lived small firms which were 10 years are more were also identified from a sample new business starts which were interviewed using face-to-face interviews between 1994 and 1997 on their finance, costs, business strategy, human capital, organisation and technical change. This third sample builds on the work of this book. These firms have been examined by Reid and Smith (2000a), Reid (1991) and Smith (1997a, b, 1998). Fifteen out of 20 were still trading (a survival rate of 75 per cent) during the further phase of fieldwork in 2001–02.

2 See Reid (1993), Reid and Andersen (1992), Reid (1996a, b) and Smith (1997a, b).

3 This created a duration variable from the point of inception, for each change that had occurred.

4 This question in structure and design format, improves on innovative aspects of the instrumentation design used in Reid and Smith (2000b) to explain changes in the management accounting system of small business enterprises using contingency theory. Cause and effect are identified here.

5 The average number of precipitators and the average number of adjustments was calculated by:

$$\sum_{c=1}^{3} P_c \bigg/ \sum_{c=1}^{3} m_c \quad \text{and} \quad \sum_{c=1}^{3} A_c \bigg/ \sum_{c=1}^{3} m_c, \text{respectively.}$$

6 The average total precipitating time and the average total adjustment time are calculated by:

$$\sum_{m=1}^{3} pt_{jm} \bigg/ \sum_{c=1}^{3} m_c \quad \text{and} \quad \sum_{m=1}^{3} at_{jm} \bigg/ \sum_{c=1}^{3} m_c, \text{respectively.}$$

7 The dimensions were generated from theory and empirical evidence from studies examining differences in the performance of long-lived small firms (see Power, 2004).

8 Rating factors along a continuum is a much easier task than ranking the list of factors from top to bottom, especially for long lists of factors. The ranks can be tied when the factors are rated. The consistency with which owner-managers rate factors on each scale item is also improved by defining the meaning respondents should assign to middle alternatives using adjectival labelling of points.

9 Our measure of labour productivity would probably be different if value added, rather than sales, were used. Alas, we lack value added figures, and our statistic has simplicity to recommend it. We doubt it would affect the results of the analysis.

10 The regressors are included in their raw count form. Existence of multi-collinearity would influence (or even destroy) the estimation of the performance equation, if the measures of agility and speed were both included as regressors in the equation, as speed is a linear function of agility.

11 Just as an option in the theory of finance confers the right (but does not impose not the obligation) to purchase a specified asset at a pre-specified price on a specified date, so a real option confers the right (but does not impose the obligation) to invest (or further invest) in an asset within the firm. The ability to delay the decision about whether to invest in a real asset increases flexibility in the face of risk (Copeland and Keenan, 1998). By adopting a 'wait and see' strategy, uncertainties regarding the true value of the asset may be resolved. The existence of a positive net present value, NPV (i.e. being 'in the money') alone should not necessarily lead to investment, if business conditions are poor. Only if conditions are favourable, should investment or further investment be made ('exercising the option'). Such an approach builds on good, or mitigates against bad fortune. As in financial options theory, real options rise in value with uncertainty, because greater variability raises the potential gains without raising the cost of accessing them. From a real options standpoint, entrepreneurs should hold a portfolio of options and adopt an incremental approach to investment (i.e. making small investments initially followed by large investments) to limit downside risks, see Bowman and Hurry (1993). In effect, the 'alert' entrepreneur takes out real options which are not obvious to others, and are therefore undervalued (McGrath, 1999).

Epilogue

We live today in an academic world in which the article (and, increasingly, the short article, or even abstract) is the predominant mode of reporting, communication and debate. Furthermore, in this globalised world, including a lively labour market for talented academics, the emphasis is on 'portable' research, that is, on research which is not country specific but, rather, generic. If you are selling your academic wares in an international market, and do not know whether you will be in Sydney, Australia; Johannesburg, South Africa; or San Francisco, California next year, why should you 'lock-in' your research agenda to a specific country?

As a result, economists have increasingly shied clear of empirical work, unless it refers to really large economies like the United States or India. It is not unusual to hear refereeing remarks like 'unfortunately, this is only about <Nigeria/Sweden/ Slovenia/Panama>', implying we can learn little from such work. A common reaction by academics who wish to hold a portable portfolio of 'academic goods' is to prefer theory to empirical work or practice. As a result, there is a very high volume of theoretical work, often of a very specialised nature, and frequently not formulated in ways which facilitate empirical testing. This is a pity, because the economic, financial and commercial world is changing so rapidly that there are many more difficult and challenging theoretical problems to tackle than there were 50 years ago, and they are of a nature that leads to empirically testable propositions, in a variety of cultural and national contexts.

The reader who has come this far will see that I am not concerned about going against the trend – as any seasoned trader knows, that can be a wise course of action. I am against the trend because this is a book, and a long one at that: not an anthology or an edited set of readings, not a handbook, and not a quick 'how to do it' book. Those who know my writings will be aware the book has emerged from the culture of articles in which I live, work and publish; but, even so, this book is on just one single theme (the new small firm) and uses just one primary dataset (which is Scottish). The book is based on a variety of theories, all of which are rigorous, and most of which can be expressed in highly formal ways, but the large body of analysis this book contains is clearly (and determinedly) empirical. So I present a long book, about a small (but proud) country called Scotland. I am clearly nailing my colours to the mast.

My riposte to criticism of this would be as follows. First, this small country, Scotland, produced the first major analysis of the enterprise economy, and was innovative in many of the institutions that in a sense 'define' the enterprise economy, like free banking, and the chartering of accountants. It is therefore an enterprise economy of great duration and depth – uniquely so. Second, there are some forms of analysis that do not come in handy bite-size units. A big problem needs a big solution. The advantage of entrepreneurship, as it has emerged in just the last two decades as a university subject, is that it is eclectic. Its many tools can therefore be turned to many ends and, as a consequence, thorough analysis may be both detailed and extensive.

Third, and finally, the Scottish economy, like the Dutch economy, or many others one might consider, is a kind of laboratory (and in my view an ideal one) for testing theories of enterprise. I see a happy coincidence of wants emerging, with good theorists becoming enthusiastic about using good 'laboratories' (like the Scottish enterprise system) for testing their theories. Indeed, I hope my extensive use of relevant theories (and tests thereof) will convince readers that this is possible. If one were *not* surprised to see articles on the Scottish economy (or the Irish, Dutch, Malawian or Hong Kong economies, for that matter) in, say, the *Journal of Political Economy*, in the next two decades, I would be mightily reassured about the solid basis of our research agenda.

My concluding remarks are not so much about why (and how and where) one does work of this sort, but about the content of the book itself. I was recently asked in an interview setting: 'You do so many things, so many projects, on so many topics – isn't there any coherence to what you are doing?' My reply was simple: 'There is *one* project, the life-cycle of the small business enterprise. Many sponsors have helped me drive this forward, for many years, and I have progressed it using many techniques and many methodologies. However, it is but one project – and a large one'.

It has been a long project too, starting in 1983, when Scotland was classified as suffering from 'entrepreneurial failure'. So much has changed since then, in an almost entirely positive way. I started seeking a better understanding of what leads individuals to found a firm, and it is in this sense that I talk of 'Foundations'. The activities of these entrepreneurs are the foundations of the enterprise economy, not this book. But I hope, nevertheless, that this book has been a guide to those foundations, in their variety, complexity and intricacy, as well as their broad sweep of dynamics, adaptation and evolution.

GCR
St Andrews
29 March 2006

Appendix on instrumentation

Pre-letters

Initial Approach

Dear ....

The small firm has become a focus of interest in the economy. Its role in employment creation, innovation and growth makes it a vital component of a dynamic, competitive economy. Scottish Business in the Community, Scottish Enterprise and the Enterprise Trust movement itself all contribute to fostering a favourable enterprise environment for small firms.

The universities too have a keen interest in small firms from the viewpoint of economic analysis. Within the universities, research is directed at creating new tools of economic analysis for the benefit of the community within which they function. For example, this research has led to innovative techniques for formulating small business strategy, and has introduced new and more effective techniques for investment appraisal within the small firm.

We are writing to request that you cooperate with a new small firms research study being undertaken within the University of St Andrews. It is under the Directorship of Professor Gavin Reid of the Centre for Research into Industry, Enterprise, Finance and the Firm (CRIEFF), within the Economics Department. His concern is with the life cycle effect within the small firm. A research team from CRIEFF will be interviewing owner managers of small firms over the next four years. They would like to make an approach to you early in the new year, with a view to conducting an interview with you at your place of work, or wherever else is mutually agreeable. This should take about an hour of your time, and the intention would be to undertake follow-up interviews at roughly yearly intervals for three further years.

It is already known of that new small firms grow faster than older, larger firms. However, what causes this slow down in growth (the 'life cycle' effect) is largely a mystery. The purpose of this research is to help unravel this mystery. If achieved, it can help research workers fashion new tools of economic analysis for predicting, and averting, if appropriate, this slow down in growth associated with the life cycle effect. Once the study is complete, respondents to the interviews will be the first to receive a summary account of CRIEFF's research findings. Of course, at all times, confidentiality will be maintained in the interviewing process.

If you have any questions concerning this involvement, please do not hesitate to contact us or Professor Reid at CRIEFF (0334 462438). We hope we can depend on your cooperation. Thank you.

Yours sincerely

First report

Date

«Title» «FirstName» «LastName» «Title1» «FirstName1» «LastName1»
«JobTitle»
«Company»
«Address1»
«Address2»
«City»
«State»«PostalCode»

Dear «Title» «LastName» «and Title1» «LastName1»

Life-cycle effects in new small Scottish firms

Last year you very kindly allowed us to interview you again about your business, thereby assisting us in the second phase of our study of small firms in Scotland. At the time, we promised to report back to you on our findings. Please now find enclosed a summary report, constructed under the headings of markets, finance, costs, business strategy, human resources, organisation and technical change. We hope it will be of interest to you.

In response to popular demand, we have also included a profile of firms that have gone out of business since year one. It should be noted that this is not necessarily because of poor performance – indeed the average profitability of these firms is somewhat higher than those that remain in business. There is evidence that these firms may have a shorter product life cycle and earlier time 'to harvest'.

In addition, we have included a fairly detailed statistical analysis of differences between firms which continued in business, and firms which ceased trading. Whilst some parts of this are for experts only, it is hoped that other parts, including the summary of key points on page 15, will be accessible to all of you.

We have explained to you that the project is on-going over four years. At the time of initial interview you were kind enough to agree to participate in later years of the study. We are now entering phase three of the project, and would like to approach you again concerning the third round of interviews. We trust we can rely once more upon your invaluable assistance, for which we are again extremely grateful. To this end, we will be contacting you in the near future to arrange an interview. The questionnaire will follow a similar line to that of last year, although it will be significantly shorter.

If you have any questions concerning this involvement, please do not hesitate to contact us at CRIEFF (01334 462438). We hope we can again depend on your cooperation, and we will be in touch with you shortly. Thank you.

Yours sincerely

Gavin C. Reid   Julia A. Smith
Professor in Economics   Research Assistant, CRIEFF
Director, CRIEFF

Encs:

Pilot study card

Date

Dear

Life-cycle effects in new small Scottish firms

Last year you very kindly allowed us to interview you about your business, thereby assisting us in the first phase of our study of small firms in Scotland. At the time, we promised to report back to you on our findings. Please now find enclosed a summary report, constructed under the headings of markets, finance, costs, business strategy, human resources, organisation and technical change. We hope it will be of interest to you.

Due to the construction of the sampling frame used for this study, you will be pleased to note that we do not require a re-interview with you. However, we should like to take this opportunity to wish you every success with your business, and to thank you again for the time you spent in helping us with our project. If there is any way in which we can expand upon the points made in the attached, please do not hesitate to let us know.

Meanwhile, thank you again for your kind cooperation.

Yours sincerely

Gavin C. Reid   Julia A. Smith
Professor in Economics   Research Assistant, CRIEFF
Director, CRIEFF

Enc:

Follow-up letter

16 September 1997

«Title» «FirstName» «LastName» «Title1» «FirstName1» «LastName1»
«JobTitle»
«Company»
«Address1»
«Address2»
«City»
«State»
«PostalCode»

Dear «Title» «LastName» «Title1» «LastName1»

Life-cycle effects in new small Scottish firms

Thank you for all the help you have given us in our study of small firms in Scotland. As usual, we said we would let you know what we found out about small firms. We now enclose a brief report of our most recent results. This summarises our findings under the headings of markets, finance, costs, business and pricing strategy, human resources, organisation and technical change. We also enclose a more complete analysis of the development and survival of new small businesses, which explores the issue of competencies in small firms quite thoroughly. We hope they will interest you.

We are now entering the next phase of the project, and would like to approach you again concerning the next round of interview. We trust we can rely once more upon your invaluable assistance, for which we are again extremely grateful. To this end, we will be contacting you in the near future to arrange an interview.

If you have any questions concerning this involvement, please do not hesitate to contact us at CRIEFF (01334 462438). We hope we can again depend on your cooperation, and we will be in touch with you shortly. Thank you.

Yours sincerely

Dr Gavin C. Reid   Dr Julia A. Smith
Professor in Economics   Research Fellow, CRIEFF
Director, CRIEFF

Enc:

References

Acar, A.C. (1993) 'The impact of key internal factors on firm performance: An empirical study of small Turkish firms', *Journal of Small Business Management* 31(4), 86–92.

Acs, Z., B. Audretsch and B. Carlsson (1990) Flexibility, plant size and restructuring, in Z. Acs, B. Audretsch and B. Carlsson (eds.), *The Economics of Small Firms: A European Challenge*. Dordrecht: Kluwer.

Acs, Z.J. and D.B. Audretsch (1993) Innovation and firm size: The new learning, in M. Dodgson and R. Rothwell (eds.), *International Journal of Technology Management*, Special Issue on Small Firms and Innovation, pp. 23–35.

Adelman, I.G. (1958) 'A stochastic analysis of the size distribution of firms', *Journal of the American Statistical Association*, 53, 893–904.

Aitchison, J. and J.A.C. Brown (1969) *The Lognormal Distribution: With Special Reference to its Uses in Economics*. Cambridge: Cambridge University Press.

Alam, I. (2005) 'Fieldwork and data collection in qualitative marketing research', *Qualitative Market Research* 8(1), 97–112.

Almus, M. (2000) 'Testing "Gibrat's Law" for young firms – empirical results for West Germany', *Small Business Economics* 15(1), 1–12.

Alum, M. (1997) Budgetary process in uncertain contexts: A study of state-owned enterprises in Bangladesh, *Management Accounting Research* 8, 147–67.

Amemiya, T. (1985) *Advanced Econometrics*. Oxford: Basil Blackwell.

Anderson, S.W. and W.N. Lanen (1999) Economic transition, strategy and the evolution of management accounting practices: The case of India, *Accounting, Organizations and Society* 24, 379–412.

Andrews, P.W.S. (1949) *Manufacturing Business*. London: Macmillan.

Ang, J.S. (1992) On the theory of finance for privately held firms, *Journal of Small Business Finance* 1(3), 185–203.

Ansoff, H.I. (1965) *Corporate Strategy: An Analytical Approach to Business Policy for Growth and Expansion*. McGraw Hill; New York.

Ashford, J.R. and R.R. Sowden (1970) Multivariate probit analysis, *Biometrics* 26, 535–46.

Atkinson, J. and N. Meager (1994) Running to stand still: The small business in the labour market, in J. Atkinson and D.J. Storey (eds.), *Employment, the Small Firm and the Labour Markets*. Routledge; London.

Audretsch, D.B., L. Klomp, E. Santarelli and A.R. Thurik. 'Gibrat's Law: Are the Services Different?', *Review of Industrial Organization* 24(3), 301–24.

Baliga, W. (1995) 'Accountants seen as information sources by small business, *Journal of Accountancy* 179(1), 15.

Barrow, C. (1986) *Routes to Success: Case Studies of 40 UK Small Business Ventures.* London: Kogan Page.

Bates, T. (1990) 'Entrepreneurial human capital inputs and small business longevity', *Review of Economics and Statistics* 72, 551–9.

Baumol, W.J. (1962) 'On the theory of the expansion of the firm', *American Economic Review* 52, 1078–87.

Becker, W.E. and P.E. Kennedy (1992) 'A graphical exposition of the ordered probit', *Econometric Theory* 8, 127–31.

Beesley, M.E. and R.T. Hamilton (1984) Small firms seedbed role and the concept of turbulence, *Journal of Industrial Economics*, 33(2), 217–231.

Beggs, S.S. Cardell and J. Hausman (1981) 'Assessing the potential demand for electric cars', *Journal of Econometrics* 17, 19–20.

Bhimani, A. (1999) Mapping methodological frontiers in cross-national management control research, *Accounting, Organizations and Society* 24(56), 413–40.

Binks, M. and J. Coynes (1983) *The Birth of Enterprise: An Analytical and Empirical Study of the Growth of Small Firms.*IEA: London.

Binks, M.R. and C.T. Ennew (1996) 'Growing firms and the credit constraint', *Small Business Economics*, 8(1), 17–27.

Binks, M.P., C.T. Ennew and G.V. Reed (1988) 'The survey by the Forum of Private Business on banks and small firms', in G. Bannock and E.V. Morgan (eds.), *Banks and Small Businesses: A Two Nation Perspective.* Forum of Private Business/National Federation of Small Business.

Birch, D. (1996) Chapter presented to the Jönköping International Business Conference on *Enterpreneurship, SME's and the Macro Economy*, 13–14th June (mimeo).

Black., J., D. De Meza and D. Jeffreys (1992) 'House prices, the supply of collateral and the enterprise economy', Discussion Paper in Economics No. 9208, Department of Economics, University of Exeter.

Blanchflower, D. and A. Oswald (1990) 'What makes an entrepreneur?' National Bureau of Economic Research Working Paper No. 3252.

Bowman, E.H. and D. Hurry (1993) 'Strategy through the options lens: An integrated view of resource investments and the incremental-choice process', *Academy of Management Review*, 24, 760–782.

Brehmer, B. (1990) 'Strategies in real-time, dynamic decision making', in R.M. Hogarth (ed.) *Insights in Decision Making: a tribute to Hillel J Einhorn.* Chicago: Chicago University Press, pp. 262–79.

Brignall, S. (1997) A contingent rationale for cost system design in services, *Management Accounting Research* 8(3), 325–46.

Brock, W.A. and D.S. Evans (1986) *The Economics of Small Business*, New York: Holmes & Meier.

Brock, W.A., and S.E. Evans (1989) 'Small business economics', *Small Business Economics*, 1(1), 7–20.

Brouthers, L.E. and G. Nakos (2005) 'The role of systematic international market selection on small firms' exporting performance', *Journal of Small Busienss Management* 43, 363–81.

Brown, C. and J. Medoff (1989) The employer size-wage effect, *Journal of Political Economy* 97, 1027–59.

Buick, I. (2003) 'Information technology in small Scottish hotels: Is it working?', *International Journal of Contemporary Hospitality Management* 15, 243–7.

Burgess, R.G. (1984) *In the Field: An Introduction for Field Research*. London: George Allen & Unwin.

Burns, T. and G. Stalker (1961) *The Management Innovation*. Tavistock Institute.

Caldeira, M.M. and J.M. Ward (2003) 'Using resource-based theory to interpret the successful adoption and use of information systems and technology in manufacturing small and medium-sized enterprises', *European Journal of Information Systems* 12(2), 127–41.

Carlsson, B. (1989) 'Flexibility and the theory of the firm,' *International Journal of Industrial Organization*, 7(2), 179–204.

Casson, M. (1994) 'Economic perspectives on business information', in L. Bud-Frierman (ed.) *Information Acumen: The Understanding and Use of Knowledge in Modern Business*, Chapter 7, London: Routledge.

Chandler, A.D. (1962) *Strategy and Structure*. MIT Press.

Chang, C.-H. and C.-W. Jevons Lee (1992) 'Information acquisition as business strategy', *Southern Economic Journal* 58(3), 750–61.

Chapman, C.S. (1997) Reflections on a contingent view of accounting, *Accounting, Organizations and Society* 22, 189–206.

Chaston, I. (1997) 'Small firm performance: Assessing the interaction between entrepreneurial style and organizational structure', *European Journal of Marketing* 31(11/12), 814.

Chaston, I., B. Badger and E. Sadler-Smith (1999) 'Small firm organizational learning: Comparing the perceptions of need and style among UK support service advisors and small firm managers', *Journal of European Industrial Training* 23, 36–42.

Chaston, I., B. Badger and E. Sadler-Smith (2000) 'Organizational learning style and competences a comparative investigation of relationship and transactionally orientated small UK manufacturing firms', *European Journal of Marketing* 34(5/6), 625.

Chaston, I., B. Badger, T. Mangles and E. Sadler-Smith (2001) 'Organisational learning style, competencies and learning systems in small, UK manufacturing firms', *International Journal of Operations and Production Management* 21(11), 1417–32.

Chittenden, F., Hall, G., and P. Hutchinson (1996) 'Small firm growth, access to capital markets and financial structure: Review of issues and an empirical investigation', *Business Economics* 8(1), 59–67.

Chow, K.W.C. and K.Y.M. Fung (1996) 'Firm dynamics and industrialization in the Chinese economy in transition: Implications for small business policy', *Journal of Business Venturing* 11(6), 489–505.

Chrisman, J.J., A. Bauerschmidt and C.W. Hofer (1998) The Determinants of New Venture Performance: An Extended Model, *Journal of Business Venturing*, Fall, 5–29.

Chung, K.L. (1967) *Markov Chains with Stationary Transition Probabilities (2nd edn)*, Berlin: Springer-Verlag.

Clay, N. and M. Cowling (1996) 'Small firms and bank relationships: A study of cultural differences between English and Scottish Banks', *Omega* 24(1), 115–20.

Coase, R.H. (1937) The nature of the firm, *Economica* 4, 386–405.

Coase, R.H. (1988) 'The nature of the firm: Origin', *Journal of Law Economics and Organization* 4, 3–17.

Collier, M. (2003) 'A micro AGV for flexible manufacturing in small enterprises', *Integrated Manufacturing Systems* 14, 442–8.

Collinson, S. (2000) 'Knowledge networks for innovation in small Scottish software firms', *Entrepreneurship and Regional Development* 12(3), 217–44.

Collinson, S. and J. Houlden (2005) Decision-making and market orientation in the internationalization process of small and medium-sized enterprises', *Management International Review* 45, 413–36.

Cooper, R.A. and A.J. Weekes (eds.) (1983) *Data, Models and Statistical Analysis*. Oxford: Philip Allan.

Copeland, T.E., and P.T. Keenan (1998) How much is flexibility worth? *The McKinsey Quarterly*, 2, 38–49.

Cressy, R.C. (1995) Borrowing and control: A theory of business types, *Small Business Economics* 7, 1–10.

Cressy, R.C. (1996a) Commitment lending under asymmetric information: Theory and tests on UK startup data, *Small Business Economics* 8, 1–12.

Cressy, R.C. (1996b), Pre-entrepreneurial income, cashflow growth and survival of startup businesses: model and tests on UK startup data, *Small Business Economics* 8(1), 49–58.

Cressy, R.C. (1996c) Are startups debt-rationed?, *The Economic Journal* 106, 1253–70.

Cressy, R. (1996) 'Commitment lending under asymmetric information: Theory and tests on UK startup data', *Small Business Economics* 8(5), 397–408.

Cressy, R.C. (1999) The Evans and Jovanovic equivalence theorem and credit rationing: Another look, *Small Business Economics*, 12(4), 295–7.

Crick, D., S. Chaudhry and B. Bradshaw (2003) 'The overseas marketing performance of successful small UK high-technology firms: an exploratory study comparing ingigenous subsidiary firm's competitiveness, *Strategic Change* 12(8), 421–33.

Cubbin, J. and D. Leech (1986) 'Growth versus profit maximization: a simultaneous equations approach to testing the Marris model', *Managerial and Decision Economics* 7, 123–31.

Cunningham, D. and W. Hornby (1993) 'Pricing decision in small firms: Theory and practice', *Management Decision* 31(7), 46–55.

Daake, D, D.D. Dawley and W.P. Anthony (2004) 'Formal data use in strategic planning: An organizational field experiment', *Journal of Managerial Issues* 16(2), 232–47.

Daly, M.A. and A. McCann (1992) How many small firms? *Employment Gazette* 100(2), 47–51.

Daudpota, N.H. (1998) 'Five steps to construct a model of data allocation for distributed database systems', *Journal of Intelligent Information Systems* 11(2), 153–68.

Davidson, R. and J.G. MacKinnon (1993) *Estimation and Inference in Econometrics*. Oxford: Oxford University Press.

De Guinea, A.O., H. Kelley and M.G. Hunter (2005) 'Information system effectiveness in small business: extending a Singaporean model in Canada', *Journal of Global Information Management* 13(3), 55–78.

DeVellis, R. (1991) *Scale Development: Theory and Applications*, Vol. 26, Applied Social Research Methods Series. London: Sage Publications.

Dobson, S. and B. Gerrard (1989) 'Growth and profitability in the Leeds engineering sector', *Scottish Journal of Political Economy* 36, 334–52.

Donaldson, G. (1961) Corporate Debt Capacity: A Study of Corporate Debt Policy and the Determinants of Corporate Debt Capacity, Division of Research, Harvard School of Business Administration, Boston, Mass., USA, mimeo.

Donaldson, L. (ed.) (1995) *Contingency Theory*. Dartmouth, Aldershot.

Dunkelberg, W.C. and A.C. Cooper (1990) Investment and capital diversity in the small enterprise, in Z. Acs and D. B. Audretsch (eds.) *The Economics of Small Firms: A European Challenge*. Dordrecht: Kluwer, pp. 119–34.

Dunn, P and L. Cheatham (1993) 'Fundamentals of small business financial management for start-up, survival, growth, and changing economic circumstances', *Managerial Finance* 19(8), 1–12.

Emmanuel, C. and D. Otley (1986) *Accounting for Management Control.* Wokingham, UK: Van Nostrand Reinhold.

Emmanuel, C., D. Otley and K. Merchant (1990) *Accounting for Management Control (2nd edn).* London: Chapman and Hall.

Epstein, M.J., and J.F. Manzoni (eds.) (2002) *Performance Measurement and Control: A Compendium of Research.* Amsterdam: JAI Press.

Evans, D.S. (1987), 'Tests of alternative theories of firm growth', *Journal of Political Economy* 95, 657–74.

Evans, D. and B. Jovanovic (1989) An estimated model of entrepreneurial choice under liquidity constraints, *Journal of Political Economy* 97, 808–27.

Evans, D.S. and L.S. Leighton (1990) Some empirical aspects of entrepreneurship, in Z.J. Acs and D.B. Audretsch (eds.), *The Economics of Small Firms: A European Challenge.* Kluwer: Dordrecht.

Everitt, B.S. (1980) *Cluster Analysis* (2nd edn). London: Heineman.

Fang, B. (1990) 'The user survey and design conception of information systems for the county of Chong Ming (Shanghai)', in Ganzhorn and Faustoferri (eds.), *Bridging the Information Gap for Small and Medium Enterprises.* Berlin: Springer-Verlag, pp. 219–27.

Feichtinger, G. and R.F. Hartl (1986) *Optimale Kontrolle Ökonomischer Prozesse.* Berlin: de Gruyter.

Fletcher, M. (1995) 'Decision-making by Scottish bank managers', *International Journal of Entrepreneurial Behaviour & Research* 1, 37–53.

Foreman-Peck, J. (1985) 'Seedcorn or Chaff? New Firms and Industrial Performance in the Interwar Economy', *Economic History Review* 38, 402–422.

Foss, N.J. and V. Mahnke (eds.) (2000) *Competence, Governance, and Entrepreneurship.* Oxford: Oxford University Press.

Frank, M.Z. (1988) 'An intemporal model of industrial exit', *Quarterly Journal of Economics* 103, 333–34.

Furrukh, I. and S. Urata (2002) 'Small firm dynamism in East Asia: An introductory overview', *Small Business Economics* 18(1–3), 1–12.

Gall, H (1990) 'Technology broker systems for SMEs in FRG', in Ganzhorn and Faustoferri (eds.), *Bridging the Information Gap for Small and Medium Enterprises,* Berlin: Springer-Verlag, pp. 151–60.

Ganugi, P., L. Grossi and G. Gozzi (2005) 'Testing Gibrat's law in Italian macro-regions: Analysis on a panel of mechanical companies', *Statistical Methods and Applications* 15(1), 101–25.

Ganugi, P., L. Grossi and L. Crosato (2004) 'Firm size distributions and stochastic growth models: A comparison between ICT and mechanical Italian Companies', *Statistical Methods and Applications* 12(3), 391–414.

Ganzhorn, K. and S. Faustoferri (eds.) (1990) *Bridging the Information Gap for Small and Medium Enterprises.* Berlin: Springer-Verlag.

Gerbing, D.W. and J.C. Andersen (1998) An updated paradigm for scale development incorporating unidimensionality and its assessment, *Journal of Marketing Research,* 25, 186–192.

Geroski, P. and K. Gugler (2004) 'Corporate growth convergence in Europe', *Oxford Economic Papers* 56(4), 597–620.

Ghemawat, P. (1991) *Commitment.* New York: The Free Press.

Gibrat (1931) *Les Inégalites Économiques.* Paris: Libraire du Recueil Sirey.

Gillespie, J.M. and J.R. Fulton (2001) 'A Markov chain analysis of the size of hog production firms in the United States', *Agribusiness* 17(4), 557–70.

Giordano, J. (2003) 'Using the survivor technique to estimate returns to scale and optimum firm size', *Topics in Economics Analysis & Policy* 3(1), 1081–1104.

Glaser, B.G. and A.L. Strauss (1967) *The Discovery of Grounded Theory: Strategies for Qualitative Research.* New York: Aldine.

Gordon, L.A. and D. Miller (1976) A contingency framework for the design of accounting information systems, *Accounting, Organizations and Society* 1, 59–70.

Greene, W.H. (1984) Estimation of the correlation coefficient in a bivariate probit model using the method of moments, *Economic Letters* 16, 285–91.

Greene, W.H. (1992) *Limdep User's Manual and Reference Guide.* Bellport, NY: Econometric Software Inc.

Greene, W.H. (1993) *Econometric Analysis* (2nd edn). Macmillan: New York.

Gregory, B.T., M.W. Rutherford, S. Oswald and L. Gardiner (2005) 'An empirical investigation of the growth cycle theory of small firm financing', *Journal of Small Business Management* 43(4), 382–92.

Groenewegen, P. (1995) *A Soaring Eagle: Alfred Marshall 1842-1924.* Aldershot, UK: Edward Elgar.

Guidici, G. and S. Paleari (2000) The provision of finance to innovation: A survey conducted among Italian technology-based small firms, *Small Business Economics* 14, 37–53.

Gul, F.A. (1991) 'The effects of management accounting systems and environmental uncertainty on small business managers' performance', *Accounting and Business Research* 22(85), 57–61.

Hair, F.J., R.E. Andersen, R.L. Tatham and W.C. Black (1995) *Multivariate Data Analysis.* New York: Prentice Hall.

Hamilton, R.T. and M.A. Fox (1998) 'The financing preferences of small firm owners', *International Journal of Entrepreneurial Behaviour & Research* 4(3), 239–48.

Hankinson, A. (2000) 'The key factors in the profiles of small owner-managers that influence business performance', *The South Coast Small Firms Survey, 1997-2000, Industrial and Commercial Training* 32(3), 94–8.

Hardman, DK and P Ayton (1997) 'Arguments for qualitative risk assessment: the StAR risk adviser', *Expert Systems* 14(1), 24–36.

Harrison, J.R. (2004) 'Models of growth in organizational ecology: A simulation assessment', *Industrial and Corporate Change* 13(1), 243–62.

Hart, P.E. (1962) 'The size and growth of firms', *Economica* 24, 29–39.

Hart, P.E. (2000) 'Theories of firms' growth and the generation of jobs', *Review of Industrial Organization* 17, 229–248.

Hart, P.E. and N. Oulton (1999) 'Gibrat, Galton and job generation', *International Journal of the Economics of Business* 6(2), 149–64.

Hartman, E.A., C.B. Tower and T.C. Sebora (1994) 'Information sources and their relationship to organizational innovation in small business', *Journal of Small Business Management* 32(1), 36–47.

Haugh, H.M. and W. Pardy (1999) 'Community entrepreneurship in north east Scotland', *International Journal of Entrepreneurial Behaviour & Research* 5(4), 163–72.

Hay, D.A. and D.J. Morris (1991) *Industrial Economics and Organization* (2nd edn). Oxford: Oxford University Press.

Hayes, D.C. and J.E. Hunton (1999) 'Building a database from scratch', *Journal of Accountancy* 188(5), 63–73.

Heckman, J. (1976) 'The common structure of statistical models of truncation, sample selection and limited dependent variables and a simple estimator for such models,' *The Annals of Economic and Social Measurement* 475–492.

Heckman, J. (1979) 'Sample selection bias as a specification error', *Econometrica* 47, 153–161.

Heshmati, A. (2001) 'On the growth of micro and small firms: Evidence from Sweden', *Small Business Economics* 17(3), 213.

Hill, J. and P. McGowan (1999) 'Small business and enterprise development: Questions about research methodology', *International Journal of Entrepreneurial Behaviour & Research* 5(1), 5.

Hilten, O van, P.M. Kort and P.J.J.M. Loon (1993) *Dynamic Policies of the Firm: An Optimal Control Approach.* Berlin, Springer-Verlag.

HMSO (1989) *Towards Scottish Enterprise.* Edinburgh: Industry Department for Scotland.

Hogarth, R.M. (ed.) (1990) *Insights in Decision-Making: A Tribute to Hillel J Einhorn,* Chicago: Chicago University Press.

Holmes, S., G. Kelly and R. Cunningham (1991) 'The small firm information cycle: A reappraisal', *International Small Business Journal* 4, 41–53.

Huck, J.F. and T. McEwan (1991) 'Competencies needed for small business success: Perceptions', *Journal of Small Business Management* 29(4), 90–3.

Hughes, A. (1993) 'Industrial concentration and small firms in the United Kingdom: The 1980s in historical perspective', in Z.J. Acs and D.B. Audretsch (eds.), *Small Firms and Entrepreneurship: An East-West Perspective,* Chapter 2. Cambridge: Cambridge University Press.

Human, S.E. and K.G. Provan (1997) 'An emergent theory of structure and outcomes in small-firm strategic manufacturing networks', *Academy of Management Journal* 40(2), 368–403.

Hume, D. (1739) *A Treatise of Human Nature,* eds. D.F. Norton and M.J. Norton. London: Oxford University Press.

Hume, D. (1752) On the Balance of Trade, in *Essays, Moral, Political and Literary.* London; Henri Frowde (1904).

Hunter, M.G. (2004) 'Information systems and small business: Research issues', *Journal of Global Information Management* 12(4), I–V.

Industry Department for Scotland (1989) Towards Highlands and Islands Enterprise. Edinburgh: HMSO.

Isaacson, D.L. and R.W. Madsen (1976) *Markov Chains, Theory and Applications.* New York, London: Wiley.

Jacobsen, L. R. (1986) 'Entrepreneurship and competitive strategy in the new small firm: An empirical investigation', Ph.D. Dissertation, University of Edinburgh, Scotland.

Jamieson, B. (2002) 'Many a meddle may make a muddle of the business', *The Scotsman,* June 13.

Jarvis, R., J. Kitching, J. Curran and G. Lightfoot (1996) *The Financial Management of Small Firms: An Alternative Perspective.* London: Certified Accountants Educational Trust.

Jefferson, P.N. (1997) 'Unemployment and financial constraints faced by small firms', *Economic Inquiry* 35, 108–119.

Jensen, M. and W. Meckling (1976) Theory of the Firm: managerial behaviour, agency costs and ownership structure, *Journal of Financial Economics* 3, 305–60.

Johnson, G. and K. Scholes (1993) *Exploring Corporate Strategy*. Prentice-Hall: Englewood Cliffs, NJ.

Jones, R. (1985) 'Building systems on a relational database', *Data Processing* 27(3), 22–4.

Jorrisen, A., E. Laveren and S. Devinck (1997a) 'Planning and control: Necessary tools for success in small and medium-sized enterprises? Empirical results of survey and core research on SMEs in Belgium', Paper presented to the 20th annual congress of the European Accounting Association.

Jorrisen, A, E. Laveren and S. Devinck (1997b) 'Planning and control: Are they necessary tools for success? Empirical results of survey and core research on small and medium-sized enterprises compared with empirical research on large enterprises'. Paper presented to the 8th World Congress of the International Association for Accounting Education and Research.

Jovanovic, B. (1982) 'Selection and the evolution of industry', *Econometrica* 50, 649–70.

Judge, E. (2002) 'Golden rule for entrepreneurs who crave success', *The Times (Business Plus Section)*, Tuesday, June 25, pp. 32.

Kalantaridis, C. (2004) 'Internationalization, strategic behavior and the small firm: A comparative investigation', *Journal of Small Business Management* 42(3), 245–62.

Kalecki, M. (1945) 'On the Gibrat distribution', *Econometrica* 13, 161–70.

Karlsson, C. and O. Olsson (1998) Product innovation in small and large enterprises, *Small Business Economics* 10, 31–46.

Kawai, H. and S. Urata (2002) 'Entry of small and medium enterprise and economic dynamism in Japan', *Small Business Economics* 18, 41–51.

Keasey, K., and R. Watson (1991) 'The state of the art in small firms failure prediction: Achievements and prognosis', *International Small Business Journal*, 9(4), 11–29.

Kent, C.A. (ed.) (1984) *The Environment for Entrepreneurship*. Lexington: D. C. Heath.

Keynes, J.M. (1921) *A Treatise on Probability*. Macmillan: London.

Kinder, T. (2000) 'Emerging e-commerce business modes: An analysis of case studies from West Lothian, Scotland', *European Journal of Information Management* 13, 130–51.

Kirzner, I. (1973) *Competition and Entrepreneurship*, Chicago: University of Chicago Press.

Kleindl, B. (2000) 'Competitive dynamics and new business models for SMEs in the virtual marketplace', *Journal of Developmental Entrepreneurship* 5(1), 73–85.

Kloot, L. (1997) Organizational learning and management control systems: responding to environmental change, *Management Accounting Research* 8, 47–73.

Knight, F.H. (1921) *Risk, Uncertainty and Profit.* Chicago: Chicago University Press (Stigler edn. 1971).

Kuo, H.C. and Y. Li (2003) 'A dynamic decision model of SMEs' FDI', *Small Business Economics* 20(3), 219–31.

Lang, J.R., R.J. Calantone and D. Gudmundson (1997) 'Small firm information seeking as a response to environmental threats and opportunities', *Journal of Small Business Management* 35(1), 11–23.

Lawrence, P.R. and J.W. Lorch (1967) *Organisation and Environment: Managing Differentiation and Integration*. Harvard University, Graduate School of Business Administration.

Lazerson, M.N. (1990) 'Transactional calculus and small business strategy', in Z.J. Acs and D.B. Audretsch (eds.), *The Economics of Small Firms: A European Challenge*, Chapter 2, Dordrecht: Kluwer.

Lee, L.F. (1982) 'Some approaches to the correction of selectivity bias', *Review of Economic Studies* 49, 335–720.

Lee, L.F. (1983) 'Generalized econometric models with selectivity bias, *Econometrica,* 51(2), 507–512.

Lee, R. (1993) 'Flexibility in a computable behavioural model of the small firm', PhD thesis, University of Edinburgh, Department of Economics.

Leighton, J. and M. Schaper (2003) Which advisers do micro-firms use? Some Australian Evidence, *Journal of Small Business and Enterprise Development* 10(2), 136–43.

Leland, H.E. (1972) 'The dynamics of a revenue maximising firm', *International Economic Review* 13, 376–85.

Lesourne, J. and R. Leban (1982) 'Control theory and the dynamics of the firm', *OR Spektrum* 4, 1–14.

Levenburg, N.M., T.C. Dandridge and S. Hong (2001) 'Marketing via the Internet: Micro-firms and e-commerce', *American Marketing Association. Conference Proceedings* 12, 97–103.

Levy, M. and P. Powell (1998) 'SME flexibility and the role of information systems', *Small Business Economics* 11 (2), 186–96.

Levy, M., P. Powell and P. Yetton (2002) 'The dynamics of SME information stations', *Small Business Economics* 19(4), 341.

Liansheng, M. (2000) 'Document database construction in China in the 1990s: A review of developments', *The Electronic Library* 18(3), 210–15.

Libby, T and J.H. Waterhouse (1996) 'Predicting change in management accounting systems', *Journal of Management Accounting Research* 8, 137–50.

Liedholm, C. (2002) 'Small firm dynamics: Evidence from Africa and Latin America', *Small Business Economics* 18(1–3), 227–40.

Lin, B., J.A. Vassar and S. Lawrence (1993) 'Information technology strategies for small business', *Journal of Applied Business Research* 9, 25.

Liu, J.-T., M.-W. Tsou and J.K. Hammitt (1999) 'Do small plants grow faster? Evidence from the Taiwan electronics industry', *Economics Letters* 65(1), 121–9.

Loasby, B. (1978) 'Whatever happened to Marshall's theory of value?', *Scottish Journal of Political Economy* 25, 1–12.

Lopez-Gracia, J. and C. Aybar-Arias (2000) An empirical approach to the financial behaviour of small and medium sized companies, *Small Business Economics* 14, 55–63.

Lu, J. and R.W. Beamish (2004) 'Network development and firm performance: A field study of internationalizing Japanese firms', *Multinational Business Review* 12, 41–61.

Lucas, R.E. (1978) On the size distribution of business firms, *Bell Journal of Economics* 9, 508–23.

Ludwig, T. (1978) *Optimale Expansionspfade der Unternehmung.* Wiesbaden: Gabler.

Luehrman, T.A. (1998) 'Strategy as a portfolio of real options', *Harvard Business Review,* Sept.-Oct., 89–99.

Lund, M. and J. Wright (1999) 'The financing of small firms in the United Kingdom', *Bank of England Quarterly Bulletin* 39(2), 195–201.

Lybaert, N. (1998) 'The information use in a SME: Its importance and some elements of influence', *Small Business Economics* 10, 171–91.

Manly, B.F.J. (1986) *Multivariate Statistical Methods: A Primer.* Chapman and Hall: London.

Markusen, A.R., and M.B. Teitz (1985) 'The world of small business: Turbulence and survival', in D.J. Storey (ed.), *Small Firms in Regional Economic Development: Britain, Ireland and the United States.* Cambridge: Cambridge University Press.

Marshall, A. (1890) *The Principles of Economics.* London: Macmillan.

Martin, G. and H. Staines (1994) 'Managerial competences in small firms', *The Journal of Management Development* 13, 23.

Mata, J. (1993) 'Small firms in Portuguese manufacturing industries', in Z. Acs and B. Audretsch (eds.), *Small Firms and Entrepreneurship: An East-West Perspective.* Cambridge, UK: Cambridge University Press.

Mata, J. and P. Portugal (2004) 'Patterns of entry, post-entry growth and survival: A comparison between domestic and foreign owned firms', *Small Business Economics* 22(3/4), 283–98.

Matlay, H. (1999) Vocational education, training and organizational change: A small business perspective, *Strategic Change* 8(5), 277–86.

McGrath, R.G. (1999) 'Falling forward: Real options reasoning and entrepreneurial failure', *Academy of Management Review*, 24, 13–30.

Meyn, S.P and R.L. Tweedie (1993) 'Stability of Markovian processes II: Continuous-time processes and sampled chains', *Advances in Applied Probability* 25(3), 487–517.

Michaelas, N., F. Chittenden and P. Poutziouris (1999) 'Financial policy and capital structure choice in UK SMEs: Empirical evidence from company panel data', *Small Business Economics* 12(2), 113–30.

Miles, M.B. and A.M. Huberman (1984) *Qualitative Data Analysis.* London: Sage Publications.

Miller, D. (1975) Towards a contingency theory of strategy formulation, *Academy of Management Proceedings*, 66–8.

Mills, D. E., and L. Schumann (1985) 'Industry structure with fluctuating demand', *American Economic Review* 75(4), 758–767.

Mintzberg, H. (1987) 'Crafting strategy', *Harvard Business Review* 60, 66–75.

Mintzberg, H. (1994) 'The fall and rise of strategic planning', *Harvard Business Review* 72, 107–114.

Mitchell, F., G.C. Reid and J.A. Smith (2000) *Information System Development in the Small Firm.* London: CIMA Publishing.

Mitra, J. (2003) 'The entrepreneurship dynamic: Origins of entrepreneurship and the evolution of industries', *Journal of Small Business and Enterprise Development* 10(2), 210–4.

Modigliani, F. and M. Miller (1958) The cost of capital, corporate finance and the theory of investment, *American Economic Review* 48(3), 291–7.

Modigliani, F. and M. Miller (1963) Taxes and the cost of capital: A correction, *American Economic Review* 53(3), 433–43.

Moore, C. (1988) Enterprise Agencies: Privatisation or partnership, *Local Economy* 3 21–30.

Morikawa, M. (2004) 'Information technology and the performance of Japanese SMEs', *Small Business Economics* 23, 171–7.

Muthen, B. (1979) A structural probit model with latent variables, *Journal of the American Statistical Association* 74, 807–11.

Myers S.C. (1984a) 'The capital structure puzzle', *Journal of Finance* 39, 581–2.

Myers, S.C. (1984b) The capital structure puzzle, *Journal of Finance* 39, 575–92.

Myers, S.C. and N. Majluf (1984) Corporate financing and investment decisions when firms have information that investors do not have', *Journal of Financial Economics* 13, 187–222.

Namiki, N. (2005) 'Successful strategies for small sized US exporters of consumer products to Japanese markets', *Southern Business Review* 31, 28–34.

Nathan, S. (1996) 'A test of the differential information hypothesis explaining the small firm effect', *Journal of Applied Business Research* 13(1), 115–20.

Nayak, A. and S. Greenfield (1997) 'The use of accounting information in managing micro businesses', Paper presented to the ACCA Policy Seminar on 'How small businesses use financial information'.

Ndimande, P.S. (2000) 'Small scale industries, job creation and labour market flexibility in South Africa: Responses to globalisation', *Management Research News* 23(2–4), 11–2.

Neijens, P. (1987) *The Choice Questionnaire: design and evaluation of an instrument for collecting informed opinions of populations*. Amsterdam: Free University Press.

Newbert, S.L. (2005) 'New firm formation: A dynamic capability perspective', *Journal of Small Business Management* 43(1), 55–77.

Newman, P. and J.N. Wolfe (1961) A model for the long-run theory of value, *Review of Economic Studies* 29(78), 51–61.

Norusis, M.J. (1994) *SPSS Professional Statistics 6.1*. Chicago: SPSS Inc.

Nunnally, J.C. (1978) *Psychometric Theory*. New York: McGraw-Hill.

Oakey, R.D. (1991) 'Government policy towards high technology: Small firms beyond the year 2000', In J. Curran and R.A. Blackburn (eds.), *Paths of Enterprise: The Future of the Small Business*. Routledge; London.

Oi, W.Y. (1983) 'Heterogeneous firms and the organization of production', *Economics Inquiry* 21, 147–71.

Oppenheim, A.N. (1992) *Questionnaire Design, Interviewing and Attitude*. London: Pinter Publishers.

Otley, D.T. (1980) The contingency theory of management accounting: Achievement and prognosis, *Accounting, Organizations and Society* 5, 413–28.

Parzen, E. (1960) *Modern Probability Theory and its Applications*. Wiley: New York.

Penrose, E.T. (1959) *The Theory of the Growth of the Firm*. Oxford: Basil Blackwell.

Perry, C.A. (1968) *Management Accounting for the Small Business* (5th impression). London: The Association of Certified Accountants.

Peston, M. (1969) *Elementary Matrices in Economics*. London, Routledge and Kegan Paul.

Petroni, A. and M. Bevilaqua (2002) 'Identifying manufacturing flexibility best practices in small and medium enterprises', *International Journal of Operations & Production Management* 22(7/8), 929–47.

Picot, G. and R. Dupuy (1998) 'Job creation by company size class: The magnitude, concentration and persistence of job gains and losses in Canada', *Small Busines Economics*, 10(2), 117–140.

Piore, M.J. and C.F. Sabel (1984) *The Second Industrial Divide: Possibilities for Prosperity*. New York: Basic Books.

Porter, M. (1980) *Competitive Strategy*. New York: Free Press.

Porter, M. (1983) *Cases in Competitive Strategy*. New York: Free Press.

Porter, M. (1985) *Competitive Advantage*. New York: Free Press.

Power, B. (2004) 'Factors which foster the survival of long-lived small firms', Ph.D. Dissertation, University of St. Andrews, Scotland.

Power, B. and Reid G.C. (2003) 'Performance, firm size and the heterogeneity of competitive strategy for long-lived small firms: A simultaneous equations analysis,' CRIEFF Discussion Chapter, Department of Economics, University of St. Andrews, No. 0307.

Prais, S.J. (1974) A new look at the growth of industrial concentration, *Oxford Economic Papers* 26(2), 273–88.

Pratten, C. (1991) *The Competitiveness of Small Firms*, Cambridge: Cambridge University Press.

Quah, D.T. (1997) 'Increasingly weightless economies', *Bank of England Quarterly Bulletin* 37(1), 49–56.

Raymond, L. and N. Magnenat-Thalmann (1982) 'Information systems in small business: Are they used in managerial decisions', *American Journal of Small Business* 6(4), 20–6.

Reid, G.C. (1987) *Theories of Industrial Organization*. Oxford: Basil Blackwell.

Reid, G.C. (1989) *Classical Economic Growth: An Analysis in the Tradition of Adam Smith*, Oxford: Basil Blackwell.

Reid, G.C. (1991) 'Staying in business', *International Journal of Industrial Organization* 9, 545–56.

Reid, G.C. (1992) Scale economies in small entrepreneurial firms, *Scottish Journal of Political Economy* 39, 39–51.

Reid, G.C. (1993) *Small Business Enterprise: An Economic Analysis.* Routledge: London.

Reid, G.C. (1995) Early life-cycle behaviour of micro-firms in Scotland, *Small Business Economics* 7, 89–95.

Reid, G.C. (1996a) Fast growing small entrepreneurial firms and their venture capital backers: An applied principal-agent analysis, *Small Business Economics* 8, 235–248.

Reid, G.C. (1996b) 'Mature micro-firms and their experience of funding shortages', *Small Business Economics* 8, 27–37.

Reid, G.C. (1998a) 'Limits to a firm's rate of growth: The Richardsonian view and its contemporary empirical significance,' in B.J. Loasby and N.J. Foss (eds.), *Capabilities and Coordination: Essays in Honour of G.B. Richardson*. London: Routledge, pp. 243–260.

Reid, G.C. (1998b) *Venture Capital Investment: An Agency Analysis of Practice.* Routledge: London.

Reid, G.C. (1999a) Complex actions and simple outcomes: How new entrepreneurs stay in business, *Small Business Economics* 13, 303–315.

Reid, G.C. (1999a) Capital structure at inception and the short-run performance of micro-firms. Chapter 7 in Z.J. Acs, B.B. Carlsson and C. Karlsson (eds.) *Entrepreneurship, Small & Medium-Sized Enterprises and the Macroeconomy.* Cambridge University Press; Cambridge, 186–205.

Reid, G.C. (1999b) 'Capital structure at inception and the short-run performance of micro-firms', in Z.J. Acs, B.B. Carlsson and C. Karlsson (eds.), *Entrepreneurship, Small & Medium-Sized Enterprises and the Macroeconomy*, Chapter 7. Cambridge: Cambridge University Press, pp. 186–205.

Reid, G.C. (1999b) Making small firms work: Policy dimensions and the Scottish context, Chapter 10 in K. Cowling (ed.) *Industrial Policy in Europe*. Routledge: London, 164–79.

Reid, G.C. (1999c) 'Making small firms work: policy dimensions and the Scottish context', in K. Cowling (ed.), *Industrial Policy in Europe*, Chapter 10. London: Routledge, pp. 164–79.

Reid, G.C. and M.E. Andersen (1992) 'A new small firms database: Sample design, instrumentation and summary statistics', CRIEFF Discussion Chapter, Department. of Economics, University of St. Andrews, No. 9207.

Reid, G.C. and L.R. Jacobsen, (1988) *The Small Entrepreneurial Firm.* Aberdeen: Aberdeen University Press.

Reid, G.C. and J.A. Smith (1999) Information system development in the small firm: Test of contingency, agency and markets & hierarchies approaches, CRIEFF Discussion Paper No. 9905, Department of Economics, University of St Andrews.

Reid, G.C. and J.A. Smith (2000a) 'What makes a new business start-up successful?', *Small Business Economics* 14(3), 165–182.

Reid, G.C. and J.A. Smith (2000b) 'The impact of contingencies on management accounting system development', *Management Accounting Research* 11, 427–450.

Reid, G.C. and J.A. Smith (2004) A coevolutionary analysis of organizational systems and processes: Quantitative applications to information system dynamics in small entrepreneurial firms, CRIEFF Discussion Paper No. 0402, Department of Economics, University of St Andrews.

Reid, G.C. and T.M. Stewart (2005) Independents Abroad: The pursuit of expansion by independent oil companies into non-traditional petroleum, CRIEFF Discussion Paper No. 0507, School of Economics & Finance, University of St Andrews.

Reid, G.C., L.R. Jacobsen and M. Andersen (1993) *Profiles in Small Business: A Competitive Strategy Approach.* London: Routledge.

Reynolds, P.D., N.M. Carter, W.B. Gartner and P.G. Greene (2004) 'The prevalence of nascent entrepreneurs in the United States: Evidence from the panel study of entrepreneurial dynamics', *Small Business Economics* 23(4), 263–84.

Richardson, G.B. (1964) 'The limits to a firm's rate of growth', *Oxford Economic Papers* 16, 9–23.

Rispas, S. (1998) Towards an interdisciplinary theory of entrepreneurship, *Small Business Economics* 10, 103–15.

Robson, M.T. (1993) 'Macroeconomic factors in the birth and death of UK firms: Evidence from quarterly VAT registrations', Working Paper No. 9209, Department of Economics, University of Newcastle upon Tyne.

Robson, M.T. (1996) Housing wealth, business creation and dissolution, in the UK regions, *Small Business Economics* 8(1), 39–48.

Romano, C.A. and J. Ratnatunga (1994) 'Growth stages of small manufacturing firms: the relationship with planning and control', *Public Policy* 13(1), 173–95.

Ross, S.A. (1977) The determination of financial structure: The incentive signalling approach, *Bell Journal of Economics and Management Science* (Spring), 23–40.

Rosti, L. and F. Chelli (2005) 'Gender discrimination, entrepreneurial talent and self-employment', *Small Business Economics* 24(2), 131–42.

Sadler-Smith, E., Y. Hampson, I. Chaston and B. Badger (2003) 'Managerial behaviour, entrepreneurial style and small firm performance', *Journal of Small Business Management* 41(1), 47–67.

Salavrakos, I.D. (1996) *An Economic and Business Strategy Analysis of Joint Ventures Between Greek Enterprises and Enterprises in the Balkan Countries and Russia from the Greek Parent Company Perspective.* PhD thesis, University of St Andrews, Scotland.

Samson, K.J. (1990) *Scientists as Entrepreneurs: Organizational Performance in Scientist-Started New Ventures.* Dordrecht: Kluwer.

Sandberg, W.R. and C.W. Hofer (1987) 'Improving new venture performance: The role of strategy, industry, structure and the entrepreneur', *Journal of Business Venturing* 2, 5–28.

Sapienza, H.J., K.J. Smith and M.J. Gannon (1988) 'Using subjective evaluations of organisational performance in small business research', *American Journal of Small Business* 12(3), 14–21.

Schütte, T. (1996) Bank lending during the transition period in Eastern Europe, *Small Business Economics* 8(1), 9–16.

Scottish Enterprise (1996) *Scottish New Business Statistics: Annual 1996*, The Committee of Scottish Clearing Banks, Glasgow.

Sekaran, U. (1992), *Research Methods for Business, A Skills Building Approach*, 2nd ed. New York: Wiley & Sons.

Shaffir, W.B. and R.A. Stebbins (eds.) (1991) *Experiencing Fieldwork: An Inside View of Qualitative Research*. London: Sage.

Simmons, J.G. (2001) 'Flexible benefits for small employers', *Journal of Accountancy* 191(3), 37–41.

Simon, H.A. (1957) *Models of Man*. New York: Wiley.

Singh, A. and G. Whittington (1968) *Growth, Profitability and Valuation*. Cambridge: Cambridge University Press.

Slater, M., (1980) The managerial limitation to the growth of firms', *Oxford Economics Papers* 90, 520–8.

Slovic, P., D. Griffin and A. Tversky (1990) 'Compatibility effects in judgement and choice', in R.M. Hogarth (ed.) (1990) *Insights in Decision-Making: A Tribute to Hillel J Einhorn*, Chicago: Chicago University Press. pp. 5–27.

Smallbone, D. (1989) 'Enterprise agencies and the survival of new business start-ups', *Local Economy* 4, 143–7.

Smallbone, D., D. North and R. Leigh (1992) 'Managing change for growth and survival: The study of mature manufacturing firms in London during the 1980s', Working Chapter No. 3, Planning Research Centre, Middlesex, Polytechnic.

Smith, A. (1776) *The Wealth of Nations*, Glasgow edition, R.H. Campbell and A. Skinner (eds.) (1976) Oxford: Oxford University Press.

Smith, J.A. (1997a) *Small Business Strategy: An Empirical Analysis of the Experience of New Scottish Firms*. PhD thesis, University of Abertay Dundee, Scotland.

Smith, J.A. (1997b) 'The behaviour and performance of young micro firms: Evidence from new businesses in Scotland', CRIEFF Discussion Paper No. 9711, Department of Economics, University of St Andrews.

Smith, J.A. (1998) 'Strategies for Start-ups', *Long Range Planning*, 31(6), 857–872.

Snell, R. and A. Lau (1994) 'Exploring local competences salient for expanding small businesses', *The Journal of Management Development* 13(4), 4–15.

St John, P.R. and D.A. Richardson (1989) *Methods of Presenting Fieldwork Data*. Sheffield: The Geographical Association.

Stigler, G.J. (1939) 'Production and distribution in the short run', *Journal of Political Economy* 47, 305–27.

Storey, D.J. (1994) *Understanding the Small Business Sector*. London: Routledge.

Sudman, S. and N.M. Bradburn (1982) *Asking Questions: A Practical Guide to Design*. Jossey-Bass: San Francisco.

Sutton, J. (1988) *Technology and Market Structure: Theory and History*. London: MIT Press.

Swartz, E. and R. Boaden (1997) 'A methodology for researching the process of information management in small firms', *International Journal of Entrepreneurial Behaviour and Research* 3(1), 53.

Teece, D.J. (1998) 'Research directions for knowledge management', *California Management Review* 40, 289–92.

Teece, D.J., G. Pisano and A. Shuen (1997) 'Dynamic capabilities and strategic management', *Strategic Management Journal* 18(7), 509–33.

Townroe, P. and K. Mallalieu (1993) 'Founding a new business in the countryside', in J. Curran and D.J. Storey (eds.), *Small Firms in Urban and Rural Locations*. London: Routledge.

Trindade, S.C. (1990) 'Preface', in K. Ganzhorn and S. Faustoferri (eds.), *Bridging the Information Gap for Small and Medium Enterprises*. Berlin: Springer-Verlag.

Tucker, J. and J. Lean (2003) 'Small firm finance and public policy', *Journal of Small Business and Enterprise Development* 10(1), 50–61.

Varian, H.R. (1992) *Microeconomic Analysis (3rd edn)*. New York: Norton.

Vaughan, L.Q. and J. Tague-Sutcliffe (1997) 'Measuring the impact of information on development: a LISREL-based study of small businesses in Shanghai', *Journal of the American Society for Information Science (1986-98)* 48(1), 917–31.

Verhees, F.J.M. and M.T. Meulenberg (2004) 'Market orientation, innovativeness, product innovation and performance in small firms', *Journal of Small Business Management* 42(2), 134–54.

Vickers, D. (1970) 'The cost of capital and the structure of the firm', *Journal of Finance* 25, 35–46.

Vickers, D. (1987) *Money Capital in the Theory of the Firm*. Cambridge, UK: Cambridge University Press.

Vijayaraman, B.S. and H.V. Ramakrishna (1993) 'Disaster preparedness of small business with micro-computer based information systems', *Journal of Systems Management* 44(6), 28–32.

von Ungern-Sternberg, T. (1990) 'The flexibility to switch between different products,' *Economica* 57, 355–69.

Wallsten, T.S. (1990) 'The costs and benefits of vague information', in RM Hogarth (ed.), *Insights in Decision Making: a tribute to Hillel J Einhorn*, Chicago: Chicago University Press, pp. 28–43.

Ward, J.H. (1963) 'Hierarchical grouping to optimize an objective function', *Journal of the American Statistical Association* 58, 236–244.

Waterhouse, J.H. and P. Tiessen (1978) A contingency framework for management accounting research, *Accounting Organizations and Society* 3, 65–76.

Weiss, C.R. (1998) 'Size, growth, and survival in the upper Austrian farm sector', *Small Business Economics* 10(4), 305–12.

Werner, O. and G.M. Schoepfle (1987) *Ethnographic Analysis and Data Management*. London: Sage.

White, H. (1980) 'A heteroskedasticity-consistent covariance matrix estimator and a direct test for heteroskedasticity', *Econometrica* 48, 817–838.

Wickham, P.A. (2001) *Strategic Entrepreneurship*. London: Pearson Education.

Wijst, N. van der, and R. Thurik (1993) Determinants of small firm debt ratios: An analysis of retail panel data, *Small Business Economics* 5, 55–65.

Williamson, O.E. (1967) 'Hierarchical control and optimum firm size', *Journal of Political Economy* 75, 123–38.

Williamson, O.E. (1975) *Markets and Hierarchies*. New York: Free Press.

Williamson, O.E. (1985) *The Economic Institutions of Capitalism*. New York: Free Press.

Willis, G.B. (2005) *Cognitive Interviewing: A Tool for Improving Design*. Thousand Oakes, CA: Sage Publications.

Winker, P. (1999) Causes and effects of financing constraints at the firm level, *Small Business Economics* 12, 169–81.

Woodward, J. (1958) *Management and Technology*, HMSO.

Woodward, J. (1965) *Industrial Organisation: Theory and Practice.* Oxford University Press.

Woolcott, H.F. (2005) *The Art of Fieldwork* (2nd edn), Walnut Creek, CA: Altamira Press.

Xiao Z. Zhong., J.R. Dyson and P.L. Powell (1996) The impact of information technology on corporate financial reporting: A contingent perspective, *The British Accounting Review* 28(3), 203–27.

Yellen, J. (1984) 'Efficiency wage models of unemployment', *American Economic Review* 74, 200–205.

Young, C. (1995) 'Financing the micro-scale enterprise: Rural craft production in Scotland 1840-1914', *Business History Review* 69, 398.

Yusuf, A. and K. Saffu (2005) 'Planning and performance of small and medium enterprise operators in a country in transition', *Journal of Small Business Management* 43(4), 480–97.

Zimmerman, R.A., M.A. Murray and D. Flaherty (2002) 'Benchmarking local firm performance', *The CPA Journal* 72(12), 54–7.

Administered questionnaire 1

MAIN STUDY

Respondent agreed to additional interview on business strategy:

Yes ☐

No ☐

Life Cycle Effects in New Small Firms

Interviewer: _____

Date and time of interview: _____

Respondent: _____

Firm Name: _____

Firm Address: _____

_____

_____

Telephone: _____

Firm Sample Area:

(1) ☐ Inverurie		(9) ☐ Grangemouth
(2) ☐ Aberdeen		(10) ☐ Stirling
(3) ☐ Dundee		(11) ☐ Glasgow
(4) ☐ Crossgates		(12) ☐ Paisley
(5) ☐ Cupar		(13) ☐ Strathkelvin
(6) ☐ Edinburgh		(14) ☐ Govan
(7) ☐ Midlothian		(15) ☐ Cumnock & Doon
(8) ☐ Alloa		

INTERVIEW AGENDA

1   Markets

2   Finance

3   Costs

4   Business Strategy

5   Human Capital

6   Organisation

7   Technical Change

ADMINISTERED QUESTIONNAIRE

LIFE-CYCLE EFFECTS IN SMALL FIRMS

1. MARKET DATA

There are seven parts to this interview. We will look at markets, finance, costs, business strategy, human capital, organisation and technical change. Either I will ask you questions directly, or I will provide you with question sheets for you to fill in yourself.

1. Market Data

1.1   How long have you been in business?   _____ months
[Answer preferably in months]

1.2   1.2.1   How would you define your *main* line of business?

              _____

              _____

      1.2.2   On this sheet, in which industrial category does your
firm lie? _____
**[Hand respondent list of Standard Industrial
Classification (SIC) codes]**
**[N.B. If several categories relevant, identify most
important by sales]**

1.3   How many people work in the business?
[N.B. If <u>none</u>, Go to Question 1.4]

      (a) Directors _____ (b) Managers _____

      (c) Full-timers _____ (d) Part-timers _____ (e) Trainees _____

1.4   What are your annual sales i.e. turnover? (based on latest estimates,
e.g. last tax year's)

      (a) Gross _____ Net _____ **[Net of taxes, VAT, etc.]**

      [N.B. VAT threshold is £80,000]

1.5   How many product *groups* or *ranges* do you produce?
[e.g. toasters, hairdriers; making two]   _____

1.6   How many *products* do you produce or supply or supply for your
markets?
**[e.g. four kinds of toasters, three kinds of hairdriers; making seven
in all]**

              _____

1.7   Do you consider your *main* market to be:
Local ☐ Regional ☐ Scottish ☐ British ☐ or International ☐?

SIC Classification Numbers

01	Agriculture and horticulture
02	Forestry
03	Fishing
11	Coal extraction and manufacture of solid fuels
12	Coke ovens
13	Extraction of mineral oil and natural gas
14	Mineral oil processing
15	Nuclear fuel processing
16	Production and distribution of electricity, gas and other forms of energy
17	Water supply industry
21	Extraction and preparation of metalliferous ores
22	Metal manufacturing
23	Extractions of other minerals
24	Manufacture of non-metallic mineral products
25	Chemical industry
26	Production of man-made fibres
31	Manufacture of other metal goods
32	Mechanical engineering
33	Manufacture of office machinery and data processing equipment
34	Electrical and electronic engineering
35	Manufacture of motor vehicles and parts
36	Manufacture of other transport equipment
37	Instrument engineering
41/42	Food, drink and tobacco manufacturing
43	Textile industry
44	Manufacture of leather and leather goods
45	Footwear and clothing industries
46	Timber and wooden furniture industries
47	Manufacture of paper and paper products, printing and publishing
48	Processing of rubber and plastics
49	Other manufacturing industries
50	Construction
61	Wholesale distribution
62	Dealing in scrap and waste metals
63	Commission agents
64/65	Retail distribution
66	Hotels and catering
67	Repair of consumer goods and vehicles
71	Railways
72	Other inland transport

74	Sea transport
75	Air transport
76	Supporting services to transport
77	Miscellaneous transport services and storage not elsewhere specified
79	Postal services and telecommunications
81	Banking and finance
82	Insurance
83	Business services
84	Renting of moveables
85	Owning and dealing in real estate
91	Public administration, national defence and compulsory social security
92	Sanitary services
93	Education
94	Research and development
95	Medical and other health services: veterinary services
96	Other services provided to the general public
97	Recreational services and other cultural services
98	Personal services
99	Domestic services

SIC Classification Numbers

01	Agriculture and horticulture
02	Forestry
03	Fishing
11	Coal extraction and manufacture of solid fuels
12	Coke ovens
13	Extraction of mineral oil and natural gas
14	Mineral oil processing
15	Nuclear fuel processing
16	Production and distribution of electricity, gas and other forms of energy
17	Water supply industry
21	Extraction and preparation of metalliferous ores
22	Metal manufacturing
23	Extractions of other minerals
24	Manufacture of non-metallic mineral products
25	Chemical industry
26	Production of man-made fibres
31	Manufacture of other metal goods
32	Mechanical engineering
33	Manufacture of office machinery and data processing equipment
34	Electrical and electronic engineering
35	Manufacture of motor vehicles and parts
36	Manufacture of other transport equipment
37	Instrument engineering
41/42	Food, drink and tobacco manufacturing
43	Textile industry
44	Manufacture of leather and leather goods
45	Footwear and clothing industries
46	Timber and wooden furniture industries
47	Manufacture of paper and paper products, printing and publishing
48	Processing of rubber and plastics
49	Other manufacturing industries
50	Construction
61	Wholesale distribution
62	Dealing in scrap and waste metals
63	Commission agents
64/65	Retail distribution
66	Hotels and catering
67	Repair of consumer goods and vehicles
71	Railways
72	Other inland transport
74	Sea transport

75	Air transport
76	Supporting services to transport
77	Miscellaneous transport services and storage not elsewhere specified
79	Postal services and telecommunications
81	Banking and finance
82	Insurance
83	Business services
84	Renting of moveables
85	Owning and dealing in real estate
91	Public administration, national defence and compulsory social security
92	Sanitary services
93	Education
94	Research and development
95	Medical and other health services: veterinary services
96	Other services provided to the general public
97	Recreational services and other cultural services
98	Personal services
99	Domestic services

1.8   1.8.1   What are your most important product *groups* or *ranges*, according to sales?
[Please rank by percentage of total sales]

                                                    % of Sales   Market Share

(a)   Most important product group

_____   _____   _____

(b)   Second most important product group

_____   _____   _____

(c)   Third most important product group

_____   _____   _____

1.8.2   What percentage of sales do each of these account for?

1.8.3   For the three most important, could you also estimate their *market share*?
[i.e. percentage of total market share in each case]

[If you cannot be precise, rough figures or 'guesstimates' will do]

[NOTE: IF A CHOICE ARISES, YOU SHOULD ANSWER THE QUESTIONS THAT FOLLOW BY REFERENCE TO YOUR *MAIN PRODUCT GROUP* BY SALES]

1.9   How many *major* rivals do you have?   _____

1.10   How many *minor* rivals do you have?   _____

1.11   How strong is competition in your main market?
        Please rank according to the categories shown, if applicable.

[Hand respondent Sheet 1.11]

		Fierce	Strong	Moderate	Weak	N/A
(a)	Price	☐	☐	☐	☐	☐
(b)	Volume	☐	☐	☐	☐	☐
(c)	Delivery	☐	☐	☐	☐	☐
(d)	Quality	☐	☐	☐	☐	☐
(e)	Design	☐	☐	☐	☐	☐
(f)	Customisation (i.e. bespoke features)	☐	☐	☐	☐	☐
(g)	Guarantee	☐	☐	☐	☐	☐
(h)	After-Sale Care	☐	☐	☐	☐	☐
(i)	Technical Progressiveness	☐	☐	☐	☐	☐
(j)	Substitutes	☐	☐	☐	☐	☐
(k)	Advertising	☐	☐	☐	☐	☐
(l)	Salesmanship	☐	☐	☐	☐	☐

[Retrieve Sheet 1.11 from respondent]

How strong is competition in your main market?
[Please rank according to the categories shown, if applicable]

		Fierce	Strong	Moderate	Weak	N/A
(a)	Price	☐	☐	☐	☐	☐
(b)	Volume	☐	☐	☐	☐	☐
(c)	Delivery	☐	☐	☐	☐	☐
(d)	Quality	☐	☐	☐	☐	☐
(e)	Design	☐	☐	☐	☐	☐
(f)	Customisation (i.e. bespoke features)	☐	☐	☐	☐	☐
(g)	Guarantee	☐	☐	☐	☐	☐
(h)	After-Sale Care	☐	☐	☐	☐	☐
(i)	Technical Progressiveness	☐	☐	☐	☐	☐
(j)	Substitutes	☐	☐	☐	☐	☐
(k)	Advertising	☐	☐	☐	☐	☐
(l)	Salesmanship	☐	☐	☐	☐	☐

Thank you. Now please return this sheet to the interviewer.

1.12   Overall, how strong is competition in your main market?

Is it:
Fierce ☐   Strong ☐   Moderate ☐ or Weak ☐?

1.13   Could you answer the following questions by reference to your main market?

1.13.1   Against how many small firms do you compete?

(a) ☐ Few   or   (b) ☐ Many?

1.13.2   Would you say that the goods which firms in your main market supply are:

(a) ☐ Similar   or   (b) ☐ Differentiated?

[N.B. 'Differentiated' means distinguished by location, presentation, packaging, presentation, etc.]

1.13.3   What is the significance of rivals' actions to your own?

Are they:

(a) ☐ Irrelevant **[i.e. you compete independently]**

(b) ☐ Conditional **[i.e. what you do depends upon what they do]**

or

(c) ☐ Agreed? **[i.e. you act together in an agreed fashion]**

1.13.4   Is there a dominant supplier or group of suppliers in your main market against whom you and other small firms compete?

(a) Yes ☐   (b) No ☐

1.14   At what market niche is your main product aimed?
[N.B. A 'niche' is a segment of a larger market that is exclusive to you]

_____

Could you elaborate **[briefly].**

_____

1.15   How long have you occupied this niche?   _____ months

Briefly, how have you fared over this period?

_____

1.16   How much longer do you think you will remain in this niche?

_____ months

Could you say, briefly, why you have this time horizon.

_____

_____

1.17   How important is *rapid* occupation of your niche to your business
strategy?

(a) Very ☐ (b) Moderately ☐ (c) Not at all ☐

1.18   **'Harvesting' a niche implies extracting all the value left in a
market segment before withdrawing from it [e.g. by a final, high-
discount sale].**

Do you have in mind a stage at which you will 'harvest' the niche your
main product group occupies?

(a) Yes ☐   (b) No ☐

1.19   **An 'end game' strategy is devised for leaving a niche in the most
profitable (or least expensive) way [e.g. by aiming to be the last
survivor, who takes what is left in the market].**

Do you have in mind such an 'end game' strategy?

(a) Yes ☐   (b) No ☐ **Go to Question 1.20**

Can you explain this briefly.

_____

_____

1.20   Do you see the quality and price of your main product line as being linked?

(a) Yes ☐   (b) No ☐

1.21   In terms of your sales strategy, is the end of the market that you aim for:

(a)   high price/high quality   ☐

(b)   high quality/low price   ☐

(c)   low price/'bare bones, no frills'   ☐

(d)   medium price/medium quality   ☐

(e)   none of these?   ☐

For which products is this strategy applied?

_____

1.22   Do you advertise?

Yes ☐ **Go to Question 1.23**

No ☐

How then, briefly, do your customers get to know about you?

_____

Go to Section 2 (FINANCE)

1.23   What form does your advertising take?
[Tick one please]

Does it:

(a)   Largely involves the provision of accurate technical
        information   ☐

(b)   Largely attempts to persuade the customer to buy   ☐
        [e.g. by lifestyle association]

(c)   Involves a mix of information and persuasion   ☐

1.24 How do you deliver your advertising messages?

(a) ☐ Radio

(b) ☐ TV

(c) ☐ Magazines

(d) ☐ Newspapers

(e) ☐ Mail-shots

(f) ☐ Posters

(g) ☐ Trade Show Displays

(h) ☐ Newsletter

(i) ☐ Trade Directory

(j) ☐ Other **[Please specify if possible]** _____

1.25 What proportion of your net sales do you allocate to advertising?

_____ %

1.26 1.26.1 If your principal rival *raised* advertising expenditure by 10%, by how much would you *raise* yours?   _____ %

  1.26.2 If your principal rival *lowered* advertising expenditure by 10%, by how much would you *lower* yours?   _____ %

  1.26.3 Does *high* demand for your main product group encourage you to *lower* advertising on it?

  (a) Yes ☐   (b) No ☐

  1.26.4 Does *lower* demand for your main product encourage you to *increase* your advertising on it?

  (a) Yes ☐   (b) No ☐

1.27 If you increased your advertising by 10%, by how much would you expect your sales to increase, assuming no reaction by your rivals?

_____ %

2. FINANCE

Thank you. Could I now turn briefly to aspects of your finance.

2. Finance

2.1   What are your current gross profits?   _____
[Give most recent annual figure]

2.2   What are your current gross sales?   _____

2.3   What are your current net profits?   _____
[Net of all costs, taxes, directors remuneration]

Please specify your deductions to get this figure

_____

_____

2.4   Do you have any debt (including business overdraft)?

      (a) Yes ☐   (b) No ☐

2.5   2.5.1   Do you have any *outside* equity?
                  [e.g. cash from a 'business angel', who has sunk money into your business]

                  (a) Yes ☐   (b) No ☐ **Go to Question 2.6**

        2.5.2   What percentage of total equity is outside equity? _____%

        2.5.3   What dividend do you pay to equity holders?   _____%

2.6   2.6.1   Did you use any outside equity to *launch* your business?

                  (a) Yes ☐

                  (b) No ☐ **Go to Question 2.6.3**

        2.6.2   What percentage of total equity was outside equity at start-up?
                                                        _____%

        2.6.3   How great was your own personal cash injection at start-up?
                                                   £ _____

2.7   2.7.1   Did you use a bank loan to help you launch your business?

                  (a) Yes ☐   (b) No ☐ **Go to Question 2.8**

        2.7.2   How large was this?   £ _____

        2.7.3   What interest rate were you charged?   _____%

2.8   2.8.1   Did you receive a grant or subsidy in starting your business?

(a) Yes ☐   (b) No ☐ **Go to Question 2.9**

2.8.2   Please specify _____

2.8.3   How much was it?   £_____

2.8.4   How important was it?

(a) crucial ☐ (b) important ☐ (c) helpful ☐

(d) unimportant ☐

2.9   What was the gearing ratio at the launch of your business?
       [i.e. debt divided by equity, typically bank loan divided by personal financial injections]

       _____

2.10   What is your gearing ratio currently?   _____

2.11   What level do you aim to get your gearing ratio to, in the next 3 years?

       _____

       Briefly, why? _____

2.12   Do you have any trade credit arrangements?

(a) Yes ☐   (b) No ☐ **Go to Question 2.15**

2.13   2.13.1   How many months of trade credit do your suppliers normally allow?   _____ months

2.13.2   What is your current balance on trade creditors?

       £_____

2.14   2.14.1   How many months of trade credit do you allow your customers?   _____ months

2.14.2   What is your current balance on trade debtors?   £_____

2.15   Do you have any extended purchase commitments?

(a) Yes ☐   (b) No ☐

2.16   Do you have any hire purchase commitments?

(a) Yes ☐   (b) No ☐

2.17   What is the gross value of your fixed assets?   _____
        [Give most recent figure]

2.18   What is the net value of your fixed assets (after depreciation)? _____

2.19   What is the value of your stocks in relation to your net assets, in
        percentage terms?   _____%

2.20   Do you have share capital in your business?

        (a) Yes ☐   (b) No ☐ **Go to Question 2.21**

        What form does this share capital take?

        _____

        _____

2.21   2.21.1 Do you use debenture finance?

        (a) Yes ☐   (b) No ☐ **Go to Section 3 (COSTS)**

        2.21.2 What ratio does this bear to your equity finance in percentage
                terms?   _____%

        2.21.3 What interest rate are you required to pay to debenture
                holders?   _____%

3. COSTS

Now we are on to the third section, which looks into the costs your business incurs.

3. Costs

3.1   3.1.1   Do you distinguish between *fixed* **[indirect]** costs and *variable* **[direct]** costs?

          (a) Yes ☐   (b) No ☐ **Go to Question 3.2**

[Note: *fixed* can be approximated by overhead costs, and *variable* by cost of sales]

     3.1.2   Which category do you regard as more important?

          (a) fixed ☐   (b) variable ☐

3.2   Are the costs you use in decision-making *actual* ☐ or *standard* ☐?

3.3   Do you monitor cost variation with output?

     (a) Yes ☐   (b) No ☐ **Go to Question 3.4**

     Briefly, explain how: _____

     _____

3.4   3.4.1   Do you have a capacity output?

          (a) Yes ☐   (b) No ☐ **Go to Question 3.5**

     3.4.2   At what percentage of your capacity do you *normally* operate?
                             _____ %

3.5   Which of the following descriptions best captures your cost structure?
[Prompt: Answer by reference to the main product in your principal product group]

[Hand respondent Sheet 3.5]

     (a)   Total cost increases in line with the amount you supply. ☐
            [i.e. for each extra unit you supply, your cost rises by the same extra amount]

     (b)   Total cost does not increase as fast as the amount you ☐
            supply.
            [i.e. the extra cost of supplying each additional unit falls, the more you supply]

(c)   Total cost increases faster than supply.   ☐
        **[i.e. each extra unit supplied adds more to cost
        than the last unit supplied]**

(d)   At first total cost does not increase as fast as supply,   ☐
        but then it increases faster than supply.
        **[i.e. the extra cost of supplying each additional
        unit initially falls, and then starts to rise]**

(e)   Total cost increases in line with supply until the   ☐
        maximum supply normally possible **[full capacity]** is
        reached. After this point, the extra cost of supplying
        another unit rises sharply.

(f)   Other **[please specify briefly]**_____   ☐

_____

[Retrieve Sheet 3.5 from respondent]

Which of the following descriptions best captures your cost structure?
**[You should answer by reference to the main product in your
most important product group]**

(a) ☐ Total cost increases in line with the amount you supply
**[i.e. for each extra unit you supply, your cost rises
by the same extra amount]**

(b) ☐ Total cost does not increase as fast as the amount you
supply **[i.e. the extra cost of supplying each
additional unit falls, the more you supply]**

(c) ☐ Total cost increases faster than supply **[i.e. each extra
unit supplied adds more to cost than the last unit
supplied]**

(d) ☐ At first total cost does not increase as fast as supply, but
then it increases faster than supply **[i.e. the extra cost
of supplying each additional unit initially falls, and
then starts to rise]**

(e) ☐ Total cost increases in line with supply until the
maximum supply normally possible **[full capacity]** is
reached. After this point, the extra cost of supplying
another unit rises sharply.

(f) ☐ Other **[please specify briefly]**_____
_____

Thank you. Now please return this sheet to the interviewer.

3.6 Which of the following elements of cost do you attribute to your products?

		Yes	No
(a)	Direct material	☐	☐
(b)	Direct labour	☐	☐
(c)	Production overhead	☐	☐
(d)	Distribution costs	☐	☐
(e)	Sales costs (including advertising)	☐	☐
(f)	Administration costs	☐	☐
(g)	Other **[please specify]**	☐	☐
	_____	☐	☐
	_____	☐	☐

3.7 On the following sheet could you say which proportions of total costs are attributable to the following, assuming *normal* levels of capacity utilisation?

First indicate which costs you incur. **[please tick]**

Then say what percentage each of those ticked accounts for.

[Hand Respondent Sheet 3.7]

		Percentage (Total 100%)
(a)	☐ Rents	_____%
(b)	☐ Wages	_____%
(c)	☐ Raw materials	_____%
(d)	☐ Energy	_____%
(e)	☐ Financing **[e.g. trade credit]**	_____%
(f)	☐ Plant and equipment	_____%
(g)	☐ Maintenance	_____%
(h)	☐ Stocks	_____%
(i)	☐ Sales and distribution	_____%
(j)	☐ Other **[please specify]** _____	_____%

[Retrieve Sheet 3.7 from Respondent]

On the following sheet could you say which proportions of total costs are attributable to the following, assuming *normal* levels of capacity utilisation?

First indicate by a tick which costs you incur.

Then say what percentage of costs is accounted for by each ticked item.

			Percentage
(a)	☐	Rents	_____%
(b)	☐	Wages	_____%
(c)	☐	Raw materials	_____%
(d)	☐	Energy	_____%
(e)	☐	Financing [e.g. trade credit]	_____%
(f)	☐	Plant and equipment	_____%
(g)	☐	Maintenance	_____%
(h)	☐	Stocks	_____%
(i)	☐	Sales and distribution	_____%
(j)	☐	Other [please specify] _____	_____%

[N.B. Percentages for ticked items, apart from (j), should add up to less than 100%. Then (j) makes the percentage up to 100%]

Thank you. Now please return this sheet to the interviewer.

3.8   Do you have a good idea of what costs your rivals have?

(a) Yes ☐   (b) No ☐

3.9   Do you think you are a *low* ☐ or *high* ☐ cost producer, compared to your principal rivals?

3.10   3.10.1 When your raw materials cost rise, do you:

(a) ☐   hold down costs elsewhere

(b) ☐   pass on costs. **Go to Question 3.11**

(c) ☐   a bit of both

3.10.2 In which areas do you then negotiate on costs?
[Tick one]

(a) ☐   Rents

(b) ☐   Wages

(c) ☐   Energy

(d) ☐   Financing **[e.g. trade credit]**

(e) ☐   Plant and equipment

(f) ☐   Maintenance

(g) ☐   Stocks

(h) ☐   Other **[please specify]** _____

_____

3.11   3.11.1 When wages rise, do you:

(a) ☐   hold down costs elsewhere

(b) ☐   pass on costs. **Go to Question 3.12**

(c) ☐   a bit of both

3.11.2 In which areas do you then negotiate on costs?
[Tick one]

(a) ☐   Rents

(b) ☐   Raw materials

(c) ☐   Energy

(d) ☐   Financing **[e.g. trade credit]**

(e) ☐   Plant and equipment

(f) ☐ Maintenance

(g) ☐ Stocks

(h) ☐ Other **[please specify]** _____

_____

3.12 3.12.1 Are you able to use your bargaining power to bid-down the costs of your supplies?

(a) Yes ☐   (b) No ☐ **Go to Question 3.13**

3.12.2 Do you think you are better at achieving this than your principal rivals?

(a) Yes ☐   (b) No ☐

3.13 Do you gain marketplace advantage by a conscious policy of extreme cost-cutting i.e. supplying your goods on a 'bare bones/no frills' basis?

(a) Yes ☐   (b) No ☐

3.14 What market share increase would you enjoy by becoming the least cost producer and pricing 10% below your principal rival? _____ %

3.15 Which strategy works better for your firm?

(a) ☐ being the least cost supplier

(b) ☐ emphasising the unique character of what you supply

4. BUSINESS STRATEGY

Good. We are about half way through the interview now. This section is largely conducted by having you fill in sheets, describing how you conduct your business strategy. This is also an area I should like to follow up separately, should you be willing.

4. Business Strategy

4.1   4.1.1   Do you have a business plan?

(a) Yes ☐   (b) No ☐ **Go to Question 4.2**

     4.1.2   Is it a formal, written plan or is it 'in your head'?

(a)   ☐   Formal, written plan.

(b)   ☐   'In your head'. **Go to Question 4.1.4**

     4.1.3   Who was involved in preparing the plan? **[Tick one]**

(a)   ☐   Yourself only

(b)   ☐   Yourself and family or friends

(c)   ☐   More than one person in the business

(d)   ☐   Outside help

(e)   ☐   Other **[please describe]** _____

_____

4.1.4   How often do you review this plan?
[answer in months]   _____ monthly

4.2   How far ahead do you look when evaluating the impact that planned decisions might have?
[answer in months]   _____ months

4.3   What was the main reason for becoming involved in this business?
[Tick one]

Was it:

(a)   ☐   as an alternative to unemployment

(b)   ☐   to 'get rich'

(c)   ☐   to take over the family business

(d)   ☐   to profit from a hobby

(e)   ☐   to be your own boss

(f)   ☐   to satisfy the need for achievement

(g)   ☐   to exploit a new market opportunity

(h)   ☐   other **[please specify]** _____

4.4   What is the *main* aim of the business? [**Tick one only**]

(a)   ☐   survival

(b)   ☐   short-term profit

(c)   ☐   long-term profit

(d)   ☐   growth

(e)   ☐   increased sales

(f)   ☐   increased market share

(g)   ☐   high rate of return

(h)   ☐   other [**please specify**] _____

4.5   Decisions can be either *strategic* [**LONG-TERM. e.g. whether or not to branch out into a new product-market niche**], or *operational* [**SHORT-TERM. e.g. which computer software to use for producing accounts**].

When making decisions, do you consider the past experience of other, similar businesses, first of all for strategic, and then for operational decisions?

4.5.1	**Strategic**	4.5.2	**Operational**
	(a) Yes ☐		(a) Yes ☐
	(b) No ☐		(b) No ☐

Are these decisions imposed upon the business by one person, or do they come about through negotiation between more than one person? Again please answer for both strategic and operational decisions.

4.5.3	**Strategic**	4.5.4	**Operational**
	(a) One person ☐		(a) One person ☐
	(b) More than one person ☐		(b) More than one person ☐

4.6   What percentage of decisions are made for *personal* reasons, and what percentage for *financial* reasons?

Personal   _____ %   **Financial**   _____ %

4.7   4.7.1   When you are constructing a new business strategy, where do you turn for help? Is it from *outside*, or is it available *'in house'*?

Could you answer for each item on this list.

[Hand respondent Sheet 4.7]

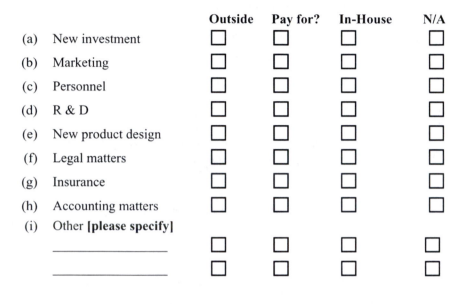

		Outside	Pay for?	In-House	N/A
(a)	New investment	☐	☐	☐	☐
(b)	Marketing	☐	☐	☐	☐
(c)	Personnel	☐	☐	☐	☐
(d)	R & D	☐	☐	☐	☐
(e)	New product design	☐	☐	☐	☐
(f)	Legal matters	☐	☐	☐	☐
(g)	Insurance	☐	☐	☐	☐
(h)	Accounting matters	☐	☐	☐	☐
(i)	Other **[please specify]**				
	_____	☐	☐	☐	☐
	_____	☐	☐	☐	☐

4.7.2   For those for which you have ticked *outside*, could you also please indicate whether you pay for that advice.

[Retrieve Sheet 4.7 from respondent]

When you are constructing a new business strategy, where do you turn for help? Is it from *outside*, or is it available *'in house'*?

Could you answer for each item on this list.

For those for which you tick *outside*, could you also please indicate whether you pay for that advice.

[Please tick where applicable]

		Outside	**Pay for?**	**In-House**	**N/A**
(a)	New investment	☐	☐	☐	☐
(b)	Marketing	☐	☐	☐	☐
(c)	Personnel	☐	☐	☐	☐
(d)	R & D	☐	☐	☐	☐
(e)	New product design	☐	☐	☐	☐
(f)	Legal matters	☐	☐	☐	☐
(g)	Insurance	☐	☐	☐	☐
(h)	Accounting matters	☐	☐	☐	☐
(i)	Other **[please specify]**				
	_____	☐	☐	☐	☐
	_____	☐	☐	☐	☐

Thank you. Now please return this sheet to the interviewer.

4.8   4.8.1   In order to make more cash available, do you:

(a)   ☐   inject more capital. **Go to Question 4.8.3**

(b)   ☐   restructure debtors'/creditors' payback terms?

4.8.2   How do you do this? **[tick one]**

(a)   ☐   Factoring **[i.e. factor takes full responsibility for the sales ledger; customer is aware of this]**

(b)   ☐   Invoice discounting **[i.e. customer pays into a trust bank account; usually confidential]**

(c)   ☐   Extending trade credit **[i.e. giving customer longer to pay]**

(d)   ☐   Other **[please specify]** _____

4.8.3   How have you raised finance in the past? **[tick all that apply]**

(a)   ☐   Personal financial injection

(b)   ☐   Loan from family or friend

(c)   ☐   Family or friend taking 'share' in business

(d)   ☐   Bank loan

(e)   ☐   Venture capital equity stake

(f)   ☐   'Business angel' equity stake

(g)   ☐   Other **[please specify]**_____

4.9   Are you willing to sacrifice a proportion of your stake in the business in order to promote growth?

(a) Yes ☐   (b) No ☐ **Go to Question 4.10**

What is the minimum stake, as a percentage of total equity, that you would be willing to hold?   _____ %

4.10   Are you willing to accept smaller profits for a time, in order to expand the business?

(a) Yes ☐   (b) No ☐

4.11   4.11.1   Do you receive any feedback from your customers about your products?

(a) Yes ☐   (b) No ☐ **Go to Question 4.12**

4.11.2   Do you (a) ask for it ☐; is it (b) given freely ☐;

or (c) both ☐?

4.11.3   How do you react to their comments? **[tick all that apply]**

(a)   ☐   Take note of them, for referral later

(b)   ☐   Discuss them with other customers

(c)   ☐   Implement changes based on their suggestions

(d)   ☐   Do nothing

(e)   ☐   Other **[please specify]** _____

4.12   4.12.1   Do you gather trade intelligence on your rivals?

(a) Yes ☐   (b) No ☐ **Go to Question 4.13**

4.12.2   What form does this information take?

		Yes	No
(a)	Market share	☐	☐
(b)	New products	☐	☐
(c)	Product quality	☐	☐
(d)	Financial performance	☐	☐
(e)	Customer relations	☐	☐
(f)	Personnel	☐	☐
(g)	Marketing methods	☐	☐
(h)	Other **[please specify]** _____	☐	☐

4.12.3   How regularly is this done or reviewed? **[answer in months]**

_____ monthly

4.12.4   How do you gather this information? **[tick all that apply]**

(a)   ☐   Electronic databases

(b)   ☐   Government publications

(c)	☐	Trade journals
(d)	☐	Library sources
(e)	☐	Newspapers
(f)	☐	Membership of trade associations
(g)	☐	Own research/conversations
(h)	☐	Other **[please specify]** _____

4.13   4.13.1   **Information technology (IT) refers to the devices businesses use to transmit, store and process information e.g. telephone, fax, PC.**

How important is information technology (IT) to your business?

Is it:

(a)	☐	scarcely. **Go to Question 4.14**
(b)	☐	moderately
(c)	☐	very important?

4.13.2   Which kinds of IT do you use?

		Yes	No
(a)	Telephone	☐	☐
(b)	Fax (facsimile)	☐	☐
(c)	Telephone answering machine	☐	☐
(d)	Electronic mail	☐	☐
(e)	Telephone conferencing	☐	☐
(f)	Video conferencing	☐	☐
(g)	Cellular telephone	☐	☐
(h)	Satellite link	☐	☐
(i)	Radio communication	☐	☐
(j)	Microfiche	☐	☐
(k)	Personal computers	☐	☐
(l)	Electronic database	☐	☐
(m)	Other **[please specify]** _____	☐	☐

4.13.3 For which of the following do you use information technology?
[tick all that apply]

(a) ☐ Tracking activities of competitors **[e.g. electronic databases]**

(b) ☐ Networking **[i.e. keeping in touch with what's going on/talking to those in the business]**

(c) ☐ Producing accounts

(d) ☐ Administration **[e.g. keeping track of buyers/suppliers]**

(e) ☐ Forecasting/producing business plan

(f) ☐ Designing new products

(g) ☐ Other **[please specify]** _____

4.14 **Total quality management (TQM) systems are installed with the help of consultants, who are employed by the business to suggest improvements in all areas. The main focus is on continuous improvement with quality being the responsibility of every employee.**

4.14.1 Have you installed such a system?

(a) Yes ☐ (b) No ☐ **Go to Question 4.15**

4.14.2 What do you gain *most* from this? **[tick one]**

(a) ☐ improved motivation

(b) ☐ improved business image

(c) ☐ increased efficiency

(d) ☐ better cost control

(e) ☐ other **[please specify]** _____

4.15 4.15.1 Are there other steps you have taken to achieve formal quality approval **[e.g. BS5750]** for the following:

		Yes	No	Please specify
(a)	Product(s)	☐	☐	_____
(b)	Operations	☐	☐	_____
(c)	Personnel	☐	☐	_____

(d)	Business as a whole	☐ ☐	_____
(e)	Other [please specify]		

_____ ☐ ☐ _____

_____ ☐ ☐ _____

[if any of the 'yes' boxes are ticked]

4.15.2 What have you gained from these approvals?

		Improved Motivation	Better Image	Increased Efficiency	Higher Benefit/ Cost	Other*	N/A
(a)	Product	☐	☐	☐	☐	☐	☐
(b)	Operations	☐	☐	☐	☐	☐	☐
(c)	Personnel	☐	☐	☐	☐	☐	☐
(d)	Business as a whole	☐	☐	☐	☐	☐	☐
(e)	Other						

[please specify]

	Improved Motivation	Better Image	Increased Efficiency	Higher Benefit/ Cost	Other*	N/A
_____	☐	☐	☐	☐	☐	☐
_____	☐	☐	☐	☐	☐	☐

* [Please elaborate, briefly]

_____

_____

_____

_____

_____

4.16   For the following, how do you rate each item, as it relates to your business, on the scale **'good'**, **'fair'** or **'could be better'**?

[Hand respondent Sheet 4.16]

		Good	Fair	Could be Better	N/A
(a)	Your adaptability	☐	☐	☐	☐
(b)	Faith in the business	☐	☐	☐	☐
(c)	Foresight/forward planning	☐	☐	☐	☐
(d)	Values of management	☐	☐	☐	☐
(e)	Plant and resources	☐	☐	☐	☐
(f)	Managers	☐	☐	☐	☐
(g)	Employees	☐	☐	☐	☐
(h)	Product quality	☐	☐	☐	☐
(i)	Product range	☐	☐	☐	☐
(j)	Organisation structure/systems	☐	☐	☐	☐
(k)	Sources of finance	☐	☐	☐	☐
(l)	Customers	☐	☐	☐	☐
(m)	Suppliers	☐	☐	☐	☐
(n)	Market share	☐	☐	☐	☐
(o)	Technological/specialist know-how	☐	☐	☐	☐
(p)	Innovativeness/new ideas	☐	☐	☐	☐
(q)	Image	☐	☐	☐	☐
(r)	Other **[please specify]**	☐	☐	☐	☐
	_____	☐	☐	☐	☐
	_____	☐	☐	☐	☐

Could you now please indicate, from the above list, which you consider to be your biggest

   strength (   ) _____

and also your biggest

   weakness (   ) _____

[Retrieve Sheet 4.16 from respondent]

For the following, how do you rate each item, as it relates to your business, on the scale **'good'**, **'fair'** or **'could be better'**?

[Please tick where applicable]

		Good	Fair	Could be Better	N/A
(a)	Your adaptability	☐	☐	☐	☐
(b)	Faith in the business	☐	☐	☐	☐
(c)	Foresight/forward planning	☐	☐	☐	☐
(d)	Values of management	☐	☐	☐	☐
(e)	Plant and resources	☐	☐	☐	☐
(f)	Managers	☐	☐	☐	☐
(g)	Employees	☐	☐	☐	☐
(h)	Product quality	☐	☐	☐	☐
(i)	Product range	☐	☐	☐	☐
(j)	Organisation structure/systems	☐	☐	☐	☐
(k)	Sources of finance	☐	☐	☐	☐
(l)	Customers	☐	☐	☐	☐
(m)	Suppliers	☐	☐	☐	☐
(n)	Market share	☐	☐	☐	☐
(o)	Technological/specialist know-how	☐	☐	☐	☐
(p)	Innovativeness/new ideas	☐	☐	☐	☐
(q)	Image	☐	☐	☐	☐
(r)	Other **[please specify]**	☐	☐	☐	☐
	_____	☐	☐	☐	☐
	_____	☐	☐	☐	☐

Could you now please indicate, from the above list, which you consider to be your biggest

      strength( ) _____

and also your biggest

      weakness ( ) _____

Thank you. Now please return this sheet to the interviewer.

4.17 How threatening are each of the following to your business, on the scale of **'weak'**, **medium'**, **'strong'**? If **'not applicable'**, you may say so.

[Hand respondent Sheet 4.17]

		weak	medium	strong	N/A
(a)	Rivals' adaptability	☐	☐	☐	☐
(b)	Rivals' forward planning	☐	☐	☐	☐
(c)	Rivals' plant/resources	☐	☐	☐	☐
(d)	Rivals' managers	☐	☐	☐	☐
(e)	Rivals' employees	☐	☐	☐	☐
(f)	Rivals' product quality	☐	☐	☐	☐
(g)	Rivals' product range	☐	☐	☐	☐
(h)	Rivals' organisation structure/systems	☐	☐	☐	☐
(i)	Rivals' customers	☐	☐	☐	☐
(j)	Rivals' suppliers	☐	☐	☐	☐
(k)	Rivals' market share	☐	☐	☐	☐
(l)	Rivals' technological/specialist know-how	☐	☐	☐	☐
(m)	Rivals' innovativeness/new ideas	☐	☐	☐	☐
(n)	Rivals' image	☐	☐	☐	☐
(o)	'Red tape'/government legislation	☐	☐	☐	☐
(p)	Breakdown of barriers to trade in EC	☐	☐	☐	☐
(q)	Substitutes	☐	☐	☐	☐
(r)	Competition	☐	☐	☐	☐
(s)	Other **[please specify]**				
	_____	☐	☐	☐	☐
	_____	☐	☐	☐	☐

From the above list, could you now please indicate which you consider to be the biggest

threat (   ) _____

to the business.

[Retrieve Sheet 4.17 from respondent]

Sheet 4.17

How threatening are each of the following to your business, on the scale of **'weak'**, **'medium'**, **'strong'**? If **'not applicable'**, you may say so.

[Please tick where applicable]

		weak	medium	strong	N/A
(a)	Rivals' adaptability	☐	☐	☐	☐
(b)	Rivals' forward planning	☐	☐	☐	☐
(c)	Rivals' plant/resources	☐	☐	☐	☐
(d)	Rivals' managers	☐	☐	☐	☐
(e)	Rivals' employees	☐	☐	☐	☐
(f)	Rivals' product quality	☐	☐	☐	☐
(g)	Rivals' product range	☐	☐	☐	☐
(h)	Rivals' organisation structure/systems	☐	☐	☐	☐
(i)	Rivals' customers	☐	☐	☐	☐
(j)	Rivals' suppliers	☐	☐	☐	☐
(k)	Rivals' market share	☐	☐	☐	☐
(l)	Rivals' technological/specialist know-how	☐	☐	☐	☐
(m)	Rivals' innovativeness/new ideas	☐	☐	☐	☐
(n)	Rivals' image	☐	☐	☐	☐
(o)	'Red tape'/government legislation	☐	☐	☐	☐
(p)	Breakdown of barriers to trade in EC	☐	☐	☐	☐
(q)	Substitutes	☐	☐	☐	☐
(r)	Competition	☐	☐	☐	☐
(s)	Other **[please specify]**				
	_____	☐	☐	☐	☐
	_____	☐	☐	☐	☐

From the above list, could you now please indicate which you consider to be the biggest

threat ( ) _____

to the business.

Thank you. Now please return this sheet to the interviewer.

4.18   How great is the business opportunity afforded to you by each of the following, on the scale 'a lot', 'some', or 'none'? If 'not applicable' you may say so.

Here, I am referring to opportunities for expansion, increased profitability, entering a new market niche, and so on.

[Hand respondent Sheet 4.18]

		A Lot	Some	None	N/A
(a)	Your adaptability	☐	☐	☐	☐
(b)	Faith in the business	☐	☐	☐	☐
(c)	Foresight/forward planning	☐	☐	☐	☐
(d)	Values of management	☐	☐	☐	☐
(e)	Plant and resources	☐	☐	☐	☐
(f)	Managers	☐	☐	☐	☐
(g)	Employees	☐	☐	☐	☐
(h)	Product quality	☐	☐	☐	☐
(i)	Product range	☐	☐	☐	☐
(j)	Organisation structure/systems	☐	☐	☐	☐
(k)	Sources of finance	☐	☐	☐	☐
(l)	Customers	☐	☐	☐	☐
(m)	Suppliers	☐	☐	☐	☐
(n)	Market share	☐	☐	☐	☐
(o)	Technological/specialist know-how	☐	☐	☐	☐
(p)	Innovativeness/new ideas	☐	☐	☐	☐
(q)	Image	☐	☐	☐	☐
(r)	Breakdown of barriers to trade in EC	☐	☐	☐	☐
(s)	Other **[please specify]**				
	_____	☐	☐	☐	☐
	_____	☐	☐	☐	☐

From the above list could you now please indicate which you consider affords the best

opportunity   (   ) _____

to the business.

[Retrieve Sheet 4.18 from respondent]

How great is the business opportunity afforded to you by each of the following, on the scale **'a lot'**, **'some'**, or **'none'**? If **'not applicable'** you may say so. Here, I am referring to opportunities for expansion, increased profitability, entering a new market niche, and so on.

[Please tick where applicable]

		A Lot	Some	None	N/A
(a)	Your adaptability	☐	☐	☐	☐
(b)	Faith in the business	☐	☐	☐	☐
(c)	Foresight/forward planning	☐	☐	☐	☐
(d)	Values of management	☐	☐	☐	☐
(e)	Plant and resources	☐	☐	☐	☐
(f)	Managers	☐	☐	☐	☐
(g)	Employees	☐	☐	☐	☐
(h)	Product quality	☐	☐	☐	☐
(i)	Product range	☐	☐	☐	☐
(j)	Organisation structure/systems	☐	☐	☐	☐
(k)	Sources of finance	☐	☐	☐	☐
(l)	Customers	☐	☐	☐	☐
(m)	Suppliers	☐	☐	☐	☐
(n)	Market share	☐	☐	☐	☐
(o)	Technological/specialist know-how	☐	☐	☐	☐
(p)	Innovativeness/new ideas	☐	☐	☐	☐
(q)	Image	☐	☐	☐	☐
(r)	Breakdown of barriers to trade in EC	☐	☐	☐	☐
(s)	Other **[please specify]**				
	_____	☐	☐	☐	☐
	_____	☐	☐	☐	☐

From the above list could you now please indicate which you consider affords the best

        opportunity   ( )_____

to the business.

Thank you. Now please return this sheet to the interviewer.

5. HUMAN CAPITAL

Now we move on to consider skills, and how they are acquired.

5. Human Capital

5.1   How long have you been directly involved in running your business?
[Provide figure in months]   _____ months

5.2   5.2.1   5.2.1.1   Did you have experience of running a business before this?

          (a) Yes ☐   (b) No ☐ **Go to Question 5.3**

         5.2.1.2   Was this:

          (a)   ☐ Your own business or

          (b)   ☐ Someone else's business? **Go to Question 5.2.3**

     5.2.2   How did you part company with your last business?
[tick one]

         (a)   ☐   Bought out

         (b)   ☐   Sold on **[i.e. trade sale]**

         (c)   ☐   Voluntary liquidation

         (d)   ☐   Involuntary liquidation

         (e)   ☐   Bankruptcy

         (f)   ☐   Other **[Please specify]** _____

     5.2.3   What aspects of your previous business experience do you think have been useful in your present business?
[tick all that apply]

         (a)   ☐   Product knowledge

         (b)   ☐   Financial knowledge

         (c)   ☐   Personnel management

         (d)   ☐   Marketing skills

         (e)   ☐   Trade networking

         (f)   ☐   'Hands On' experience

         (g)   ☐   Training courses

         (h)   ☐   None

         (i)   ☐   Other **[Please Specify]** _____

5.3   How many years of secondary education did you receive? _____ years

5.4   5.4.1   Did you go to college or university?

                  (a) Yes ☐   (b) No ☐ **Go to Question 5.5**

      5.4.2   How long did you spend at college or university? ___ months
                  [Give time in months]

      5.4.3   Was the first college or university qualification you earned:

                  (a)   ☐   A diploma

                  (b)   ☐   A certificate

                  (c)   ☐   An ordinary degree

                  (d)   ☐   An honours degree

                  (e)   ☐   Did not graduate

                  (f)   ☐   Other **[Please specify]** _____

      5.4.4   Do you have further college or university qualifications?

                  (a) Yes ☐   (b) No ☐ **Go to Question 5.5**

      5.4.5   Do you have:

                  (a)   ☐   A higher diploma

                  (b)   ☐   An advanced certificate

                  (c)   ☐   A masters postgraduate degree

                  (d)   ☐   A postgraduate diploma

                  (e)   ☐   A doctoral degree

                  (f)   ☐   Other **[Please specify]** _____

5.5   Do you have a professional association membership which was awarded by examination, or some other evidence of skill?

      (a) Yes ☐   (b) No ☐ **Go to Question 5.6**

      [please specify]

_____

_____

5.6   How many hours a week do you typically devote to this business?
                                    _____ hours

5.7   How many hours a week do you devote to this business outside of your 'normal' working hours?   _____ hours

5.8   Looking at your typical week, what proportion of your time would you say you allocate to the activities listed on this sheet?

First, please tick those that are relevant. Then say what percentage you allocate to each of those that are ticked.

[Hand respondent Sheet 5.8]

Percentage (Total 100%)

(a)	☐ Production	_____ %
(b)	☐ Management	_____ %
(c)	☐ Marketing	_____ %
(d)	☐ Planning	_____ %
(e)	☐ Doing deals	_____ %
(f)	☐ Sales	_____ %
(g)	☐ Other [Please specify] _____	_____ %
	_____	_____ %

[Retrieve Sheet 5.8 from respondent]

5.9   5.9.1   Do you run any other businesses?

(a) Yes ☐   (b) No ☐ **Go to Question 5.10**

5.9.2   How many other businesses do you run?   _____

5.9.3   What proportion of the total time you allot to all your various business involvements do you devote to this business itself? **[i.e. the business you have been questioned about for the last half hour]**   _____ %

5.9.4   What is your principal motive for running more than one business?

(a)	☐	Extra profit
(b)	☐	Risk spreading
(c)	☐	Strategic flexibility
(d)	☐	Tax efficiency
(e)	☐	Other [Please specify] _____

5.10   5.10.1   Do you formally train your employees?

               (a) Yes ☐   (b) No ☐ **Go to Question 5.11**

       5.10.2   What proportion of your employees' time is devoted to training?

               [e.g. per annum?]   _____ %

Sheet 5.8

Looking at your typical week, what proportion of your time would you say you allocate to the activities listed on this sheet?

First, please tick those that are relevant. Then say what percentage you allocate to each of those that are ticked.

Percentage (Total 100%)

(a) ☐ Production _____ %

(b) ☐ Management _____ %

(c) ☐ Marketing _____ %

(d) ☐ Planning _____ %

(e) ☐ Doing Deals _____ %

(f) ☐ Sales _____ %

(g) ☐ Other **[Please specify]** _____ _____ %

_____ _____ %

Thank you. Now please return this sheet to the interviewer.

5.11   5.11.1   Do your employees acquire skills on the job?

(a) Yes ☐   (b) No ☐ **Go to Section 6**
                                      (ORGANISATION)

Could you give an example

_____

5.11.2   How important is 'on the job' skill acquisition to your employees' productivity?

Is it:

Slightly ☐   Significantly ☐   or Very ☐ important?

5.12   What is the wage rate for your best skilled full-time workers? **[monthly]**

£_____ /month

6. ORGANISATION

Thank you for your help so far. We are well on the way. Could I now turn to how you organise your business? If you are a very small business much of this may not be relevant, and we will move on rapidly to the next section.

6. Organisation

6.1 In a legal sense, how would you define your business?

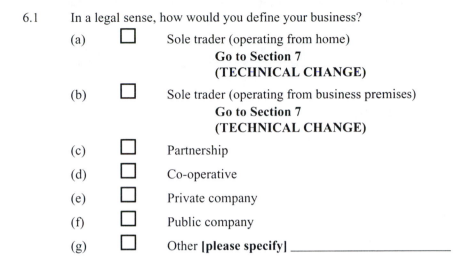

(a) ☐ Sole trader (operating from home)
Go to Section 7
(TECHNICAL CHANGE)

(b) ☐ Sole trader (operating from business premises)
Go to Section 7
(TECHNICAL CHANGE)

(c) ☐ Partnership

(d) ☐ Co-operative

(e) ☐ Private company

(f) ☐ Public company

(g) ☐ Other **[please specify]** _____

6.2 I should like to know how many people are involved in running your business, from the top **[most senior level]** to the bottom **[most junior level]**. Could you also indicate what multiple of the lowest wages or salaries the higher ones are?

[Hand Respondent Sheet 6.2]

		Number of Persons	**Salary Multiple**
(a)	Top level	_____	_____
(b)	Second level	_____	_____
(c)	Third level	_____	_____
(d)	Fourth level	_____	_____
(e)	Further levels	_____	_____

[Retrieve Sheet 6.2 from Respondent]

6.3 At which of these levels does the day-to-day running of your business take place? _____

6.4   Is authority always exercised through the next level down [**i.e. through immediate subordinates**], or is there discretion for a superior to intervene selectively at lower levels?

(a)   ☐   Only next level

(b)   ☐   Can intervene selectively

6.5   On, average, how often does a superior review his or her immediate subordinates?   _____ months

6.2.1   I should like to know how many people are involved in running your business, from the top [**most senior level**] to the bottom [**most junior level**]. Please indicate below the number of persons at each level.

6.2.2   Could you also indicate for each level how many times greater the average salary or wage is, compared to the bottom level. [**e.g. if a person at the bottom level is paid £400 p.m., and a person at the level above is paid £500 p.m. (on average), the higher payment is 1¼ times greater than the lower**]

		Number of Persons	**Salary Multiple**
(a)	Top level	_____	_____
(b)	Second level	_____	_____
(c)	Third level	_____	_____
(d)	Fourth level	_____	_____
(e)	Further levels	_____	_____
_____	_____	_____	
_____	_____	_____	

Thank you. Now please return this sheet to the interviewer.

6.6   How much discretion does a superior typically have over his or her
       subordinates' workplace activities?

       Is it:
       (a)   ☐   Extensive
       (b)   ☐   Considerable
       (c)   ☐   Moderate
       (d)   ☐   Limited
       (e)   ☐   None
       (f)   ☐   Not applicable

6.7   Are there standard procedures for superiors to monitor subordinates,
       or is monitoring discretionary?

       (a)   ☐   Standard
       (b)   ☐   Discretionary
       (c)   ☐   Not applicable

6.8   Is monitoring of subordinates by superiors typically done at regular
       known intervals, or is it in some measure unpredictable?
       (a)   ☐   Regular
       (b)   ☐   Unpredictable
       (c)   ☐   Not applicable

6.9   In the superior/subordinate relations within your firm, would you say
       that typically the superior gets his subordinate to *understand and act
       on what he wants*

       mostly ☐ frequently ☐ sometimes ☐ rarely ☐?

6.10   When subordinates do not fully *understand and act on* superiors'
       instructions, how relevant are the following factors?

[Hand Respondent Sheet 6.10]

		Important	**Unimportant**	**Irrelevant**
(a)	Unclear instructions	☐	☐	☐
(b)	Unfair instructions	☐	☐	☐
(c)	Subordinate indiscipline	☐	☐	☐

(d)	Superior indiscipline	☐ ☐ ☐
(e)	Demarcation disputes	☐ ☐ ☐
(f)	Loyalty conflicts	☐ ☐ ☐
(g)	Inadequate subordinate's skills	☐ ☐ ☐
(h)	Dissatisfaction with work conditions	☐ ☐ ☐
(i)	Dissatisfaction with pay conditions	☐ ☐ ☐
(j)	Other [please specify]	☐ ☐ ☐
	_____	☐ ☐ ☐
	_____	☐ ☐ ☐

[Retrieve Sheet 6.10 from Respondent]

6.11   How *precisely* are areas of specialisation defined in your firm?

(a)   ☐   Exactly

(b)   ☐   Reasonably clearly

(c)   ☐   Loosely

6.12   Are different specialists in your firm knowledgeable about each others' skills?

(a) Yes ☐   (b) No ☐

6.13   Are different specialists in your firm expected to take on each others' tasks in certain circumstances?

(a) Yes ☐   (b) No ☐

When subordinates do not fully *understand and act on* superiors' instructions, how relevant are the following factors?

[Please tick where applicable]

		Important	Unimportant	Irrelevant
(a)	Unclear instructions	☐	☐	☐
(b)	Unfair instructions	☐	☐	☐
(c)	Subordinate indiscipline	☐	☐	☐
(d)	Superior indiscipline	☐	☐	☐
(e)	Demarcation disputes	☐	☐	☐
(f)	Loyalty conflicts	☐	☐	☐
(g)	Inadequate subordinate's skills	☐	☐	☐
(h)	Dissatisfaction with work conditions	☐	☐	☐
(i)	Dissatisfaction with pay conditions	☐	☐	☐
(j)	Other **[please specify]**	☐	☐	☐
	_____	☐	☐	☐
	_____	☐	☐	☐

Thank you. Now please return this sheet to the interviewer.

6.14   Who decides to hire and dismiss personnel in your firm?

    (a)   ☐   You

    (b)   ☐   Your partner

    (c)   ☐   Your subordinates or fellow director
                      [e.g. personnel manager: please specify] _____

    (d)   ☐   All of you **[i.e. group decision]**

    (e)   ☐   Other **[please specify]** _____

6.15   For which of the following reasons does dismissal occur?

    [Please tick where relevant]

                 [Hand Respondent Sheet 6.15]

		Reason for Dismissal	Percentage
(a)	Disciplinary problems	☐	_____ %
(b)	Job no longer needed	☐	_____ %
(c)	Employee no longer suitable for job	☐	_____ %
(d)	Other **[please specify]**		
	_____	☐	_____ %
	_____	☐	_____ %

Could you also please say what percentage of dismissals the above (ticked) reasons account for.

            [Retrieve Sheet 6.15 from Respondent]

For which of the following reasons does dismissal occur?

[Please tick where relevant]

		Reason for Dismissal	**Percentage**
(a)	Disciplinary problems	☐	_____ %
(b)	Job no longer needed	☐	_____ %
(c)	Employee no longer suitable for job	☐	_____ %
(d)	Other **[please specify]**		
	_____	☐	_____ %
	_____	☐	_____ %

Could you also please say what percentage of dismissals the above (ticked) reasons account for.

Thank you. Now please return this sheet to the interviewer.

7. TECHNICAL CHANGE

Good. Thank you for bearing with me. This is the final, and rather short, section of the questionnaire.

7. Technical Change

7.1   A *process* is a way you do things **[e.g. how you cut a component; how you advise a client; how you overhaul an engine]**.

    7.1.1   Since you started your business, what best describes the extent of innovation in your use of processes?
[tick one]

        (a) ☐   No change **[we kept all our processes the same]**
                  Go to Question 7.1.3

        (b) ☐   Slight change
                  [we modified a few processes in minor ways]

        (c) ☐   Significant change
                  [we modified a few processes in major ways]

        (d) ☐   Important change
                  [we modified many processes in major ways]

    7.1.2   What best describes *why* you had *process* innovation to the extent you have just described? **[tick one]**

        (a) ☐   Imitation of rivals

        (b) ☐   Hints from trade or professional journals etc

        (c) ☐   Suggestions from customers

        (d) ☐   Suggestions from within firm

        (e) ☐   Suggestions from suppliers

        (f) ☐   New staff 'carrying in' knowledge

        (g) ☐   Other **[please specify]** _____

        (h) ☐   Not applicable

    7.1.3   How much process innovation is undertaken by your principal rivals?
[tick one]

        (a) ☐   None

        (b) ☐   A little

        (c) ☐   A lot

7.1.4 How much competitive pressure is put on you by process innovation of your principal rivals?
[tick one]

(a) ☐ None

(b) ☐ A little

(c) ☐ A lot

7.2 7.2.1 A new product or *product innovation* is a new good or service that you can sell to meet a newly discovered customer need. How many new products have you developed since you started your business?
[tick one]

(a) ☐ None

(b) ☐ 1–5

(c) ☐ 6–10

(d) ☐ 11–20

(e) ☐ More than twenty

7.2.2 How much product innovation is undertaken by your rivals?
[tick one]

(a) ☐ None

(b) ☐ A little

(c) ☐ A lot

(d) ☐ Don't know

7.2.3 How much competitive pressure is put on you by product innovation of your principal rivals?
[tick one]

(a) ☐ None

(b) ☐ A little

(c) ☐ A lot

7.3 7.3.1 Has there been a lot of technical change in your industry in the last few years?

(a) Yes ☐   (b) No ☐ **Go to Question 7.4**

7.3.2 Who have been the prime initiators of technical change?
[tick one]

(a) ☐ Acknowledged leader in the industry

(b) ☐ Newly emerging innovators in the industry

(c) ☐ Forces outside the industry
[e.g. government constructed incentives]

(d) ☐ Other **[please specify briefly]** _____

7.4 How important are the following methods for protecting innovations *in your industry*?
[tick one for each row]

		Unimportant	Important	Very Important
(a)	Patents	☐	☐	☐
(b)	Copyright	☐	☐	☐
(c)	Trademarks	☐	☐	☐
(d)	Exploiting innovation rapidly **[i.e. before rivals can respond**	☐	☐	☐
(e)	Other **[please specify]**			
	_____	☐	☐	☐
	_____	☐	☐	☐

7.5 How important are the following in your search for technical knowledge which is relevant to new products or processes?
[tick one box in each row]

[Hand Respondent Sheet 7.5]

		Unimportant	Important	Very Important
(a)	Trade journals	☐	☐	☐
(b)	Technical or scientific journals	☐	☐	☐
(c)	Government bodies	☐	☐	☐

(d)	Suppliers	☐	☐	☐
(e)	Customers	☐	☐	☐
(f)	Licensed technologies	☐	☐	☐
(g)	Consultants	☐	☐	☐
(h)	Universities	☐	☐	☐
(i)	Rival firms	☐	☐	☐
(j)	Other [please specify]			
	_____	☐	☐	☐
	_____	☐	☐	☐

[Retrieve Sheet 7.5 from Respondent]

How important are the following in your search for technical knowledge which is relevant to new products or processes?

[tick one box in each row]

		Unimportant	Important	Very Important
(a)	Trade journals	☐	☐	☐
(b)	Technical or scientific journals	☐	☐	☐
(c)	Government bodies	☐	☐	☐
(d)	Suppliers	☐	☐	☐
(e)	Customers	☐	☐	☐
(f)	Licensed technologies	☐	☐	☐
(g)	Consultants	☐	☐	☐
(h)	Universities	☐	☐	☐
(i)	Rival firms	☐	☐	☐
(j)	Other **[please specify]**			
	_____	☐	☐	☐
	_____	☐	☐	☐

Thank you. Now please return this sheet to the interviewer.

7.6 Which of the following statements best reflects your experience of using new production technologies in your firm?
[N.B. relate this to your experience since start-up, by reference to developments like automation, robotics, numerically controlled machines]
[tick one only]

[Hand Respondent Sheet 7.6]

(a) ☐ We haven't used new production technologies.

(b) ☐ We have implemented new production technologies, but rarely successfully.

(c) ☐ We have implemented new production technologies, but not always successfully.

(d) ☐ We have generally been successful in implementing new production technologies.

[Retrieve Sheet 7.6 from Respondent]

7.7 Do you expect your business to grow over the next 3 years?

(a) Yes ☐   (b) No ☐

7.8 Have you derived satisfaction from setting up a new business?

(a) Yes ☐   (b) No ☐

That is the end of the questionnaire. Thank you very much for your assistance. Again I would emphasise the confidentiality surrounding the collection of data in this study.

Signature of Interviewer _____

Time and date of end of interview_____

Sheet 7.6

Which of the following statements best reflects your experience of using new production technologies in your firm?

[N.B. relate this to your experience since start-up, by reference to developments like automation, robotics, numerically controlled machines]

[tick one only]

(a) ☐ We haven't used new production technologies.

(b) ☐ We have implemented new production technologies, but rarely successfully.

(c) ☐ We have implemented new production technologies, but not always successfully.

(d) ☐ We have generally been successful in implementing new production technologies.

Thank you. Now please return this sheet to the interviewer.

Form for forwarding address

Should your business change name or address before we next contact you, we would be most grateful if you could fill in and return to us the following information:

Previous Firm Name	
Previous Address	

Current Firm Name	
Current Address	
Telephone	

This will enable us to keep our records in order, and it will also help us when sending you summary reports of our findings. Please return to the address below:

Centre for Research into Industry, Enterprise, Finance and the Firm (CRIEFF)
Department of Economics
University of St Andrews
St Salvator's College
St Andrews
Fife
KY16 8XP

Professor Gavin C Reid ☎ 0334 62431 / 62439
Director, CRIEFF

Miss Julia A Smith ☎ 0334 62438
Research Assistant, CRIEFF

Miss Marianne Nilkes ☎ 0334 62440
Research Trainee, CRIEFF

Administered questionnaire 4

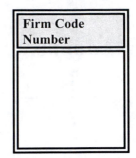

Firm Code Number

Life Cycle Effects in New Small Firms

Interviewer: _____

Date and time
of interview: _____

Respondent: _____

Firm Name: _____

Firm Address: _____

_____

_____

Telephone: _____

Mobile: _____

INTERVIEW AGENDA

1   Markets

2   Finance

3   Costs

4   Business Strategy

5   Development of MAS

6   Human Capital

7   Organisation

8   Technical Change

LIFE-CYCLE EFFECTS IN SMALL FIRMS

1. MARKET DATA

There are eight parts to this interview. We will look at markets, finance, costs, business strategy, development of management accounting systems, human capital, organisation and technical change. Either I will ask you questions directly, or I will provide you with question sheets for you to fill in yourself.

1. Market Data

1.2   1.2.1   Has your main line of business changed since last year? If so, what is it now?

_____

_____

1.3   How many people work in the business?
[N.B. If none, Go to Question 1.4]

(a) Directors/owner manager _____ (b) Managers (as employees) _____

(c) Full-timers employees_____ (d) Part-time employees _____

(e) Trainees _____

1.4   1.4.1   What are your annual sales *i.e.* turnover? (based on latest estimates, *e.g.* last tax year's)

£ _____ **[incl. VAT?]**

1.4.2   If you set a target level for sales, what was it, and how often is it (re)set?

£ _____   every_____ months

[N.B. VAT threshold is £47,000]

1.5   How many product *groups* or *ranges* do you produce?
[e.g. toasters, hairdriers; making two]

_____

1.6   How many *products* do you produce or supply or supply for your markets?
[e.g. four kinds of toasters, three kinds of hairdriers; making seven in all]

_____

1.7   Do you consider your *main* market to be:
Local ☐   Regional ☐   Scottish ☐   British ☐   or International ☐?

1.8 1.8.1 What is your most important product *group* or *range*, according to sales?

_____

1.8.2 What is your market share for this? What did you target it to be? How often do you set this target?
[Tick box if NOT applicable]

Current Market Share **Target Market Share** ☐ **Target Set** ☐

_____ % _____ % every _____ months

1.8.3 How important is this appraisal of market share to managing your firm?
[1 = Low, 5 = High]

1 ☐ 2 ☐ 3 ☐ 4 ☐ 5 ☐

[NOTE: IF A CHOICE ARISES, YOU SHOULD ANSWER THE QUESTIONS THAT FOLLOW BY REFERENCE TO YOUR *MAIN PRODUCT GROUP* BY SALES]

1.9 How many *major* rivals do you have? _____

1.10 How many *minor* rivals do you have? _____

1.11   How strong is competition in your main market?
        Please rank according to the categories shown, if applicable.

[Hand respondent Sheet 1.11]

		Fierce	Strong	Moderate	Weak	N/A
(a)	Price	☐	☐	☐	☐	☐
(b)	Volume	☐	☐	☐	☐	☐
(c)	Delivery	☐	☐	☐	☐	☐
(d)	Quality	☐	☐	☐	☐	☐
(e)	Design	☐	☐	☐	☐	☐
(f)	Customisation (i.e. bespoke features)	☐	☐	☐	☐	☐
(g)	Guarantee	☐	☐	☐	☐	☐
(h)	After-Sale Care	☐	☐	☐	☐	☐
(i)	Technical Progressiveness	☐	☐	☐	☐	☐
(j)	Substitutes	☐	☐	☐	☐	☐
(k)	Advertising	☐	☐	☐	☐	☐
(l)	Salesmanship	☐	☐	☐	☐	☐

[Retrieve Sheet 1.11 from respondent]

1.12   Overall, how strong is competition in your main market?

        Is it:

        Fierce ☐   Strong ☐   Moderate ☐ or Weak ☐?

Sheet 1.11

How strong is competition in your main market?
[Please rank according to the categories shown, if applicable]

		Fierce	Strong	Moderate	Weak	N/A
(a)	Price	☐	☐	☐	☐	☐
(b)	Volume	☐	☐	☐	☐	☐
(c)	Delivery	☐	☐	☐	☐	☐
(d)	Quality	☐	☐	☐	☐	☐
(e)	Design	☐	☐	☐	☐	☐
(f)	Customisation (i.e. bespoke features)	☐	☐	☐	☐	☐
(g)	Guarantee	☐	☐	☐	☐	☐
(h)	After-Sale Care	☐	☐	☐	☐	☐
(i)	Technical Progressiveness	☐	☐	☐	☐	☐
(j)	Substitutes	☐	☐	☐	☐	☐
(k)	Advertising	☐	☐	☐	☐	☐
(l)	Salesmanship	☐	☐	☐	☐	☐

Thank you. Now please return this sheet to the interviewer.

1.13   Again by reference to your main market:

1.13.1   Against how many small firms do you compete?
(a) ☐ Few or   (b) ☐ Many?

1.13.2   Would you say that the goods which firms in your main market supply are:
(a) ☐ Similar   or (b) ☐ Differentiated?
[N.B. 'Differentiated' means distinguished by location, presentation, packaging, presentation etc]

1.13.3   What is the significance of rivals' actions to your own?
Are they:
(a)   ☐ Irrelevant **[i.e. you compete independently]**
(b)   ☐ Conditional **[i.e. what you do depends upon what they do]**

or

(c)   ☐ Agreed? **[i.e. you act together in an agreed fashion]**

1.13.4   Is there a dominant rival or group of rivals in your main market against whom you and other small firms compete?
(a) Yes ☐   (b) No ☐

1.14   At what market niche is your main product aimed?
[N.B. A 'niche' is a segment of a larger market that is exclusive to you]

_____

_____

_____

1.15   How long have you occupied this niche?   _____ months

Briefly, how have you fared over this period?

_____

1.16   How much longer do you think you will remain in this niche?

_____ months

Could you say, briefly, why you have this time horizon.

_____

_____

1.17   How important is *rapid* occupation of your niche to your business strategy?

(a) Very ☐, (b) Moderately ☐, (c) Not at all ☐

1.18   **'Harvesting' a niche implies extracting all the value left in a market segment before withdrawing from it [e.g. by a final, high-discount sale].**

Do you have in mind a stage at which you will 'harvest' the niche your main product group occupies?

(a) Yes ☐   (b) No ☐

1.19   **An 'end game' strategy is devised for leaving a niche in the most profitable (or least expensive) way [e.g. by aiming to be the last survivor, who takes what is left in the market].**

Do you have in mind such an 'end game' strategy?

(a) Yes ☐   (b) No ☐ **Go to Question 1.20**

Can you explain this briefly.

_____

_____

1.20   Do you see the quality and price of your main product line as being linked?

(a) Yes ☐   (b) No ☐

1.21   In terms of price and quality, what is the end of the market that you aim for?

(a) High price/high quality   ☐

(b) High quality/low price   ☐

(c) Low price/low quality   ☐

(d) Medium price/medium quality ☐

(e) High quality/medium or fair price ☐

(f) Other ☐

For which products is this strategy applied?

_____

1.22 Do you advertise?

Yes ☐ **Go to Question 1.23**

No ☐

How then, briefly, do your customers get to know about you?

_____

Go to Section 2 (FINANCE)

1.23 What form does your advertising take?
[Tick one please]

Does it:
(a) Largely involve the provision of accurate technical information

☐

(b) Largely attempt to persuade the customer to buy ☐
[e.g. by lifestyle association]

(c) Involve a mix of information and persuasion ☐

1.24 How do you deliver your advertising messages?

(a) ☐ Radio

(b) ☐ TV

(c) ☐ Magazines

(d) ☐ Newspapers

(e) ☐ Mail-shots

(f) ☐ Posters

(g) ☐ Trade Show Displays

(h) ☐ Newsletter

(i) ☐ Trade Directory

(j) ☐ Other **[Please specify if possible]** _____

1.25   1.25.1 What do you spend on advertising (in a year)?   £_____

        (1.25.2 Proportion of net sales allocated to advertising   _____%)

1.26   1.26.1 If your principal rival *raised* advertising expenditure by 10%, by how much would you *raise* yours?

        _____ %

       1.26.2 If your principal rival *lowered* advertising expenditure by 10%, by how much would you *lower* yours?

        _____ %

       1.26.3 Does *high* demand for your main product group encourage you to *lower* advertising on it?

       (a) Yes ☐   (b) No ☐

       1.26.4 Does *lower* demand for your main product encourage you to *increase* your advertising on it?

       (a) Yes ☐   (b) No ☐

1.27   If you increased your advertising by 10%, by how much would you expect your sales to increase, assuming no reaction by your rivals?

        _____ %

2. FINANCE

Thank you. Could I now turn briefly to aspects of your finance.

2. Finance

2.1   What are your current gross profits?   £_____
       [Give most recent annual figure]

2.2   What are your current gross sales?   £_____

2.3   What are your current net profits?   £_____
       [Net of all costs, taxes, directors remuneration]

2.4   Do you have any debt (including business overdraft)?

       (a) Yes ☐   (b) No ☐

2.5   2.5.1   Do you have any *outside* equity?
                **[e.g. cash from a 'business angel', who has backed your
                business by putting   money into it]**

                (a) Yes ☐   (b) No ☐ **Go to Question 2.6**

       2.5.2   What percentage of total equity is outside equity? _____%

       2.5.3   What dividend do you pay to equity holders?   _____%

2.6   2.6.1   In an operational sense, have you ever had cash flow
                difficulties?

                (a) Yes ☐   (b) No ☐ **Go to Question 2.6.4**

       2.6.2   Which one of the following contributed most to your cash
                flow difficulties?

                (a) ☐ Non-payment by customers

                (b) ☐ Non-delivery by suppliers

                (c) ☐ Over-investment (e.g. in stocks or capital equipment)

                (d) ☐ Insufficient overdraft facility

       2.6.3   When did you have your most severe cash flow crisis (m/y)?

                _____

       2.6.4   In a strategic sense, do you sometimes wish you had access to
                more finance for the business?

                (a) Yes ☐   (b) No ☐ **Go to Question 2.7**

2.6.5 Why do you feel this shortfall mostly occurs?

(a) ☐ Lack of funds generated within the business

(b) ☐ Shortage of interested outside investors (e.g. family & friends)

(c) ☐ Unwillingness of bank manager to advance further funding

(d) ☐ Lack of grant support

2.6.7 When has this shortfall been most acute (m/y)? _____

2.7   2.7.1 Have you used a bank loan or overdraft facility since last year?

(a) Yes ☐   (b) No ☐ **Go to Question 2.8**

2.7.2 How large was this?   £_____

2.7.3 What interest rate were you charged?   _____ %
[or percentage above base rate?]

2.8   2.8.1 Have you received a grant or subsidy for running your business since last year?

(a) Yes ☐   (b) No ☐ **Go to Question 2.9**

2.8.2 Please specify _____

2.8.3 How much was it?   £_____

2.8.4 How important was it?
(a) crucial ☐ (b) important ☐ (c) helpful ☐
(d) unimportant ☐

2.10   What is your gearing ratio currently?   _____

[i.e. debt divided by equity, typically bank loan divided by personal financial injections]

2.11   What level do you aim to get your gearing ratio to, in the next three years?   _____

Briefly, why? _____

2.12   Do you have any trade credit arrangements?

(a) Yes ☐   (b) No ☐ **Go to Question 2.15**

2.13   2.13.1   How many months of trade credit do your suppliers normally allow?   _____ months

           2.13.2   What is your current balance on trade creditors?   £_____

           2.13.3   What's the maximum amount of credit you take, and how often do you revise this figure?

Credit Limit   **Revised**

£ _____   every _____ months

2.14   2.14.1   How many months of trade credit do you allow your customers?   _____ months

           2.14.2   What is your current balance on trade debtors?   £_____

           2.14.3   What's the maximum balance on trade debtors you allow, and how often do you revise this figure?

Credit Limit   **Revised**

£ _____   every _____ months

           2.14.4   How important is it to make sure that trade debtors keep within the limit you set?
                 [1 = Low, 5 = High]

         1 ☐   2 ☐   3 ☐   4 ☐   5 ☐

2.15   Do you have any extended purchase commitments?

(a) Yes ☐   (b) No ☐

2.16   Do you have any hire purchase commitments?

(a) Yes ☐   (b) No ☐

           2.16.1   Do you have any lease purchase commitments?

(a) Yes ☐   (b) No ☐

2.17   What is the gross value of your fixed assets?   £_____
        [Give most recent figure]

2.18   What is the net value of your fixed assets (after depreciation)?

                                                                     £_____

2.19   2.19.1   What level of stocks do you hold?   £_____

        2.19.2   What is your target level for this?   ☐£_____

        2.19.3   How often do you set it?   every _____ months
                  [Tick box if NOT applicable]

        2.19.4   How important is your analysis of stock levels and their
                  targets to the managing of your firm?
                  [1 = Low, 5 = High]
                  1 ☐   2 ☐   3 ☐   4 ☐   5 ☐

        *(2.19.5 Ratio of value of stocks to net assets _____% for database
        only)*

2.20   Do you have share capital in your business?
        (a) Yes ☐   (b) No ☐ **Go to Question 2.21**

        What form does this share capital take?

        _____

        _____

2.21   2.21.1   Do you raise loan finance by issuing bonds or debentures?
                  (a) Yes ☐   (b) No ☐ **Go to Section 3 (COSTS)**

        2.21.2   What ratio does this bear to your equity finance in percentage
                  terms?   _____%

        2.21.3   What interest rate are you required to pay to debenture
                  holders?   _____%

3. COSTS

Now we are on to the third section, which looks into the costs your business incurs.

3. Costs

3.1   3.1.1   Do you distinguish between *fixed* **[indirect]** costs and *variable* **[direct]** costs?

(a) Yes ☐   (b) No ☐ **Go to Question 3.2**

[Note: *fixed* do not vary in short run, *variable* do]

3.1.2   Which category do you regard as more important for day-to-day decisions?

(a) fixed ☐   (b) variable ☐

3.2   Are the costs you use in decision-making *actual* ☐ or *standard* ☐?

3.3   Do you monitor cost variation with output?

(a) Yes ☐   (b) No ☐ **Go to Question 3.4**

Briefly, explain how: _____

_____

3.4   At what percentage of your capacity are you working?   _____ %

What is your target level for this   ☐ _____ %

and how often do you set it?   every _____ months
[Tick box if NOT applicable]

3.5   Which of the following descriptions best captures your cost structure?
[Prompt: Answer by reference to the main product in your principal product group]

[Hand respondent Sheet 3.5]

(a)   Total cost increases in line with the amount you supply   ☐
[i.e. for each extra unit you supply, your cost rises by the same extra amount]

(b)   Total cost does not increase as fast as the amount you   ☐
supply
[i.e. the extra cost of supplying each additional unit falls, the more you supply]

(c)   Total cost increases faster than supply **[i.e. each extra unit supplied adds more to cost than the last unit supplied]**   ☐

(d)   At first total cost does not increase as fast as supply, but then it increases faster than supply **[i.e. the extra cost of supplying each additional unit initially falls, and then starts to rise]**   ☐

(e)   Total cost increases in line with supply until the maximum supply normally possible **[full capacity]** is reached. After this point, the extra cost of supplying another unit rises sharply.   ☐

(f)   Other **[please specify briefly]** _____   ☐

[Retrieve Sheet 3.5 from respondent]

Sheet 3.5

Which of the following descriptions best captures your cost structure?
[You should answer by reference to the main product in your most important product group]

(a) ☐ Total cost increases in line with the amount you supply **[i.e. for each extra unit you supply, your cost rises by the same extra amount]**

(b) ☐ Total cost does not increase as fast as the amount you supply **[i.e. the extra cost of supplying each additional unit falls, the more you supply]**

(c) ☐ Total cost increases faster than supply **[i.e. each extra unit supplied adds more to cost than the last unit supplied]**

(d) ☐ At first total cost does not increase as fast as supply, but then it increases faster than supply **[i.e. the extra cost of supplying each additional unit initially falls, and then starts to rise]**

(e) ☐ Total cost increases in line with supply until the maximum supply normally possible **[full capacity]** is reached. After this point, the extra cost of supplying another unit rises sharply.

(f) ☐ Other **[please specify briefly]** _____

_____

Thank you. Now please return this sheet to the interviewer.

3.6   Which of the following elements of cost do you attribute to your products?

	Yes	No
(a) Direct material	☐	☐
(b) Direct labour	☐	☐
(c) Production overhead	☐	☐
(d) Distribution costs	☐	☐
(e) Sales costs (including advertising)	☐	☐
(f) Administration costs	☐	☐
(g) Other [please specify]	☐	☐
_____	☐	☐
_____	☐	☐

3.7   What do you spend on each of the following? What targets do you set for these, if any? And how often do you set them?
[Tick box if NOT applicable]

		Actual	Target	Frequency Set
(a)	Rent & rates	£____	£____	every ____ months
(b)	Wages & salaries	£____	£____	every ____ months
(c)	Raw materials	£____	£____	every ____ months

TOTAL COSTS £____

3.8   Do you have a good idea of what costs your rivals have?
(a) Yes ☐   (b) No ☐

3.9   Do you think you are a *low* ☐ or *high* ☐ cost producer, compared to your principal rivals?

3.12   3.12.1   Are you able to use your bargaining power to bid-down the costs of your supplies?
(a) Yes ☐   (b) No ☐ **Go to Question 3.13**

3.12.2   Do you think you are better at achieving this than your principal rivals?
(a) Yes ☐   (b) No ☐

3.13 Do you gain marketplace advantage by a conscious policy of extreme cost-cutting?

(a) Yes ☐   (b) No ☐

3.14 What market share increase would you enjoy by becoming the least cost producer and pricing 10% below your principal rival? _____ %

3.15 Which strategy works better for your firm?

(a) ☐ Being the least cost supplier

(b) ☐ Emphasising the unique character of what you supply

4. BUSINESS STRATEGY

Good. We are about half way through the interview now. This section is largely conducted by having you fill in sheets, describing how you conduct your business strategy.

4. Business Strategy

4.1 4.1.1 Do you have a business plan?

(a) Yes ☐   (b) No ☐ **Go to Question 4.2**

4.1.2 Is it a formal, written plan or is it 'in your head'?

(a) ☐ Formal, written plan.

(b) ☐ 'In your head'.

4.1.3 How often do you review this plan?
[answer in months]   _____ monthly

4.2 How far ahead do you look when evaluating the impact that planned decisions might have?
[answer in months]   _____ months

4.3 What is the *main* aim of the business? **[Tick one only]**

(a) ☐ Survival

(b) ☐ Short-term profit

(c) ☐ Long-term profit

(d) ☐ Growth

(e) ☐ Increased sales

(f) ☐ Increased market share

(g) ☐ High rate of return

(h) ☐ Other **[please specify]** _____

4.4 Are you willing to sacrifice a proportion of your stake in the business in order to promote growth?

(a) Yes ☐   (b) No ☐ **Go to Question 4.5**

What is the minimum stake, as a percentage of total equity, that you would be willing to hold?   _____ %

4.5 Are you willing to accept smaller profits for a time, in order to expand the business?

(a) Yes ☐   (b) No ☐

4.6   Are you contemplating junior market listing?

(a) Yes ☐   (b) No ☐

On what time scale? _____ months/years from now

4.6   4.6.1   **Information Technology (IT) refers to the devices businesses use to transmit, store and process information e.g. telephone, fax, PC.**

How important is information technology (IT) to your business?

Is it:

(a) ☐ Scarcely. **Go to Question 4.7**

(b) ☐ Moderately

(c) ☐ Very important?

4.6.2   Which kinds of IT do you use?

		Yes	No
(a)	Telephone	☐	☐
(b)	Fax	☐	☐
(c)	Telephone answering machine	☐	☐
(d)	Electronic mail	☐	☐
(e)	Telephone conferencing	☐	☐
(f)	Video conferencing	☐	☐
(g)	Cellular telephone	☐	☐
(h)	Satellite link	☐	☐
(i)	Radio communication	☐	☐
(j)	Microfiche	☐	☐
(k)	Personal computers	☐	☐
(l)	Electronic database	☐	☐
(m)	Other **[please specify]**		
	_____	☐	☐

5. DEVELOPMENT OF MAS

5. Development of MAS

5.1 Who prepares accounting information within your firm?
     [Tick all that apply and enter years in digits]

Staff Involved	Qualification:(articled/trainee, school, college/university, professional)				Years of Accounting Experience	
	Art.	Schl.	Col.	Prof.	Within this firm	Since Completing training
(a) ☐ Owner						
(b) ☐ Accountant						
(c) ☐ Manager						
(d) ☐ Partner						
(e) ☐ Director						
(f) ☐ Executive						
(g) ☐ Clerk						
(h) ☐ Supervisor						
(i) ☐ Secretary						
(j) ☐ Assistant						
(k) ☐ Another						

5.1.1   What proportion of their time does the principle preparer of accounting information allocate to this task within a week?

_____ %

5.2 Which of the following types of information are available within your firm?

	Set as budget/ target?		Recorded as actual amount?		Frequency of measurement? (e.g. every 2/3/6 months)	Importance in managing the firm? (1=lo, 5=hi)				
	Yes	No	Yes	No		1	2	3	4	5
(a) Profit & loss										
(b) Balance sheet										
(c) Cash flow										
(d) Bank balance										

5.3   Could you tell me if you use any of the following methods to decide
        about capital investment? When did you first use them (month/year)?

                                                        Used?   When?

(a) Return on investment i.e. a measure of profit ÷   ☐   _____
    a measure of investment

(b) Residual income i.e. net surplus on a project   ☐   _____

(c) Net present value i.e. net discounted project   ☐   _____
    cash flow

(d) Internal rate of return project   ☐   _____

(e) Payback period i.e. years to +ve net cash flow   ☐   _____

5.4   I shall describe some methods for managing costs. For those methods
        that you do use, could you tell me when they were first implemented
        (m/y)?

                                                        Used?   When?

(a) Modern production practices   ☐   _____
e.g. JIT, automated manufacturing

(b) Modern accounting practices   ☐   _____
e.g. ABC, throughput accounting

(c) Quantitative risk analysis   ☐   _____
e.g. expected outcomes, decision trees

(d) Value analysis   ☐   _____
e.g. by identifying products or activities
that do not add value

(e) Strategic pricing   ☐   _____
e.g. product life-cycle pricing, price
discrimination

(f) Transfer pricing   ☐   _____
e.g. using profit centres, pricing of
components

5.5 The next question is concerned with how information flows around your
business.

    5.5.1   Do you think about your business as being split up into
            groups or divisions, or simply as being just a single unit?

    (a) Groups/Divisions/Branches ☐   (b) Single unit ☐

If (a), when (m/y) did you first start viewing your business in this way?

_____

5.5.2   For the various types of information available within your business (e.g. sales, profit, cash flow, work effort, bank balance), do you ever segment them on any of the following bases?

(a) ☐ Product or product group

(b) ☐ Department of division of workgroup

(c) ☐ Geographical area

(d) ☐ Customer

(e) ☐ Any other (please specify)

5.5.3   Do you use spreadsheets or other computer software for handling information within your business?

(a) Yes ☐   (b) No ☐

If 'Yes', for which of the following do you use this technique, and when (m/y) did you first start doing so?

	Used?	When first used?
(a) Storing data	☐	_____
(b) Project appraisal e.g. NPV, IRR	☐	_____
(c) Financial modelling	☐	_____
(d) Forecasting and simulation	☐	_____
(e) Sensitivity analysis	☐	_____

5.6.1   Do management get regular accounting information which:

(a) ☐ Measures performance?

(b) ☐ Contains budget targets?

(c) ☐ Shows the financial implications of specific decisions?

(d) ☐ Other **[please specify]** _____

Not applicable☐ **Go to Q. 5.7**

5.6.2   Has this information developed over time?

(a) Yes ☐   (b) No ☐ **Go to Q. 5.7**

5.6.3   In what important ways has it changed?

_____

_____

_____

_____

5.7   Would you say any of the following factors have influenced the introduction/development of accounting information?

(a) ☐ Growth in sales?

(b) ☐ Growth in number of employees?

(c) ☐ Growth in product lines?

(d) ☐ Change in organisational structure?

(e) ☐ Experiencing problems in performance?

(f) ☐ Increasing complexity in the operational process?

(g) ☐ The introduction of new capital (equity or loan)?

5.8   I am interested in the complexity of your use of accounting information, so could I ask you whether you use such accounting information for:
[Please tick all that apply, otherwise leave blank]

5.9.1   *Effective Planning and Analysis?* **Do you do this to:**

(a) ☐ Keep within budget

(b) ☐ Identify cost-cutting opportunities

(c) ☐ Identify productivity raising opportunities

(d) ☐ Identify possibilities for improving product design

(e) ☐ Identify growth opportunities

(f) ☐ Reach specified levels of profit

(g) ☐ Motivate employees by setting targets

(h) ☐ Analyse business performance against projected or target values

(i) ☐ Justify proposed expenditures

(j) ☐ Measure performance of individual employees

(k) ☐ Measure performance of teams of employees

5.9.2   *Activation and Direction of Daily Operations?* **Do you do this to:**

(a) ☐ Identify trends

(b) ☐ Assess and manage stock levels

(c) ☐ Evaluate product performance

(d) ☐ Calculate effects of marginal changes in costs and revenue

(e) ☐ Identify standards within the firm which need revision

(f) ☐ Identify operations which have become inefficient

(g) ☐ Ensure products conform to quality standards

(h) ☐ Measure customer service/satisfaction

(i) ☐ Measure use of work time

(j) ☐ Measure speed of production

5.9.3   *Problem Solving and Decision-Making?* **Do you do this to:**

(a) ☐ Evaluate or choose between alternative actions

(b) ☐ Assess a new project or investment

(c) ☐ Fix prices

(d) ☐ Determine output levels

(e) ☐ Determine schedule of production

(f) ☐ Determine balance between in-house production and sub-contracting

(g) ☐ Analyse riskiness of a new idea

(h) ☐ Decide whether or not to shut down whole or part of the business

(i) ☐ Decide whether to sell off assets or part of the business

(j) ☐ Decide whether to replace old assets with new assets

(k) ☐ Determine number of products

(l) ☐ Determine remuneration of staff

(m) ☐ Assess staff for promotion/demotion

5.10.1   Do you consider accounting information produced for you to be reliable?

(a) Yes ☐   (b) No ☐   (c) not applicable ☐ **Go to next Section**

5.10.2   Why?

_____

_____

_____

_____

5.11.1   Do you have difficulty in using accounting information?

   (a) Yes ☐   (b) No ☐   (c) not applicable ☐ **Go to next Section**

5.11.2   Why?

_____

_____

_____

_____

6. HUMAN CAPITAL

Now we move on to consider skills, and how they are acquired.

6. Human Capital

6.4   6.4.1   Have you gained a college or university qualification since last year?

(a) Yes ☐   (b) No ☐ **Go to Question 6.5**

6.4.2   How much time did you devote to this last year?
[Give time in months] _____months

6.4.3   Was the qualification you earned:

(a) ☐ A diploma

(b) ☐ A certificate

(c) ☐ An ordinary degree

(d) ☐ An honours degree

(e) ☐ Did not graduate

(f) ☐ Other **[Please specify]** _____

6.4.4   Or was it a higher qualification?

(a) Yes ☐   (b) No ☐ **Go to Question 6.5**

6.4.5   Which of these was it?

(a) ☐ A higher diploma

(b) ☐ An advanced certificate

(c) ☐ A masters postgraduate degree

(d) ☐ A postgraduate diploma

(e) ☐ A doctoral degree

(f) ☐ Other **[Please specify]** _____

6.5   Have you gained a professional association membership (which was awarded by examination, or some other evidence of skill) since last year?

(a) Yes ☐   (b) No ☐ **Go to Question 6.6**

[please specify]

_____

_____

6.6   How many hours a week do you typically devote to this business?

                                                                                 _____ hours

6.7   How many of the hours a week that you devote to this business do you consider to be outside of 'normal' working hours? (e.g. outside the hours you would expect a full time employee to work?)

                                                                                 _____ hours

6.8   Looking at your typical week, what proportion of your time would you say you allocate to the activities listed on this sheet?

First, please tick those that are relevant. Then say what percentage you allocate to each of those that are ticked.

[Hand respondent Sheet 6.8]

                                                       Percentage (Total 100%)

(a) ☐ Production   _____ %

(b) ☐ Management   _____ %

(c) ☐ Marketing   _____ %

(d) ☐ Planning   _____ %

(e) ☐ Doing deals   _____ %

(f) ☐ Sales   _____ %

(g) ☐ Other **[Please specify]**_____   _____ %

                                    _____   _____ %

[Retrieve Sheet 6.8 from respondent]

6.9   6.9.1   Do you run any other businesses?

                    (a) Yes ☐   (b) No ☐ **Go to Question 6.10**

        6.9.2   How many other businesses do you run?   _____

        6.9.3   What proportion of the total time you allot to all your various business involvements do you devote to this business itself? **[i.e. the business you have been questioned about for the last half hour]**   _____ %

6.9.4   What is your principal motive for running more than one business?

(a) ☐ Extra profit

(b) ☐ Risk spreading

(c) ☐ Strategic flexibility

(d) ☐ Tax efficiency

(e) ☐ Other **[Please specify]** _____

6.10   6.10.1   Do you *formally* train your employees?

(a) Yes ☐   (b) No ☐ **Go to Question 6.11**

6.10.2   What proportion of your employees' time is devoted to training? **[e.g. per annum?]**   _____ %

Sheet 6.8

Looking at your typical week, what proportion of your time would you say you allocate to the activities listed on this sheet?

First, please tick those that are relevant. Then say what percentage you allocate to each of those that are ticked.

Percentage (Total 100%)

(a) ☐ Production   _____ %

(b) ☐ Management   _____ %

(c) ☐ Marketing   _____ %

(d) ☐ Planning   _____ %

(e) ☐ Doing deals   _____ %

(f) ☐ Sales   _____ %

(g) ☐ Other **[Please specify]**_____ _____ %

                                         _____ _____ %

Thank you. Now please return this sheet to the interviewer.

6.11   6.11.1   Do your employees acquire skills on the job?

(a) Yes ☐   (b) No ☐ **Go to Section 7 (ORGANISATION)**

Could you give an example

_____

6.11.2   How important is 'on the job' skill acquisition to your employees' productivity?

Is it:

Slightly ☐   Significantly ☐   or Very ☐   important?

6.12   What is the wage rate for your best skilled full-time workers? **[monthly]**
[N.B. Note whether per hour, per week _etc_, then convert to per month, based on 40 hour week, 4 week month]

£_____ /month

7. ORGANISATION

Thank you for your help so far. We are well on the way. Could I now turn to how you organise your business? If you are a very small business much of this may not be relevant, and we will move on rapidly to the next section.

7. Organisation

7.1   In a legal sense, how would you define your business?

    (a) ☐ Sole trader (operating from home).

    (b) ☐ Sole trader (operating from business premises).

    (c) ☐ Partnership

    (d) ☐ Co-operative

    (e) ☐ Private limited company

    (f) ☐ Public company

    (g) ☐ Other [please specify] _____

[N.B. If no employees, go to Section 8]

7.2   I should like to know how many people are involved in running your business, from the top [**most senior level**] to the bottom [**most junior level**]. Could you also indicate what multiple of the lowest wages or salaries the higher ones are?

[Hand Respondent Sheet 7.2]

	Number of Persons	Salary Multiple
(a) Top level	_____	_____
(b) Second level	_____	_____
(c) Third level	_____	_____
(d) Fourth level	_____	_____
(e) Further levels	_____	_____

[Retrieve Sheet 7.2 from Respondent]

7.3   At which of these levels does the day-to-day running of your business take place? _____

7.4   Is authority always exercised through the next level down [**i.e. through immediate subordinates**], or is there discretion for a superior to intervene selectively at lower levels?

    (a) ☐ Only next level

    (b) ☐ Can intervene selectively

    (c) ☐ There is no authority system [**Go to Question 7.11**]

7.5   On, average, how often does a superior review his or her immediate
        subordinates?

       7.5.1 Formally?   _____ months

       7.5.2 Informally?   _____ months

Sheet 7.2

7.2.1   I should like to know how many people are involved in running your business, from the top [**most senior level**] to the bottom [**most junior level**]. Please indicate below the number of persons at each level.

7.2.2   Could you also indicate for each level how many times greater the average salary or wage is, compared to the bottom level. [**e.g. if a person at the bottom level is paid £400 p.m., and a person at the level above is paid £500 p.m. (on average), the higher payment is 1¼ times greater than the lower**]

	Number of Persons	**Salary Multiple**
(a) Top level	_____	_____
(b) Second level	_____	_____
(c) Third level	_____	_____
(d) Fourth level	_____	_____
(e) Further levels	_____	_____
_____	_____	_____
_____	_____	_____

Thank you. Now please return this sheet to the interviewer.

7.6　　How much discretion does a superior typically have over his or her subordinates' workplace activities?

Is it:

(a) ☐ Extensive

(b) ☐ Considerable

(c) ☐ Moderate

(d) ☐ Limited

(e) ☐ None

(f) ☐ Not applicable

7.7　　Are there standard procedures for superiors to monitor subordinates, or is monitoring discretionary?

(a) ☐ Standard

(b) ☐ Discretionary

(c) ☐ Not applicable

7.8　　Is monitoring of subordinates by superiors typically done at regular known intervals, or is it in some measure unpredictable?

(a) ☐ Regular

(b) ☐ Unpredictable

(c) ☐ Not applicable

7.9　In the superior/subordinate relations within your firm, would you say that typically the superior gets his subordinate to *understand and act* on what he wants

☐ mostly **[Go to Question 7.11]**　　　　　　☐ frequently

☐ sometimes　　　　　　　　　　　　　　　　☐ rarely?

7.10   When subordinates do not fully *understand and act on* superiors' instructions, how relevant are the following factors?

[Hand Respondent Sheet 7.10]

		Important	**Unimportant**	**Irrelevant**
(a)	Unclear instructions	☐	☐	☐
(b)	Unfair instructions	☐	☐	☐
(c)	Subordinate indiscipline	☐	☐	☐
(d)	Superior indiscipline	☐	☐	☐
(e)	Demarcation disputes	☐	☐	☐
(f)	Loyalty conflicts	☐	☐	☐
(g)	Inadequate subordinate's skills	☐	☐	☐
(h)	Dissatisfaction with work conditions	☐	☐	☐
(i)	Dissatisfaction with pay conditions	☐	☐	☐
(j)	Other **[please specify]**	☐	☐	☐
	_____	☐	☐	☐
	_____	☐	☐	☐

[Retrieve Sheet 7.10 from Respondent]

7.11   How *precisely* are areas of specialisation defined in your firm?

(a) ☐ Exactly

(b) ☐ Reasonably clearly

(c) ☐ Loosely

7.12   Are different specialists in your firm knowledgeable about each others' skills?

(a) Yes ☐   (b) No ☐

7.13   Are different specialists in your firm expected to take on each others' tasks in certain circumstances?

(a) Yes ☐   (b) No ☐

When subordinates do not fully *understand and act on* superiors' instructions, how relevant are the following factors?

[Please tick where applicable]

		Important	Unimportant	Irrelevant
(a)	Unclear instructions	☐	☐	☐
(b)	Unfair instructions	☐	☐	☐
(c)	Subordinate indiscipline	☐	☐	☐
(d)	Superior indiscipline	☐	☐	☐
(e)	Demarcation disputes	☐	☐	☐
(f)	Loyalty conflicts	☐	☐	☐
(g)	Inadequate subordinate's skills	☐	☐	☐
(h)	Dissatisfaction with work conditions	☐	☐	☐
(i)	Dissatisfaction with pay conditions	☐	☐	☐
(j)	Other **[please specify]**	☐	☐	☐
	_____	☐	☐	☐
	_____	☐	☐	☐

Thank you. Now please return this sheet to the interviewer.

7.14   Who decides to hire and dismiss personnel in your firm?
        [Tick all that apply]

        (a) ☐ You

        (b) ☐ Your partner

        (c) ☐ Your subordinates or fellow director
             [e.g. personnel manager: please specify] _____

        (d) ☐ All of you **[*i.e.* group decision]**

        (e) ☐ Other **[please specify]** _____

7.15   For which of the following reasons does dismissal occur?

        [Please tick where relevant]

        [Hand Respondent Sheet 7.15]

	Reason for Dismissal	**Percentage**
(a) Disciplinary problems	☐	_____ %
(b) Job no longer needed	☐	_____ %
(c) Employee no longer suitable for job	☐	_____ %
(d) Other **[please specify]**		
_____	☐	_____ %
_____	☐	_____ %

Could you also please say what percentage of dismissals the above (ticked) reasons account for.

[Retrieve Sheet 7.15 from Respondent]

For which of the following reasons does dismissal occur?

[Please tick where relevant]

		Reason for Dismissal	**Percentage**
(a)	Disciplinary problems	☐	_____ %
(b)	Job no longer needed	☐	_____ %
(c)	Employee no longer suitable for job	☐	_____ %
(d)	Other **[please specify]**		
	_____	☐	_____ %
	_____	☐	_____ %

Could you also please say what percentage of dismissals the above (ticked) reasons account for.

Thank you. Now please return this sheet to the interviewer.

8. TECHNICAL CHANGE

Good. Thank you for bearing with me. This is the final, and rather short, section of the questionnaire.

8. Technical Change

8.1   A *process* is a way you do things [e.g. **how you cut a component; how you advise a client; how you overhaul an engine**].

      8.1.1   Since last year, what best describes the extent of innovation in your use of processes? **[tick one]**

            (a) ☐ No change   **[we kept all our processes the same]**

                                            Go to Question 8.1.3

            (b) ☐ Slight change   **[we modified a few processes in minor ways]**

            (c) ☐ Significant change   **[we modified a few processes in major ways]**

            (d) ☐ Important change   **[we modified many processes in major ways]**

      8.1.2   What best describes *why* you had *process* innovation to the extent you have just described? **[tick one]**

            (a) ☐ Imitation of rivals

            (b) ☐ Hints from trade or professional journals etc

            (c) ☐ Suggestions from customers

            (d) ☐ Suggestions from within firm

            (e) ☐ Suggestions from suppliers

            (f) ☐ New staff 'carrying in' knowledge

            (g) ☐ Other **[please specify]** _____

            (h) ☐ Not applicable

      8.1.3   How much process innovation is undertaken by your principal rivals? **[tick one]**

            (a) ☐ None

            (b) ☐ A little

            (c) ☐ A lot

            (d) ☐ Don't know

8.1.4   How much competitive pressure is put on you by process innovation of your principal rivals?
[tick one]

(a) ☐ None

(b) ☐ A little

(c) ☐ A lot

8.2   8.2.1   A new product or *product innovation* is a new good or service that you can sell to meet a newly discovered customer need. How many new products have you developed since last year?
[tick one]

(a) ☐ None

(b) ☐ 1–5

(c) ☐ 6–10

(d) ☐ 11–20

(e) ☐ More than twenty

8.2.2   How much product innovation is undertaken by your rivals?
[tick one]

(a) ☐ None

(b) ☐ A little

(c) ☐ A lot

(d) ☐ Don't know

8.2.3   How much competitive pressure is put on you by product innovation of your principal rivals?
[tick one]

(a) ☐ None

(b) ☐ A little

(c) ☐ A lot

8.3   8.3.1   Has there been a lot of technical change in your industry since last year?

(a) Yes ☐   (b) No ☐ **Go to Question 8.4**

8.3.2   Who have been the prime initiators of technical change?
         [tick one]

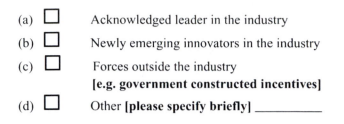

         (a) ☐   Acknowledged leader in the industry
         (b) ☐   Newly emerging innovators in the industry
         (c) ☐   Forces outside the industry
                  [e.g. government constructed incentives]
         (d) ☐   Other **[please specify briefly]** _____

8.4 How important are the following methods for protecting innovations *in your industry*?
    [tick one for each row]

		Unimportant	Important	Very Important
(a)	Patents	☐	☐	☐
(b)	Copyright	☐	☐	☐
(c)	Trademarks	☐	☐	☐
(d)	Exploiting innovation rapidly **[i.e. before rivals can respond]**	☐	☐	☐
(e)	Other **[please specify]**	☐	☐	☐
	_____	☐	☐	☐
	_____	☐	☐	☐

8.5 How important are the following in your search for technical knowledge which is relevant to new products or processes?
    [tick one box in each row]

[Hand Respondent Sheet 8.5]

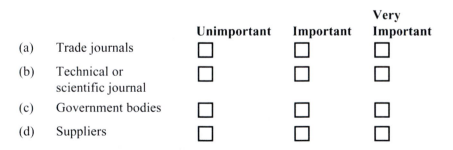

		Unimportant	Important	Very Important
(a)	Trade journals	☐	☐	☐
(b)	Technical or scientific journal	☐	☐	☐
(c)	Government bodies	☐	☐	☐
(d)	Suppliers	☐	☐	☐

(e)	Customers	☐	☐	☐
(f)	Licensed technologies	☐	☐	☐
(g)	Consultants	☐	☐	☐
(h)	Universities	☐	☐	☐
(i)	Rival firms	☐	☐	☐

(j) Other
[please specify]

_____ ☐ ☐ ☐

_____ ☐ ☐ ☐

[Retrieve Sheet 8.5 from Respondent]

How important are the following in your search for technical knowledge which is relevant to new products or processes?
[tick one box in each row]

		Unimportant	Important	Very Important
(a)	Trade journals	☐	☐	☐
(b)	Technical or scientific journal	☐	☐	☐
(c)	Government bodies	☐	☐	☐
(d)	Suppliers	☐	☐	☐
(e)	Customers	☐	☐	☐
(f)	Licensed technologies	☐	☐	☐
(g)	Consultants	☐	☐	☐
(h)	Universities	☐	☐	☐
(i)	Rival firms	☐	☐	☐
(j)	Other **[please specify]** _____	☐	☐	☐
	_____	☐	☐	☐

Thank you. Now please return this sheet to the interviewer.

8.6   Which of the following statements best reflects your experience of using new production technologies in your firm?
[N.B. relate this to your experience since the last interview, by reference to developments like automation, robotics, numerically controlled machines]
[tick one only]

[Hand Respondent Sheet 8.6]

(a) ☐   We haven't used new production technologies.

(b) ☐   We have implemented new production technologies, but rarely successfully.

(c) ☐   We have implemented new production technologies, but not always successfully.

(d) ☐   We have generally been successful in implementing new production technologies.

If (b), (c) or (d), when was your most important implementation of new production technologies since start-up?

_____ month/year

[Retrieve Sheet 8.6 from Respondent]

8.7   Do you expect your business to grow over the next three years?

(a) Yes ☐   (b) No ☐

8.8   Have you derived satisfaction from running your business over the last year?

(a) Yes ☐   (b) No ☐

That is the end of the questionnaire. Thank you very much for your assistance. Again I would emphasise the confidentiality surrounding the collection of data in this study.

Signature of Interviewer _____

Time and date of end of interview _____

Sheet 8.6

Which of the following statements best reflects your experience of using new production technologies in your firm?

[N.B. relate this to your experience since the last interview, by reference to developments like automation, robotics, numerically controlled machines]

[tick one only]

(a) ☐ We haven't used new production technologies.

(b) ☐ We have implemented new production technologies, but rarely successfully.

(c) ☐ We have implemented new production technologies, but not always successfully.

(d) ☐ We have generally been successful in implementing new production technologies.

If (b), (c) or (d), when was your most important implementation of new production technologies since start-up?

_____ month/year

Thank you. Now please return this sheet to the interviewer.

Form for forwarding address

Should your business change name or address before we next contact you, we would be most grateful if you could fill in and return to us the following information:

Previous Firm Name	
Previous Address	

Current Firm Name	
Current Address	
Telephone	

This will enable us to keep our records in order, and it will also help us when sending you summary reports of our findings. Please return to the address below:

Centre for Research into Industry, Enterprise, Finance and the Firm (CRIEFF)
Department of Economics
University of St Andrews
St Salvator's College
St Andrews
Fife
KY16 9AL

Professor Gavin C Reid   ☎01334 462431   **FAX:** 01334 462438
Director, CRIEFF

Professor Falconer Mitchell   ☎0131 650 8340   **FAX:** 0131 650 8340
University of Edinburgh

Dr Julia A Smith   ☎01334 462438   **FAX:** 01334 462438
Research Fellow, CRIEFF

e-mail: *js3@st-andrews.ac.uk*
www: *http://www.st-and.ac.uk/~www_crieff/CRIEFF.html*

Index